Pandora Hearts

Jun Mochizuki

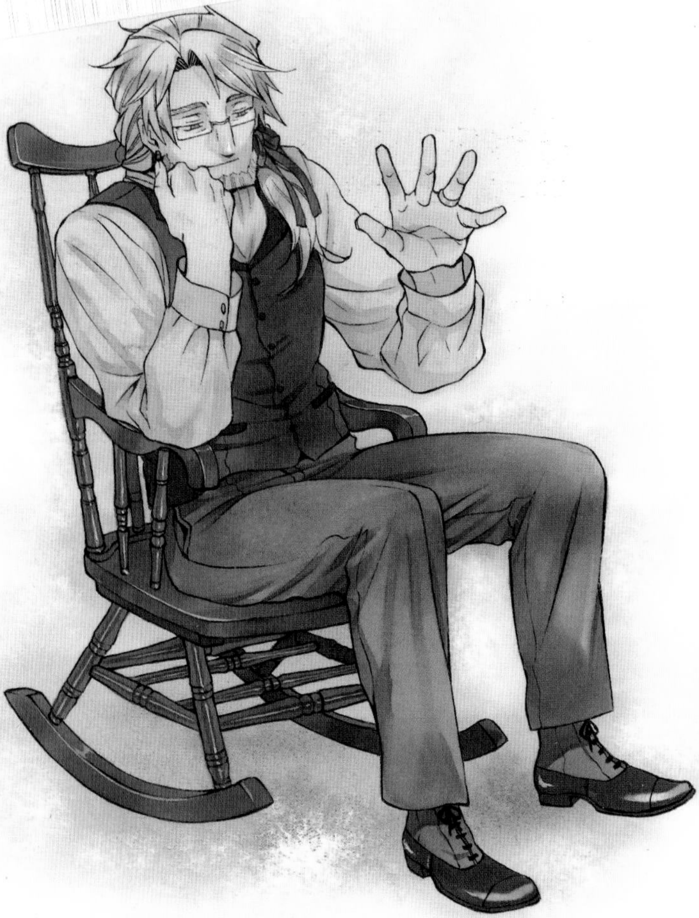

CONTENTS

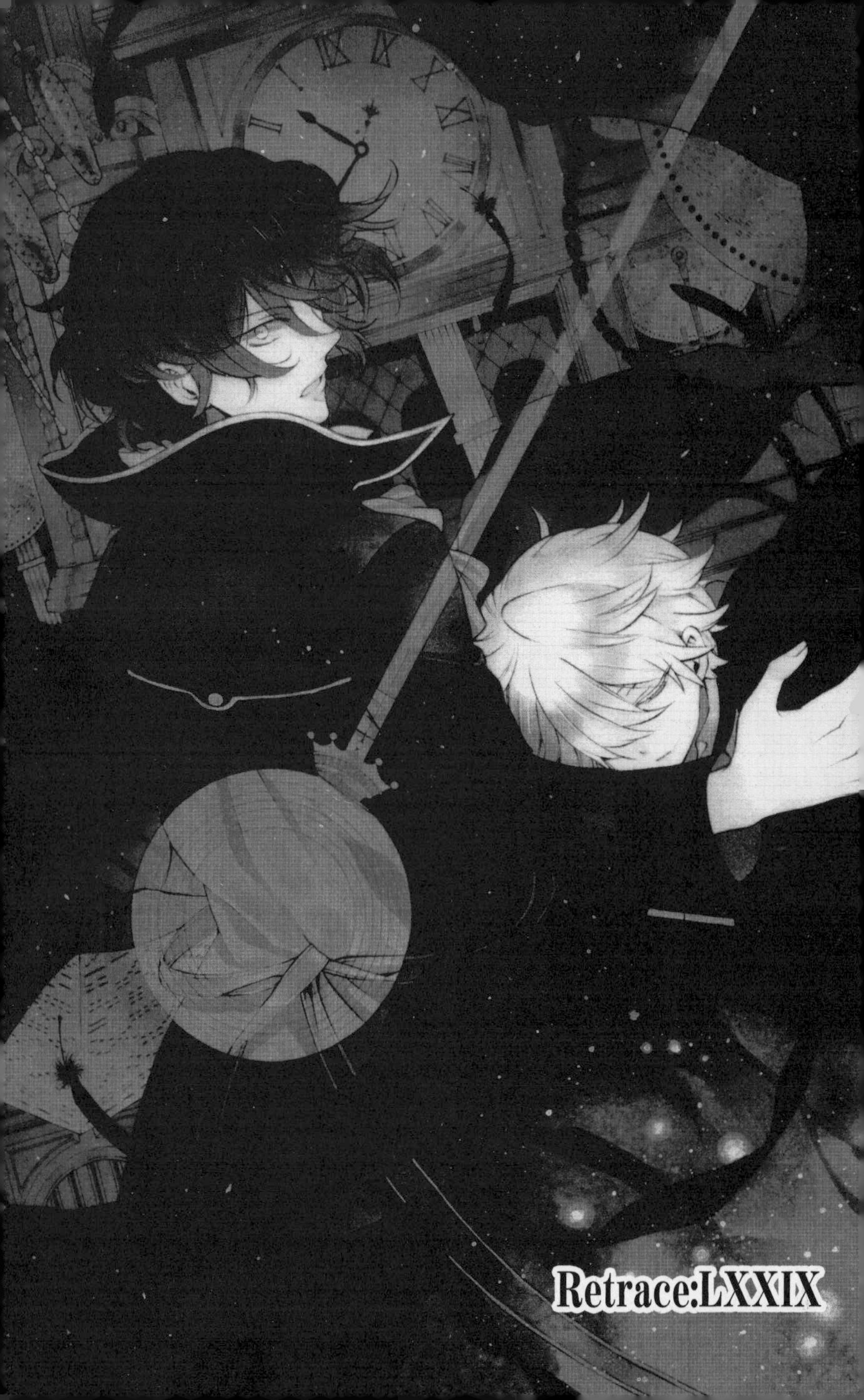
Retrace:LXXIX

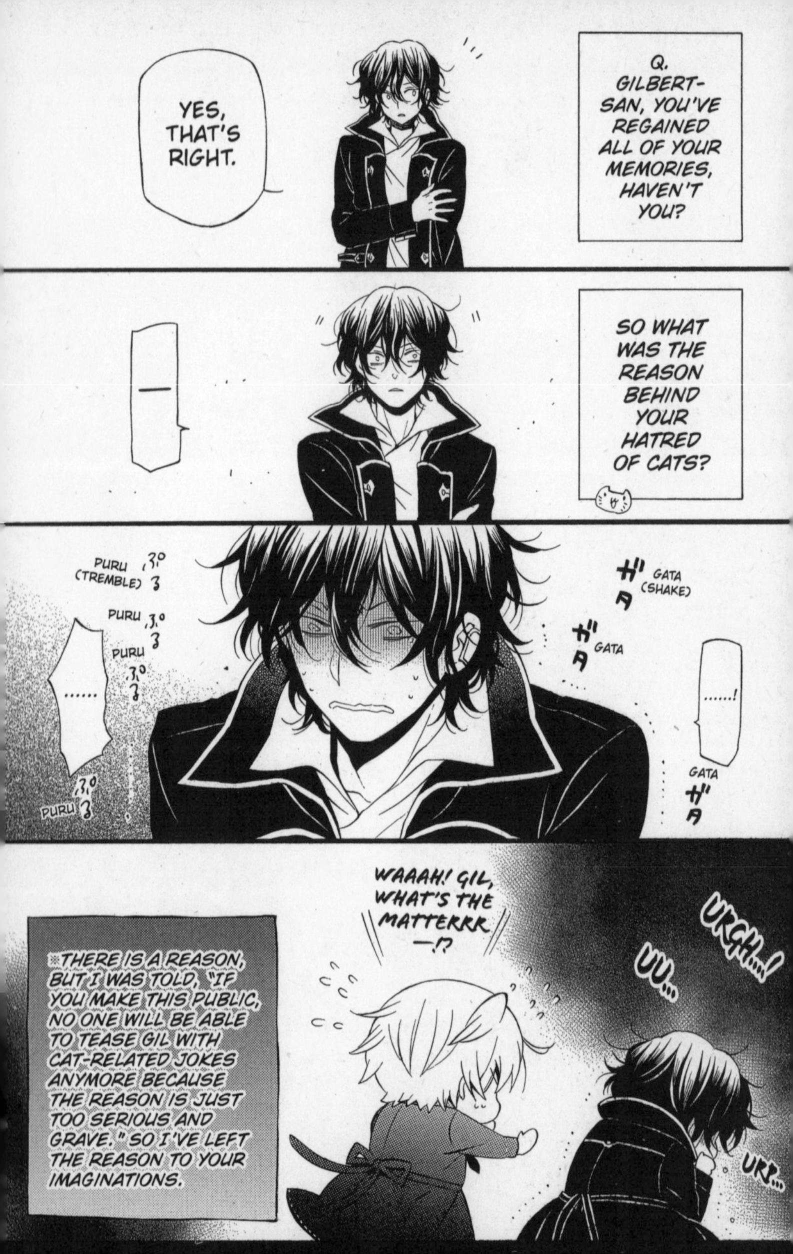
Q. GILBERT-SAN, YOU'VE REGAINED ALL OF YOUR MEMORIES, HAVEN'T YOU?
YES, THAT'S RIGHT.
SO WHAT WAS THE REASON BEHIND YOUR HATRED OF CATS?
—
ガタ GATA (SHAKE)
ガタ GATA
......!
ガタ GATA
PURU (TREMBLE)
PURU
PURU
......
PURU
URGH...!
UU...
URP...
WAAAH! GIL, WHAT'S THE MATTERRR—!?
※THERE IS A REASON, BUT I WAS TOLD, "IF YOU MAKE THIS PUBLIC, NO ONE WILL BE ABLE TO TEASE GIL WITH CAT-RELATED JOKES ANYMORE BECAUSE THE REASON IS JUST TOO SERIOUS AND GRAVE." SO I'VE LEFT THE REASON TO YOUR IMAGINATIONS.

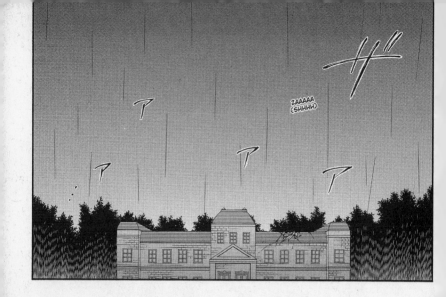

ZAAAAA
(SHHHH)

WHAT HAVE YOU DONE...!? HOW COULD YOU BURN OFF YOUR ARM...!?

GIL...

GIL!

HAH...

HAH...!

VINCE.

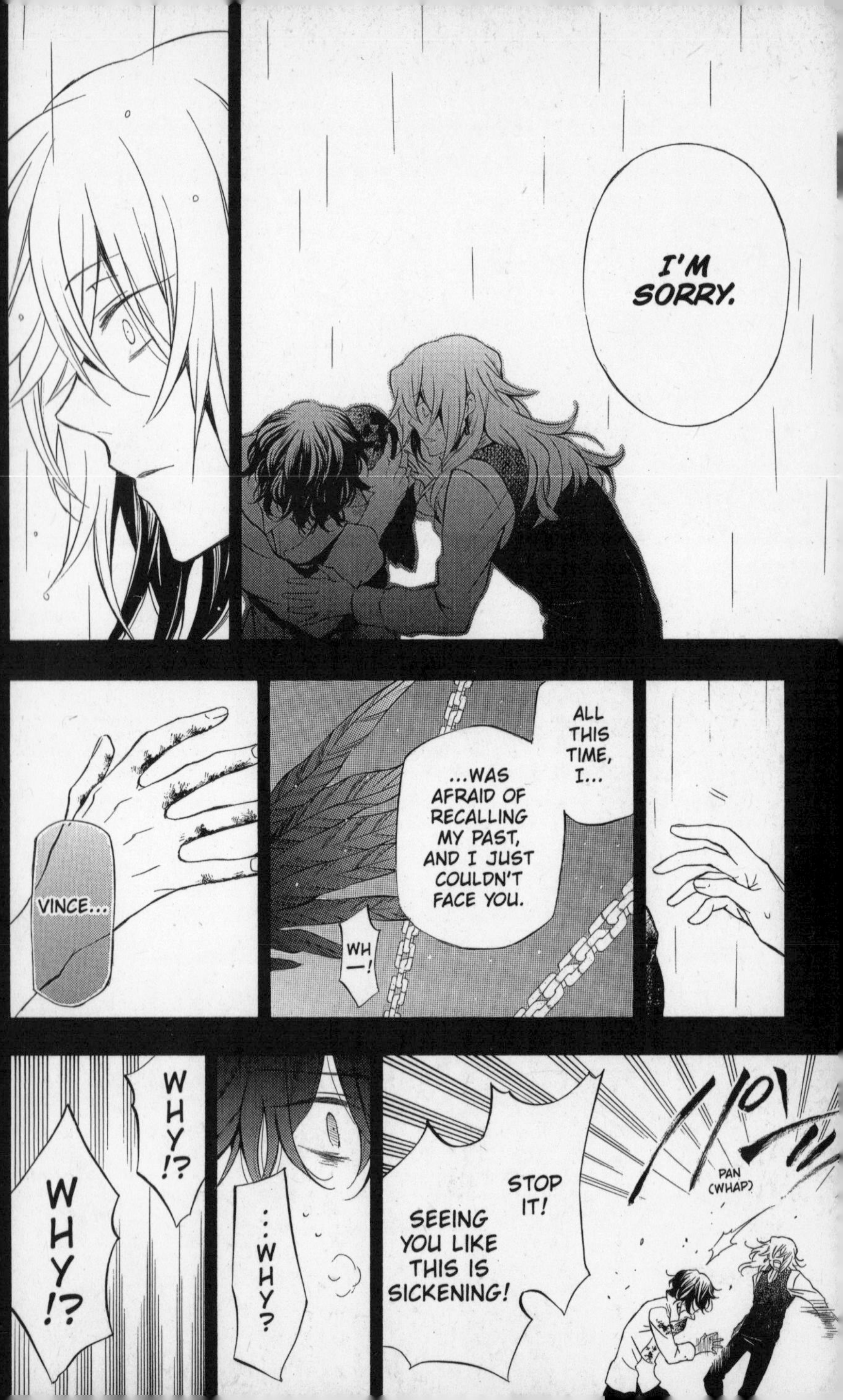
I'M SORRY.
ALL THIS TIME, I...
...WAS AFRAID OF RECALLING MY PAST, AND I JUST COULDN'T FACE YOU.
WH—!
VINCE...
PAN (WHAP)
STOP IT!
SEEING YOU LIKE THIS IS SICKENING!
...WHY?
WHY!?
WHY!?

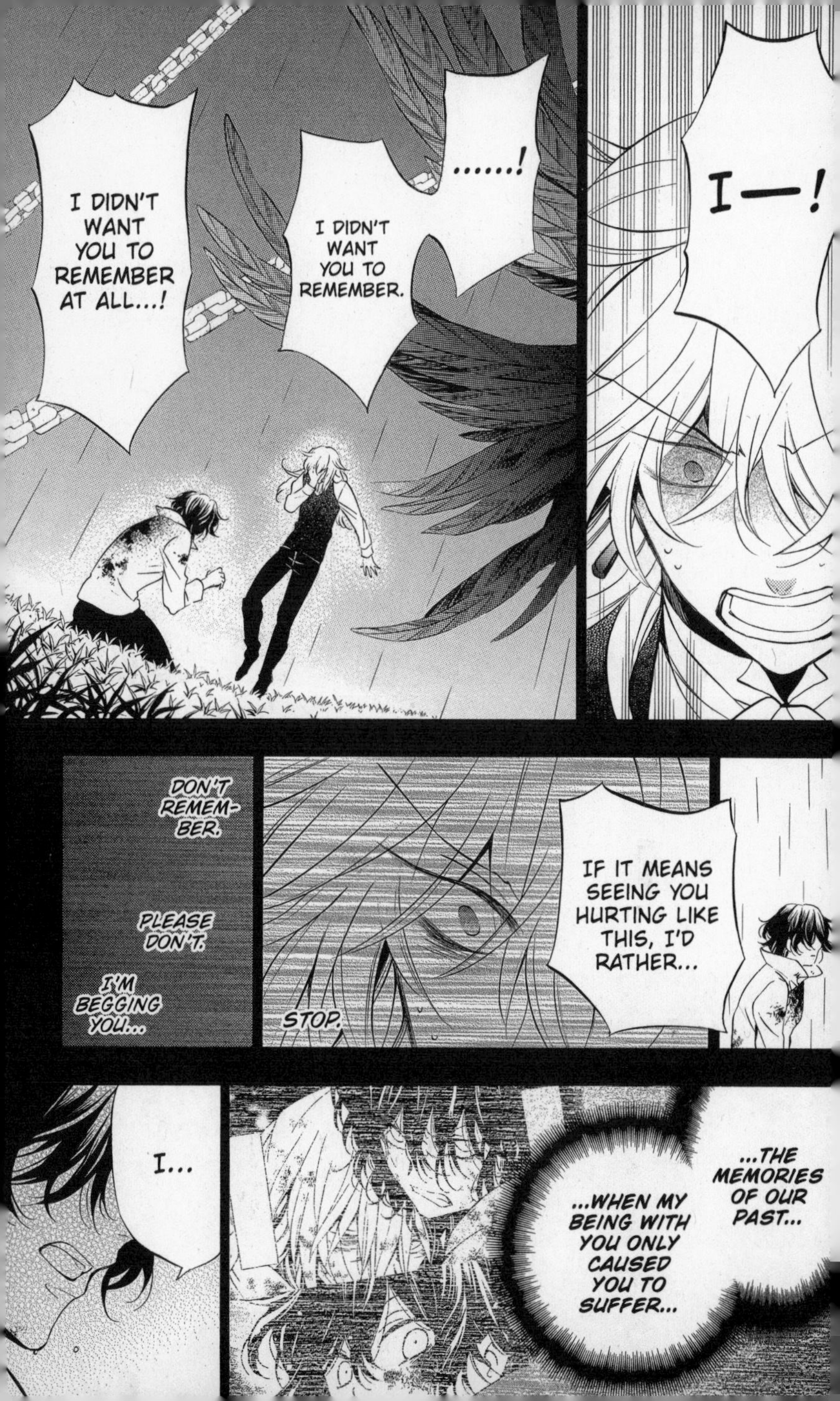
I—!
......!
I DIDN'T WANT YOU TO REMEMBER.
I DIDN'T WANT YOU TO REMEMBER AT ALL...!
IF IT MEANS SEEING YOU HURTING LIKE THIS, I'D RATHER...
STOP.
DON'T REMEMBER.
PLEASE DON'T.
I'M BEGGING YOU...
...THE MEMORIES OF OUR PAST...
...WHEN MY BEING WITH YOU ONLY CAUSED YOU TO SUFFER...
I...

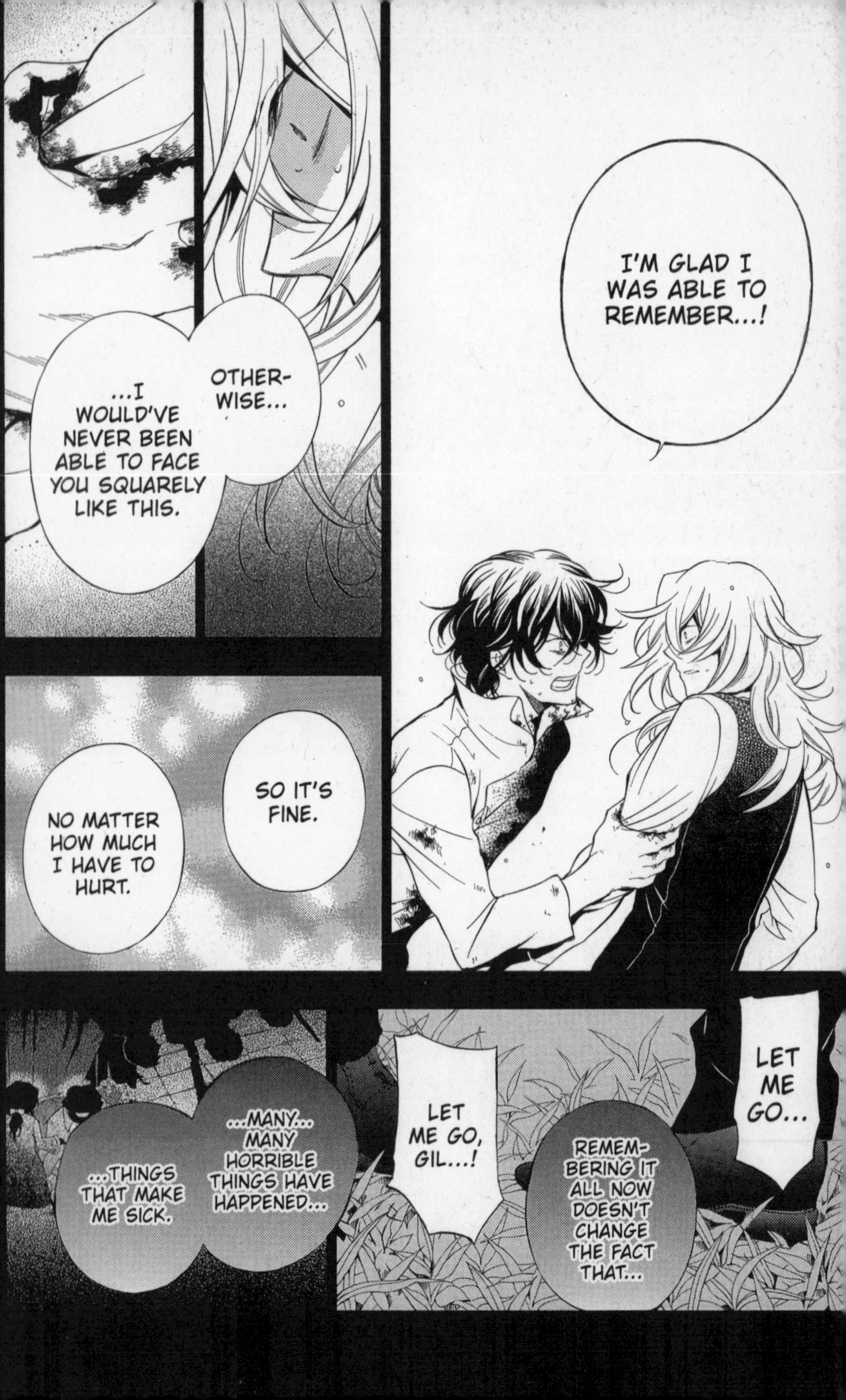
I'M GLAD I WAS ABLE TO REMEMBER...!
OTHER-WISE...
...I WOULD'VE NEVER BEEN ABLE TO FACE YOU SQUARELY LIKE THIS.
SO IT'S FINE.
NO MATTER HOW MUCH I HAVE TO HURT.
LET ME GO...
LET ME GO, GIL...!
REMEM-BERING IT ALL NOW DOESN'T CHANGE THE FACT THAT...
...MANY... MANY HORRIBLE THINGS HAVE HAPPENED...
...THINGS THAT MAKE ME SICK.

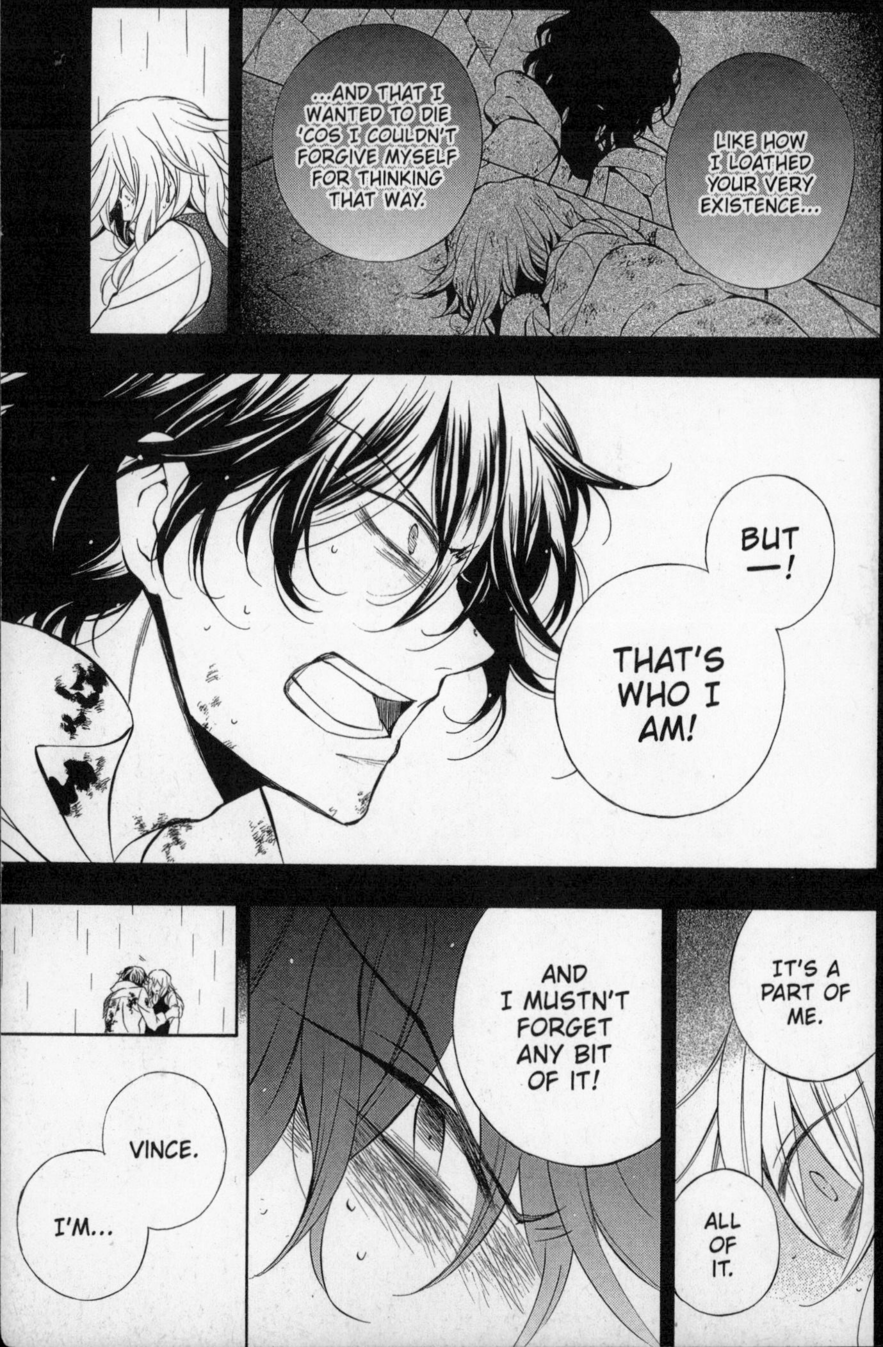
LIKE HOW I LOATHED YOUR VERY EXISTENCE...
...AND THAT I WANTED TO DIE 'COS I COULDN'T FORGIVE MYSELF FOR THINKING THAT WAY.
BUT—!
THAT'S WHO I AM!
IT'S A PART OF ME.
ALL OF IT.
AND I MUSTN'T FORGET ANY BIT OF IT!
VINCE.
I'M...

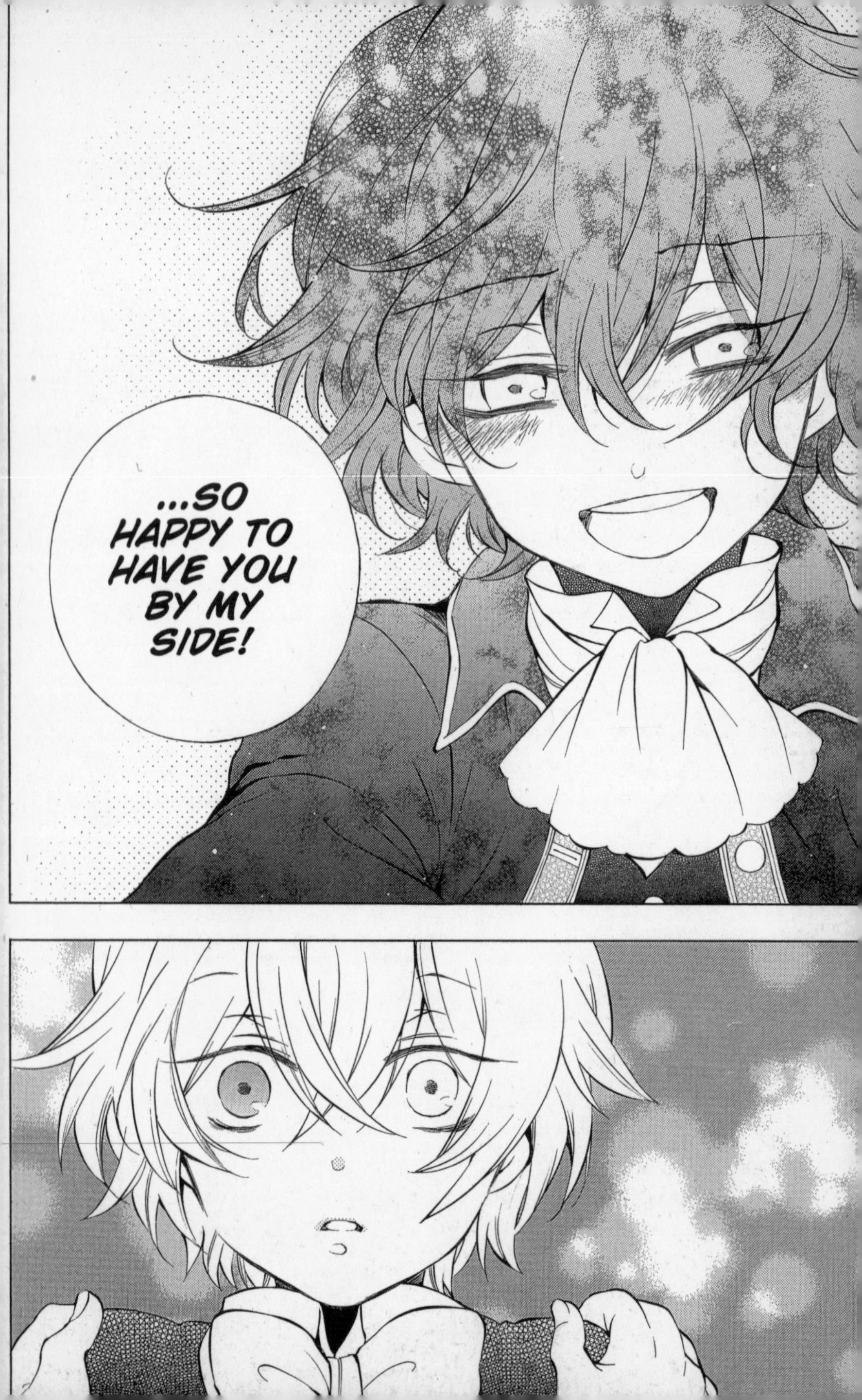
...SO HAPPY TO HAVE YOU BY MY SIDE!

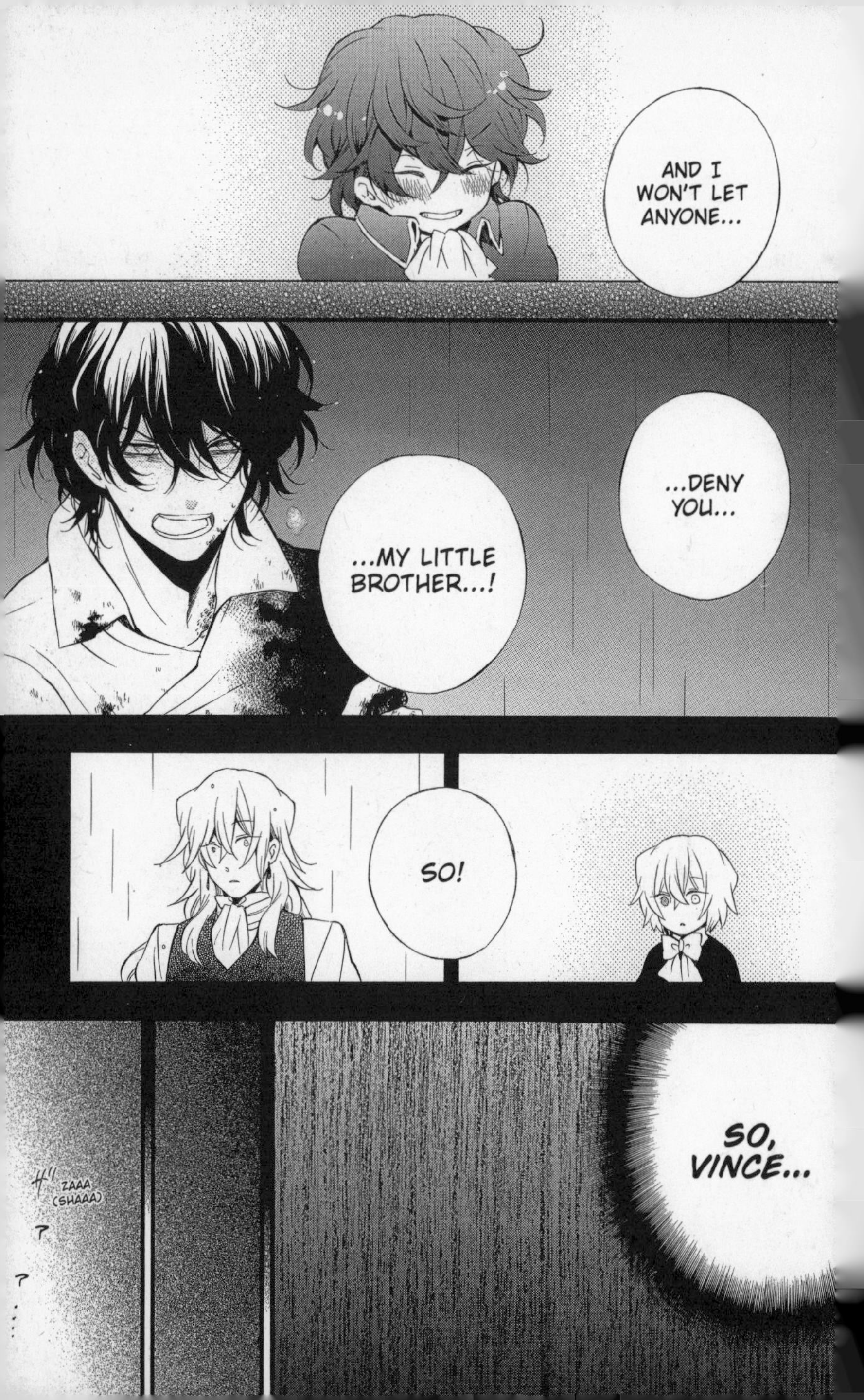
AND I WON'T LET ANYONE...
...DENY YOU...
...MY LITTLE BROTHER...!
SO!
SO, VINCE...
ZAAA (SHAAA)

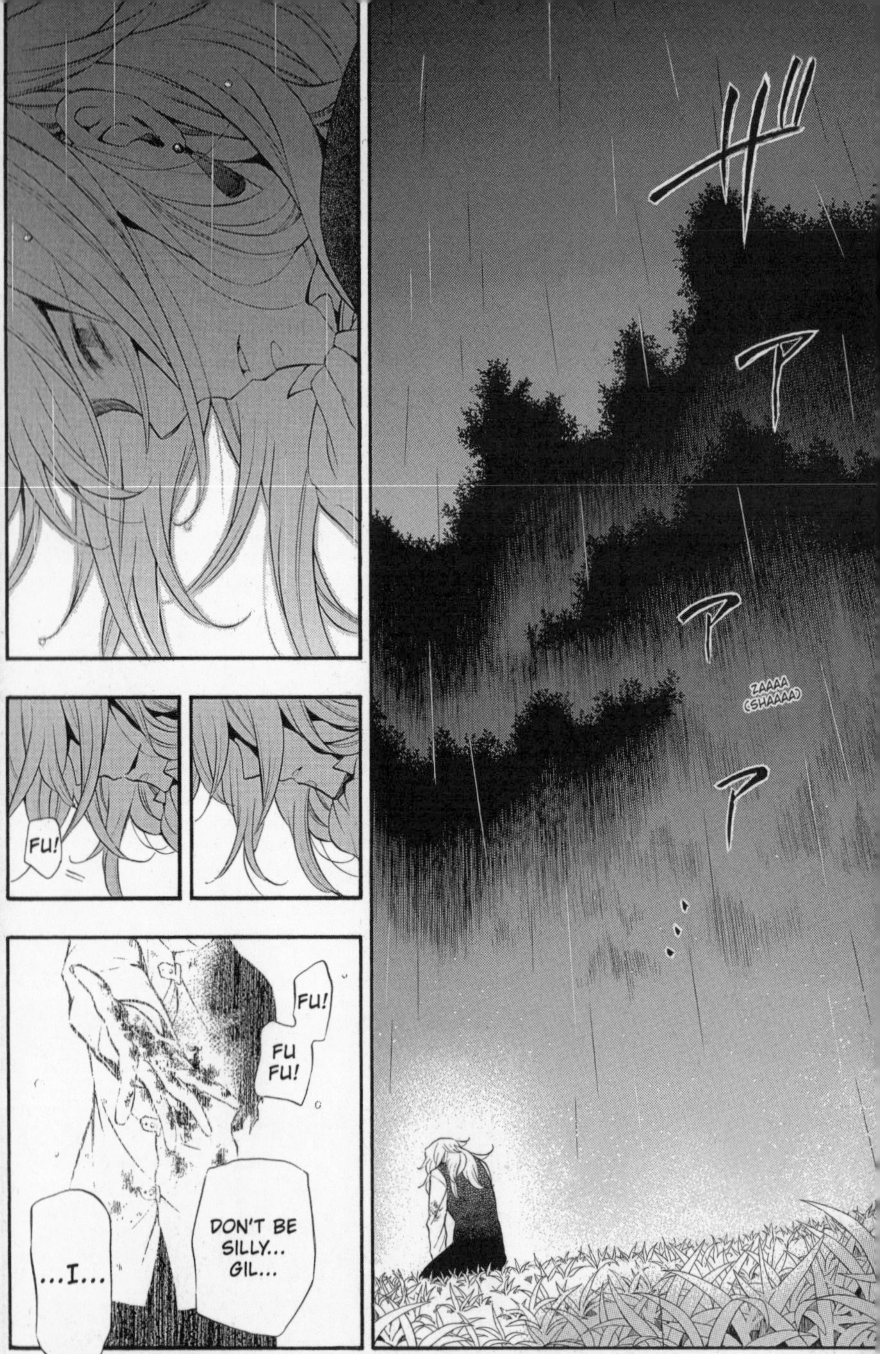
ザァァァ…
ZAAAA (SHAAAA)
FU!
FU!
FU FU!
DON'T BE SILLY... GIL...
...I...

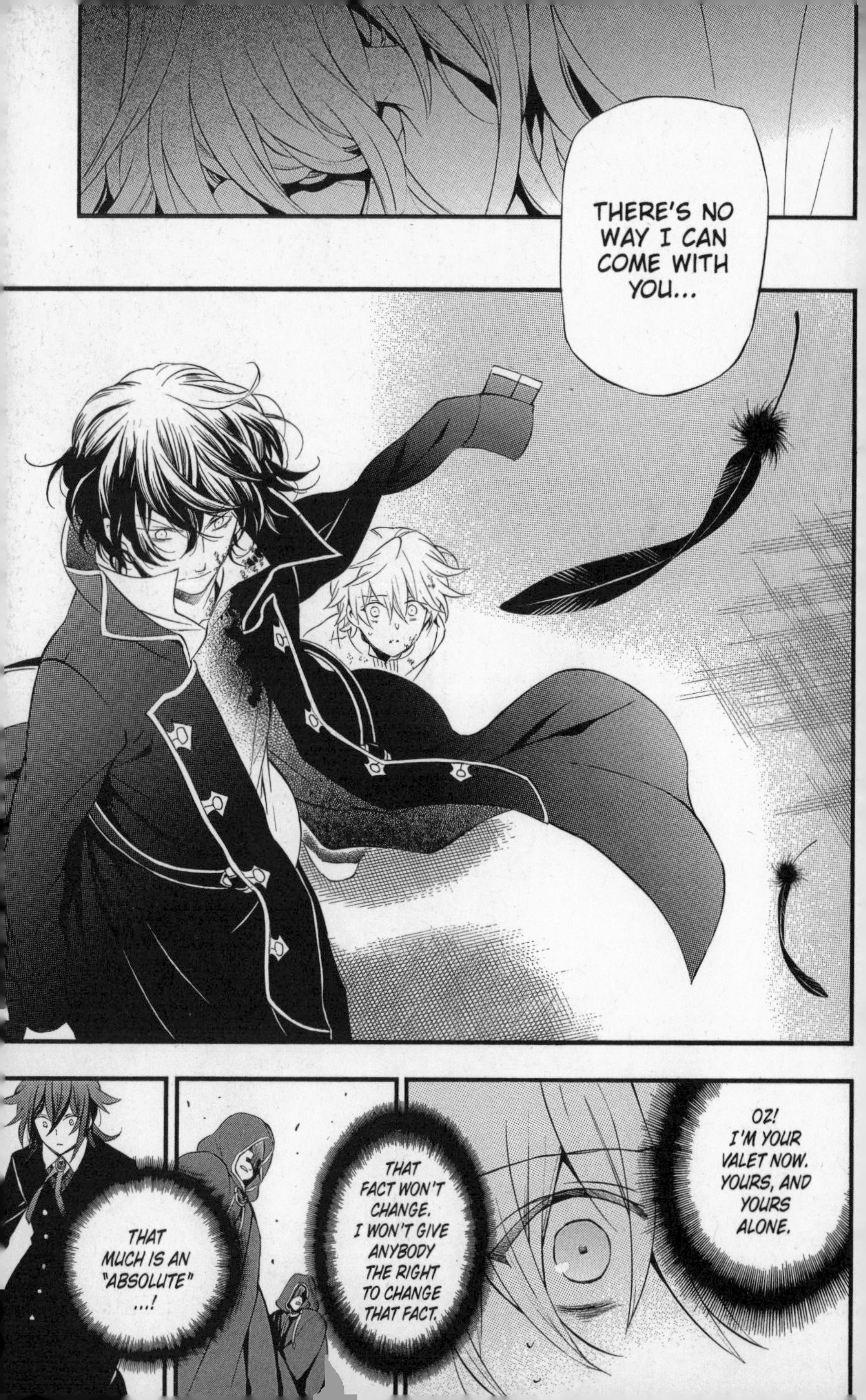
THERE'S NO WAY I CAN COME WITH YOU...
OZ! I'M YOUR VALET NOW. YOURS, AND YOURS ALONE.
THAT FACT WON'T CHANGE. I WON'T GIVE ANYBODY THE RIGHT TO CHANGE THAT FACT.
THAT MUCH IS AN "ABSOLUTE" ...!

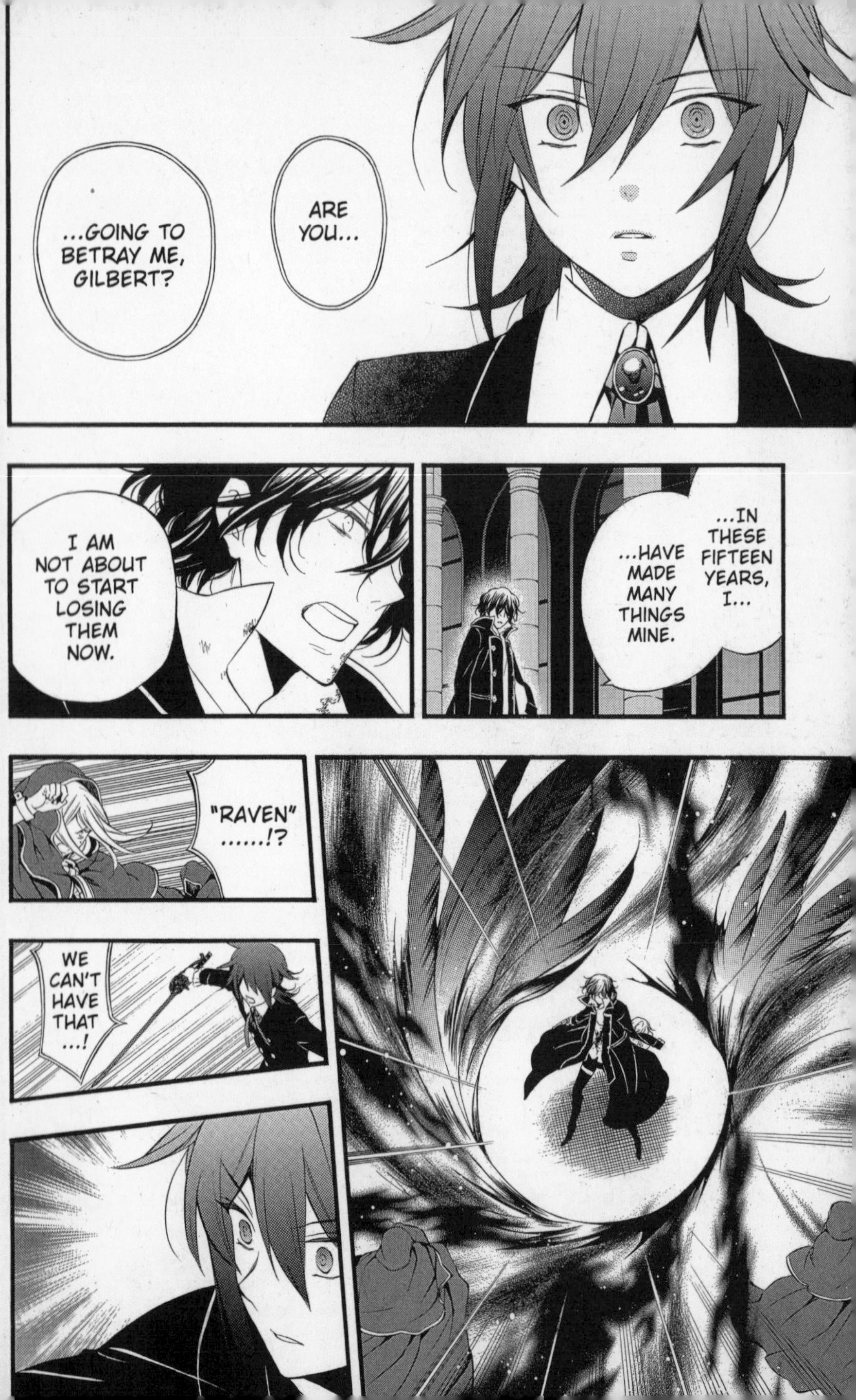
ARE YOU...
...GOING TO BETRAY ME, GILBERT?
...IN THESE FIFTEEN YEARS, I...
...HAVE MADE MANY THINGS MINE.
I AM NOT ABOUT TO START LOSING THEM NOW.
"RAVEN" ......!?
WE CAN'T HAVE THAT ...!

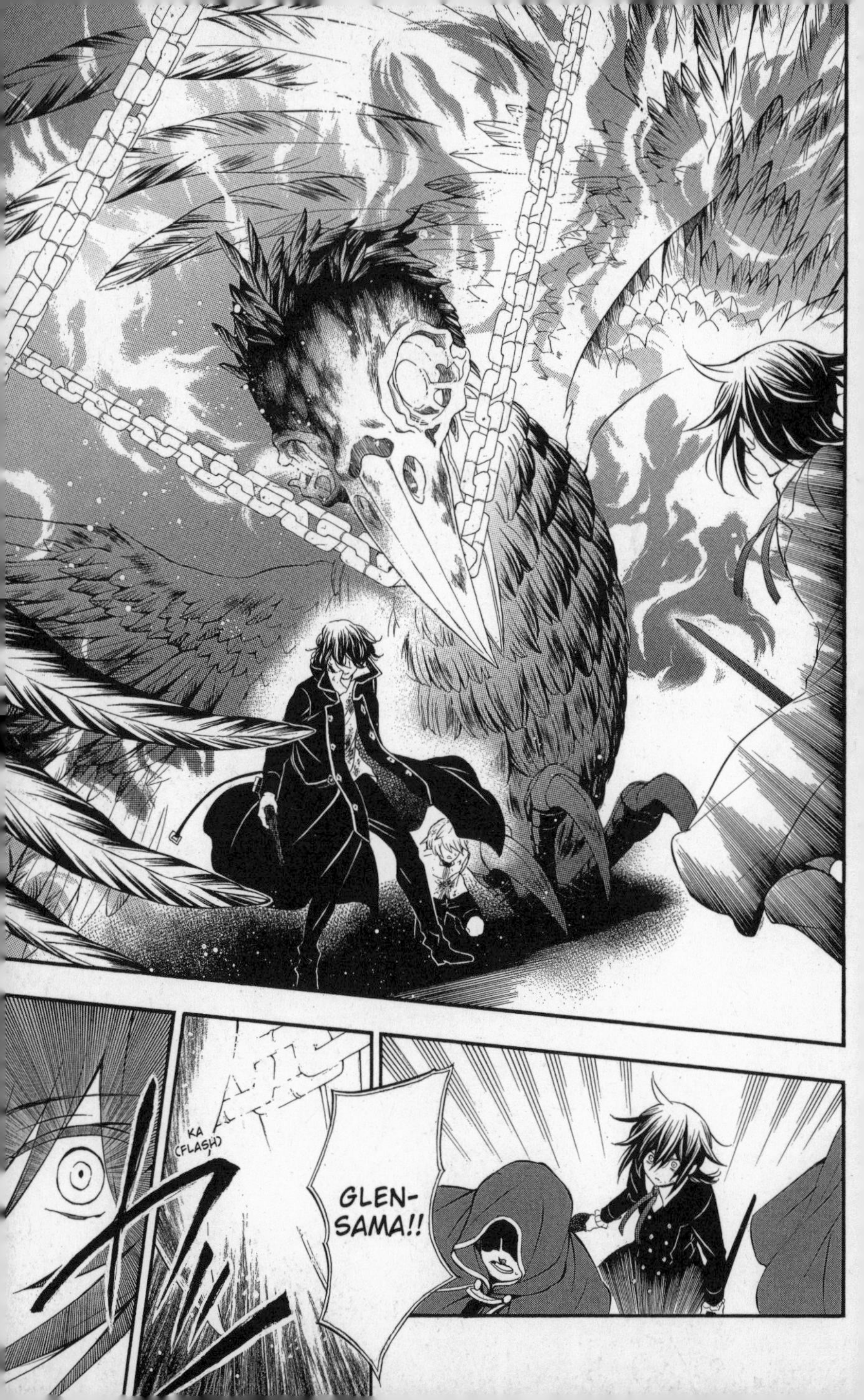
GLEN-
SAMA!!
KA
(FLASH)

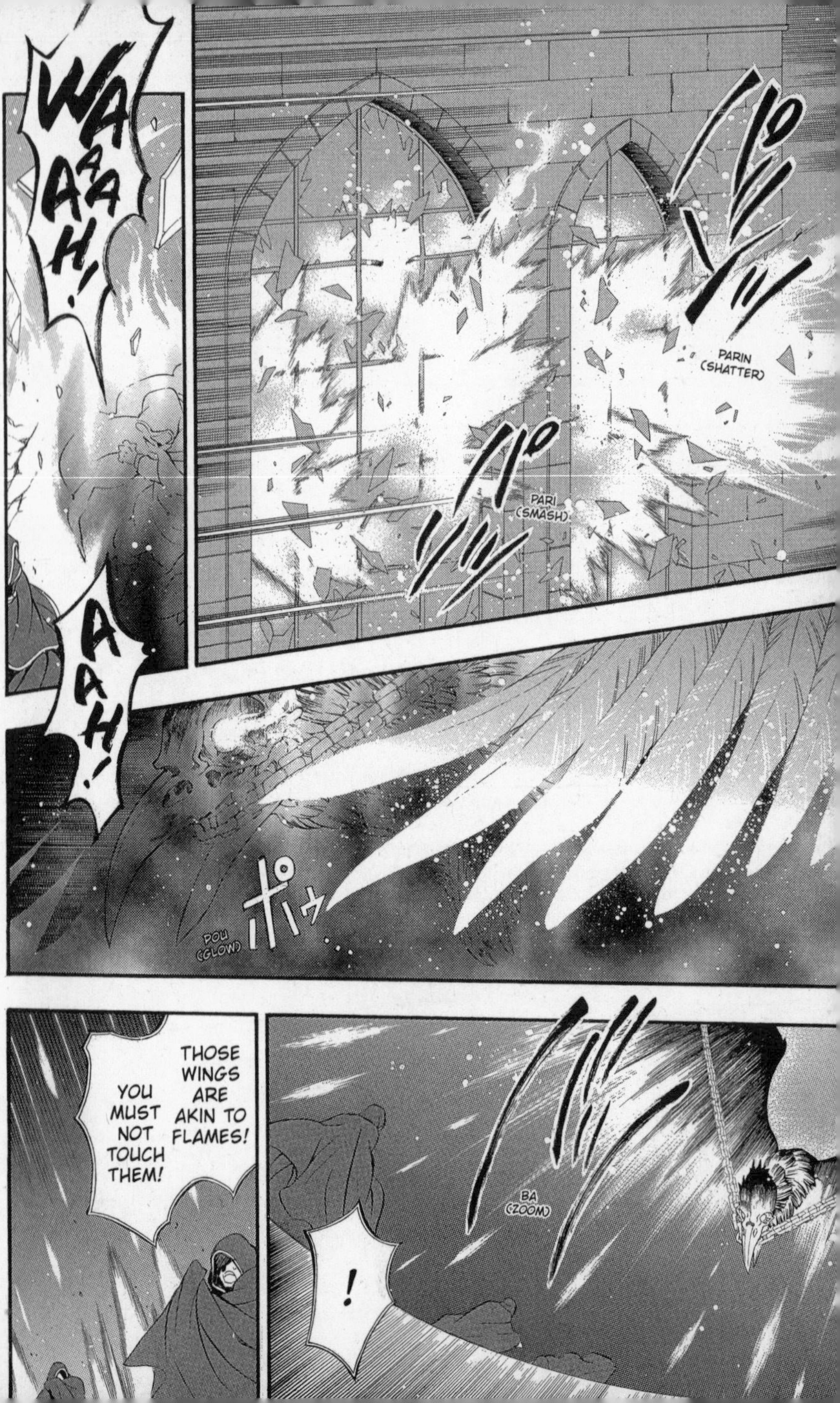
PARIN (SHATTER)
PARI (SMASH)
POU (GLOW)
WAAAAAH!
AAAH!
BA (ZOOM)
!
THOSE WINGS ARE AKIN TO FLAMES!
YOU MUST NOT TOUCH THEM!

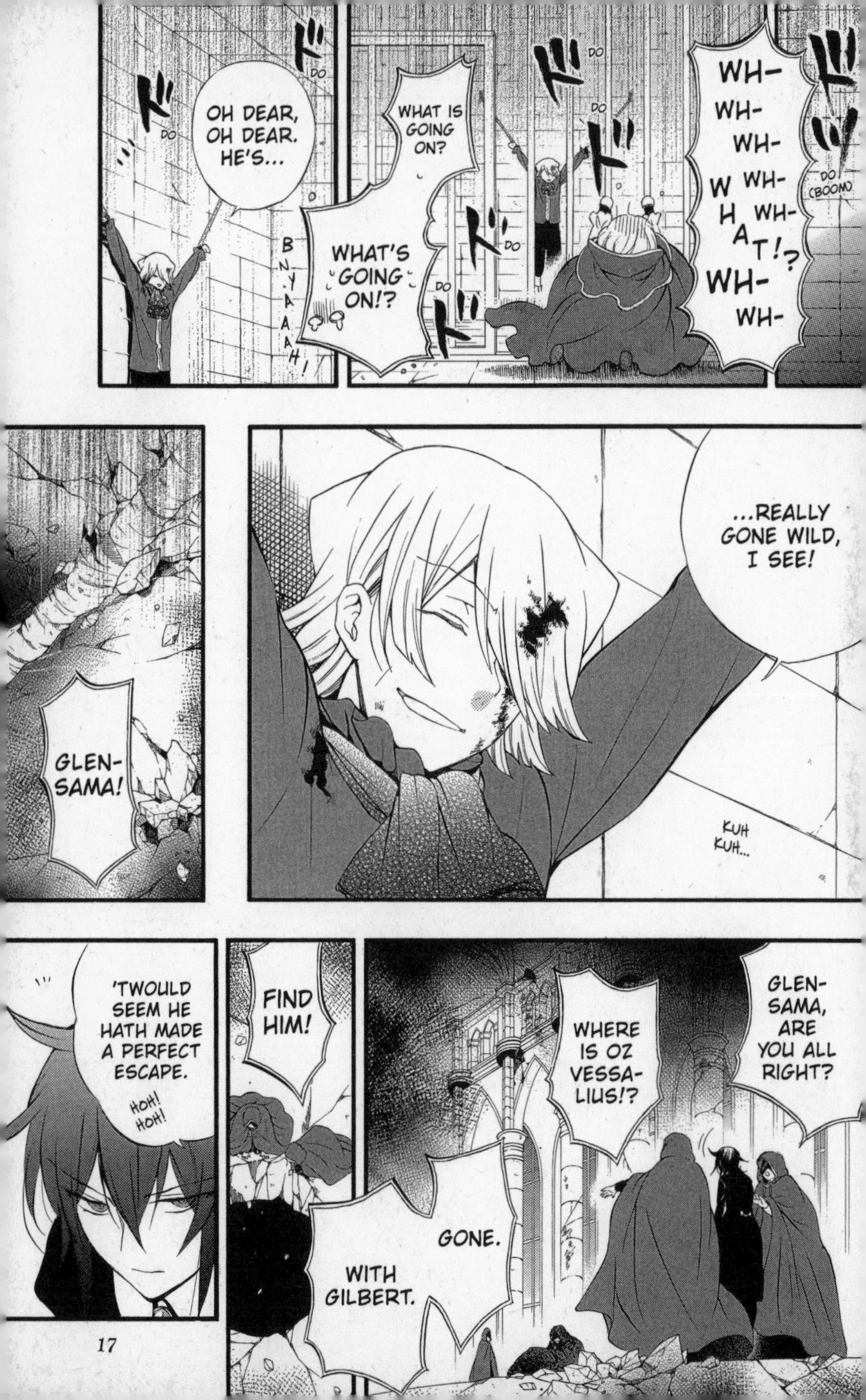

DO (BOOM)
WH- WH- WH- WH- WH- WHAT!? WH- WH-
DO
DO
WHAT IS GOING ON?
DO
DO
WHAT'S GOING ON!?
DO
OH DEAR, OH DEAR. HE'S...
DO
BNYAAAAH!
...REALLY GONE WILD, I SEE!
KUH KUH...
GLEN-SAMA!
GLEN-SAMA, ARE YOU ALL RIGHT?
WHERE IS OZ VESSALIUS!?
GONE.
WITH GILBERT.
FIND HIM!
'TWOULD SEEM HE HATH MADE A PERFECT ESCAPE.
HOH! HOH!

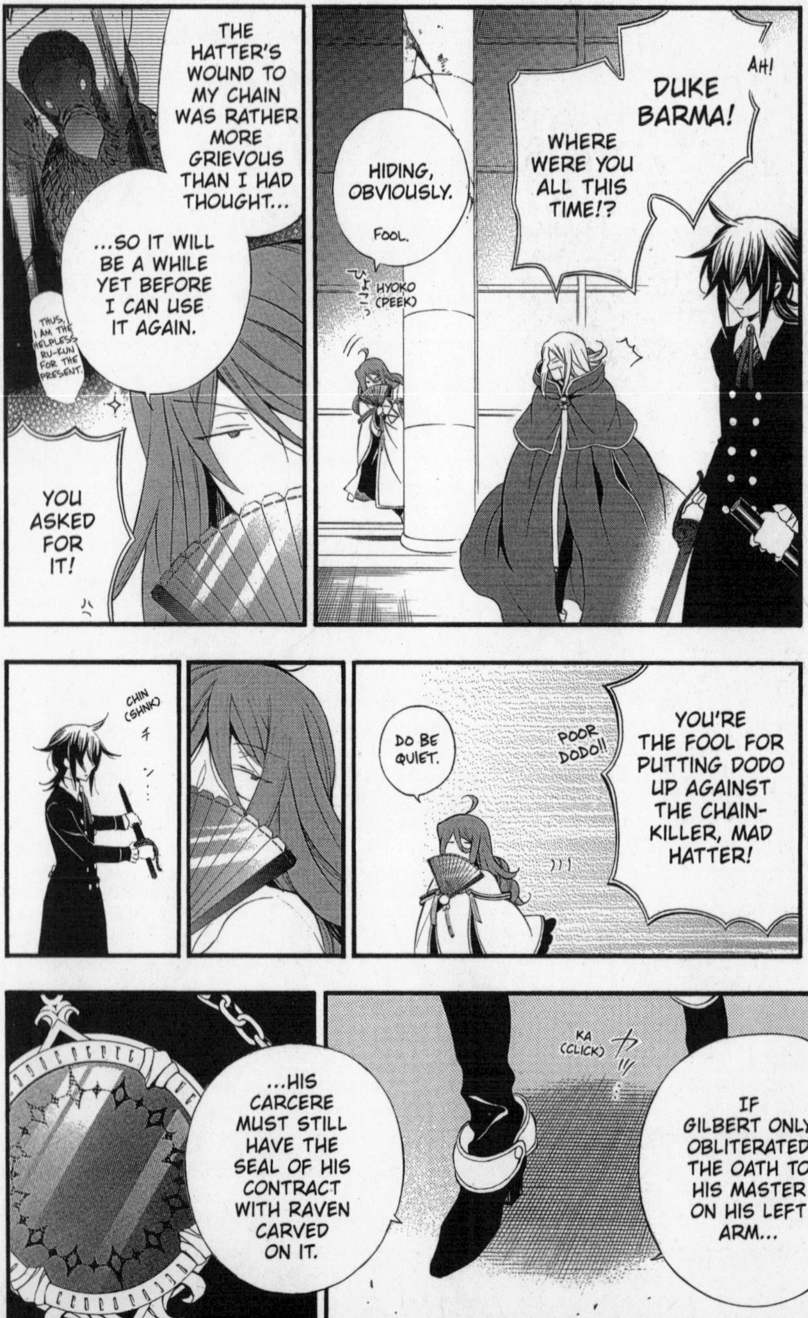
AH!
DUKE BARMA!
WHERE WERE YOU ALL THIS TIME!?
HIDING, OBVIOUSLY.
FOOL.
HYOKO (PEEK)
THE HATTER'S WOUND TO MY CHAIN WAS RATHER MORE GRIEVOUS THAN I HAD THOUGHT...
...SO IT WILL BE A WHILE YET BEFORE I CAN USE IT AGAIN.
THUS, I AM THE HELPLESS RU-KUN FOR THE PRESENT.
YOU ASKED FOR IT!
YOU'RE THE FOOL FOR PUTTING DODO UP AGAINST THE CHAIN-KILLER, MAD HATTER!
POOR DODO!!
DO BE QUIET.
CHIN (SHNK)
KA (CLICK)
IF GILBERT ONLY OBLITERATED THE OATH TO HIS MASTER ON HIS LEFT ARM...
...HIS CARCERE MUST STILL HAVE THE SEAL OF HIS CONTRACT WITH RAVEN CARVED ON IT.

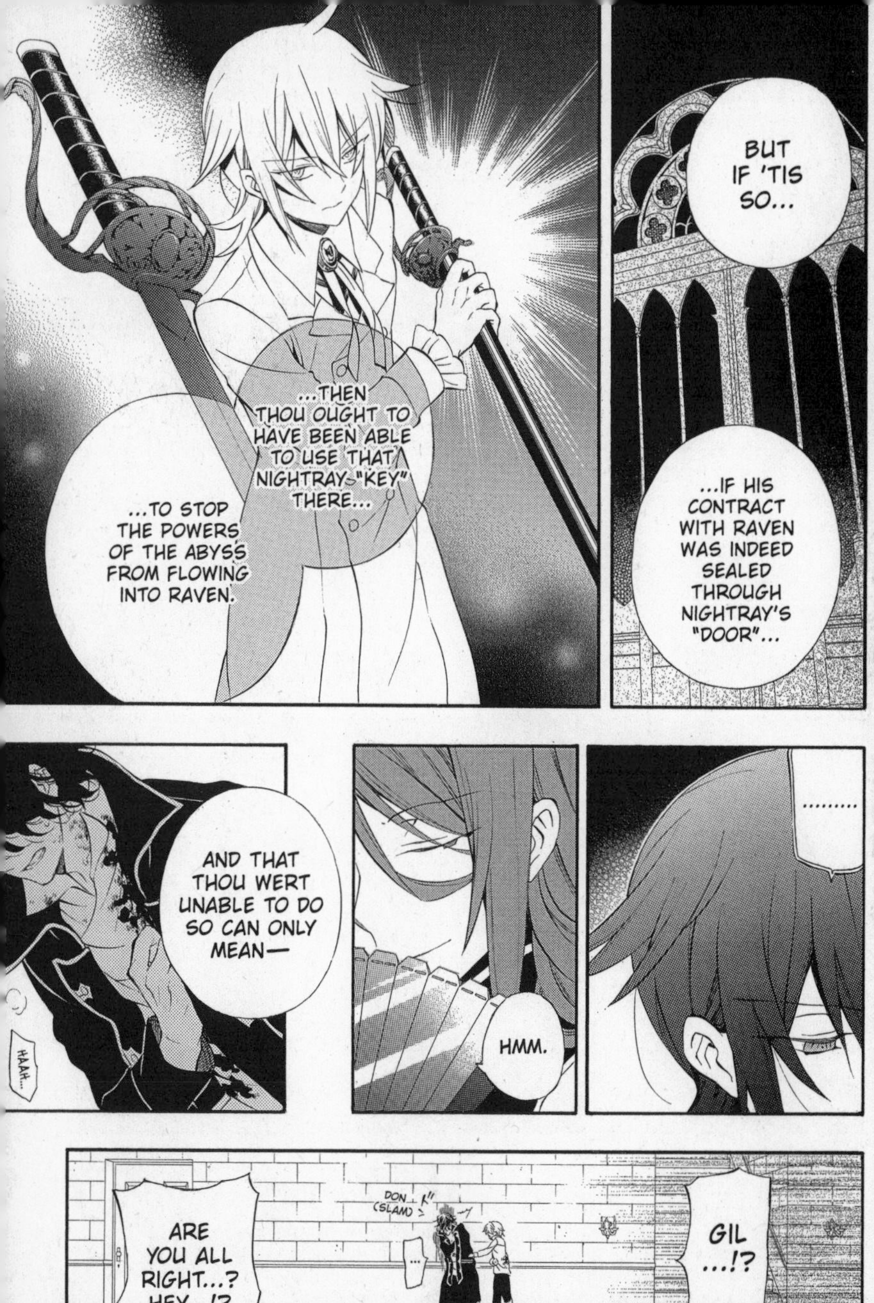
BUT IF 'TIS SO...
...IF HIS CONTRACT WITH RAVEN WAS INDEED SEALED THROUGH NIGHTRAY'S "DOOR"...
...THEN THOU OUGHT TO HAVE BEEN ABLE TO USE THAT NIGHTRAY "KEY" THERE...
...TO STOP THE POWERS OF THE ABYSS FROM FLOWING INTO RAVEN.
....
HMM.
AND THAT THOU WERT UNABLE TO DO SO CAN ONLY MEAN—
HAAH...
GIL ...!?
DON (SLAM)
...
ARE YOU ALL RIGHT...? HEY...!?

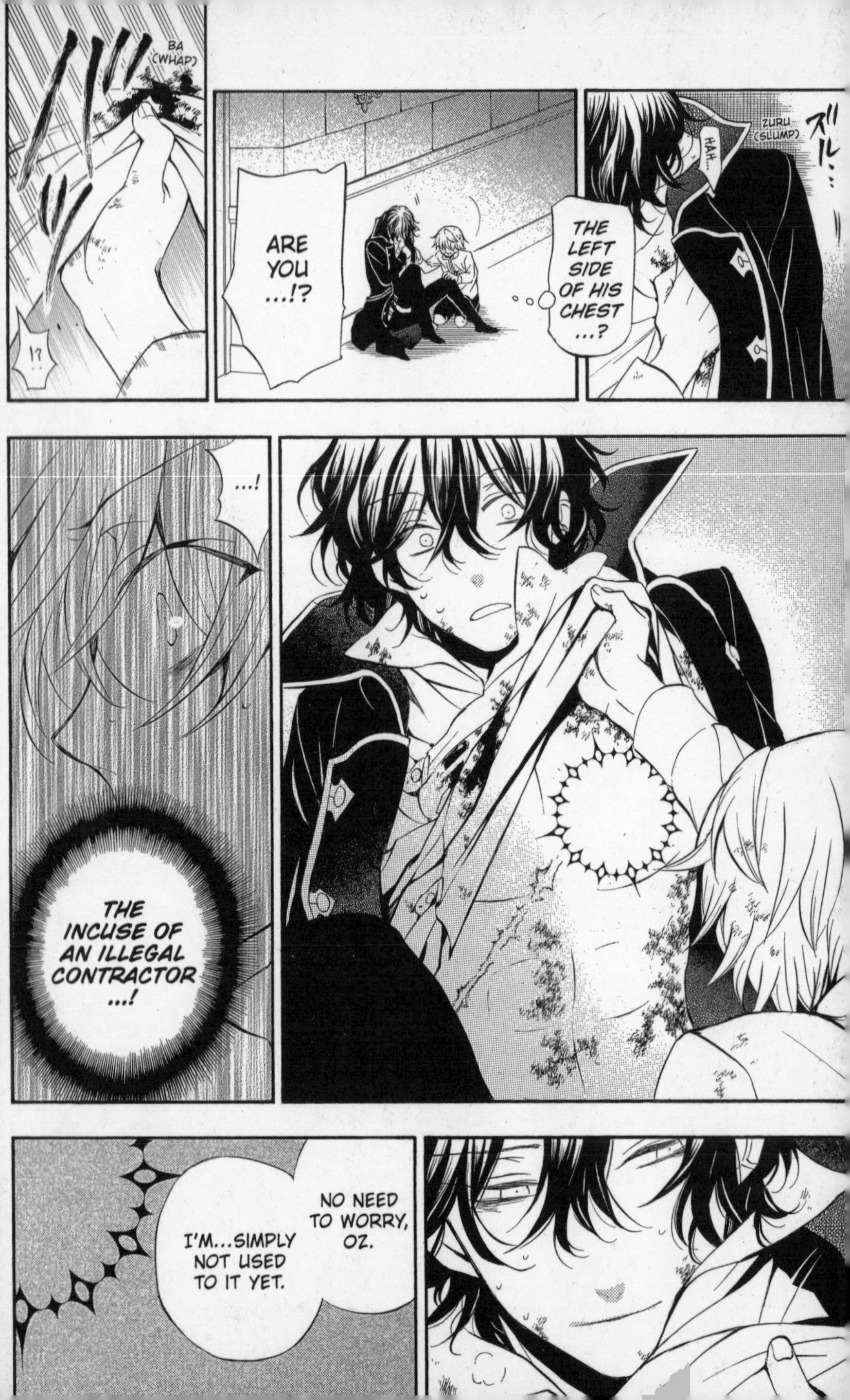
ZURU (SLUMP)
ズル…
HAH...
THE LEFT SIDE OF HIS CHEST ...?
ARE YOU ...!?
BA (WHAP)
!?
...!
THE INCUSE OF AN ILLEGAL CONTRACTOR ...!
NO NEED TO WORRY, OZ.
I'M...SIMPLY NOT USED TO IT YET.

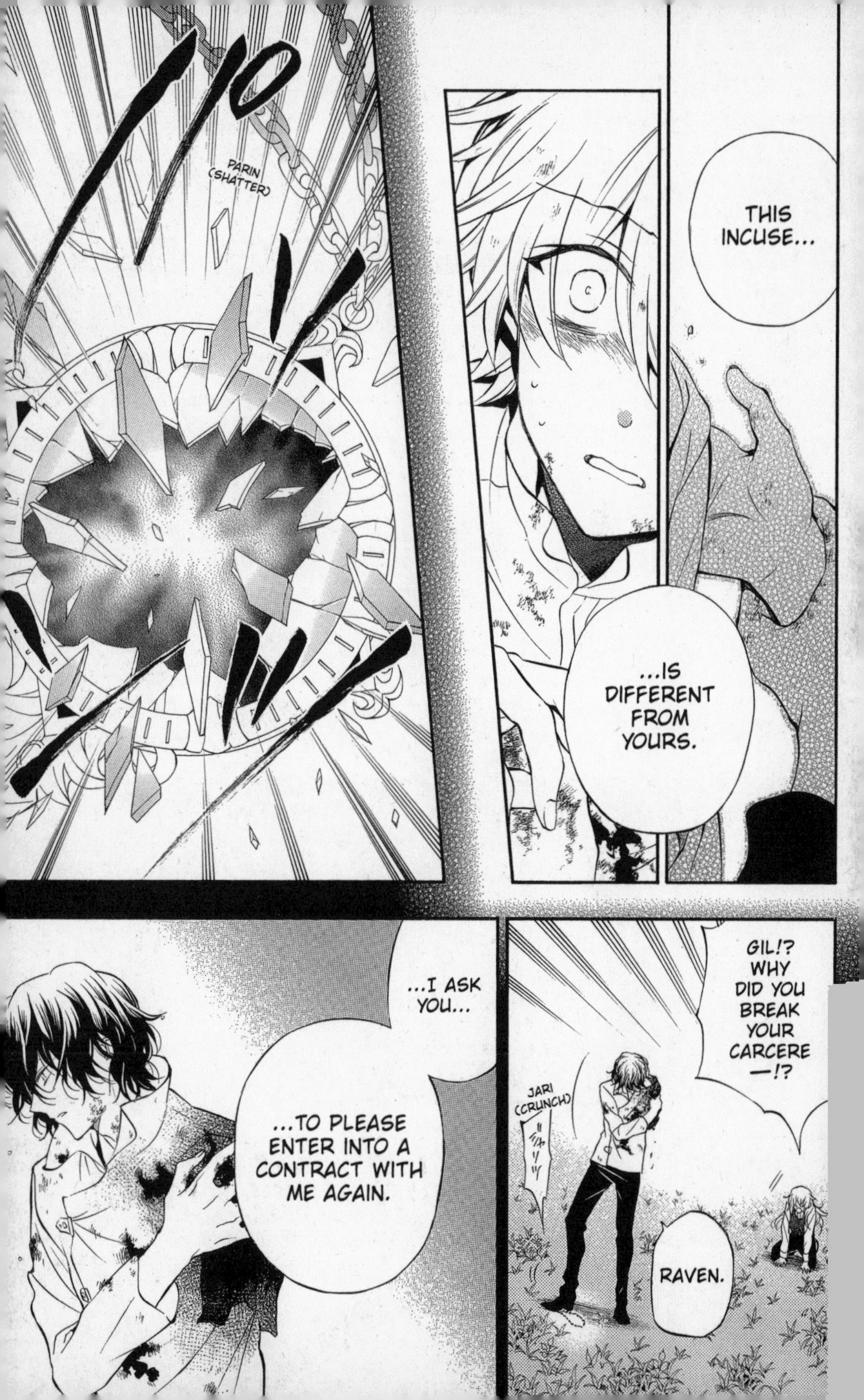
THIS INCUSE...
...IS DIFFERENT FROM YOURS.
PARIN (SHATTER)
GIL!? WHY DID YOU BREAK YOUR CARCERE—!?
JARI (CRUNCH)
RAVEN.
...I ASK YOU...
...TO PLEASE ENTER INTO A CONTRACT WITH ME AGAIN.

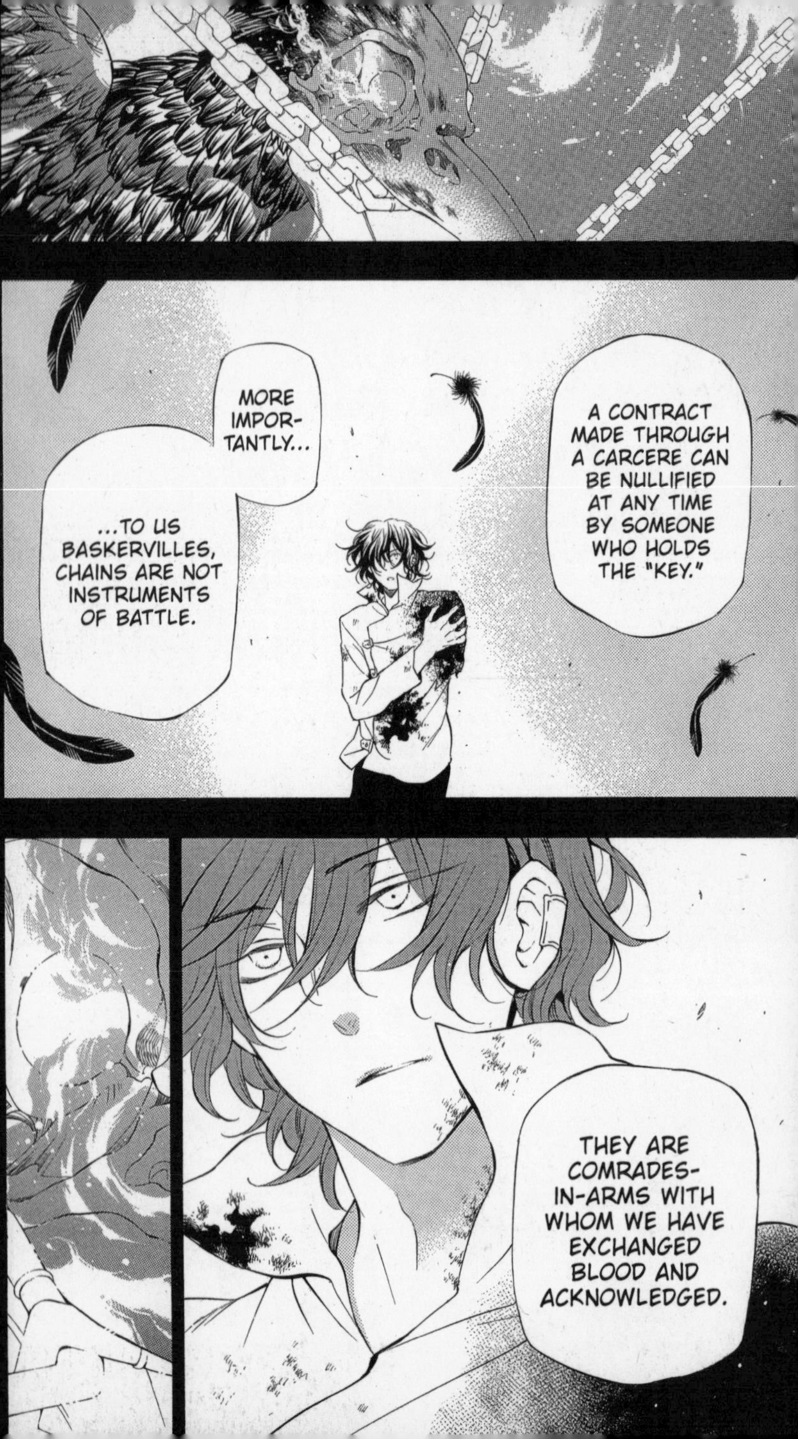
A CONTRACT MADE THROUGH A CARCERE CAN BE NULLIFIED AT ANY TIME BY SOMEONE WHO HOLDS THE "KEY."
MORE IMPOR-TANTLY...
...TO US BASKERVILLES, CHAINS ARE NOT INSTRUMENTS OF BATTLE.
THEY ARE COMRADES-IN-ARMS WITH WHOM WE HAVE EXCHANGED BLOOD AND ACKNOWLEDGED.

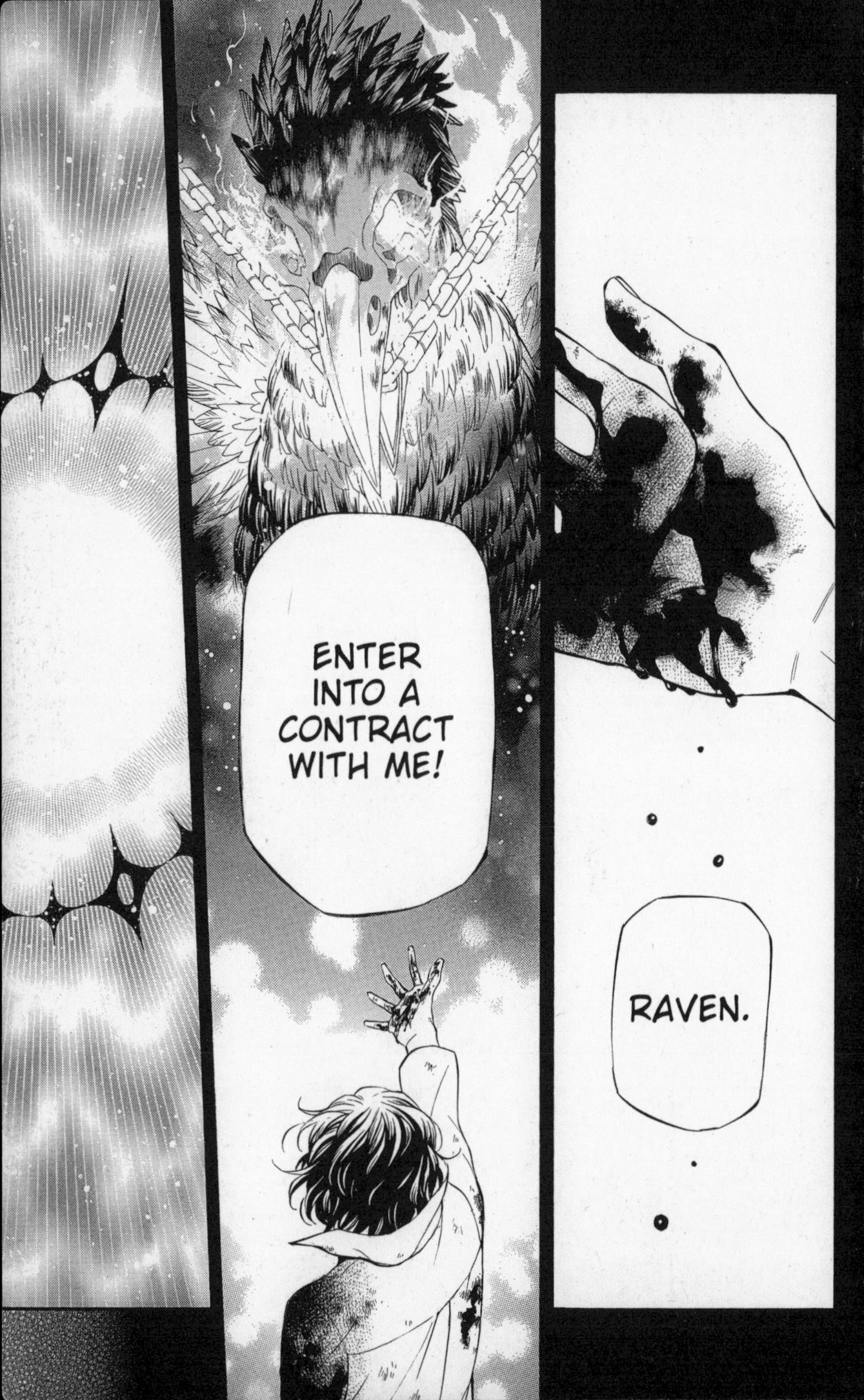
RAVEN.
ENTER INTO A CONTRACT WITH ME!

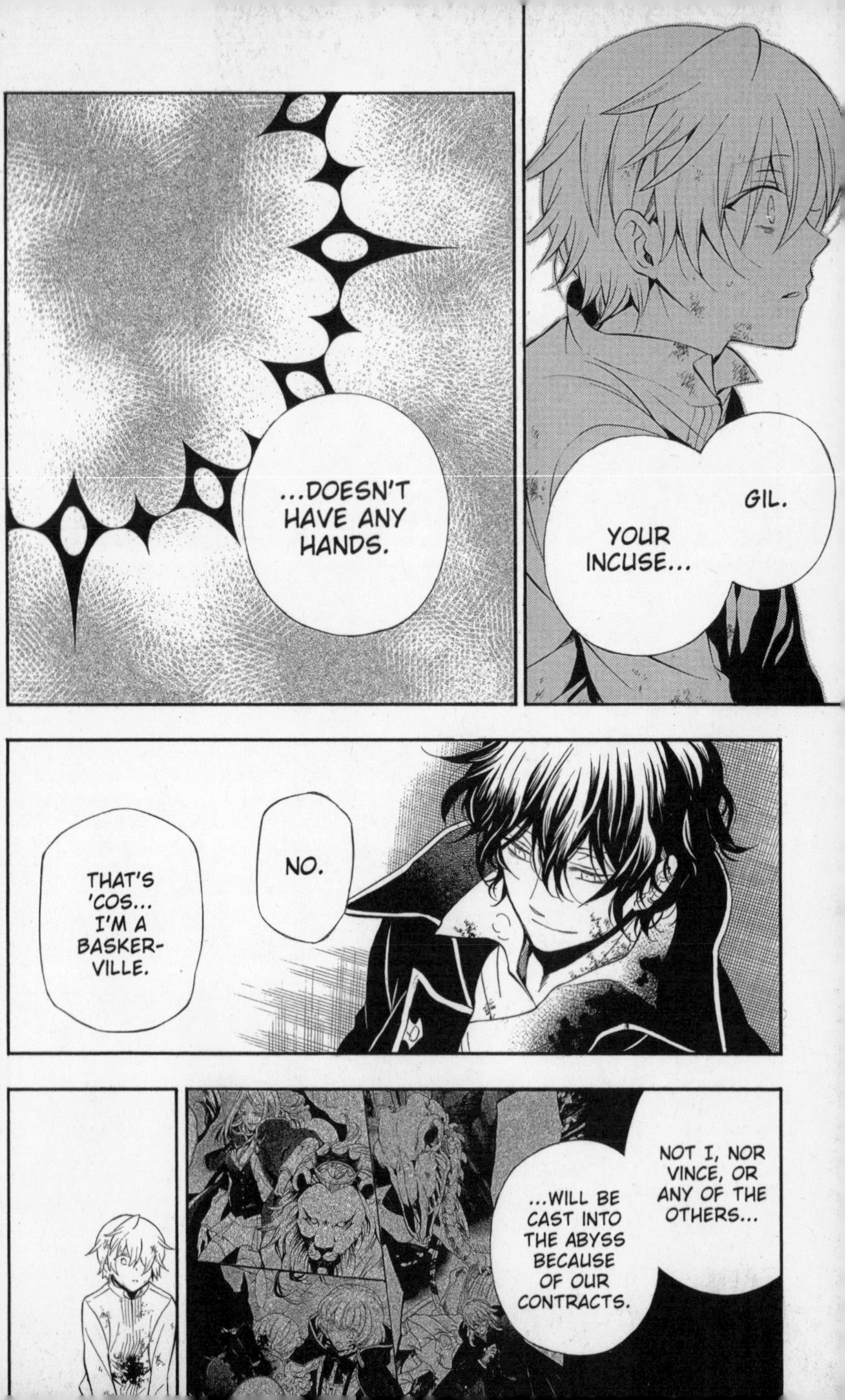
GIL.
YOUR INCUSE...
...DOESN'T HAVE ANY HANDS.
NO.
THAT'S 'COS... I'M A BASKER-VILLE.
NOT I, NOR VINCE, OR ANY OF THE OTHERS...
...WILL BE CAST INTO THE ABYSS BECAUSE OF OUR CONTRACTS.

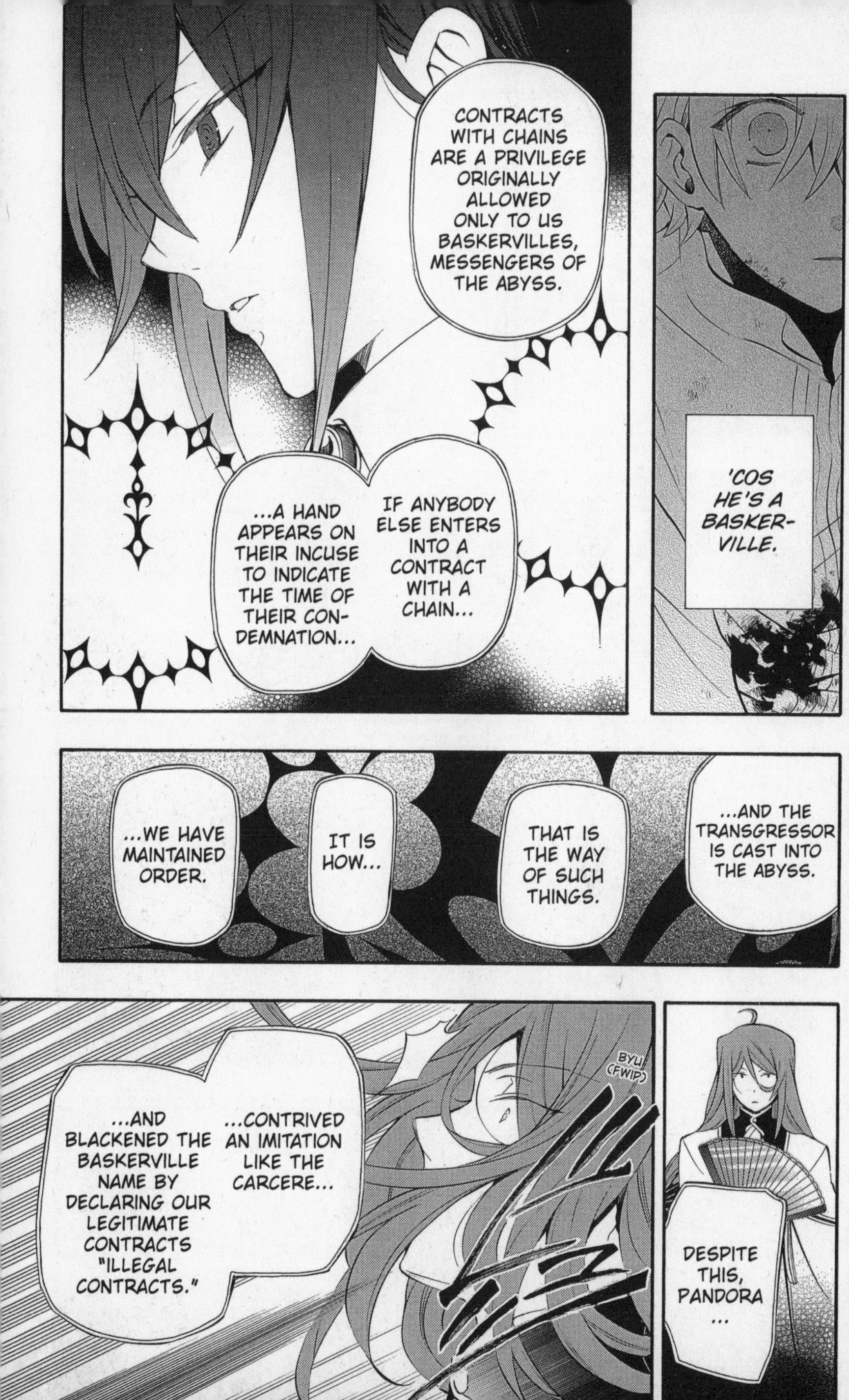

'COS HE'S A BASKER-VILLE.
CONTRACTS WITH CHAINS ARE A PRIVILEGE ORIGINALLY ALLOWED ONLY TO US BASKERVILLES, MESSENGERS OF THE ABYSS.
IF ANYBODY ELSE ENTERS INTO A CONTRACT WITH A CHAIN...
...A HAND APPEARS ON THEIR INCUSE TO INDICATE THE TIME OF THEIR CON-DEMNATION...
...AND THE TRANSGRESSOR IS CAST INTO THE ABYSS.
THAT IS THE WAY OF SUCH THINGS.
IT IS HOW...
...WE HAVE MAINTAINED ORDER.
DESPITE THIS, PANDORA...
BYU (FWIP)
...CONTRIVED AN IMITATION LIKE THE CARCERE...
...AND BLACKENED THE BASKERVILLE NAME BY DECLARING OUR LEGITIMATE CONTRACTS "ILLEGAL CONTRACTS."

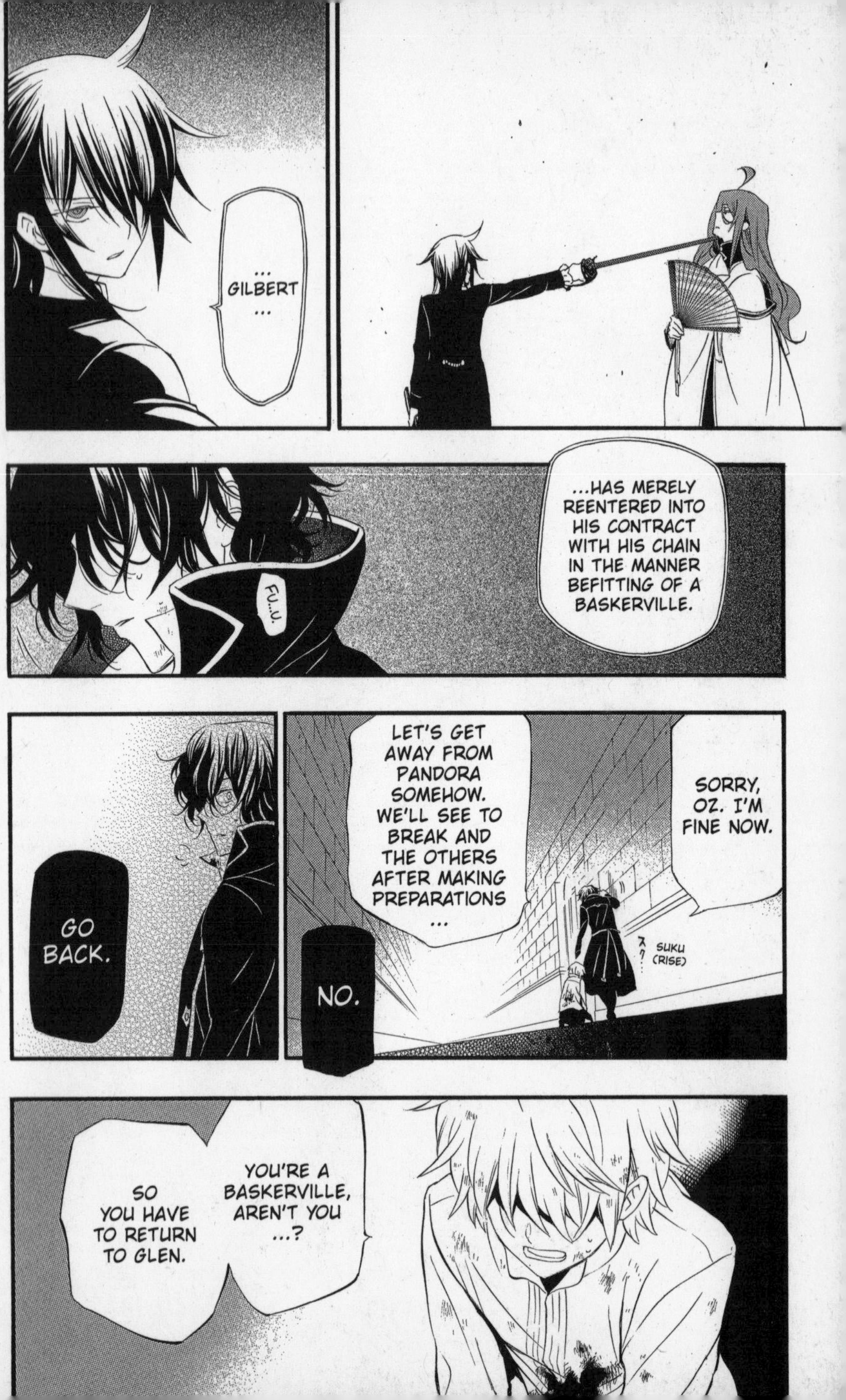

... GILBERT ...
...HAS MERELY REENTERED INTO HIS CONTRACT WITH HIS CHAIN IN THE MANNER BEFITTING OF A BASKERVILLE.
FU...U.
SORRY, OZ. I'M FINE NOW.
LET'S GET AWAY FROM PANDORA SOMEHOW. WE'LL SEE TO BREAK AND THE OTHERS AFTER MAKING PREPARATIONS ...
SUKU (RISE)
NO.
GO BACK.
YOU'RE A BASKERVILLE, AREN'T YOU ...?
SO YOU HAVE TO RETURN TO GLEN.

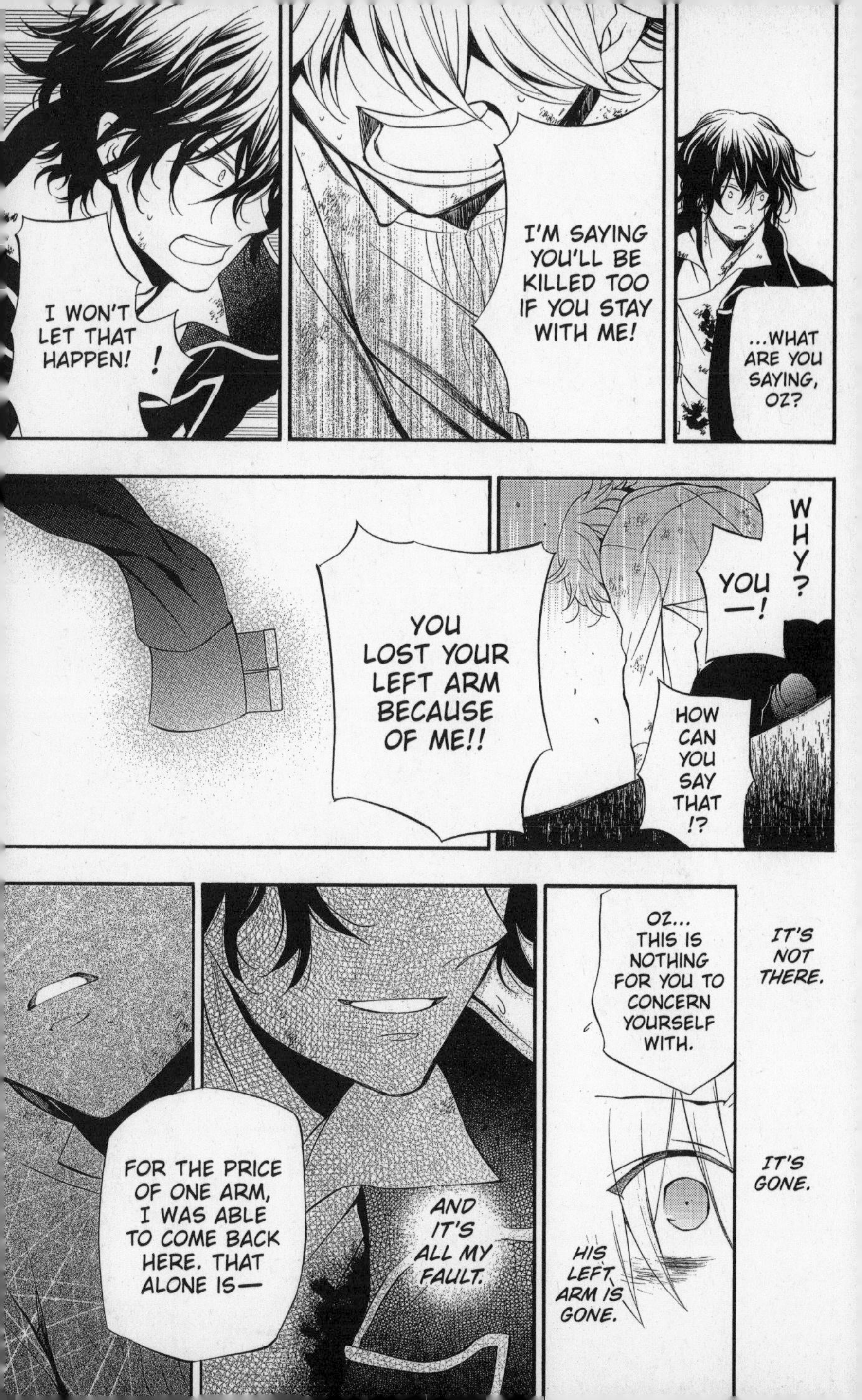
...WHAT ARE YOU SAYING, OZ?
I'M SAYING YOU'LL BE KILLED TOO IF YOU STAY WITH ME!
I WON'T LET THAT HAPPEN!
!
WHY?
YOU—!
HOW CAN YOU SAY THAT!?
YOU LOST YOUR LEFT ARM BECAUSE OF ME!!
IT'S NOT THERE.
OZ... THIS IS NOTHING FOR YOU TO CONCERN YOURSELF WITH.
IT'S GONE.
HIS LEFT ARM IS GONE.
AND IT'S ALL MY FAULT.
FOR THE PRICE OF ONE ARM, I WAS ABLE TO COME BACK HERE. THAT ALONE IS—

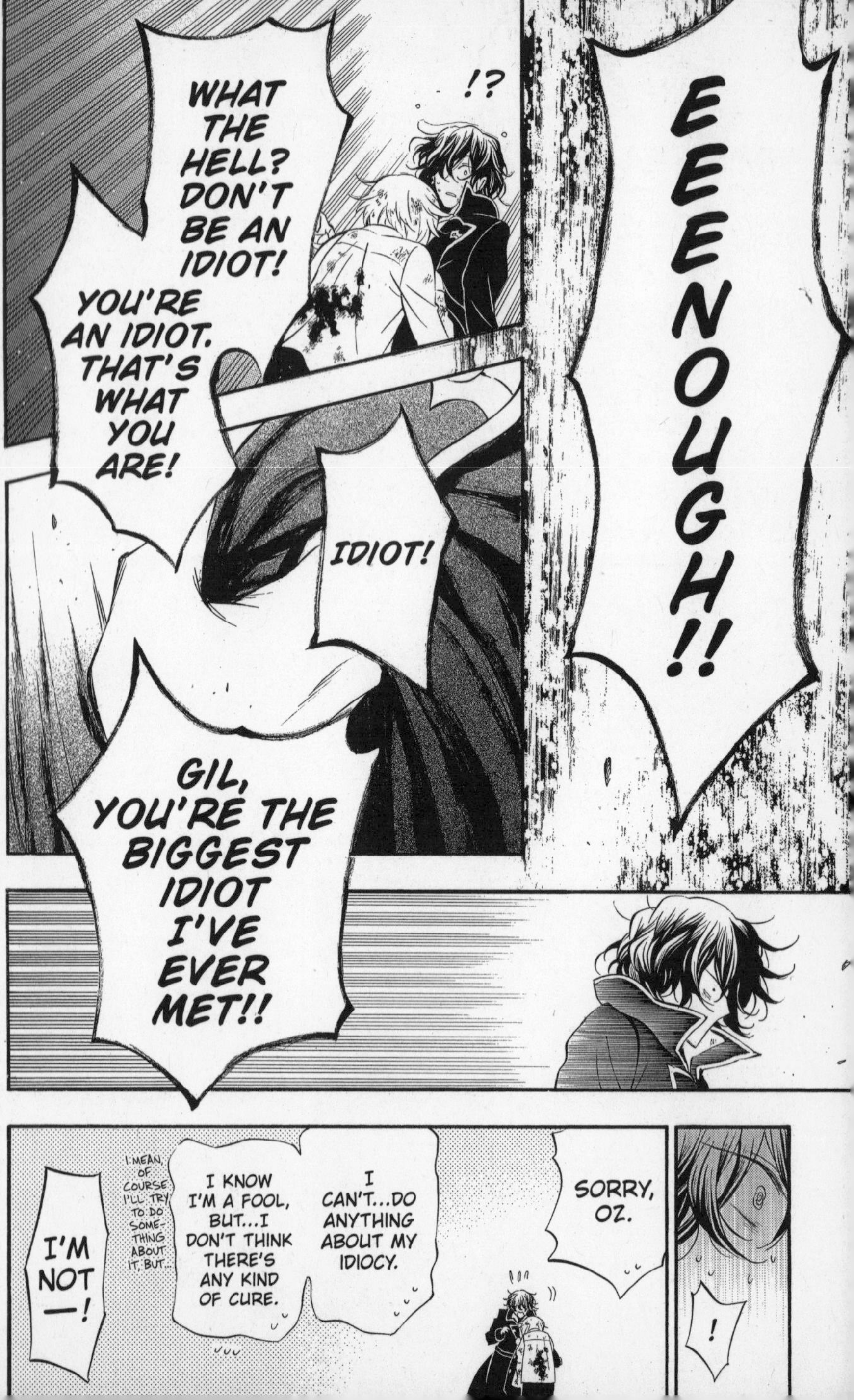
EEEENOUGH!!
!?
WHAT THE HELL? DON'T BE AN IDIOT!
YOU'RE AN IDIOT. THAT'S WHAT YOU ARE!
IDIOT!
GIL, YOU'RE THE BIGGEST IDIOT I'VE EVER MET!!
!
SORRY, OZ.
I CAN'T...DO ANYTHING ABOUT MY IDIOCY.
I KNOW I'M A FOOL, BUT...I DON'T THINK THERE'S ANY KIND OF CURE.
I MEAN, OF COURSE I'LL TRY TO DO SOMETHING ABOUT IT, BUT...
I'M NOT—!

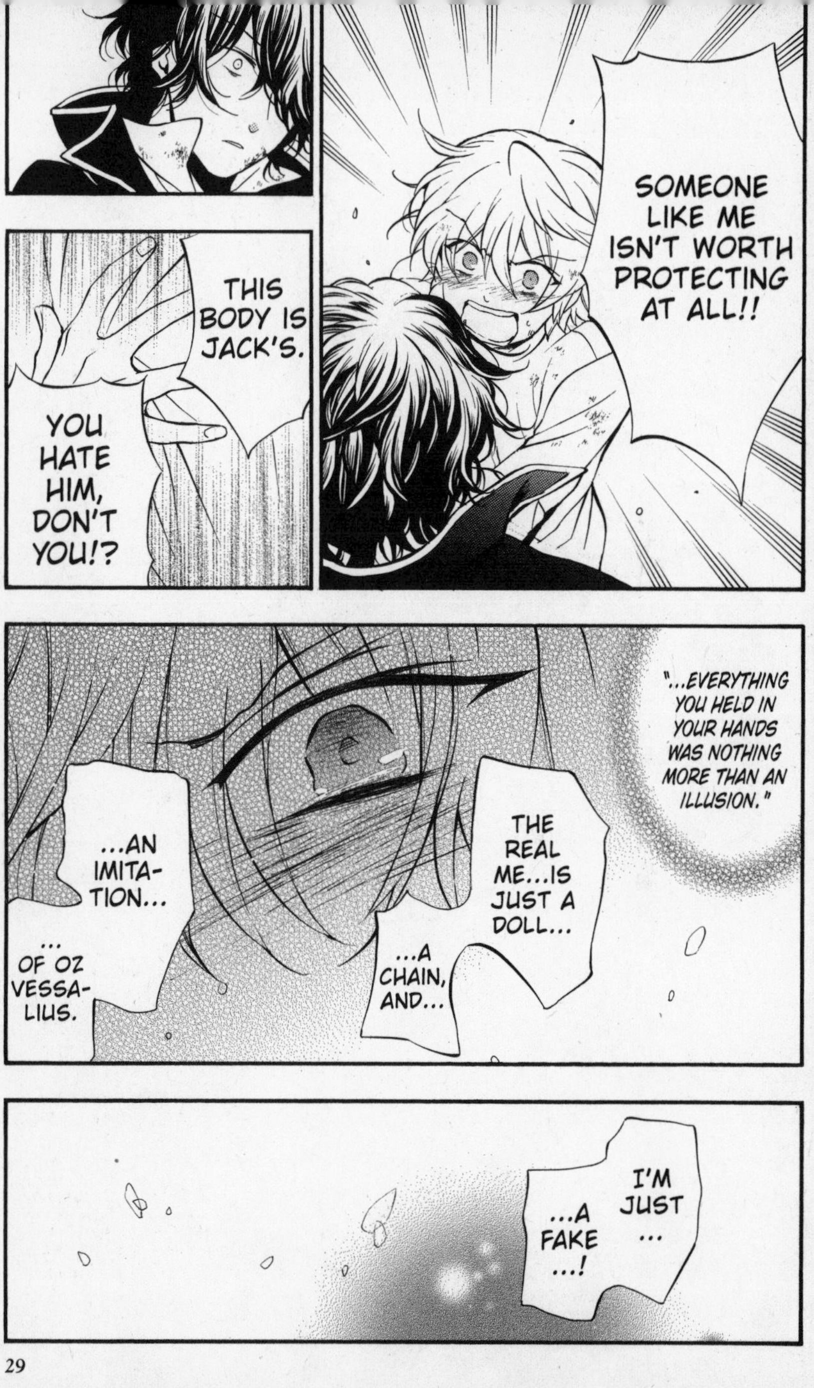
SOMEONE LIKE ME ISN'T WORTH PROTECTING AT ALL!!
THIS BODY IS JACK'S.
YOU HATE HIM, DON'T YOU!?
"...EVERYTHING YOU HELD IN YOUR HANDS WAS NOTHING MORE THAN AN ILLUSION."
THE REAL ME...IS JUST A DOLL...
...A CHAIN, AND...
...AN IMITATION...
...OF OZ VESSALIUS.
I'M JUST...
...A FAKE...!

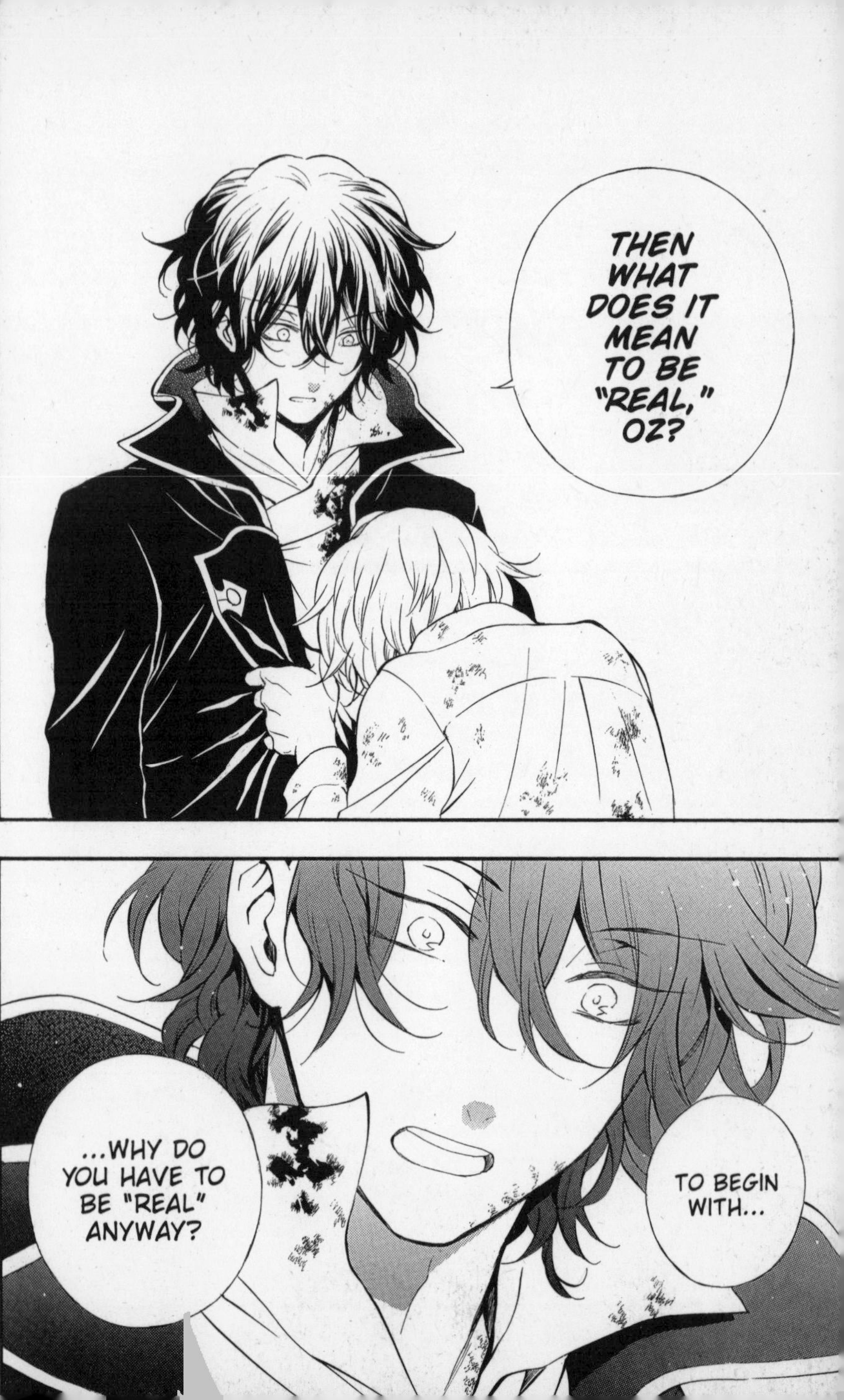
THEN WHAT DOES IT MEAN TO BE "REAL," OZ?
TO BEGIN WITH...
...WHY DO YOU HAVE TO BE "REAL" ANYWAY?

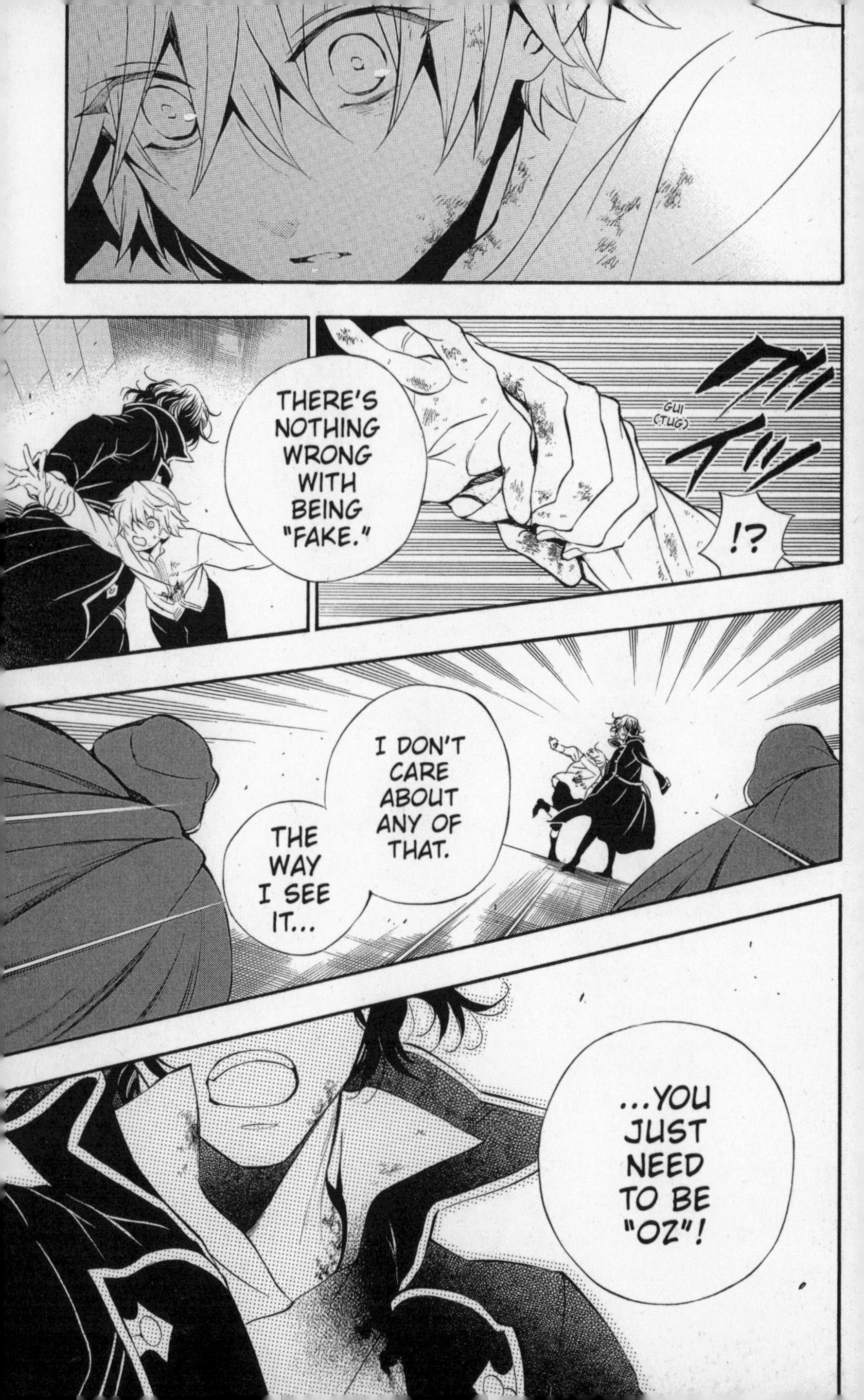

GUI (TUG)
!?
THERE'S NOTHING WRONG WITH BEING "FAKE."
I DON'T CARE ABOUT ANY OF THAT.
THE WAY I SEE IT...
...YOU JUST NEED TO BE "OZ"!

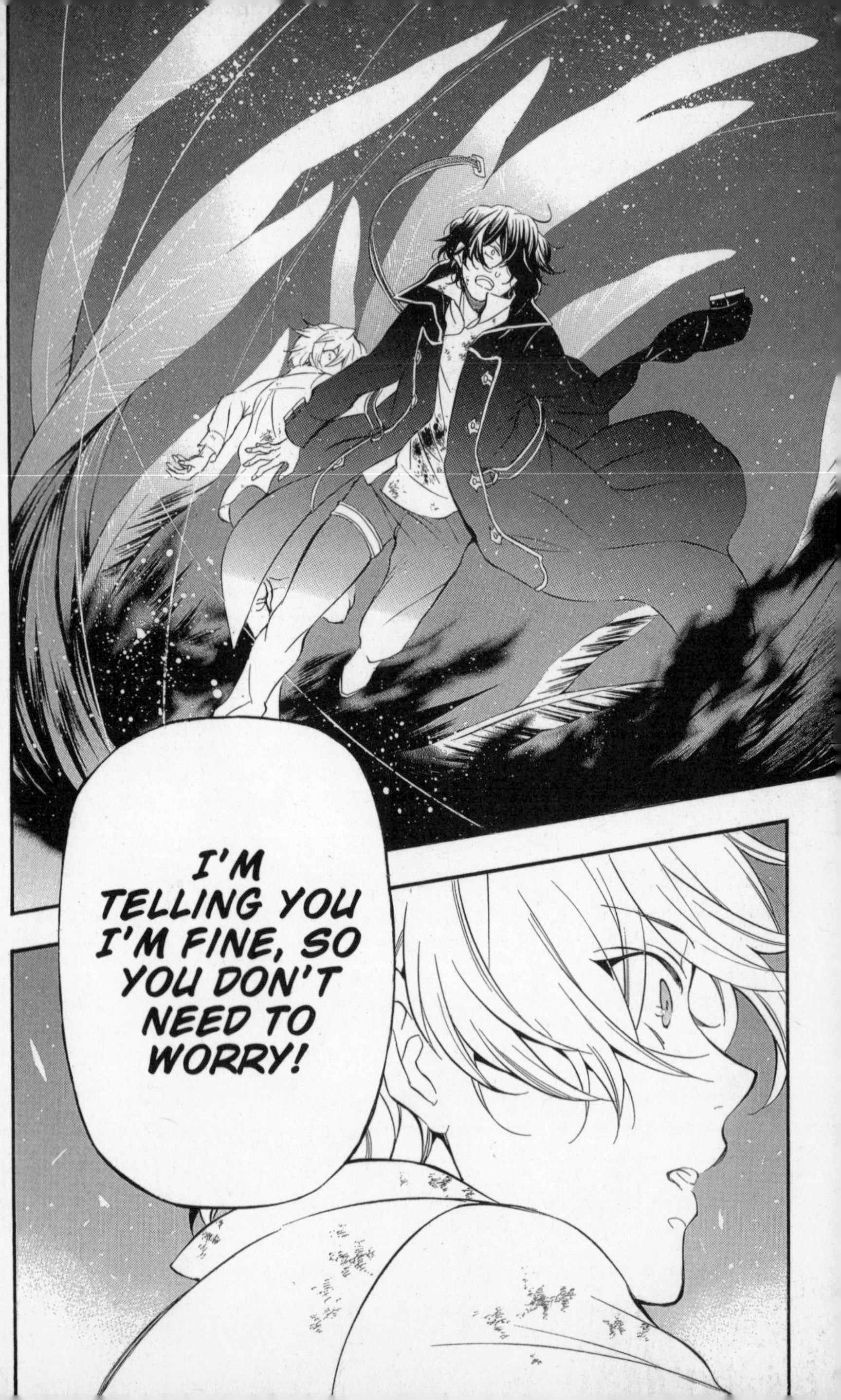
I'M TELLING YOU I'M FINE, SO YOU DON'T NEED TO WORRY!

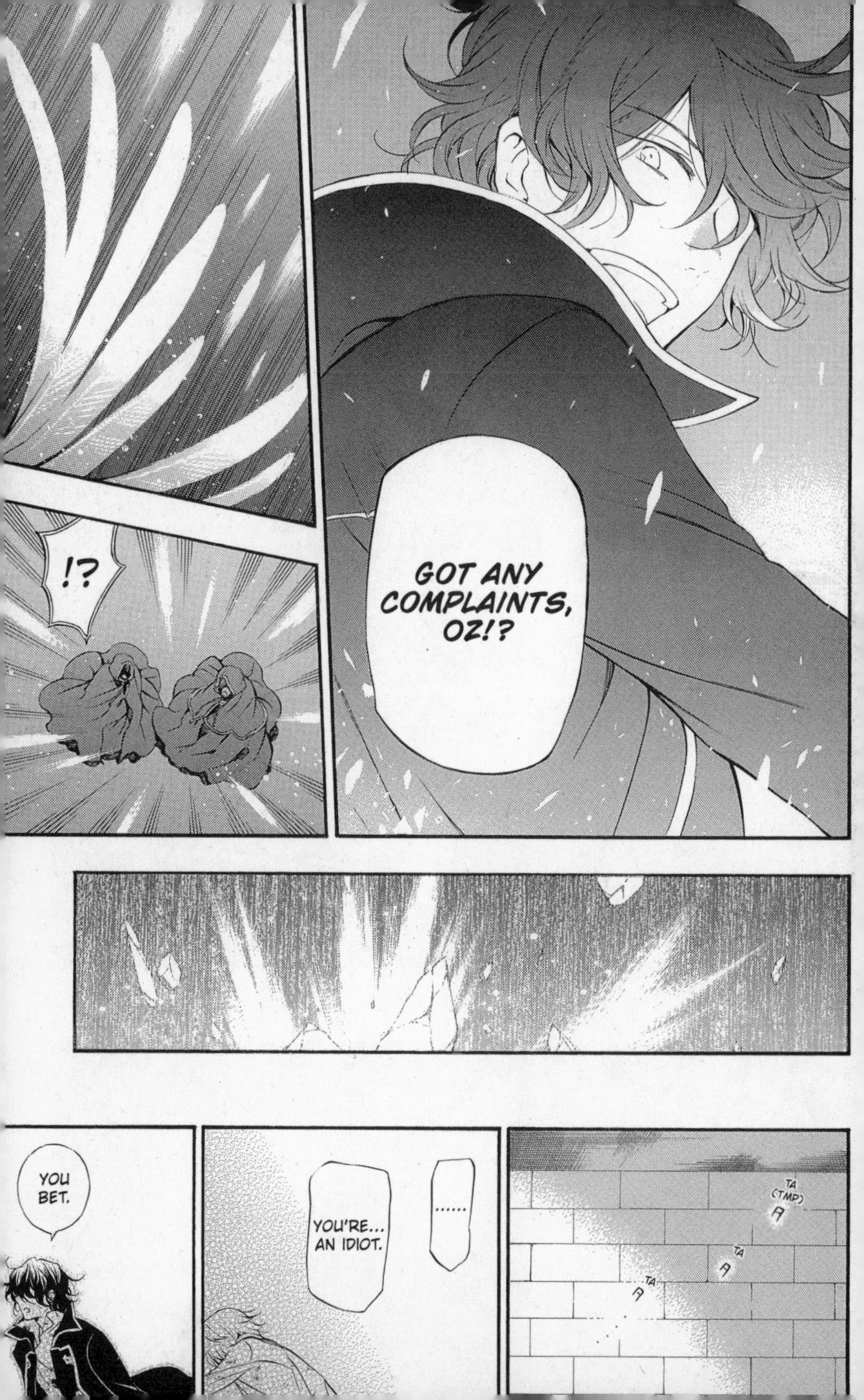
GOT ANY COMPLAINTS, OZ!?
!?
TA (TMP)
TA
TA
......
YOU'RE... AN IDIOT.
YOU BET.

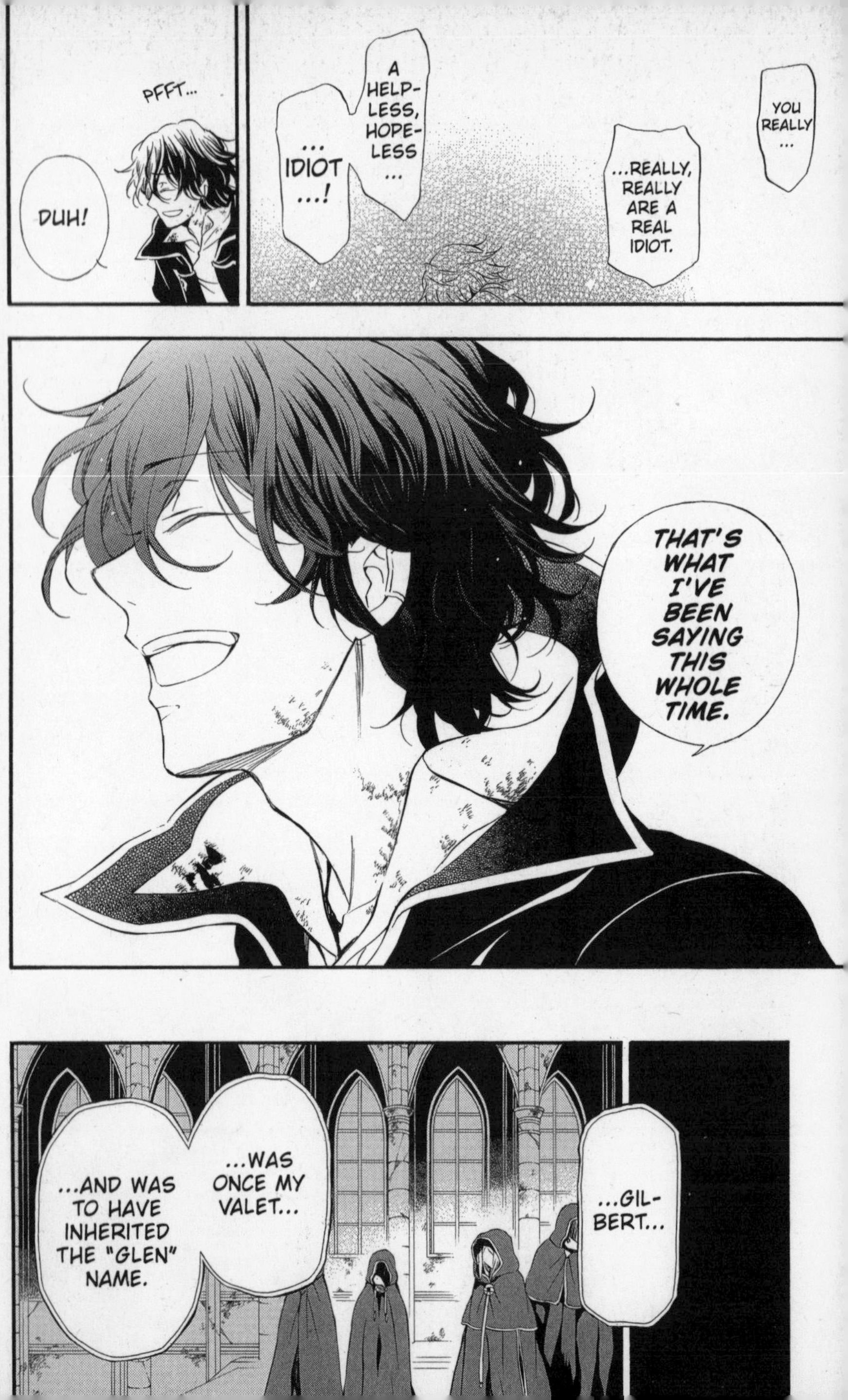
YOU REALLY ...
...REALLY, REALLY ARE A REAL IDIOT.
A HELPLESS, HOPELESS ...
... IDIOT ...!
PFFT...
DUH!
THAT'S WHAT I'VE BEEN SAYING THIS WHOLE TIME.
...GILBERT...
...WAS ONCE MY VALET...
...AND WAS TO HAVE INHERITED THE "GLEN" NAME.

BUT NOW HE IS NOTHING MORE THAN A FOOLISH TRAITOR.

KILL HIM.

ALONG WITH OZ VESSALIUS —!

KATSU (CLICK)

!

OZ. GILBERT.

ARE YOU THERE!?

KATSU

KATSU

SHH... OZ...

!

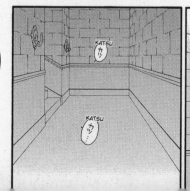

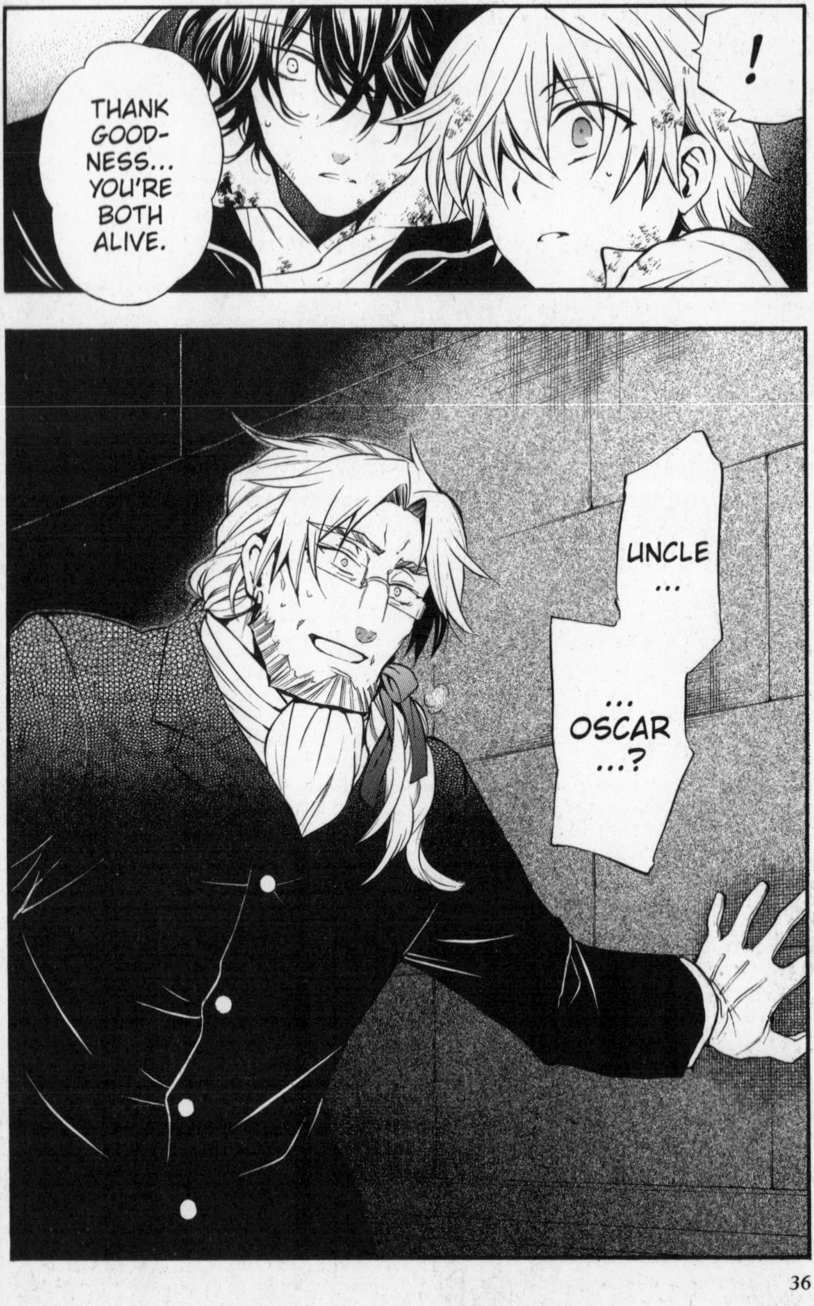
!
THANK GOODNESS... YOU'RE BOTH ALIVE.
UNCLE ...
... OSCAR ...?

Retrace:LXXIX Falling

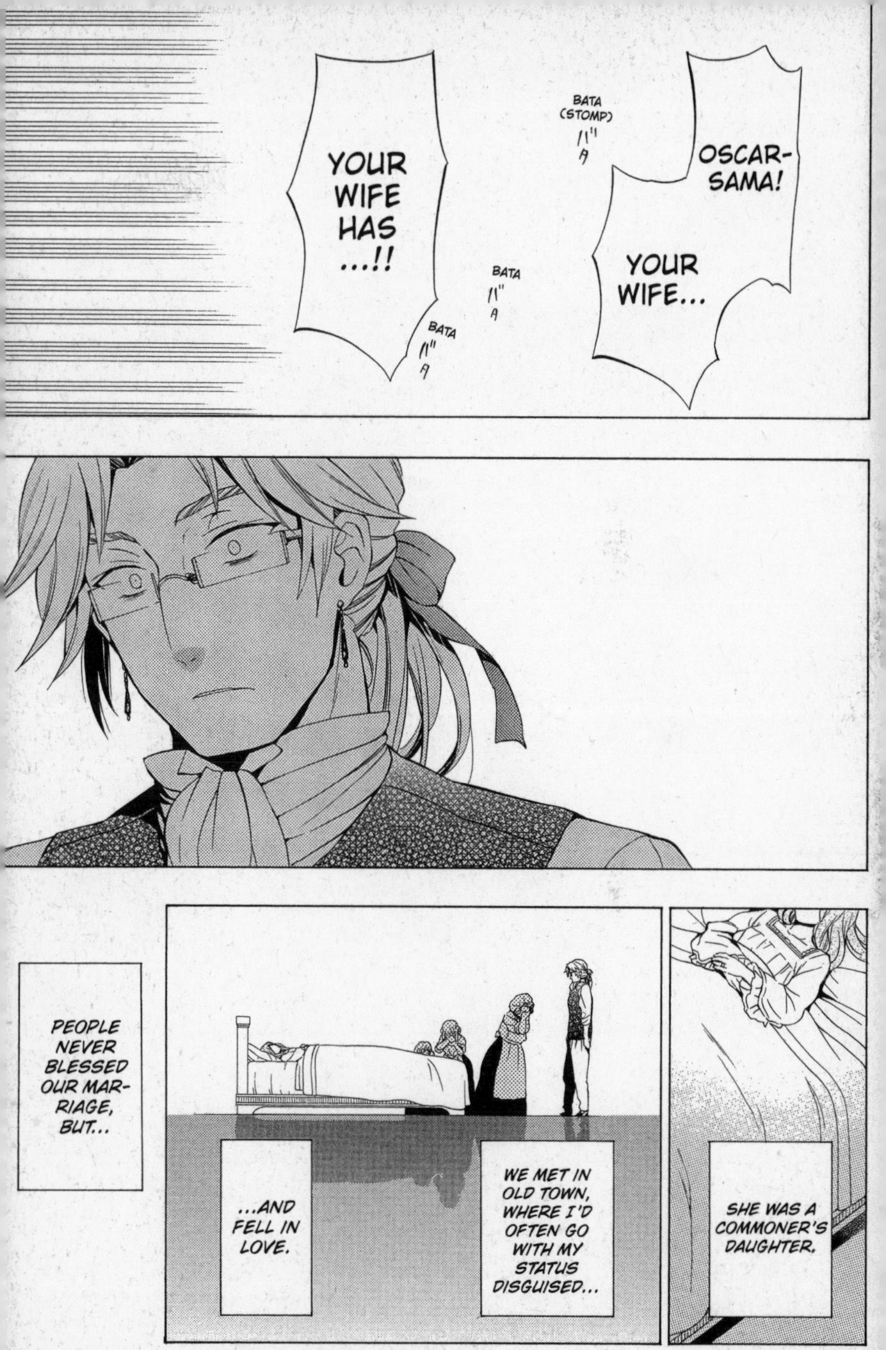
OSCAR-SAMA!
YOUR WIFE...
BATA (STOMP)
バタ
YOUR WIFE HAS ...!!
BATA
バタ
BATA
バタ
SHE WAS A COMMONER'S DAUGHTER.
WE MET IN OLD TOWN, WHERE I'D OFTEN GO WITH MY STATUS DISGUISED...
...AND FELL IN LOVE.
PEOPLE NEVER BLESSED OUR MAR-RIAGE, BUT...

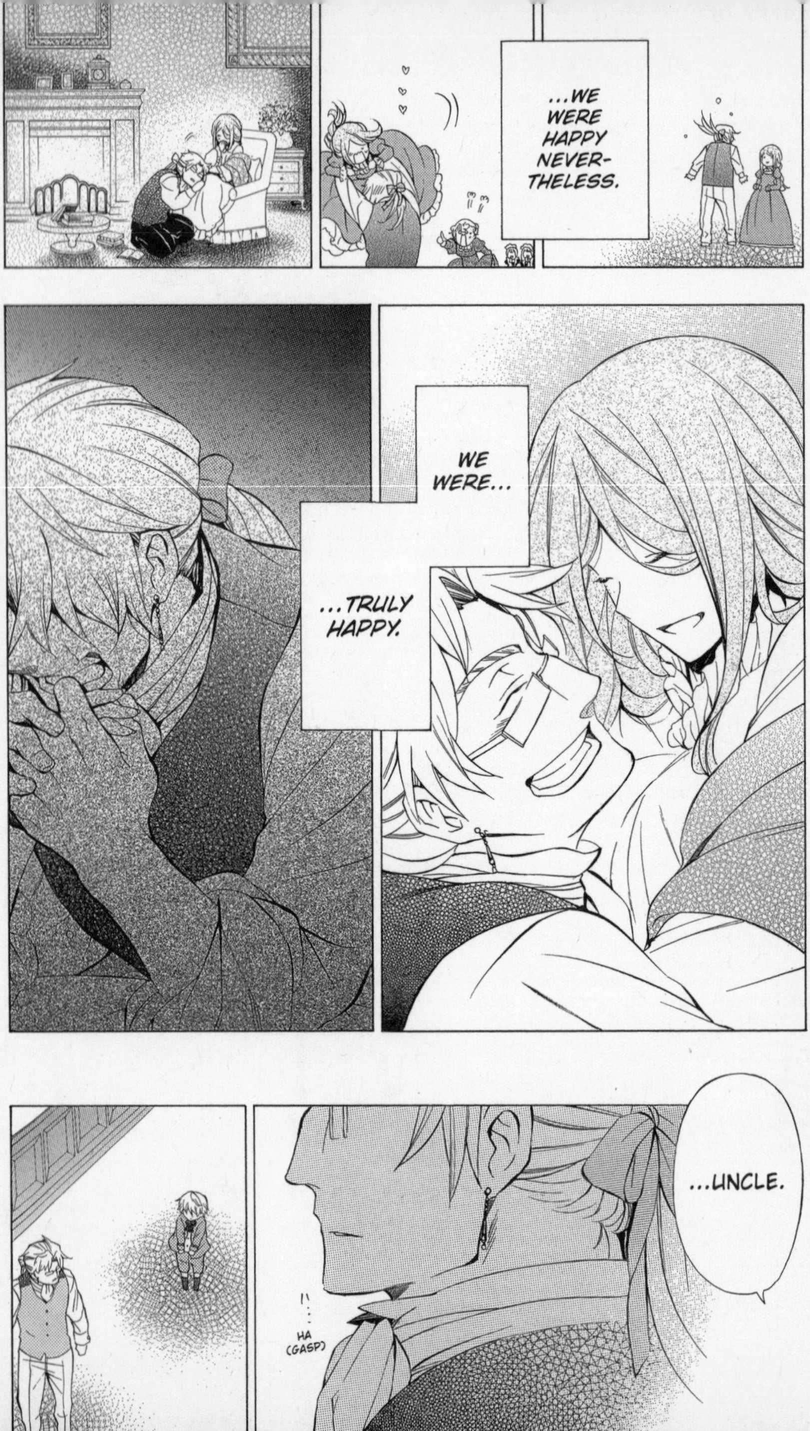
...WE WERE HAPPY NEVER-THELESS.
WE WERE...
...TRULY HAPPY.
...UNCLE.
HA (GASP)

OZ.

YOU COULDN'T HAVE KNOWN.

WHENEVER YOU CLUNG TO ME WITH YOUR LITTLE HANDS...

...FOR ME, THAT WAS...

...SUCH...

...SUCH—

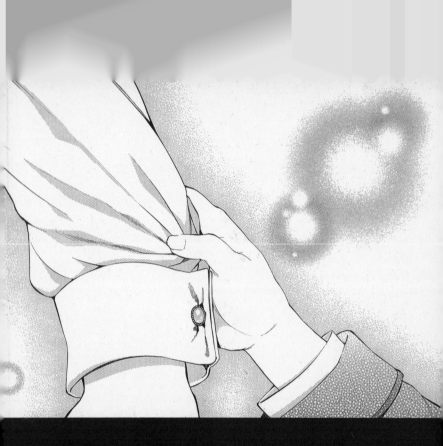

Retrace:LXXX

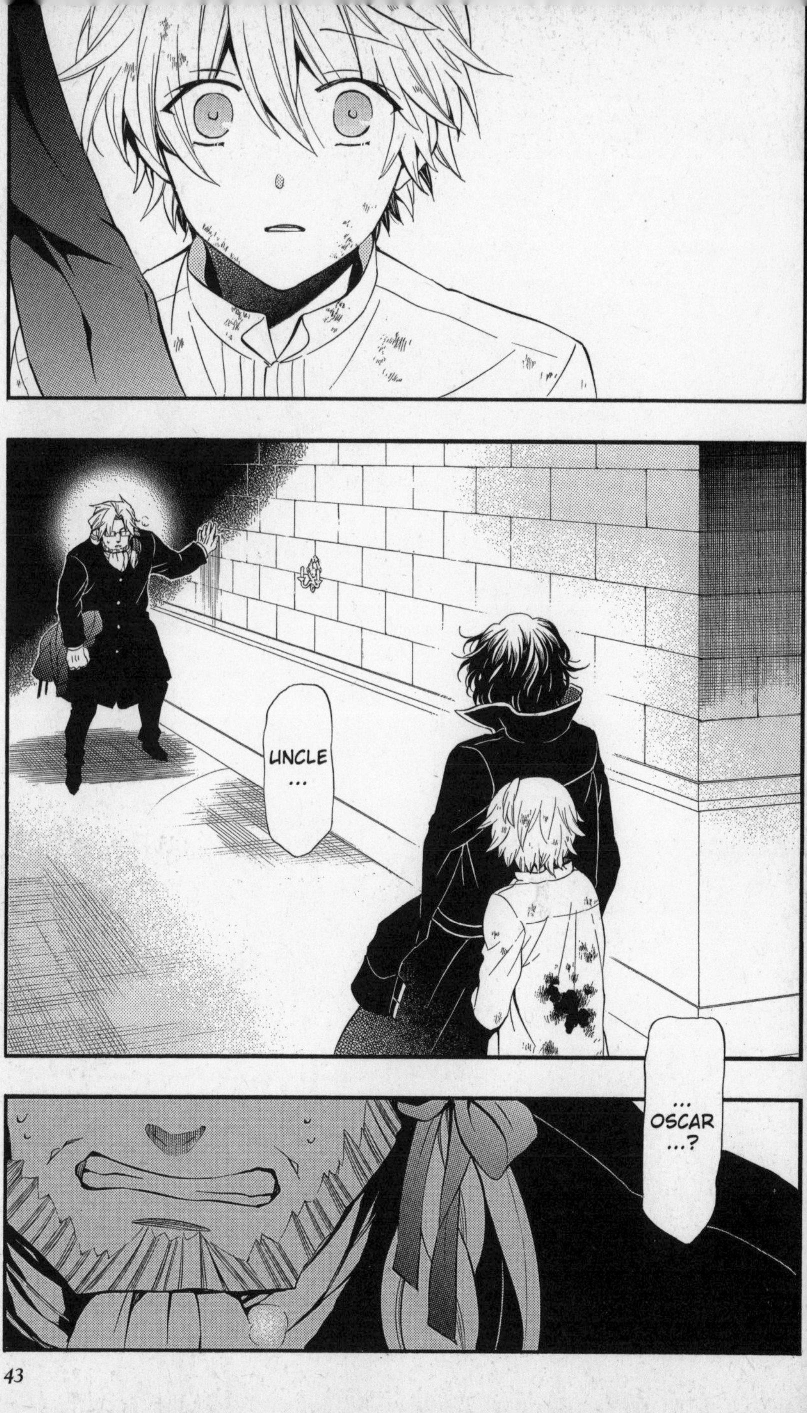
UNCLE ...
... OSCAR ...?

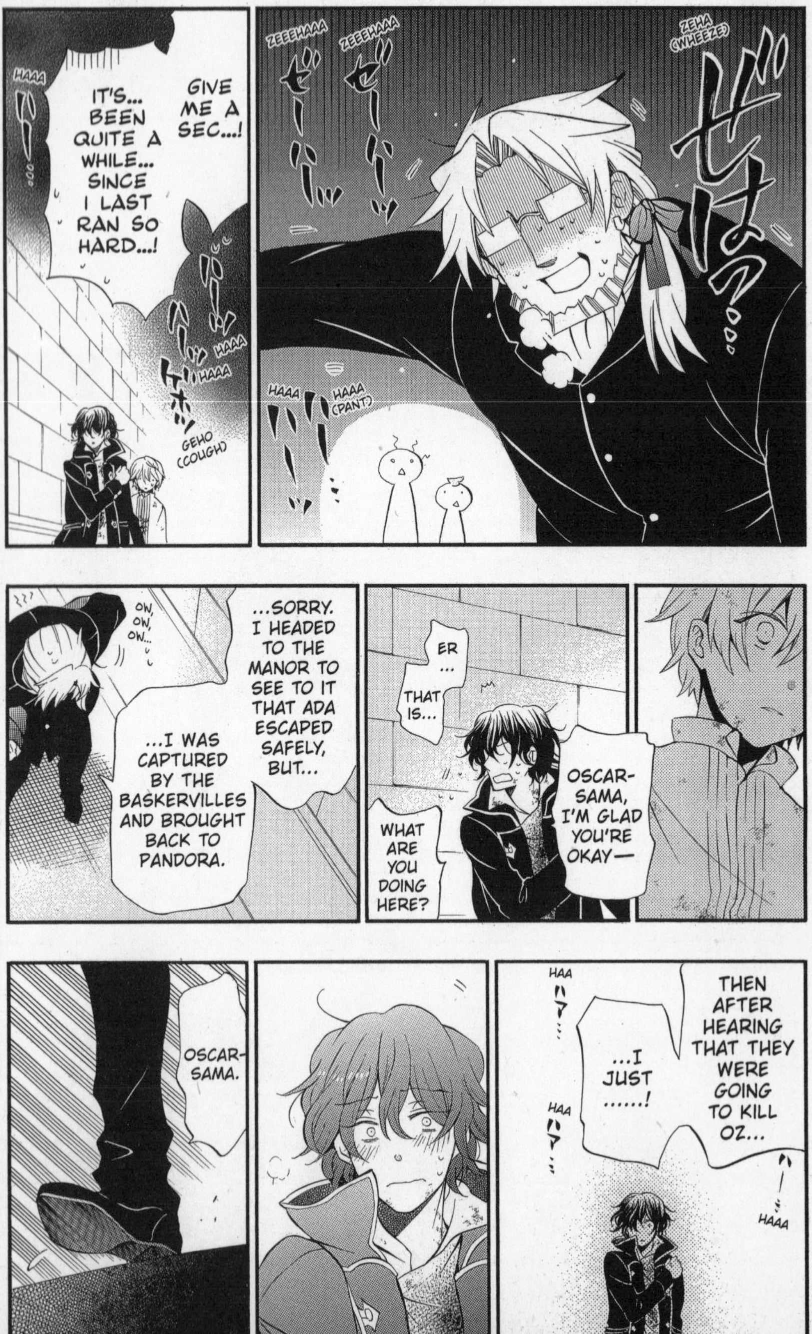
ZEHA (WHEEZE)
ZEEEHAAA
ZEEEHAAA
HAAA (PANT)
HAAA
GIVE ME A SEC...!
IT'S... BEEN QUITE A WHILE... SINCE I LAST RAN SO HARD...!
HAAA
HAAA
HAAA
GEHO (COUGH)
OSCAR-SAMA, I'M GLAD YOU'RE OKAY—
ER ... THAT IS...
WHAT ARE YOU DOING HERE?
...SORRY. I HEADED TO THE MANOR TO SEE TO IT THAT ADA ESCAPED SAFELY, BUT...
...I WAS CAPTURED BY THE BASKERVILLES AND BROUGHT BACK TO PANDORA.
OW, OW, OW...
THEN AFTER HEARING THAT THEY WERE GOING TO KILL OZ...
...I JUST ......!
HAA
HAA
HAAA
OSCAR-SAMA.

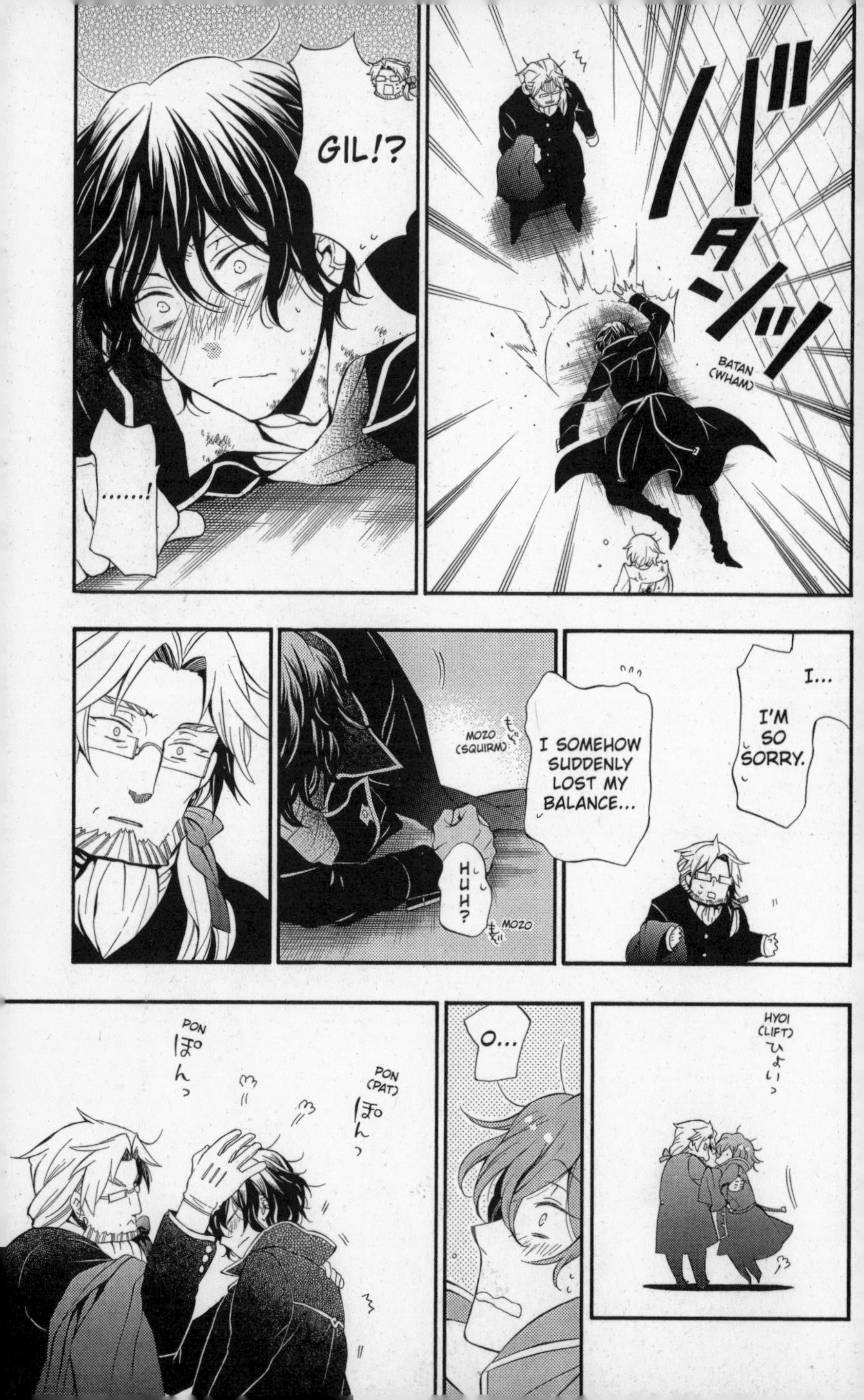

バタンッ
BATAN (WHAM)
GIL!?
......!
I...
I'M SO SORRY.
MOZO (SQUIRM)
I SOMEHOW SUDDENLY LOST MY BALANCE...
HUH?
MOZO
HYOI (LIFT)
ひょいっ
O...
PON (PAT)
ぽんっ
PON
ぽんっ

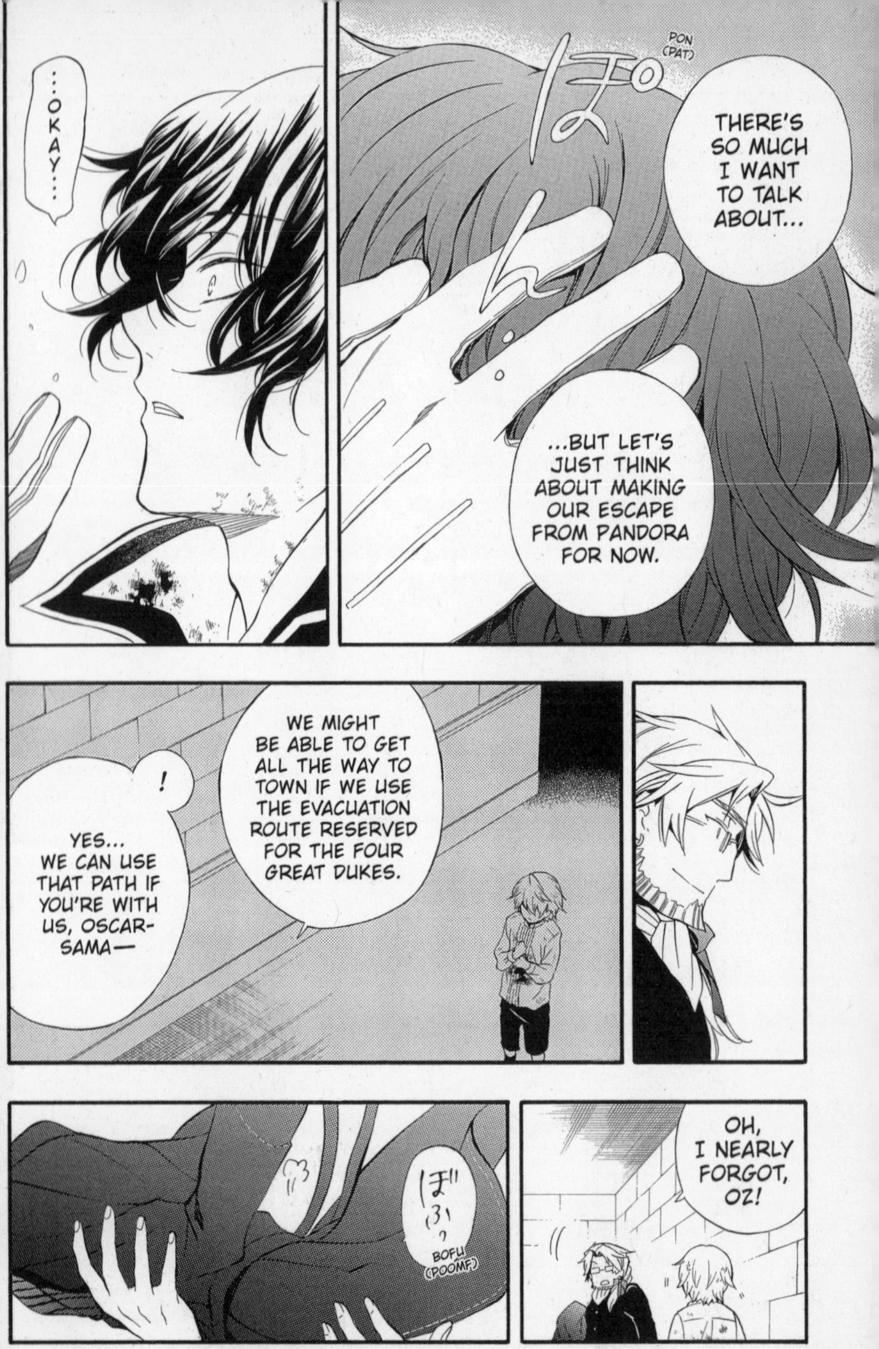
ぽん
PON (PAT)
THERE'S SO MUCH I WANT TO TALK ABOUT...
...BUT LET'S JUST THINK ABOUT MAKING OUR ESCAPE FROM PANDORA FOR NOW.
...OKAY...
WE MIGHT BE ABLE TO GET ALL THE WAY TO TOWN IF WE USE THE EVACUATION ROUTE RESERVED FOR THE FOUR GREAT DUKES.
!
YES... WE CAN USE THAT PATH IF YOU'RE WITH US, OSCAR-SAMA—
OH, I NEARLY FORGOT, OZ!
ぼふっ
BOFU (POOMF)

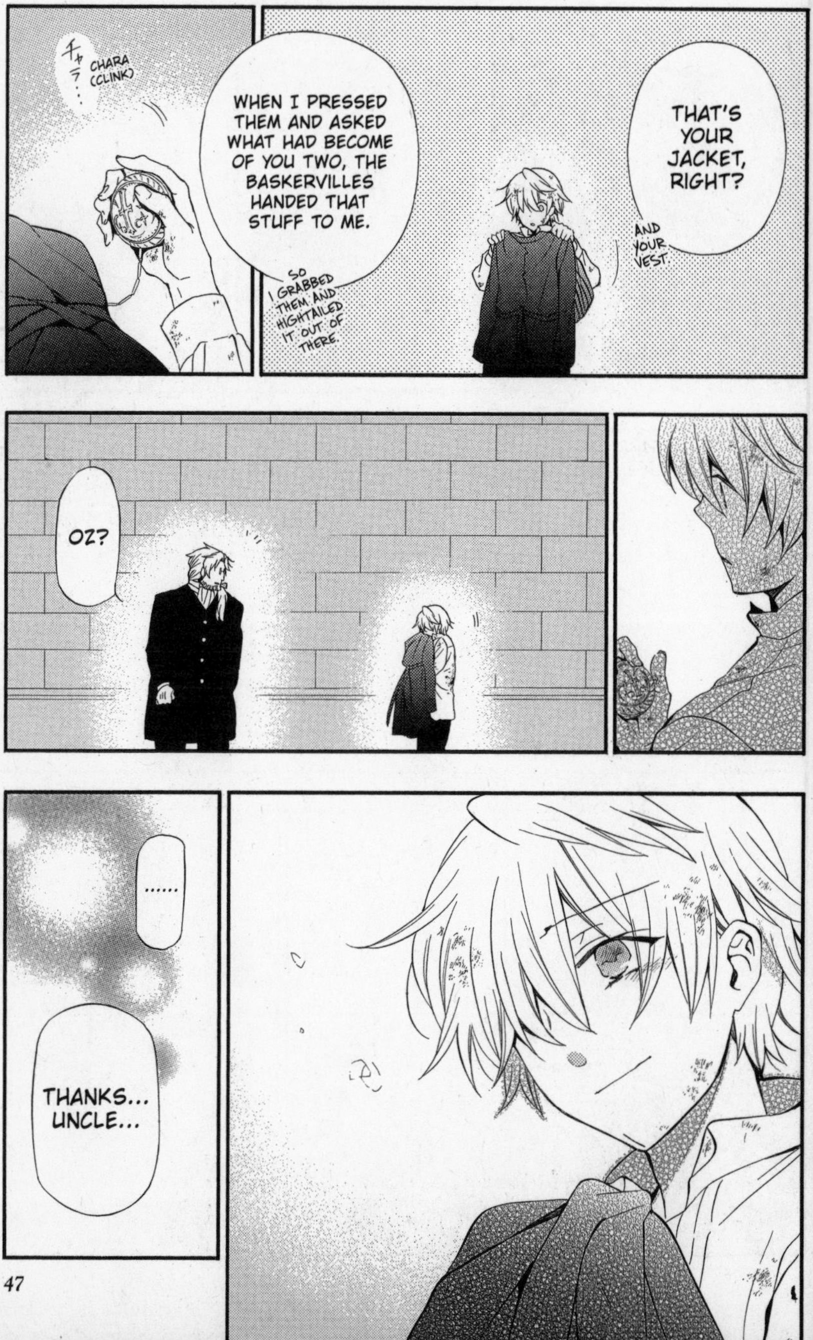
THAT'S YOUR JACKET, RIGHT?
AND YOUR VEST.
WHEN I PRESSED THEM AND ASKED WHAT HAD BECOME OF YOU TWO, THE BASKERVILLES HANDED THAT STUFF TO ME.
SO I GRABBED THEM AND HIGHTAILED IT OUT OF THERE.
チャラ…
CHARA (CLINK)
OZ?
......
THANKS... UNCLE...

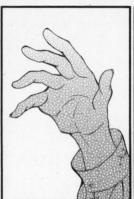

UNCLE
...? ......

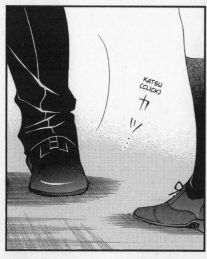

KATSU
(CLICK)

IT'S NOTH- ING.

......

OSCAR- SAMA.

YOU MUST HAVE REALIZED...

OSCAR.

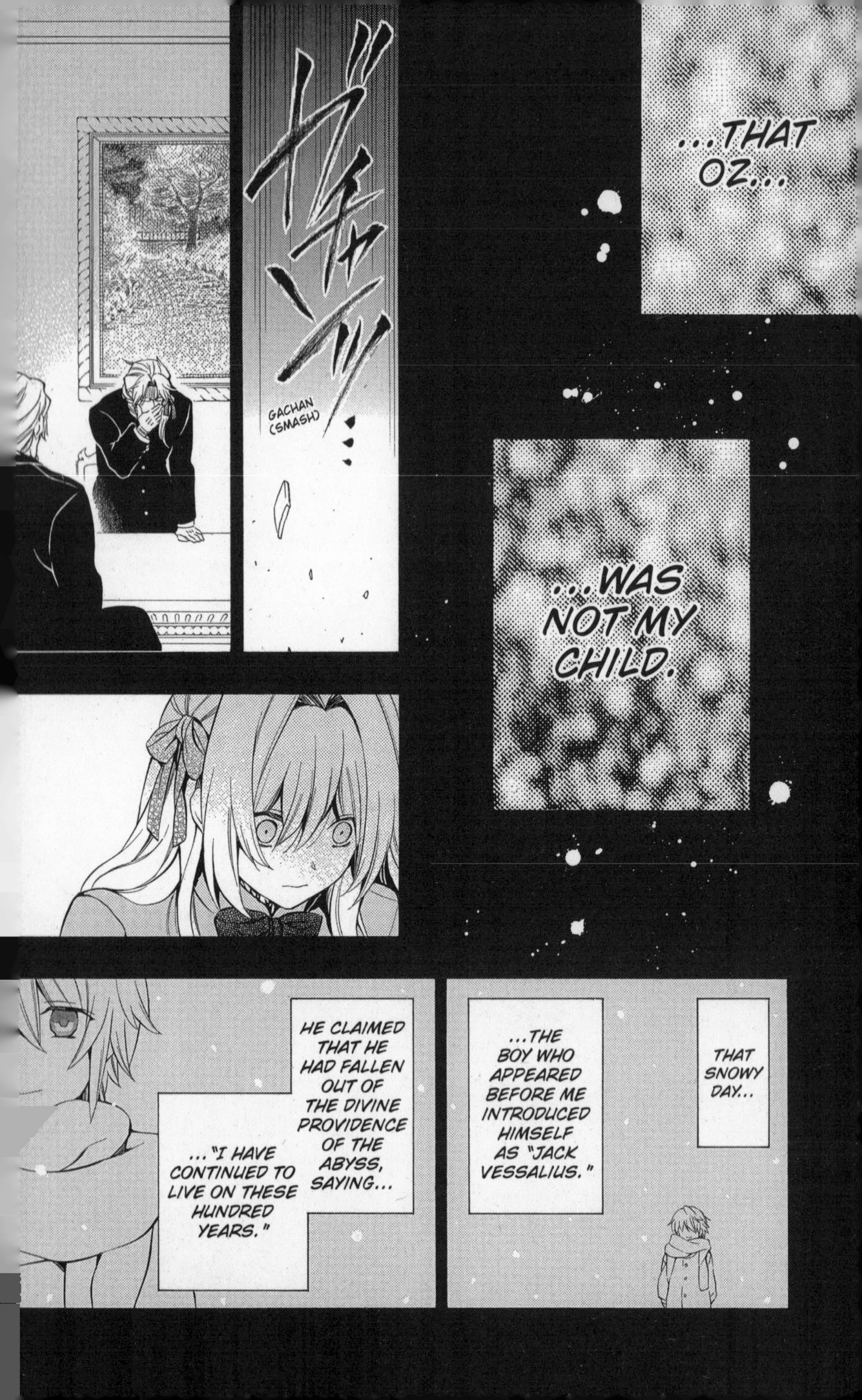
...THAT OZ...
GACHAN (SMASH)
...WAS NOT MY CHILD.
THAT SNOWY DAY...
...THE BOY WHO APPEARED BEFORE ME INTRODUCED HIMSELF AS "JACK VESSALIUS."
HE CLAIMED THAT HE HAD FALLEN OUT OF THE DIVINE PROVIDENCE OF THE ABYSS, SAYING...
..."I HAVE CONTINUED TO LIVE ON THESE HUNDRED YEARS."

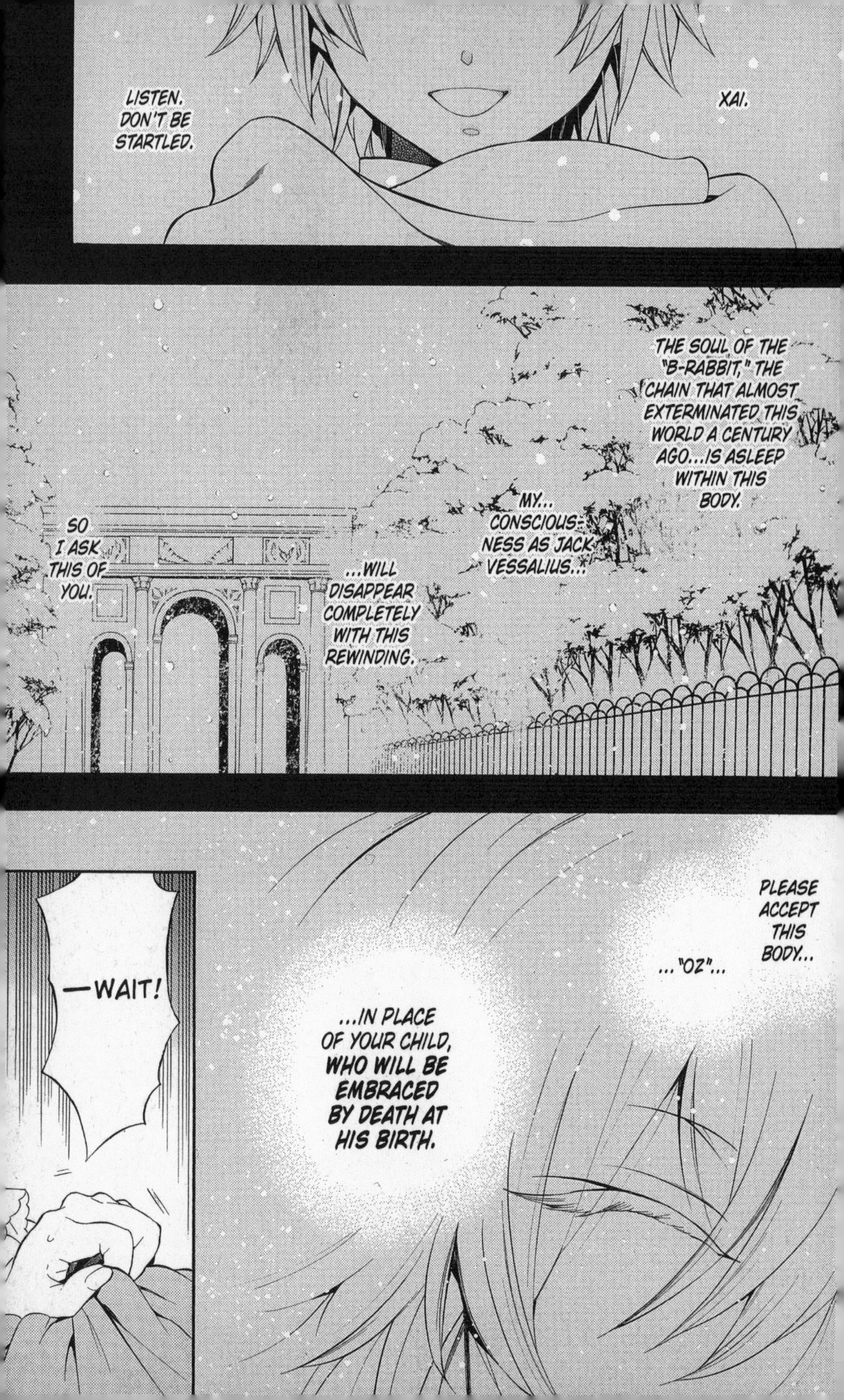
XAI.
LISTEN. DON'T BE STARTLED.
THE SOUL OF THE "B-RABBIT," THE CHAIN THAT ALMOST EXTERMINATED THIS WORLD A CENTURY AGO...IS ASLEEP WITHIN THIS BODY.
MY... CONSCIOUS-NESS AS JACK VESSALIUS...
...WILL DISAPPEAR COMPLETELY WITH THIS REWINDING.
SO I ASK THIS OF YOU.
PLEASE ACCEPT THIS BODY...
..."OZ"...
...IN PLACE OF YOUR CHILD, WHO WILL BE EMBRACED BY DEATH AT HIS BIRTH.
—WAIT!

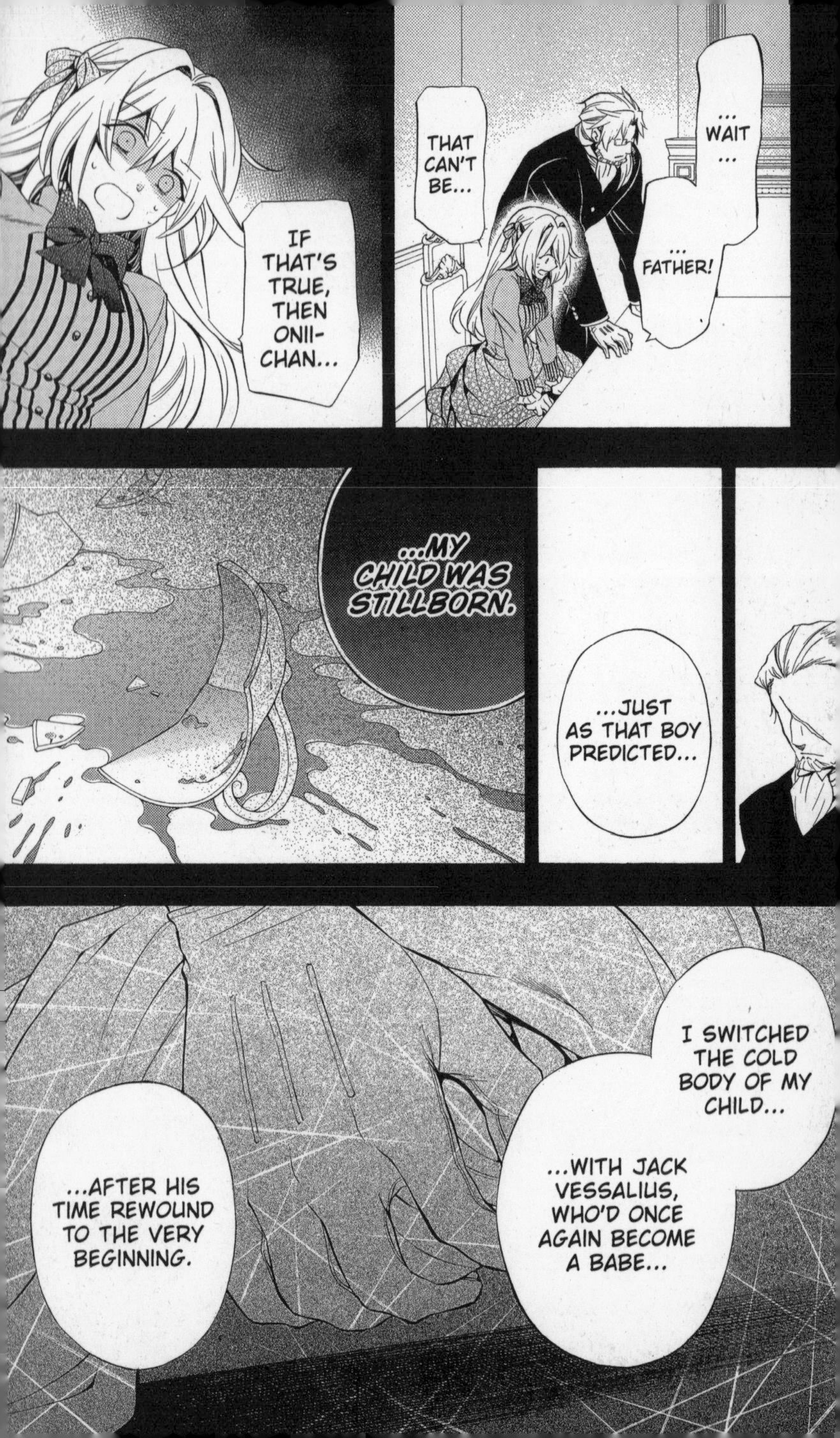
...WAIT...
...FATHER!
THAT CAN'T BE...
IF THAT'S TRUE, THEN ONII-CHAN...
...JUST AS THAT BOY PREDICTED...
...MY CHILD WAS STILLBORN.
I SWITCHED THE COLD BODY OF MY CHILD...
...WITH JACK VESSALIUS, WHO'D ONCE AGAIN BECOME A BABE...
...AFTER HIS TIME REWOUND TO THE VERY BEGINNING.

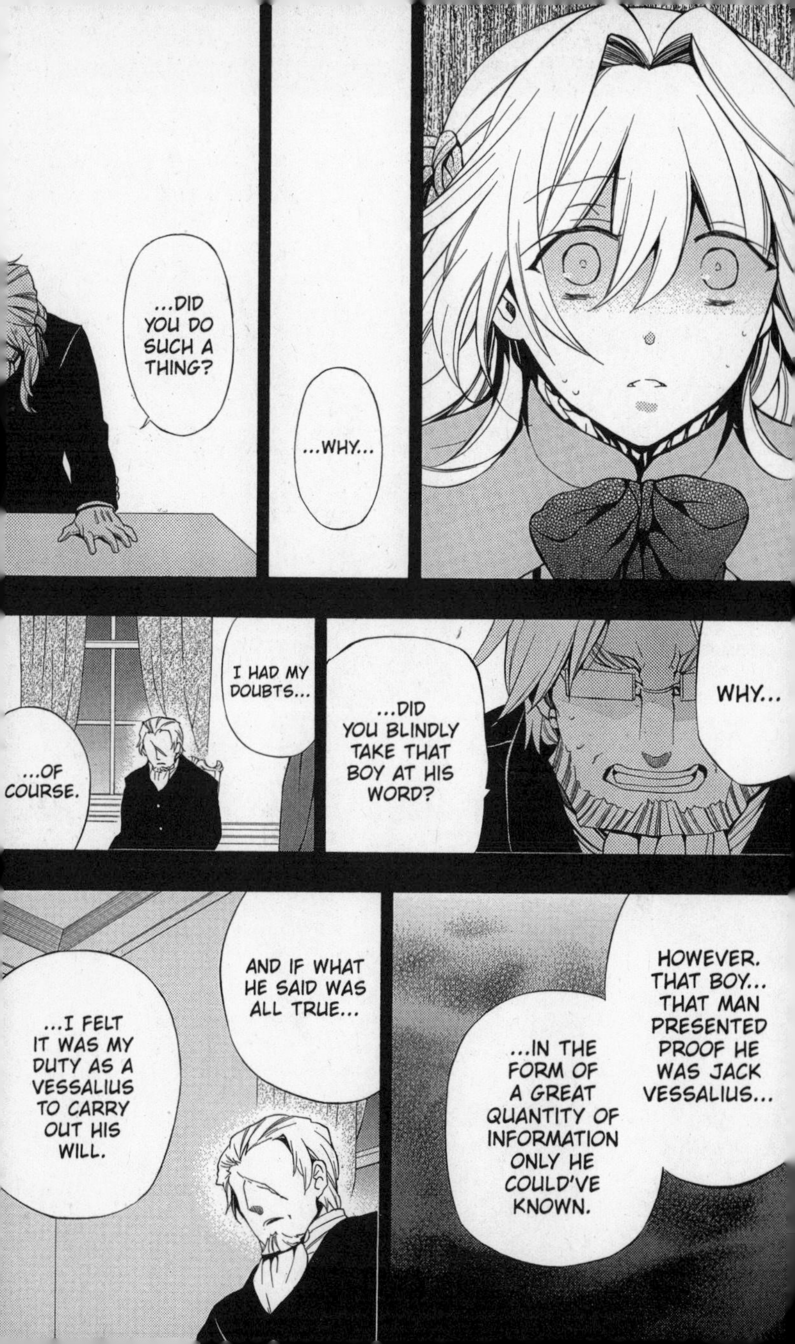
...WHY...
...DID YOU DO SUCH A THING?
WHY...
...DID YOU BLINDLY TAKE THAT BOY AT HIS WORD?
I HAD MY DOUBTS...
...OF COURSE.
HOWEVER. THAT BOY... THAT MAN PRESENTED PROOF HE WAS JACK VESSALIUS...
...IN THE FORM OF A GREAT QUANTITY OF INFORMATION ONLY HE COULD'VE KNOWN.
AND IF WHAT HE SAID WAS ALL TRUE...
...I FELT IT WAS MY DUTY AS A VESSALIUS TO CARRY OUT HIS WILL.

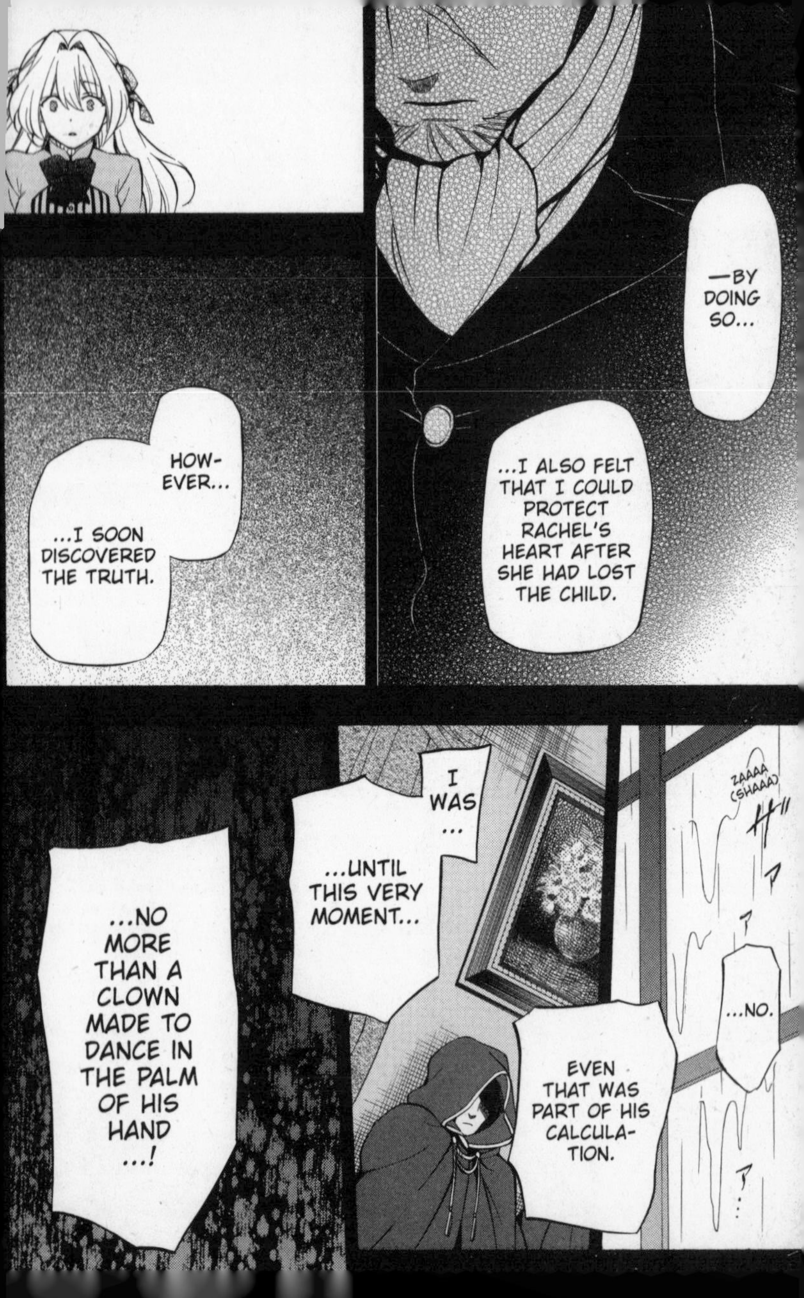
—BY DOING SO...
...I ALSO FELT THAT I COULD PROTECT RACHEL'S HEART AFTER SHE HAD LOST THE CHILD.
HOW-EVER...
...I SOON DISCOVERED THE TRUTH.
ZAAAA (SHAAA)
...NO.
EVEN THAT WAS PART OF HIS CALCULA-TION.
I WAS...
...UNTIL THIS VERY MOMENT...
...NO MORE THAN A CLOWN MADE TO DANCE IN THE PALM OF HIS HAND...!

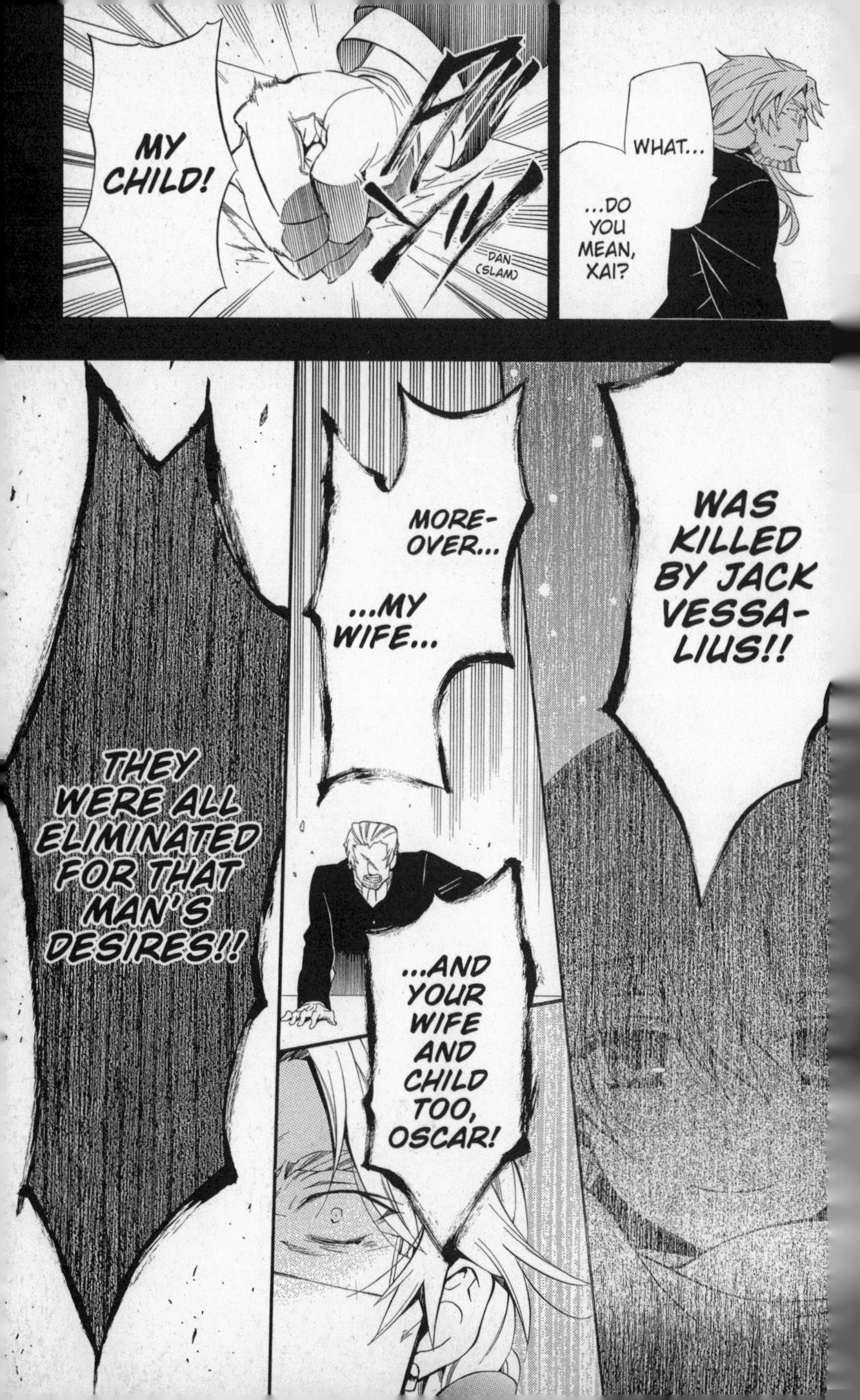
WHAT...
...DO YOU MEAN, XAI?
MY CHILD!
DAN (SLAM)
WAS KILLED BY JACK VESSALIUS!!
MORE-OVER...
...MY WIFE...
...AND YOUR WIFE AND CHILD TOO, OSCAR!
THEY WERE ALL ELIMINATED FOR THAT MAN'S DESIRES!!

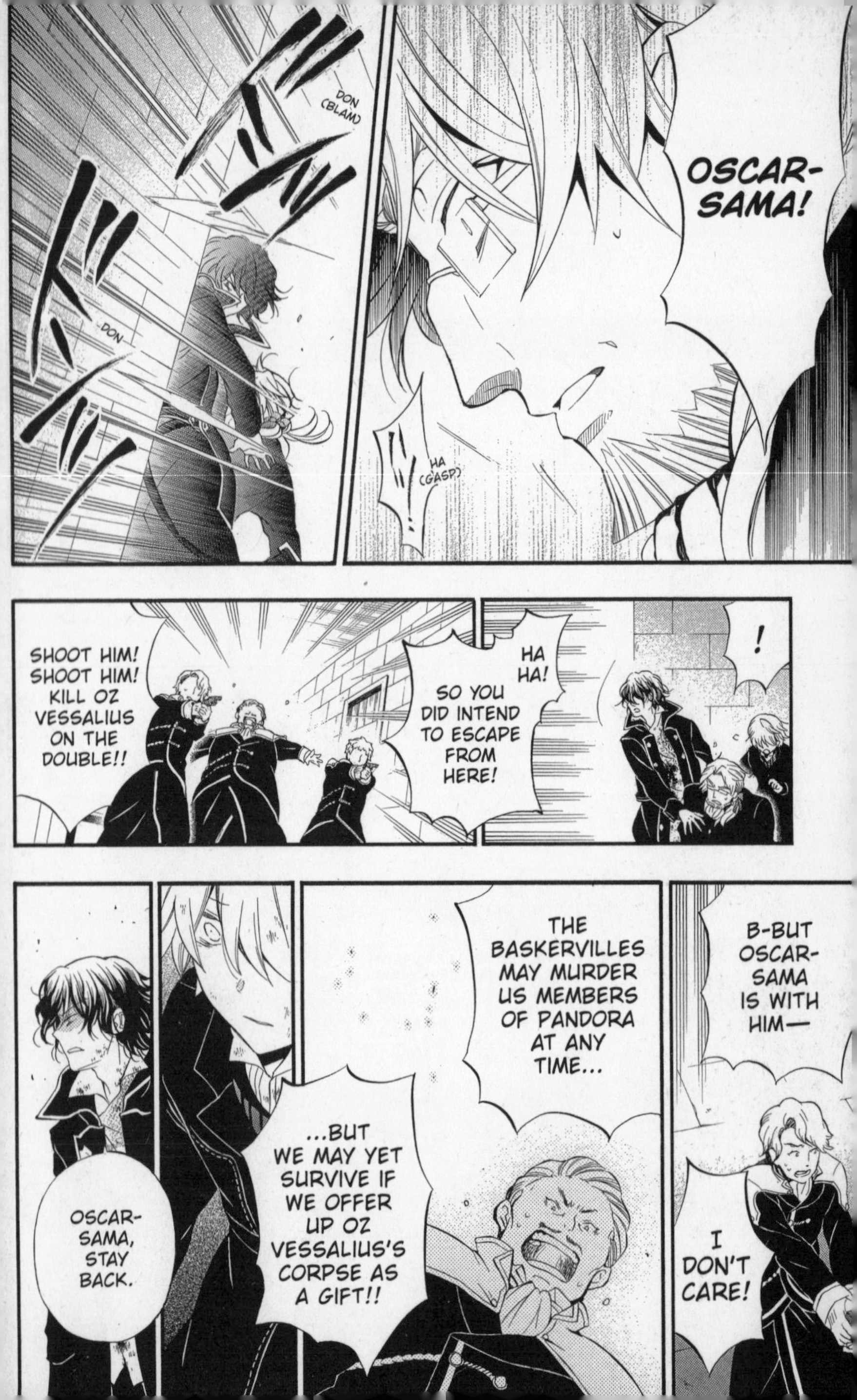
OSCAR-SAMA!
HA (GASP)
DON (BLAM)
DON
!
HA HA!
SO YOU DID INTEND TO ESCAPE FROM HERE!
SHOOT HIM! SHOOT HIM! KILL OZ VESSALIUS ON THE DOUBLE!!
B-BUT OSCAR-SAMA IS WITH HIM—
I DON'T CARE!
THE BASKERVILLES MAY MURDER US MEMBERS OF PANDORA AT ANY TIME...
...BUT WE MAY YET SURVIVE IF WE OFFER UP OZ VESSALIUS'S CORPSE AS A GIFT!!
OSCAR-SAMA, STAY BACK.

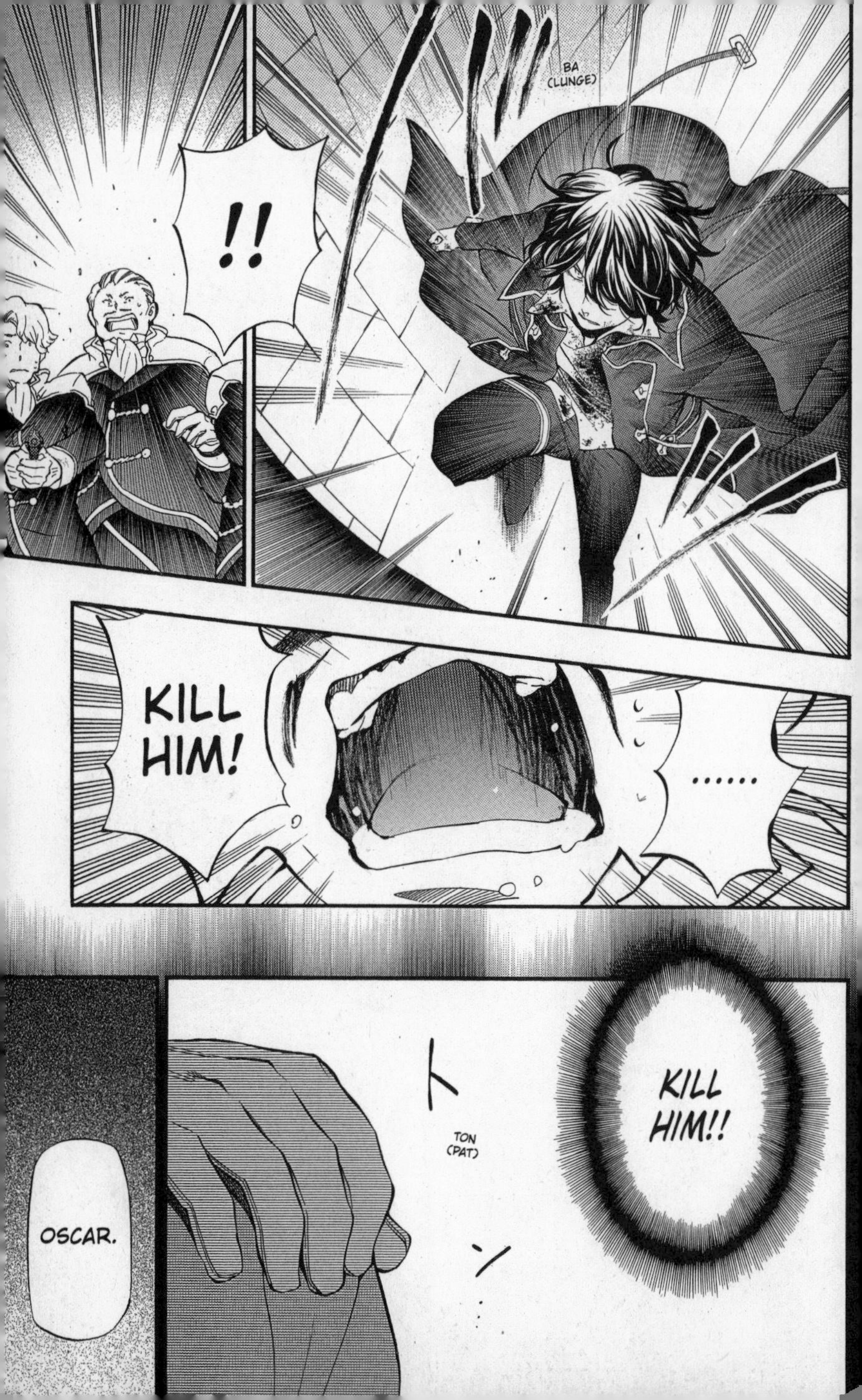

BA (LUNGE)
!!
......
KILL HIM!
KILL HIM!!
トン
TON (PAT)
OSCAR.

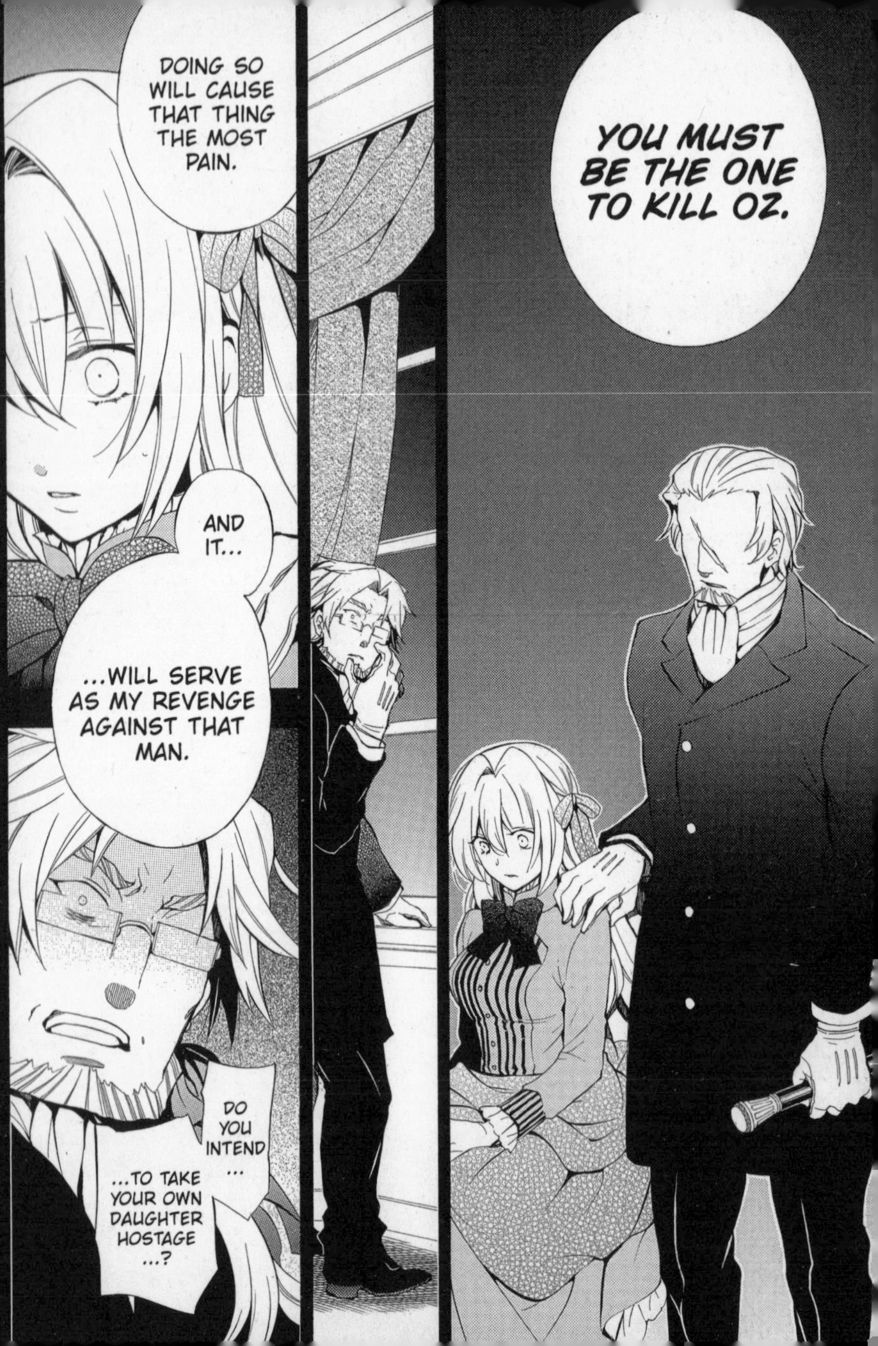
YOU MUST BE THE ONE TO KILL OZ.
DOING SO WILL CAUSE THAT THING THE MOST PAIN.
AND IT...
...WILL SERVE AS MY REVENGE AGAINST THAT MAN.
DO YOU INTEND ...
...TO TAKE YOUR OWN DAUGHTER HOSTAGE ...?

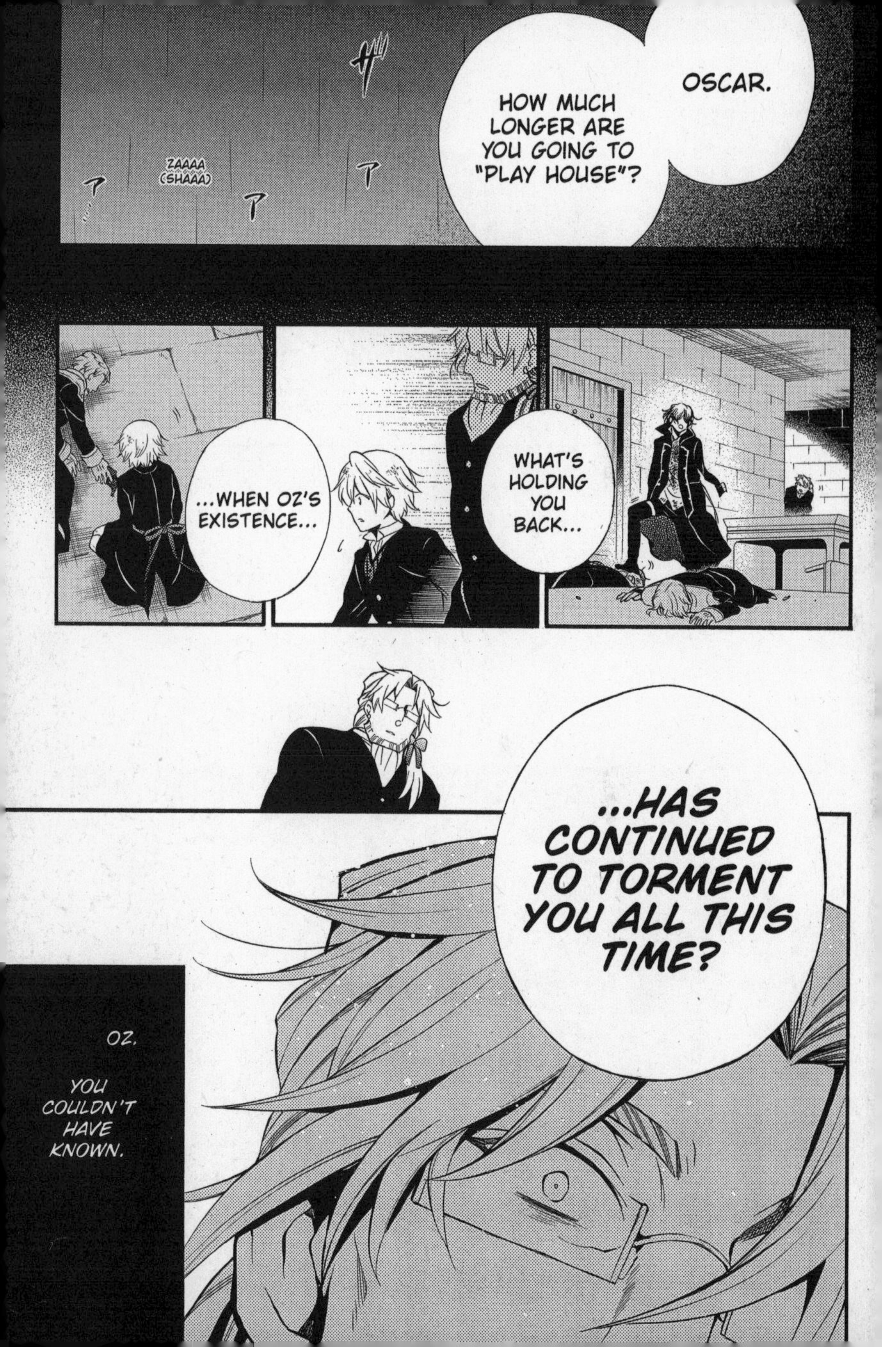
OSCAR.
HOW MUCH LONGER ARE YOU GOING TO "PLAY HOUSE"?
ZAAAA (SHAAA)
WHAT'S HOLDING YOU BACK...
...WHEN OZ'S EXISTENCE...
...HAS CONTINUED TO TORMENT YOU ALL THIS TIME?
OZ.
YOU COULDN'T HAVE KNOWN.

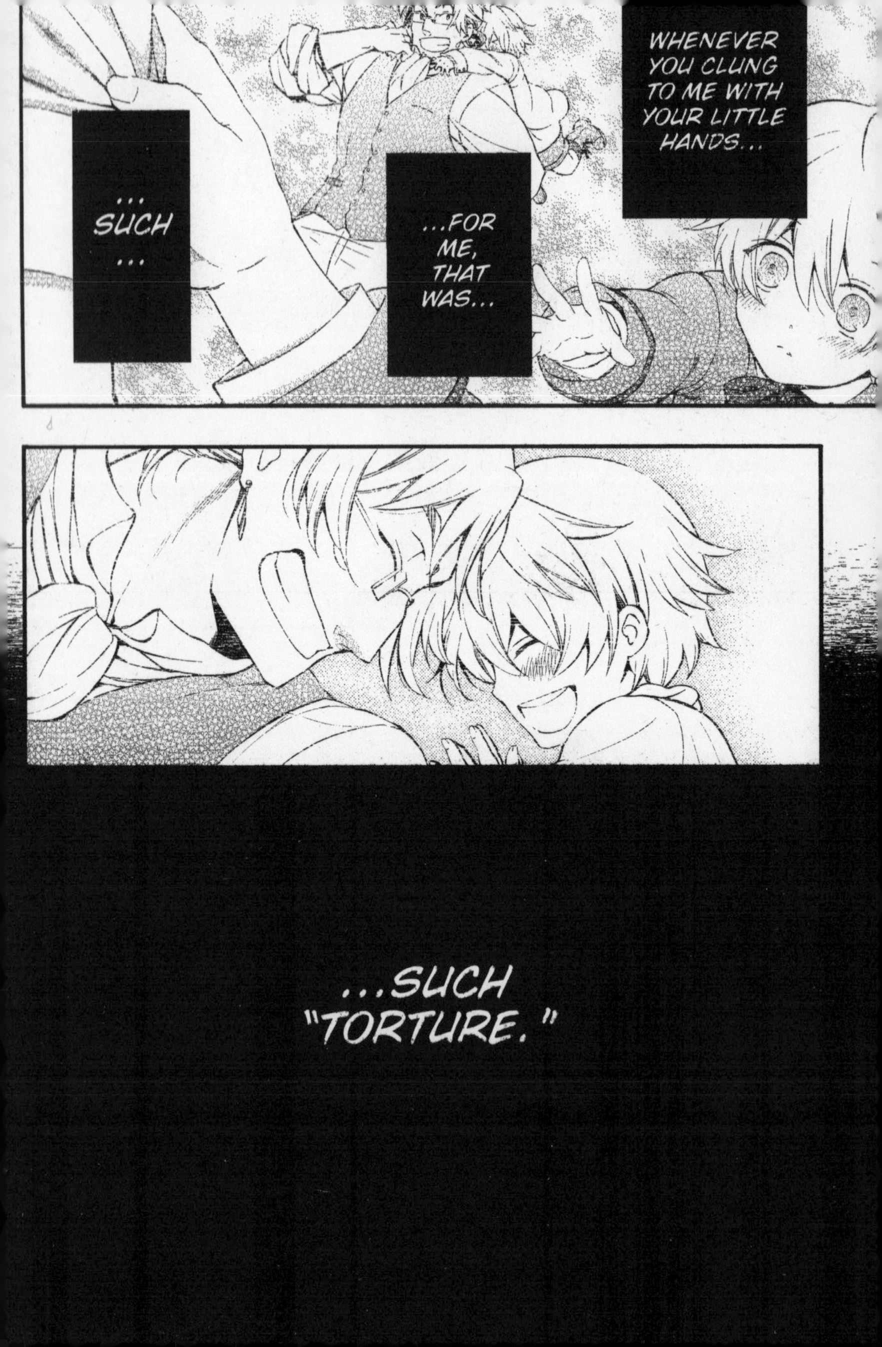
WHENEVER YOU CLUNG TO ME WITH YOUR LITTLE HANDS...
...FOR ME, THAT WAS...
... SUCH ...
...SUCH "TORTURE."

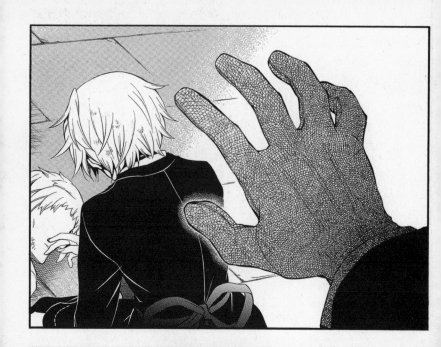

HOLD IT.

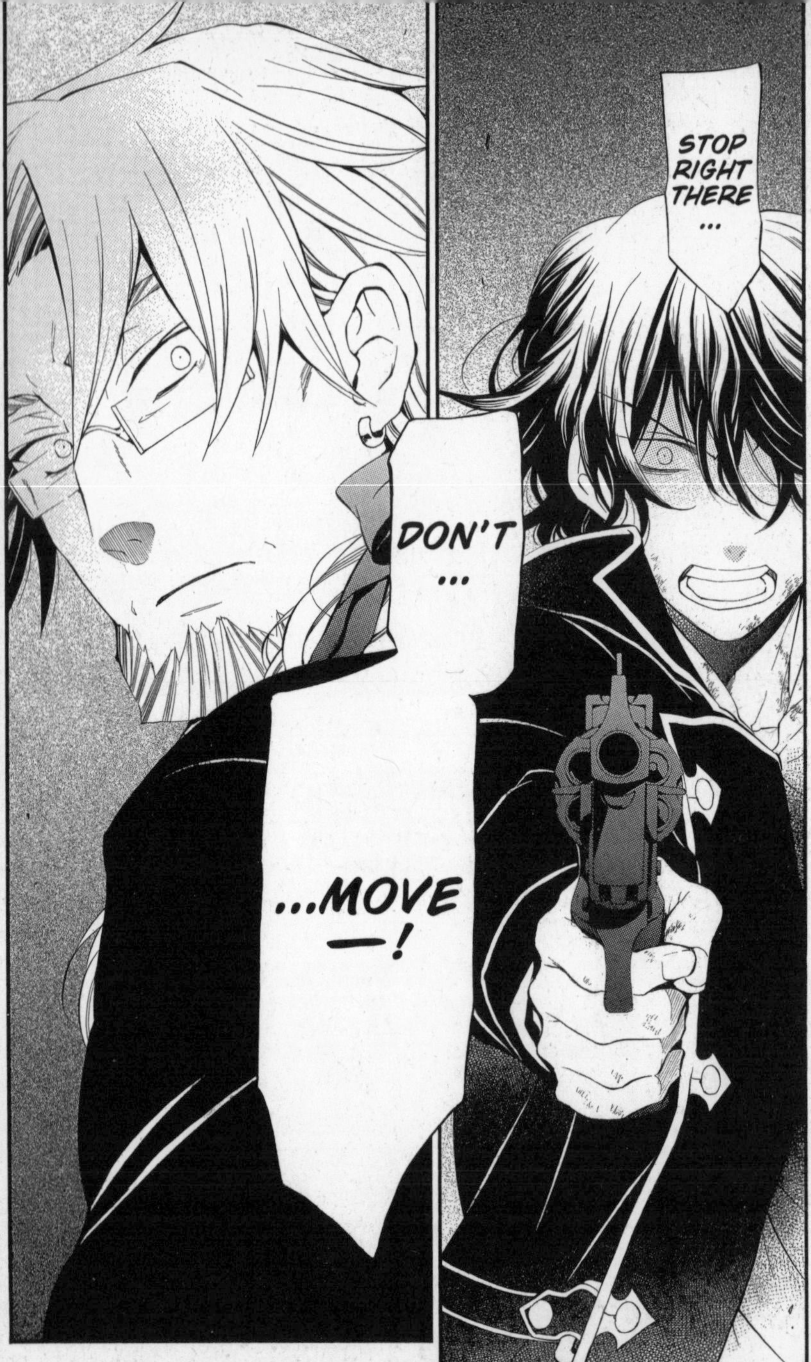
STOP RIGHT THERE ...
DON'T ...
...MOVE —!

Retrace:LXXX   Oscar Vessalius

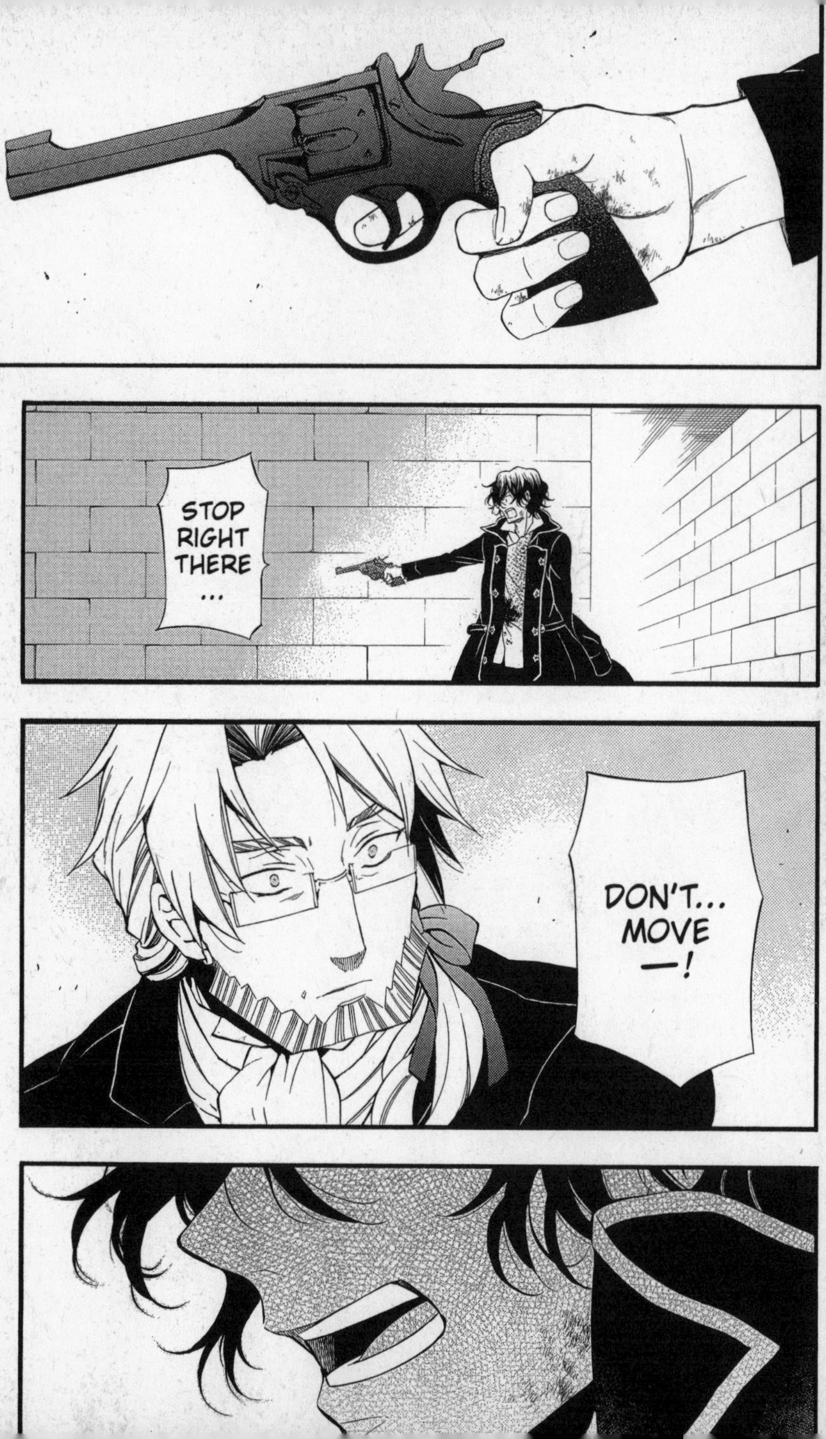
STOP RIGHT THERE ...
DON'T... MOVE —!

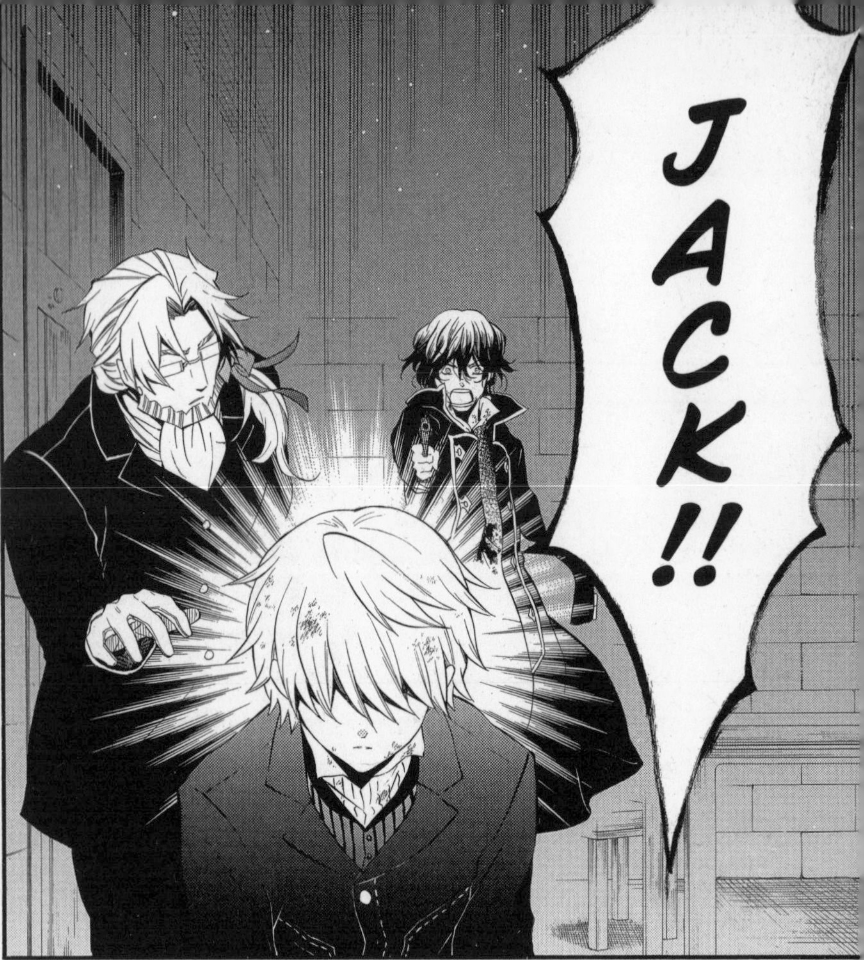
JACK!!
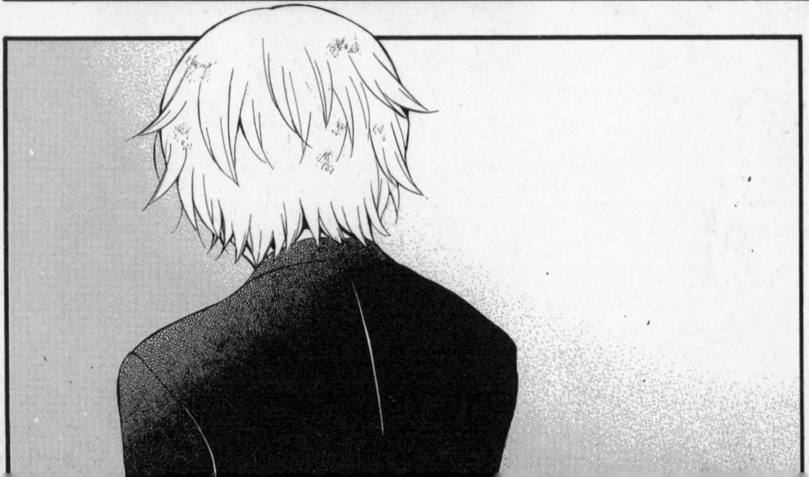

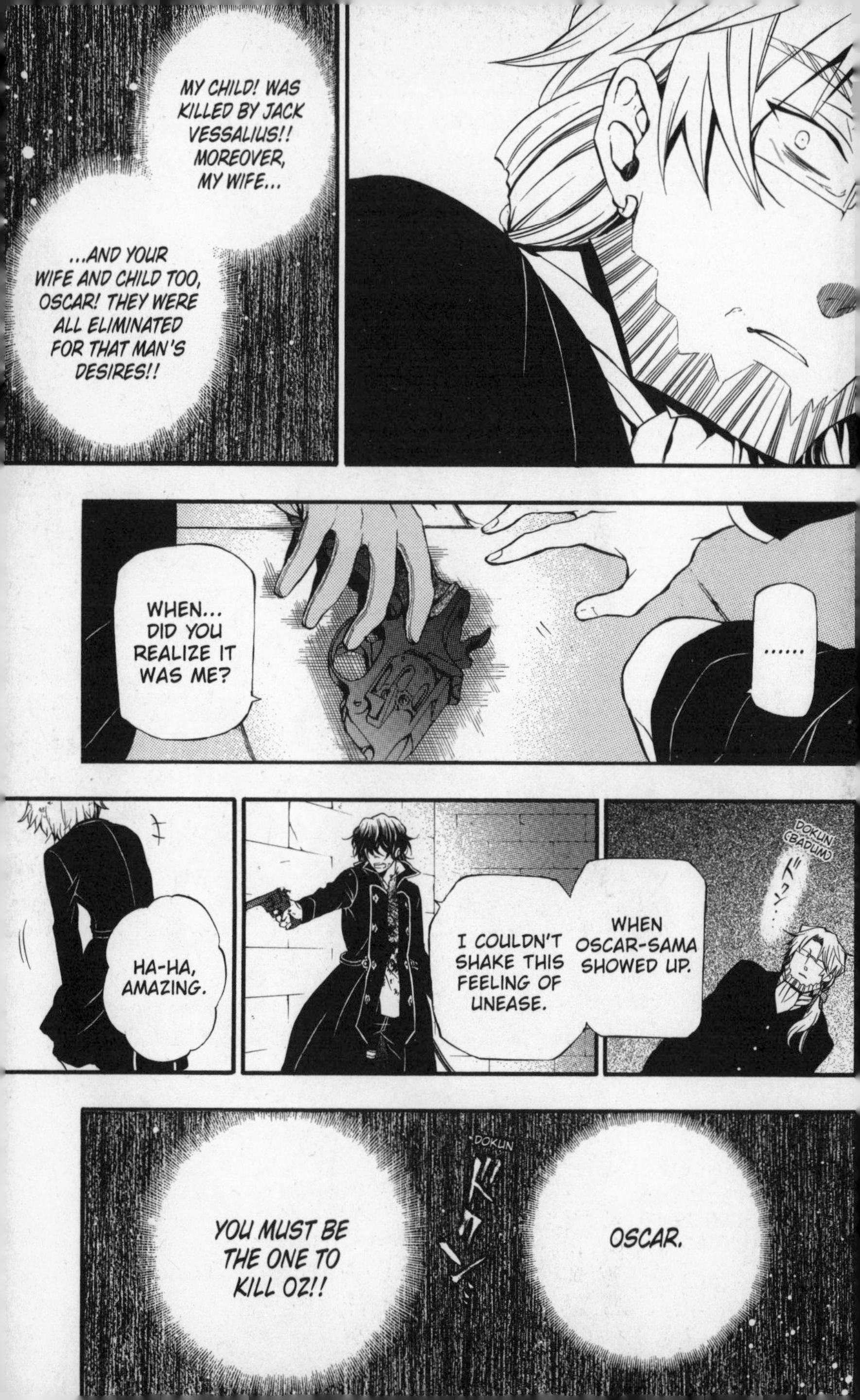
MY CHILD! WAS KILLED BY JACK VESSALIUS!! MOREOVER, MY WIFE...
...AND YOUR WIFE AND CHILD TOO, OSCAR! THEY WERE ALL ELIMINATED FOR THAT MAN'S DESIRES!!
......
WHEN... DID YOU REALIZE IT WAS ME?
DOKUN (BADUM)
WHEN OSCAR-SAMA SHOWED UP.
I COULDN'T SHAKE THIS FEELING OF UNEASE.
HA-HA, AMAZING.
OSCAR.
DOKUN
YOU MUST BE THE ONE TO KILL OZ!!

Retrace:LXXXI

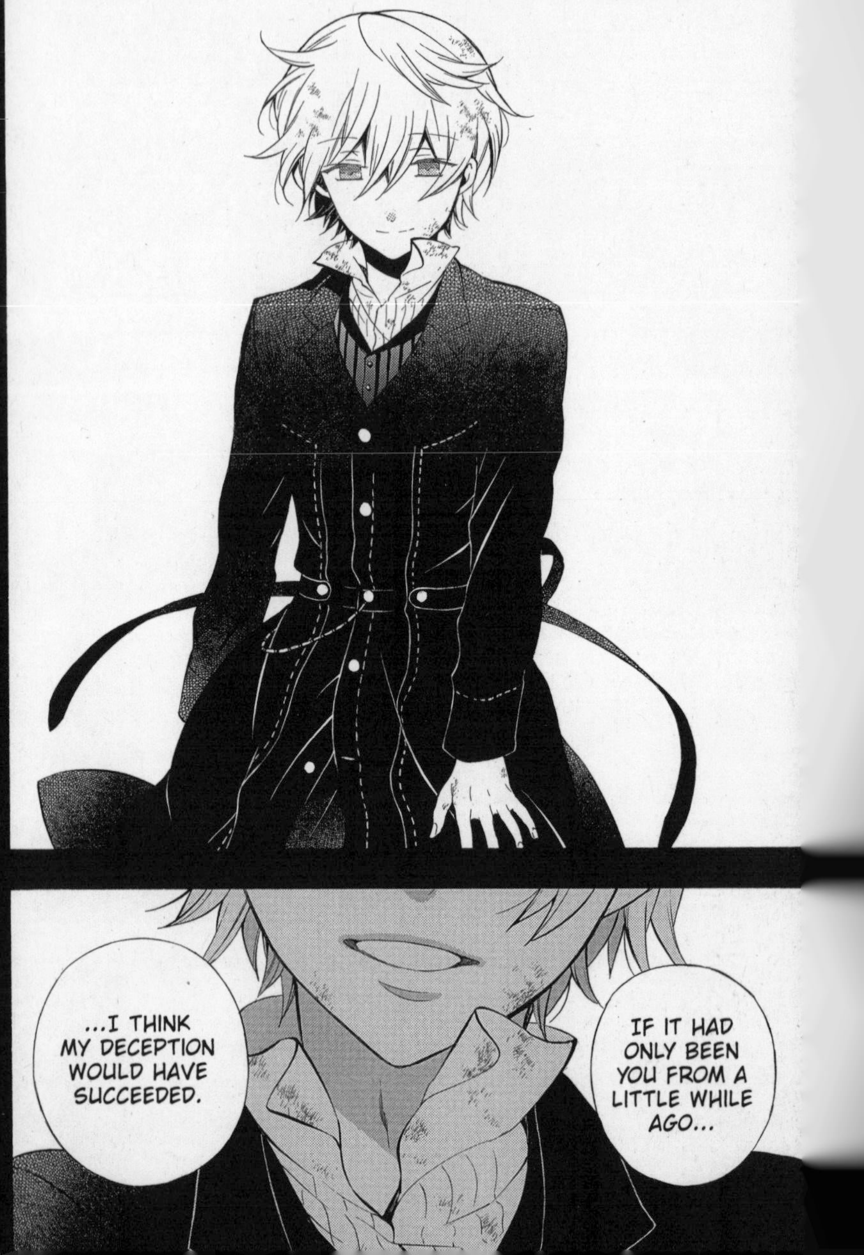
IF IT HAD ONLY BEEN YOU FROM A LITTLE WHILE AGO...
...I THINK MY DECEPTION WOULD HAVE SUCCEEDED.

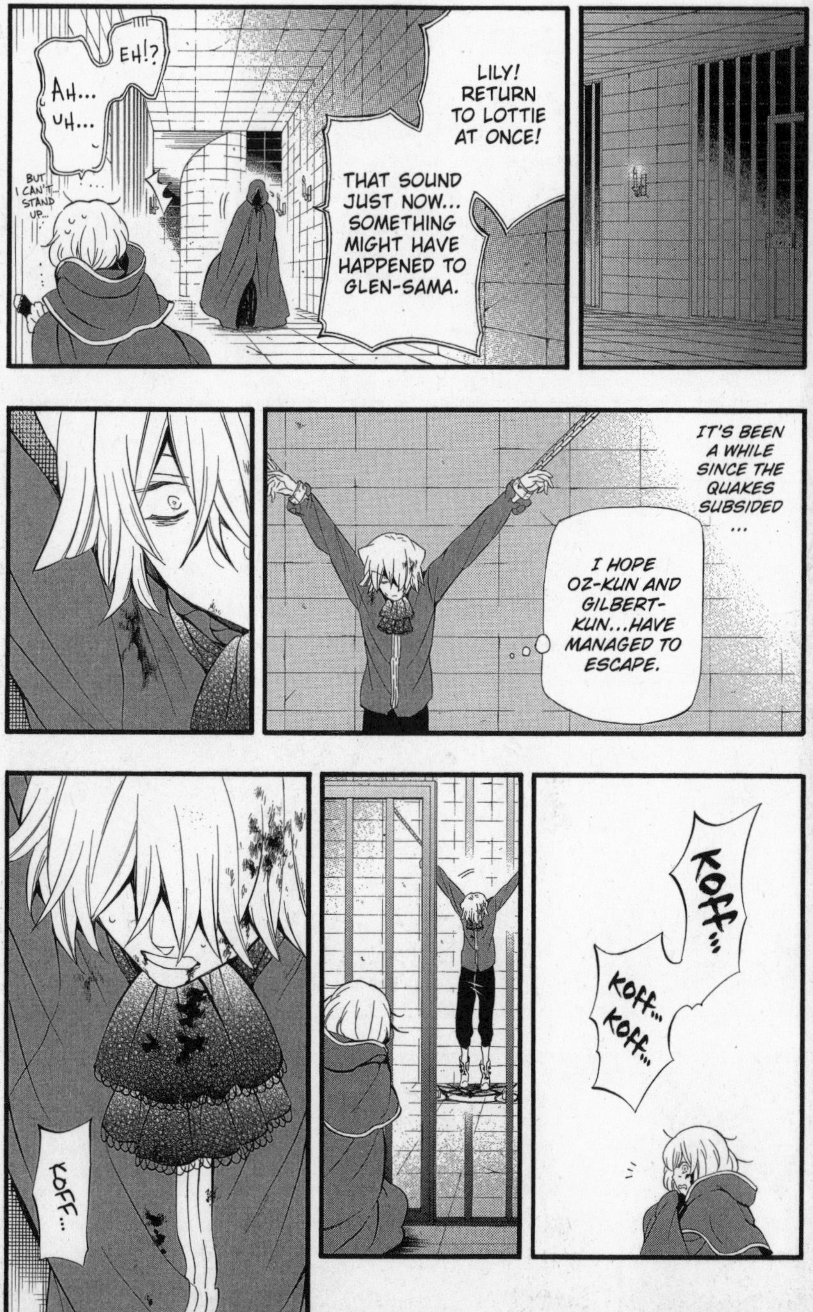
LILY! RETURN TO LOTTIE AT ONCE!
THAT SOUND JUST NOW... SOMETHING MIGHT HAVE HAPPENED TO GLEN-SAMA.
EH!?
AH... UH...
...
BUT I CAN'T... STAND UP...
IT'S BEEN A WHILE SINCE THE QUAKES SUBSIDED...
I HOPE OZ-KUN AND GILBERT-KUN...HAVE MANAGED TO ESCAPE.
KOFF...
KOFF... KOFF...
KOFF...

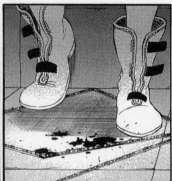

SO YOU'RE GONNA DIE.

OHH.

...STILL...

I'M...

...BE RIDICULOUS.

PLEASE DON'T...

GICHI
(STRAIN)

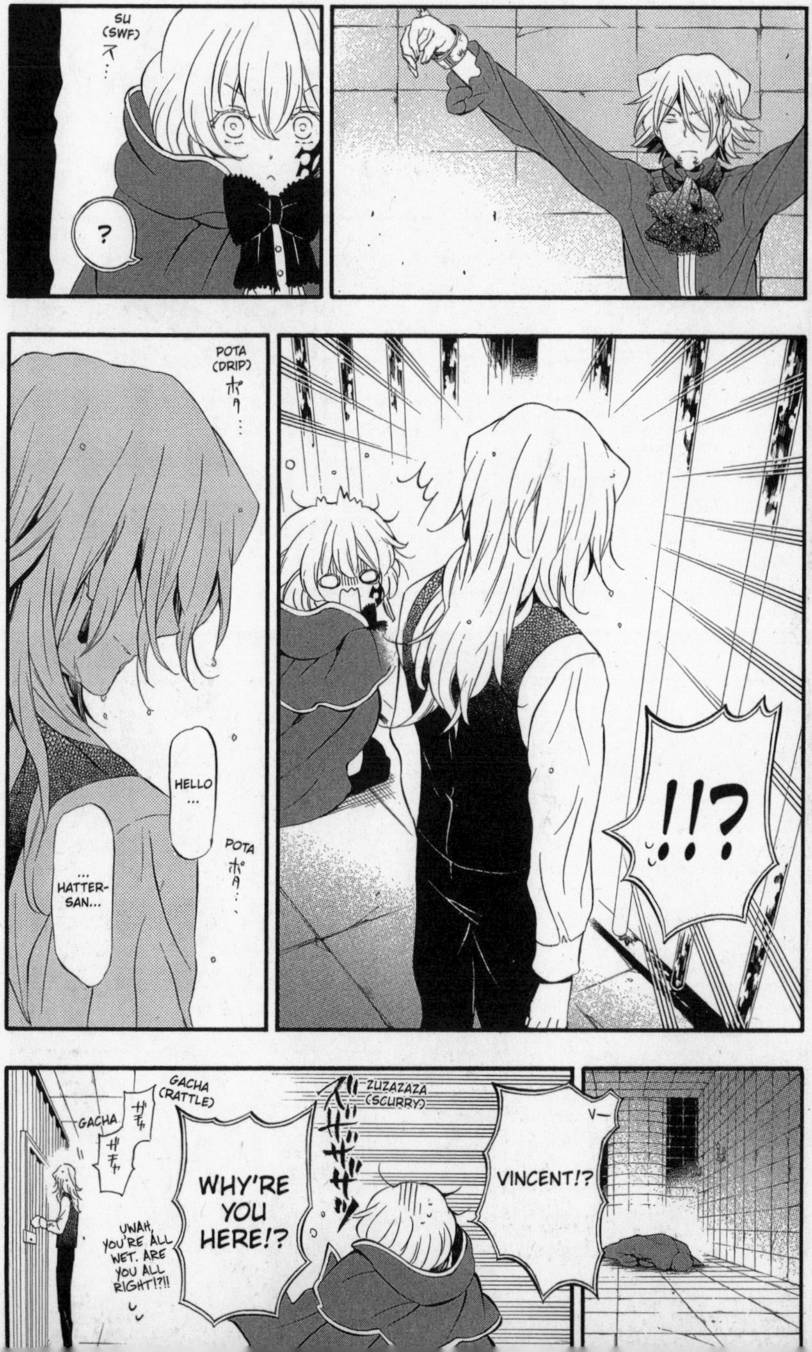
SU (SWF)
ス…
?
!!?
POTA (DRIP)
ポタ…
HELLO…
…HATTER-SAN…
POTA
ポタ…
V—
VINCENT!?
ZUZAZAZA (SCURRY)
ズザザザッ
WHY'RE YOU HERE!?
GACHA (RATTLE)
ガチャ
GACHA
ガチャ
UWAH, YOU'RE ALL WET. ARE YOU ALL RIGHT!?!!

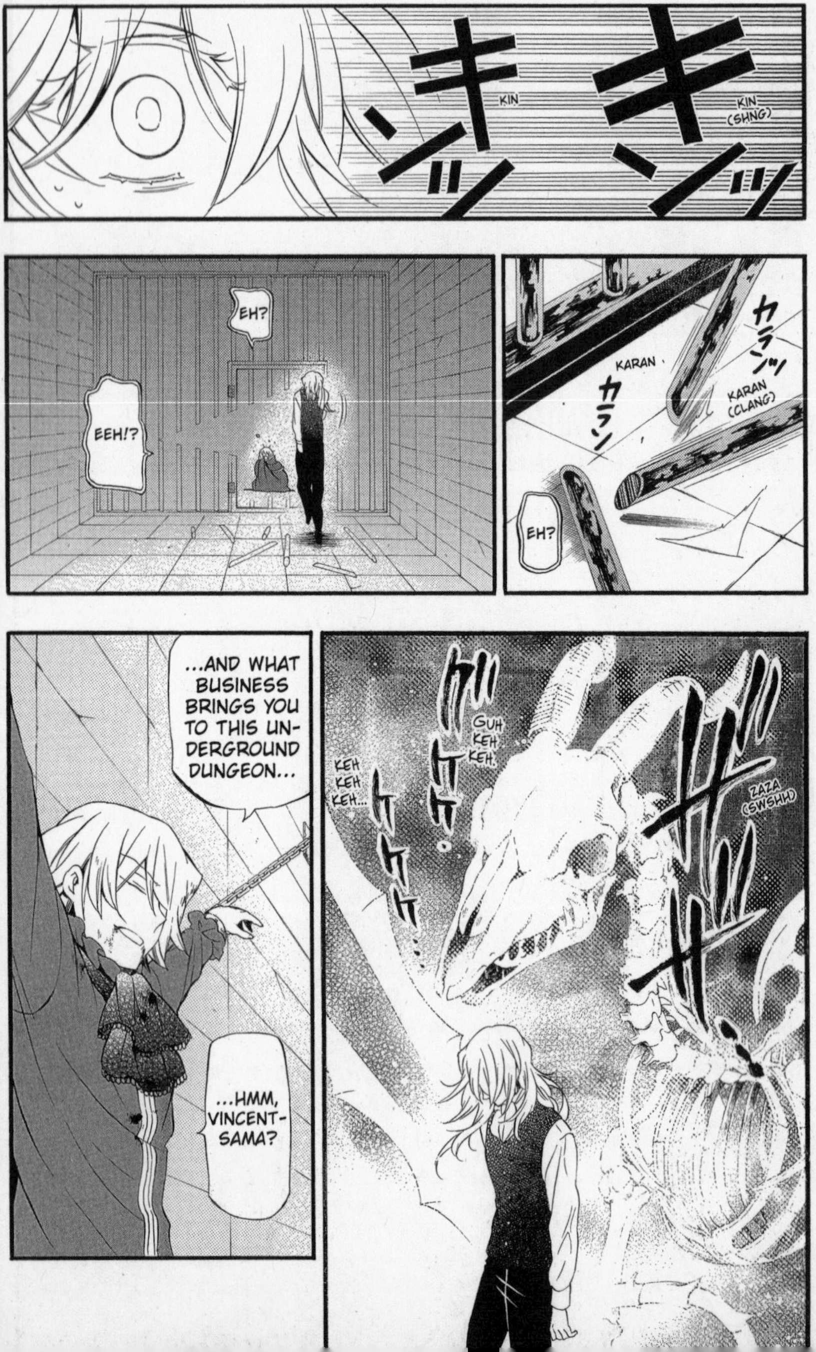
KIN (SHNG)
KIN
KARAN (CLANG)
KARAN
EH?
EH?
EEH!?
ZAZA (SWSHH)
GUH KEH KEH.
KEH KEH KEH...
...AND WHAT BUSINESS BRINGS YOU TO THIS UN-DERGROUND DUNGEON...
...HMM, VINCENT-SAMA?

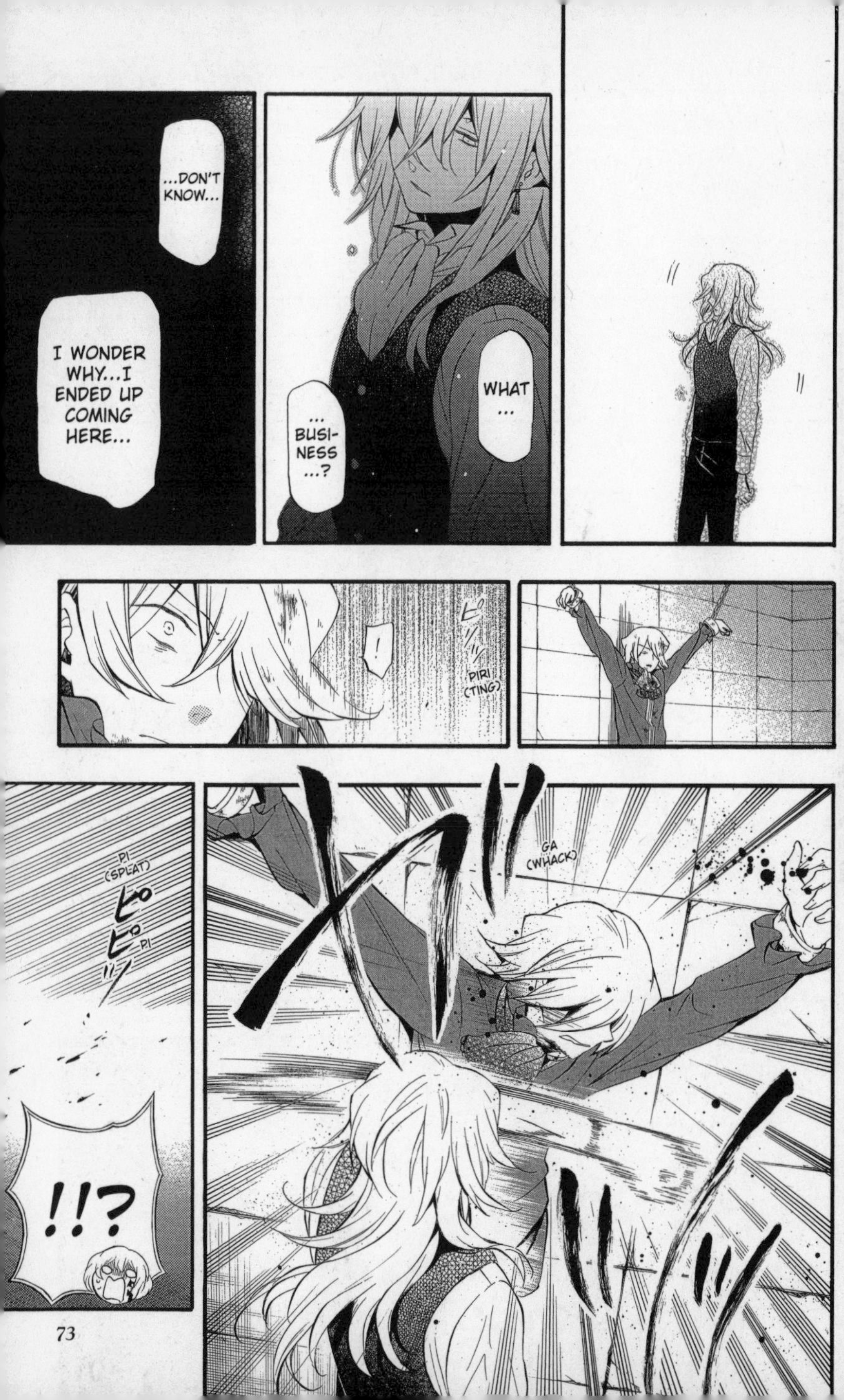
WHAT ...
... BUSI-NESS ...?
...DON'T KNOW...
I WONDER WHY...I ENDED UP COMING HERE...
!
PIRI (TING)
GA (WHACK)
PI (SPLAT)
PI
!!?

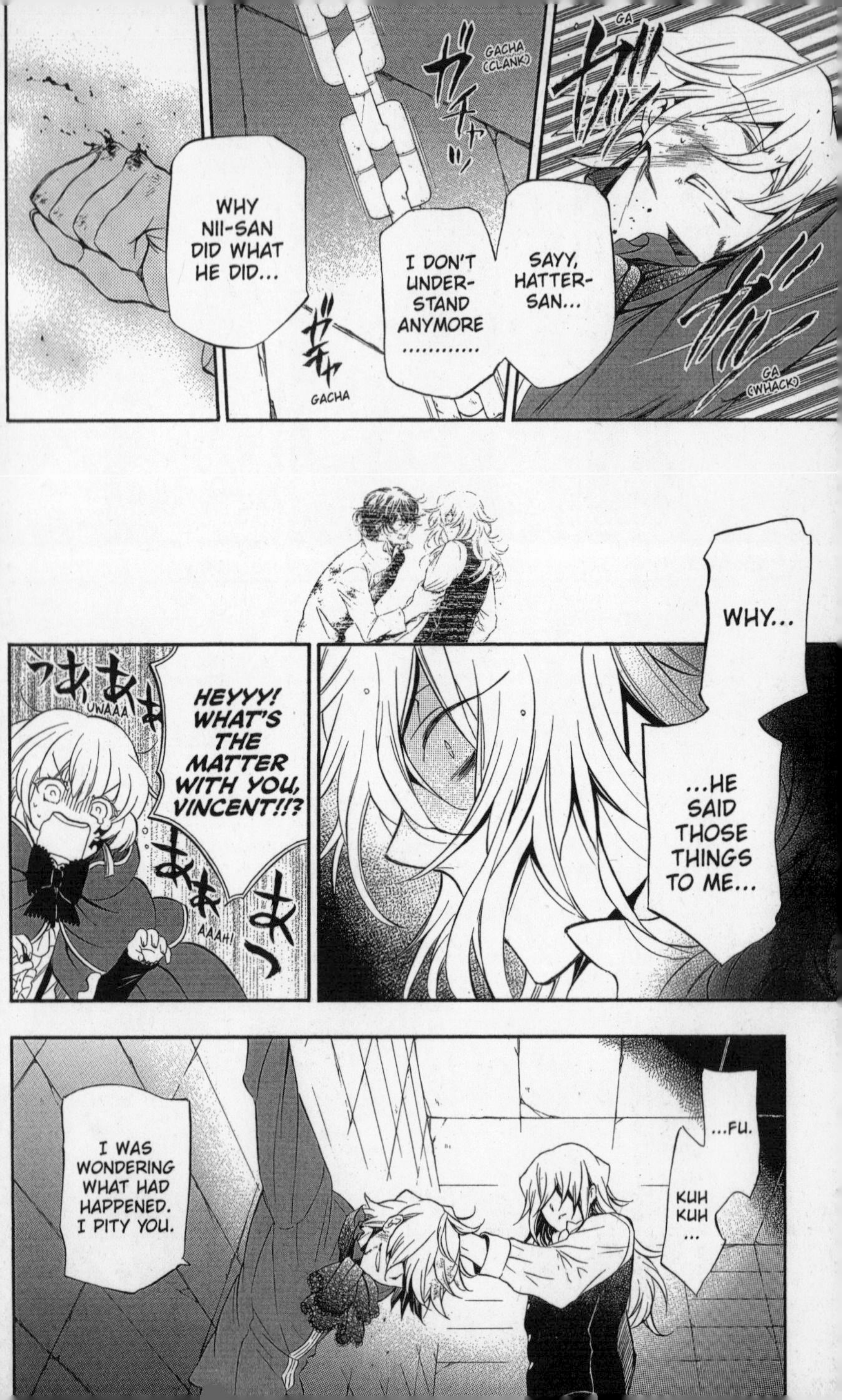
GA
GA (WHACK)
GACHA (CLANK)
SAYY, HATTER-SAN...
I DON'T UNDER-STAND ANYMORE ....
GACHA
WHY NII-SAN DID WHAT HE DID...
WHY...
...HE SAID THOSE THINGS TO ME...
UNAAA
HEYYY! WHAT'S THE MATTER WITH YOU, VINCENT!!?
AAAH!
...FU.
KUH KUH ...
I WAS WONDERING WHAT HAD HAPPENED. I PITY YOU.

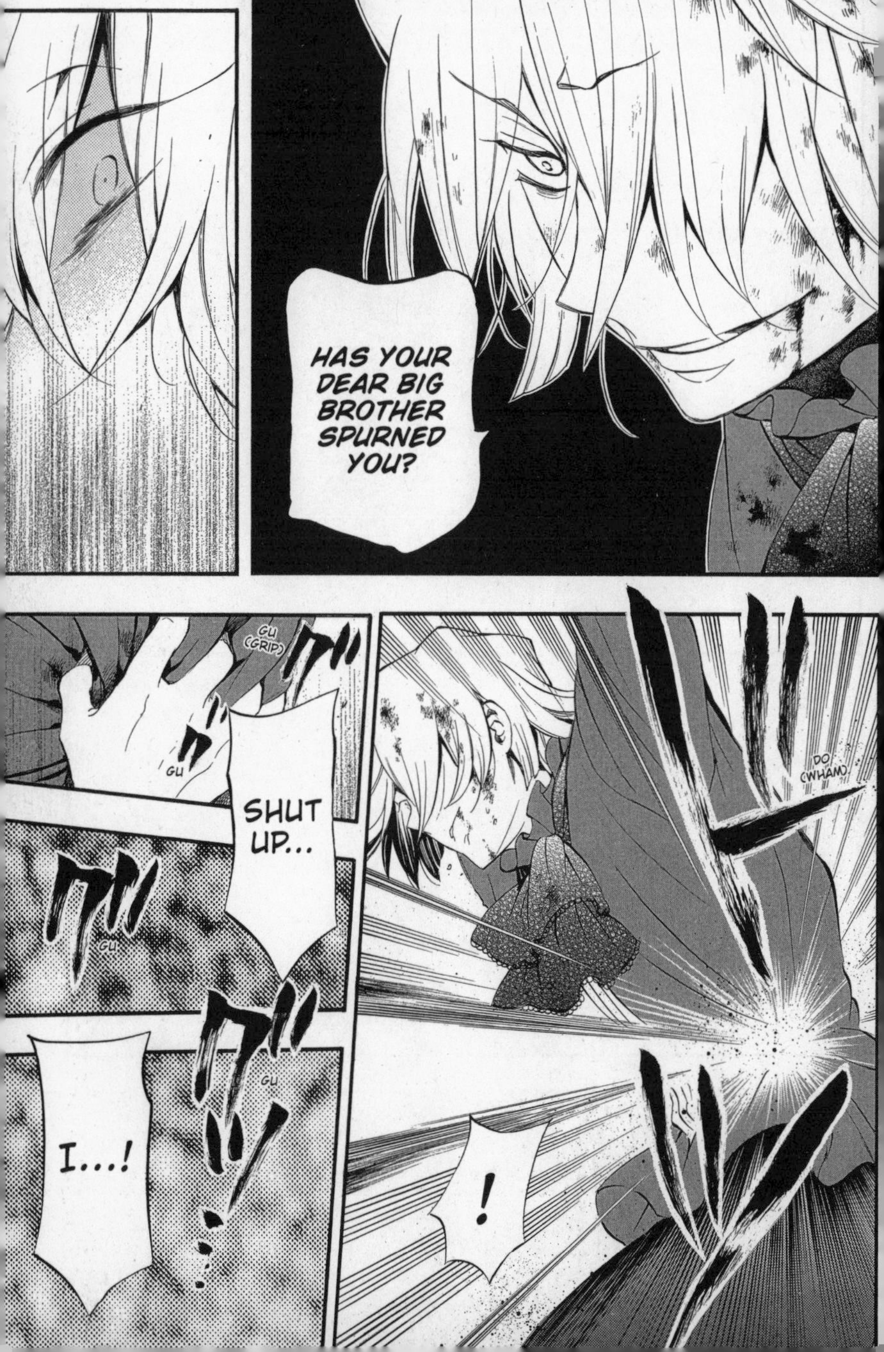
HAS YOUR DEAR BIG BROTHER SPURNED YOU?
DO (WHAM)
!
GU (GRIP)
GU
SHUT UP...
GU
GU
I...!

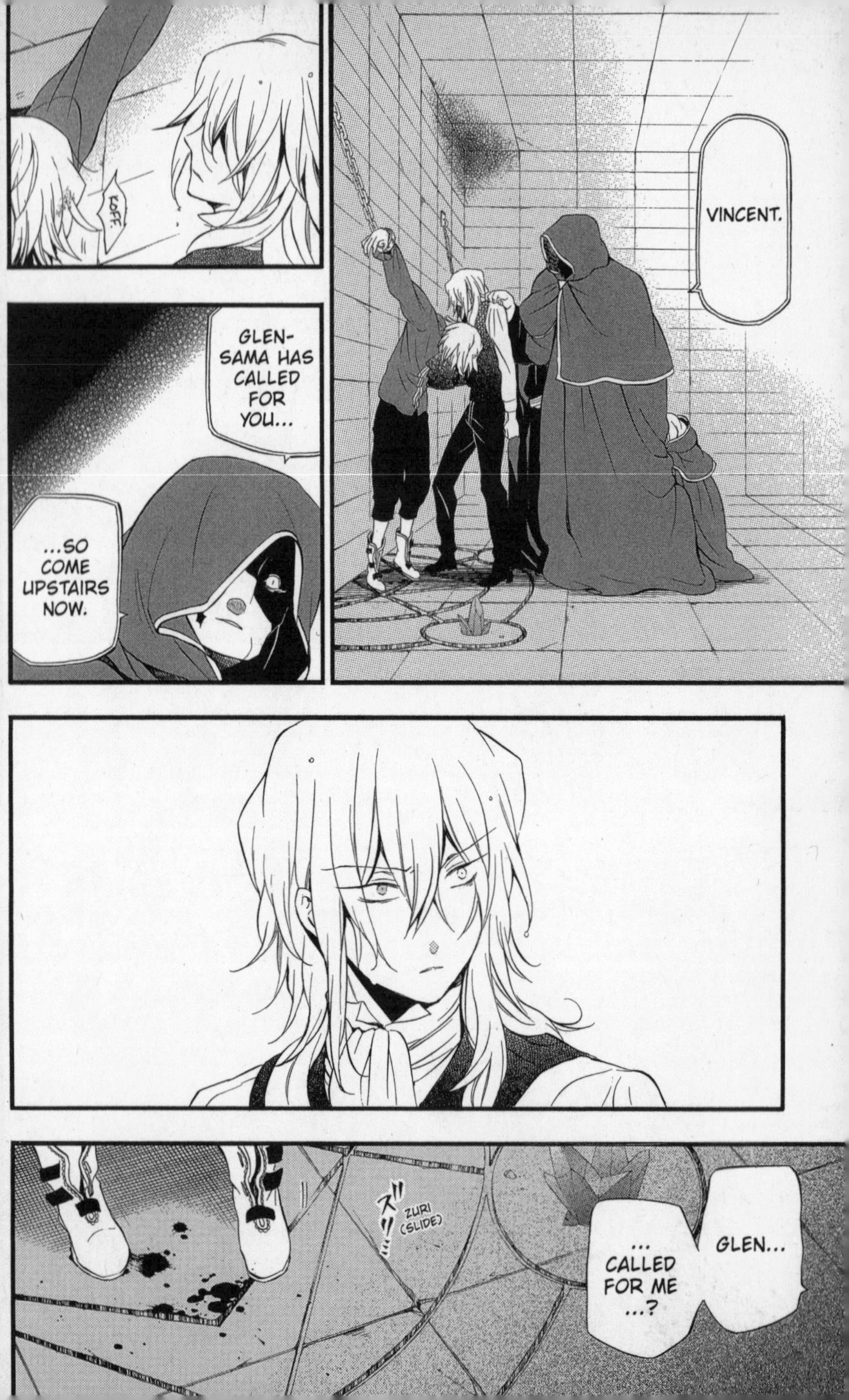
VINCENT.
KOFF
GLEN-SAMA HAS CALLED FOR YOU...
...SO COME UPSTAIRS NOW.
GLEN...
...CALLED FOR ME...?
ZURI (SLIDE)

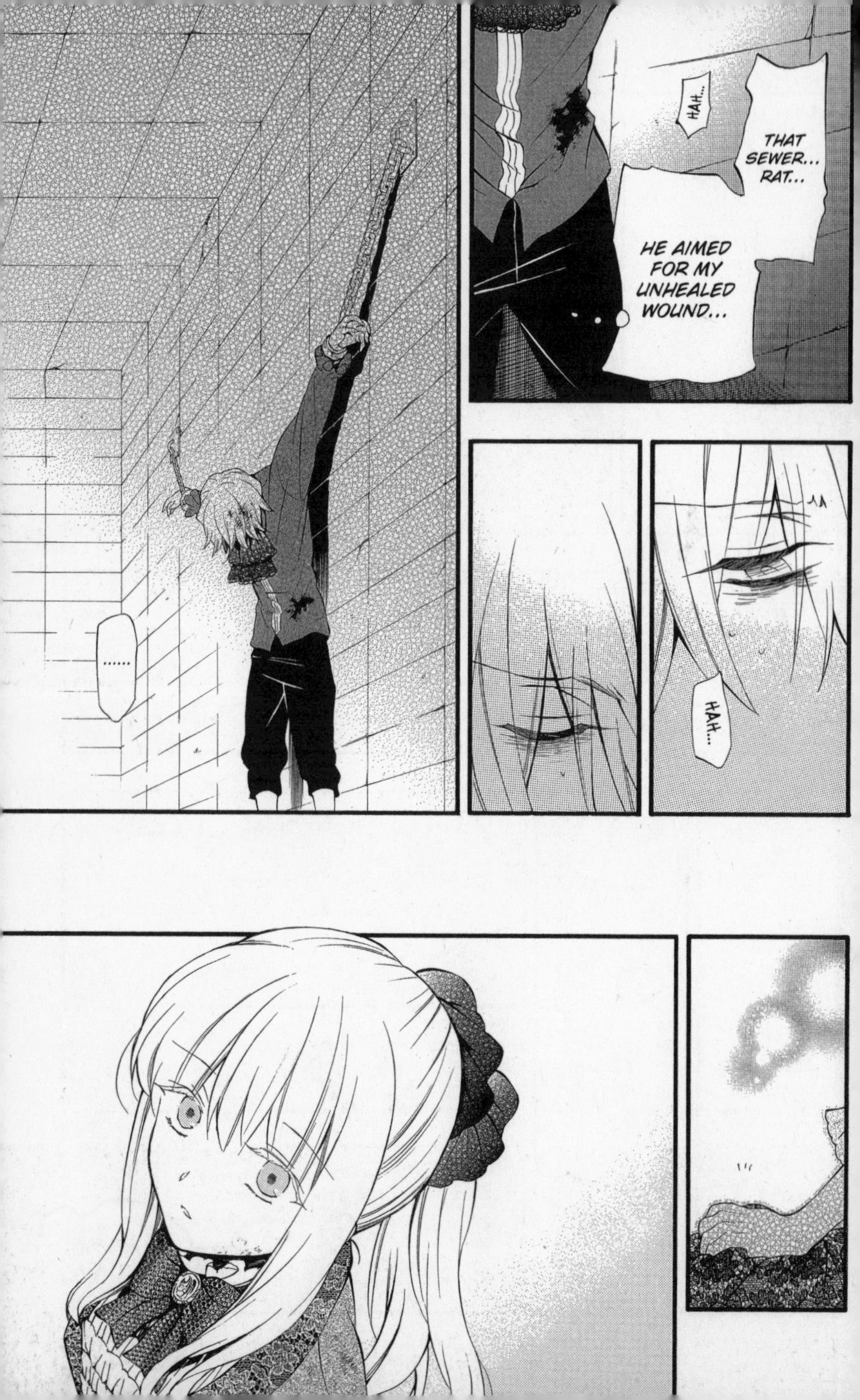
THAT SEWER... RAT...
HAH...
HE AIMED FOR MY UNHEALED WOUND...
HAH...
......

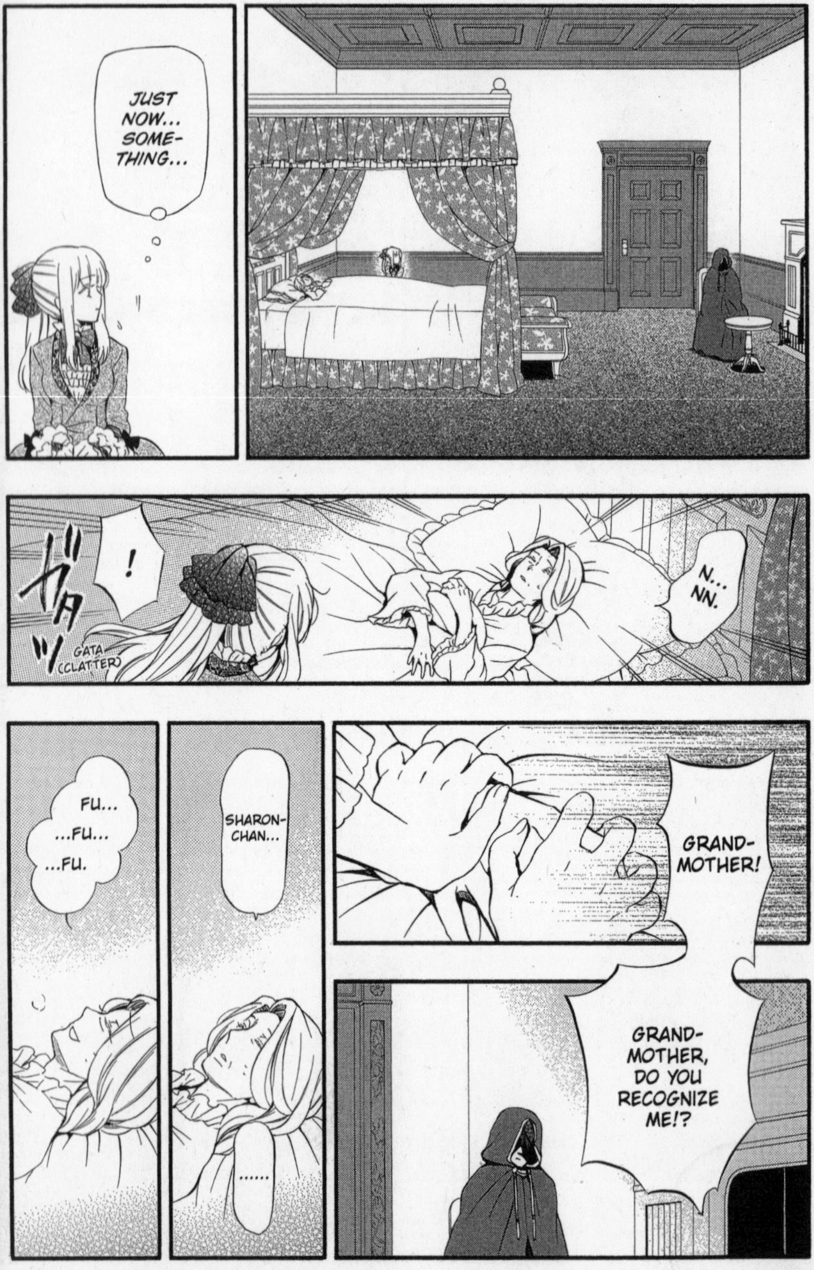
JUST NOW... SOMETHING...
N... NN.
!
GATA (CLATTER)
GRAND-MOTHER!
GRAND-MOTHER, DO YOU RECOGNIZE ME!?
SHARON-CHAN...
......
FU... ...FU... ...FU.

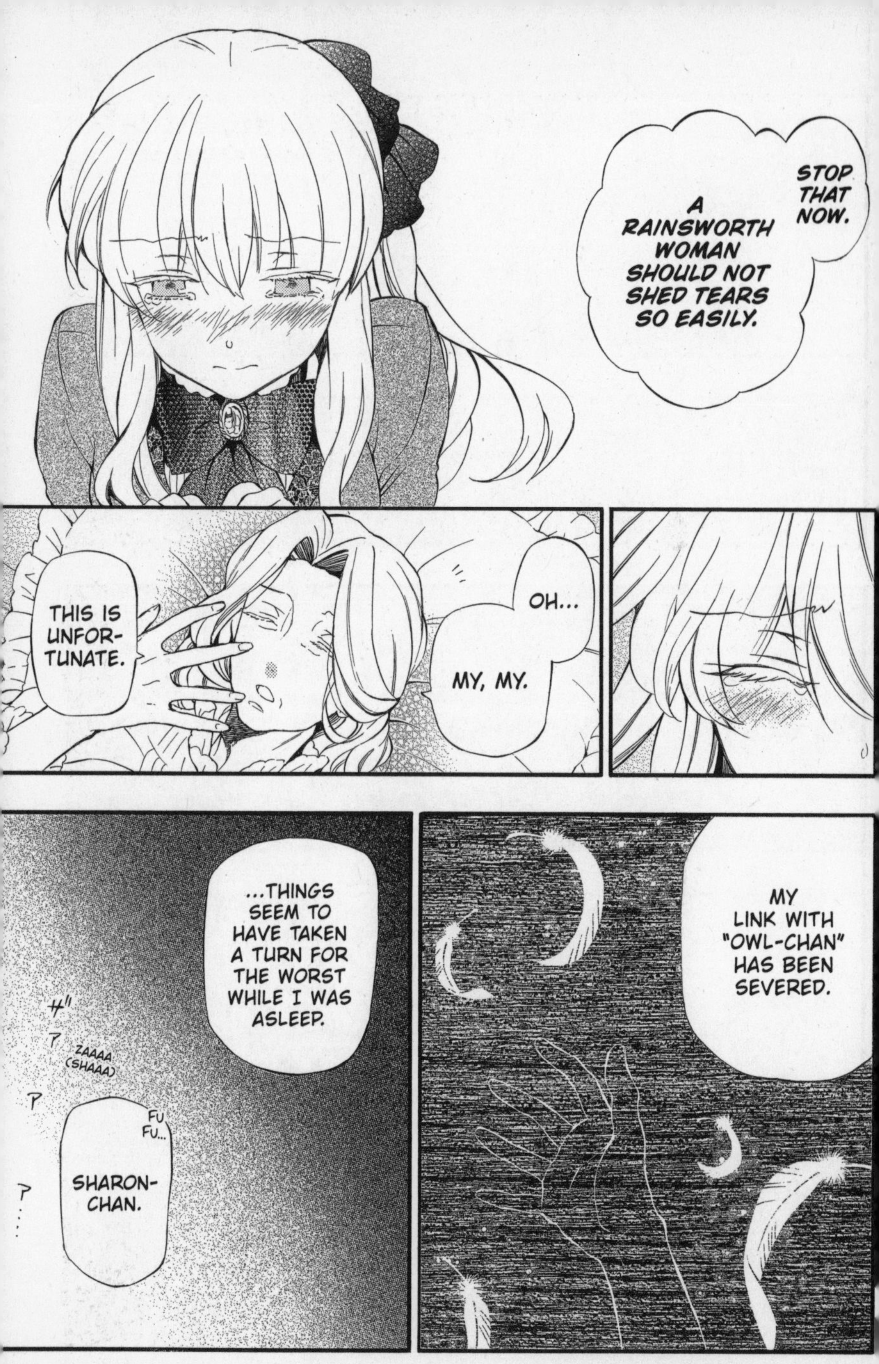
STOP THAT NOW.
A RAINSWORTH WOMAN SHOULD NOT SHED TEARS SO EASILY.
OH...
MY, MY.
THIS IS UNFORTUNATE.
MY LINK WITH "OWL-CHAN" HAS BEEN SEVERED.
...THINGS SEEM TO HAVE TAKEN A TURN FOR THE WORST WHILE I WAS ASLEEP.
ZAAAA (SHAAA)
FU FU...
SHARON-CHAN.

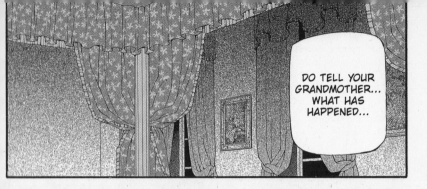

DO TELL YOUR GRANDMOTHER... WHAT HAS HAPPENED...
DO (BOOM)
DO
IS IT ANOTHER EARTH-QUAKE?
THEY'RE SO FREQUENT NOWADAYS.
DO
PARIN (CRACKLE)
PARIN

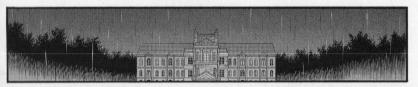

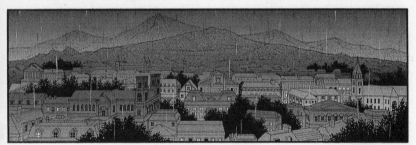

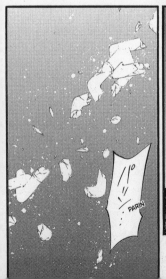

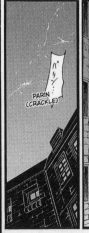

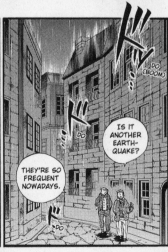

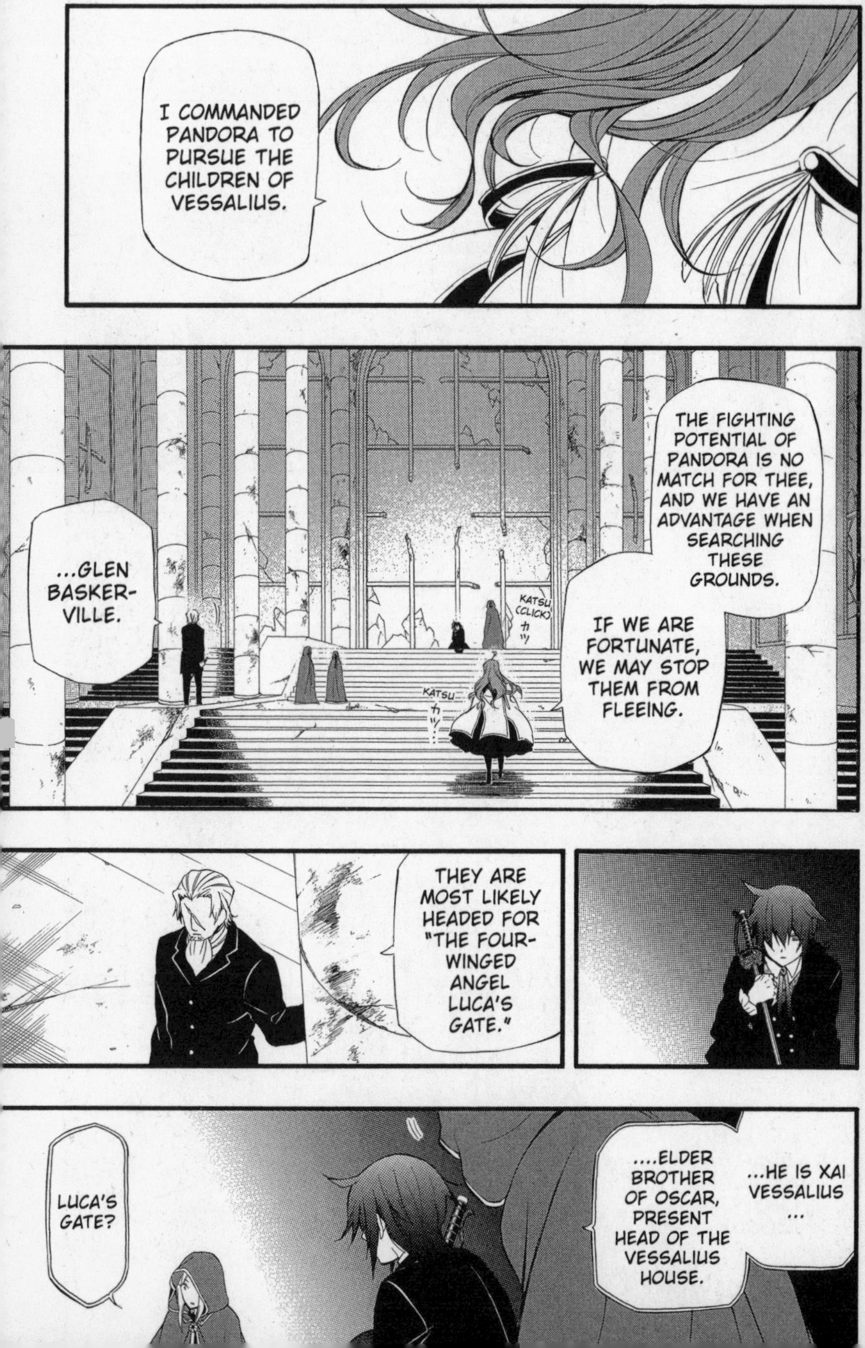
I COMMANDED PANDORA TO PURSUE THE CHILDREN OF VESSALIUS.
THE FIGHTING POTENTIAL OF PANDORA IS NO MATCH FOR THEE, AND WE HAVE AN ADVANTAGE WHEN SEARCHING THESE GROUNDS.
IF WE ARE FORTUNATE, WE MAY STOP THEM FROM FLEEING.
KATSU (CLICK) カツ
KATSU カツ
...GLEN BASKER-VILLE.
THEY ARE MOST LIKELY HEADED FOR "THE FOUR-WINGED ANGEL LUCA'S GATE."
...HE IS XAI VESSALIUS ...
....ELDER BROTHER OF OSCAR, PRESENT HEAD OF THE VESSALIUS HOUSE.
LUCA'S GATE?

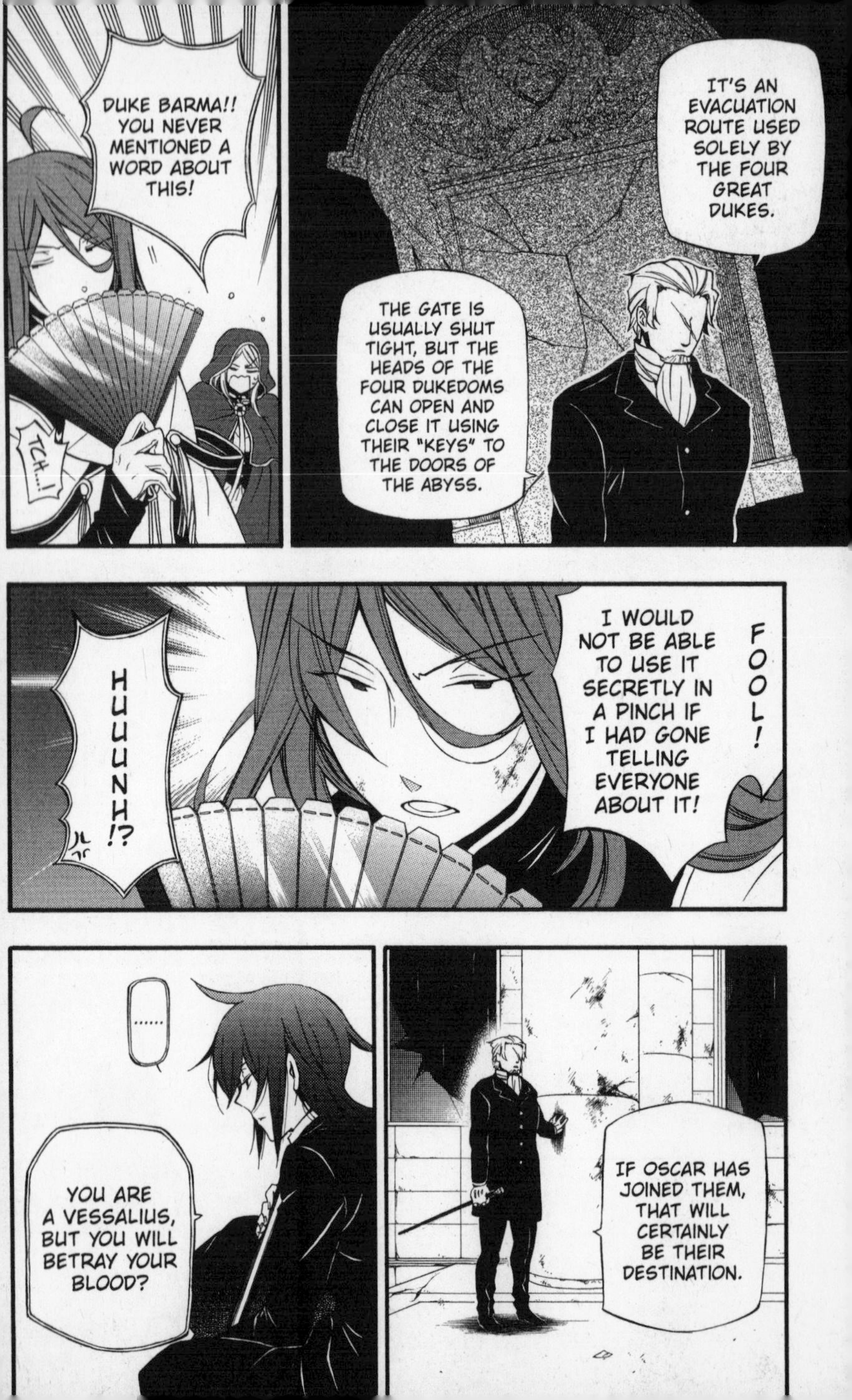
IT'S AN EVACUATION ROUTE USED SOLELY BY THE FOUR GREAT DUKES.
THE GATE IS USUALLY SHUT TIGHT, BUT THE HEADS OF THE FOUR DUKEDOMS CAN OPEN AND CLOSE IT USING THEIR "KEYS" TO THE DOORS OF THE ABYSS.
DUKE BARMA!! YOU NEVER MENTIONED A WORD ABOUT THIS!
TCH...!
FOOL!
I WOULD NOT BE ABLE TO USE IT SECRETLY IN A PINCH IF I HAD GONE TELLING EVERYONE ABOUT IT!
HUUUNH!?
IF OSCAR HAS JOINED THEM, THAT WILL CERTAINLY BE THEIR DESTINATION.
......
YOU ARE A VESSALIUS, BUT YOU WILL BETRAY YOUR BLOOD?

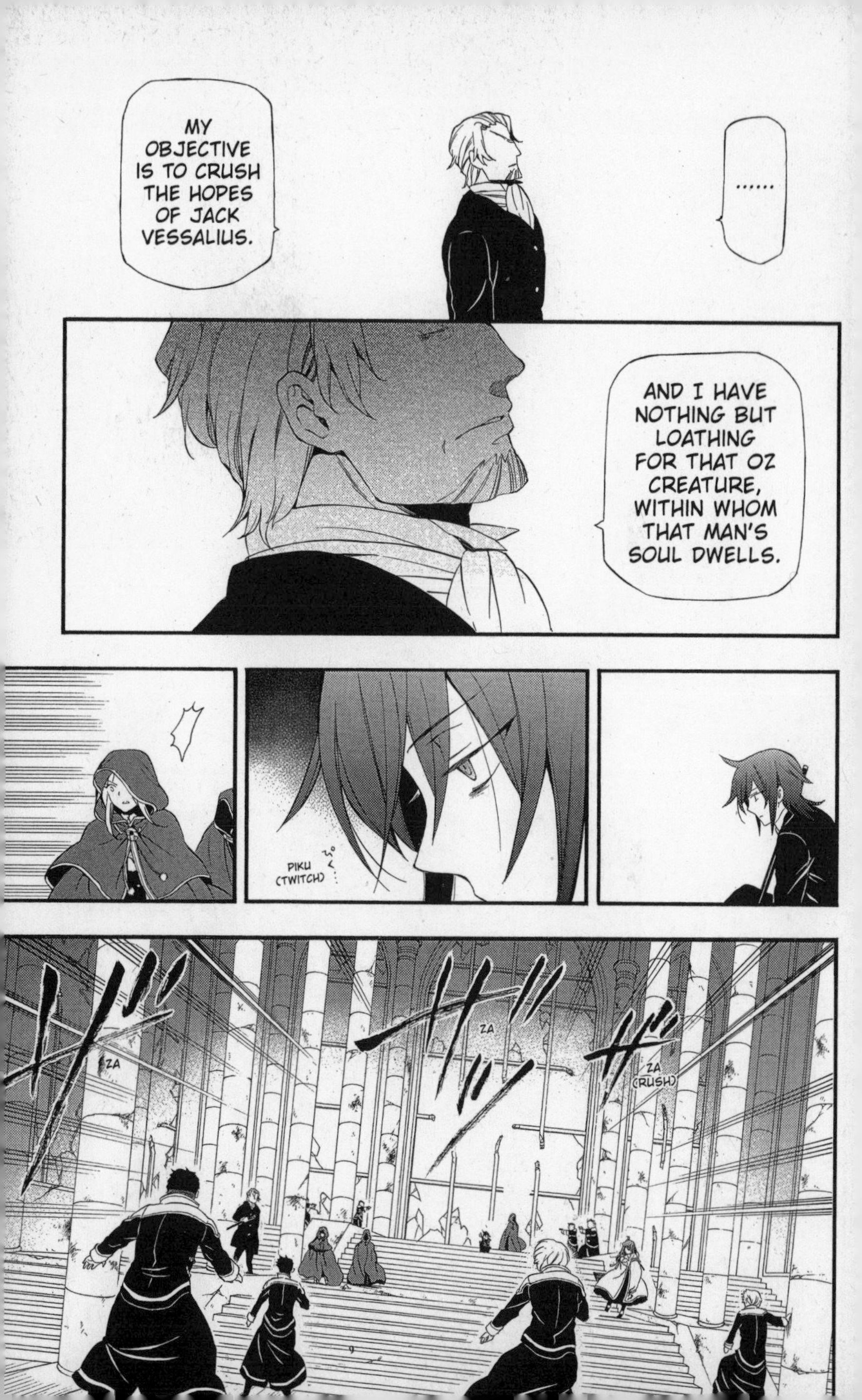
......
MY OBJECTIVE IS TO CRUSH THE HOPES OF JACK VESSALIUS.
AND I HAVE NOTHING BUT LOATHING FOR THAT OZ CREATURE, WITHIN WHOM THAT MAN'S SOUL DWELLS.
PIKU (TWITCH)
ZA (RUSH)
ZA
ZA

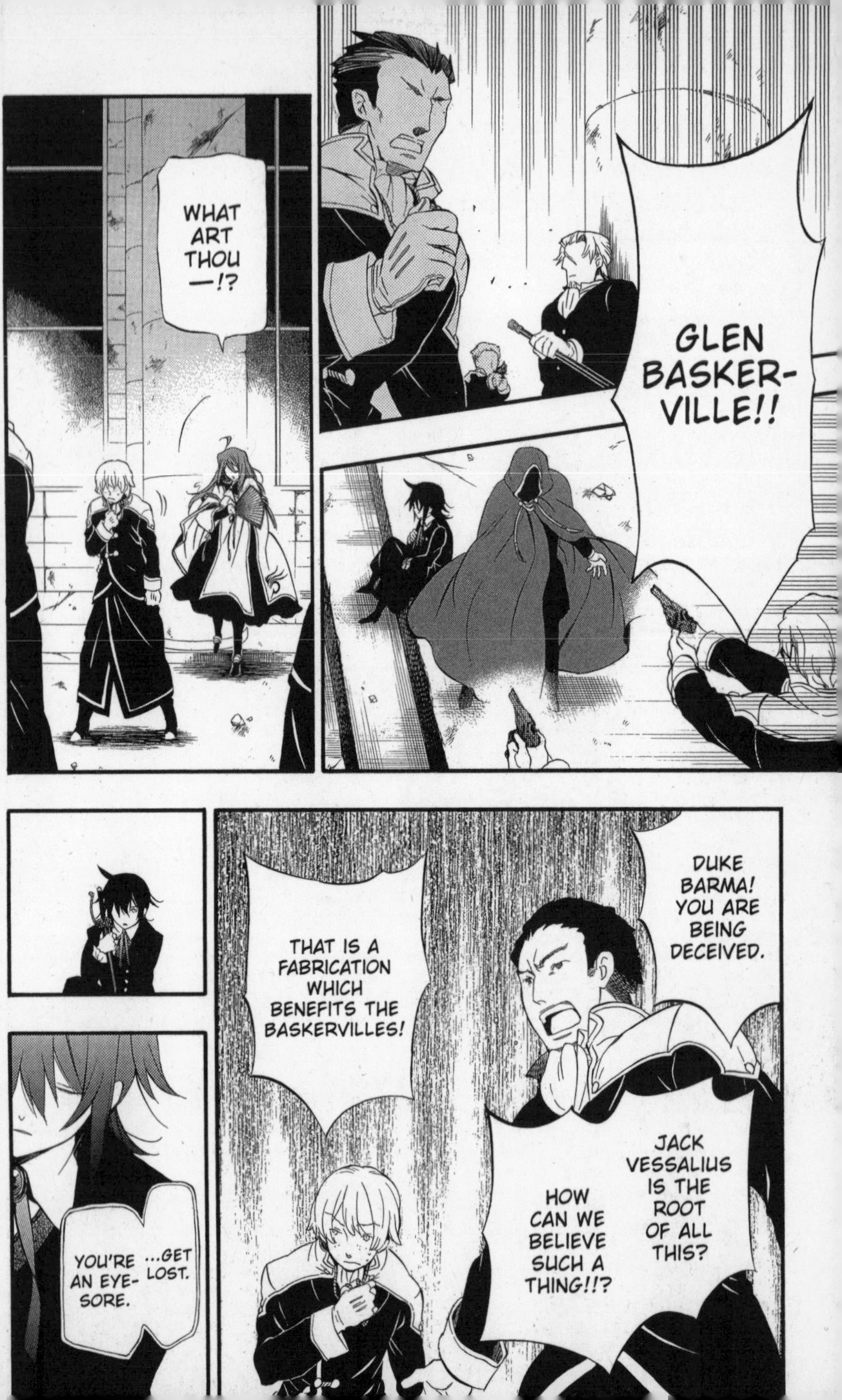
GLEN BASKERVILLE!!
WHAT ART THOU—!?
DUKE BARMA! YOU ARE BEING DECEIVED.
THAT IS A FABRICATION WHICH BENEFITS THE BASKERVILLES!
JACK VESSALIUS IS THE ROOT OF ALL THIS? HOW CAN WE BELIEVE SUCH A THING!!?
...GET LOST.
YOU'RE AN EYE-SORE.

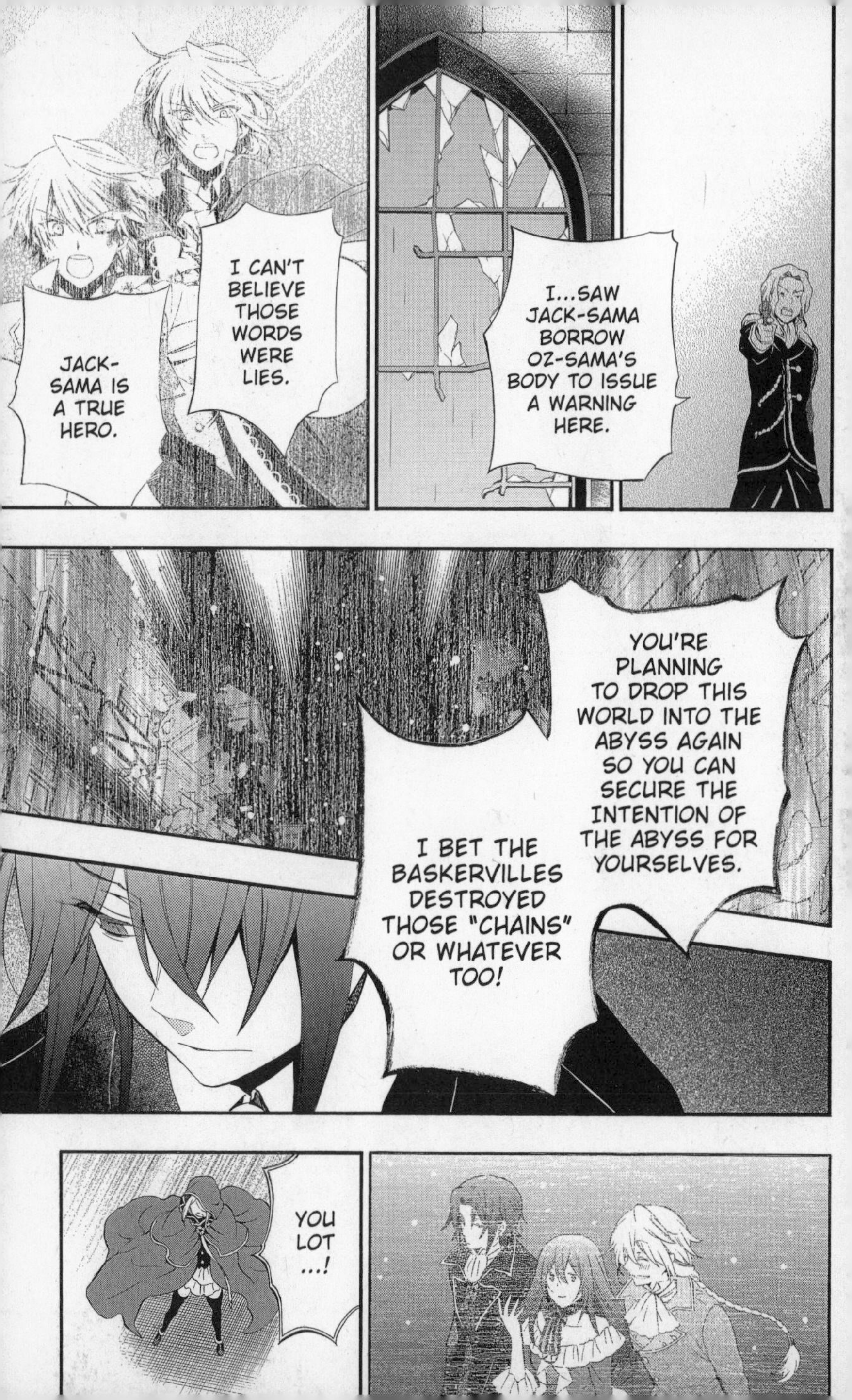
I...SAW JACK-SAMA BORROW OZ-SAMA'S BODY TO ISSUE A WARNING HERE.
I CAN'T BELIEVE THOSE WORDS WERE LIES.
JACK-SAMA IS A TRUE HERO.
YOU'RE PLANNING TO DROP THIS WORLD INTO THE ABYSS AGAIN SO YOU CAN SECURE THE INTENTION OF THE ABYSS FOR YOURSELVES.
I BET THE BASKERVILLES DESTROYED THOSE "CHAINS" OR WHATEVER TOO!
YOU LOT ...!

KUH
KUH
KUH
...

HA-HA-
HA-HA-
HA-HA!

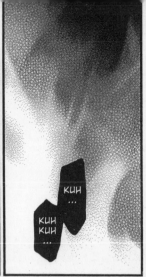

KUH
...

KUH
KUH
...

YES...
THAT'S...

...WHAT
JACK IS.

KATSU
(CLICK)

KATSU

GLEN-
SAMA
...?

HA
...

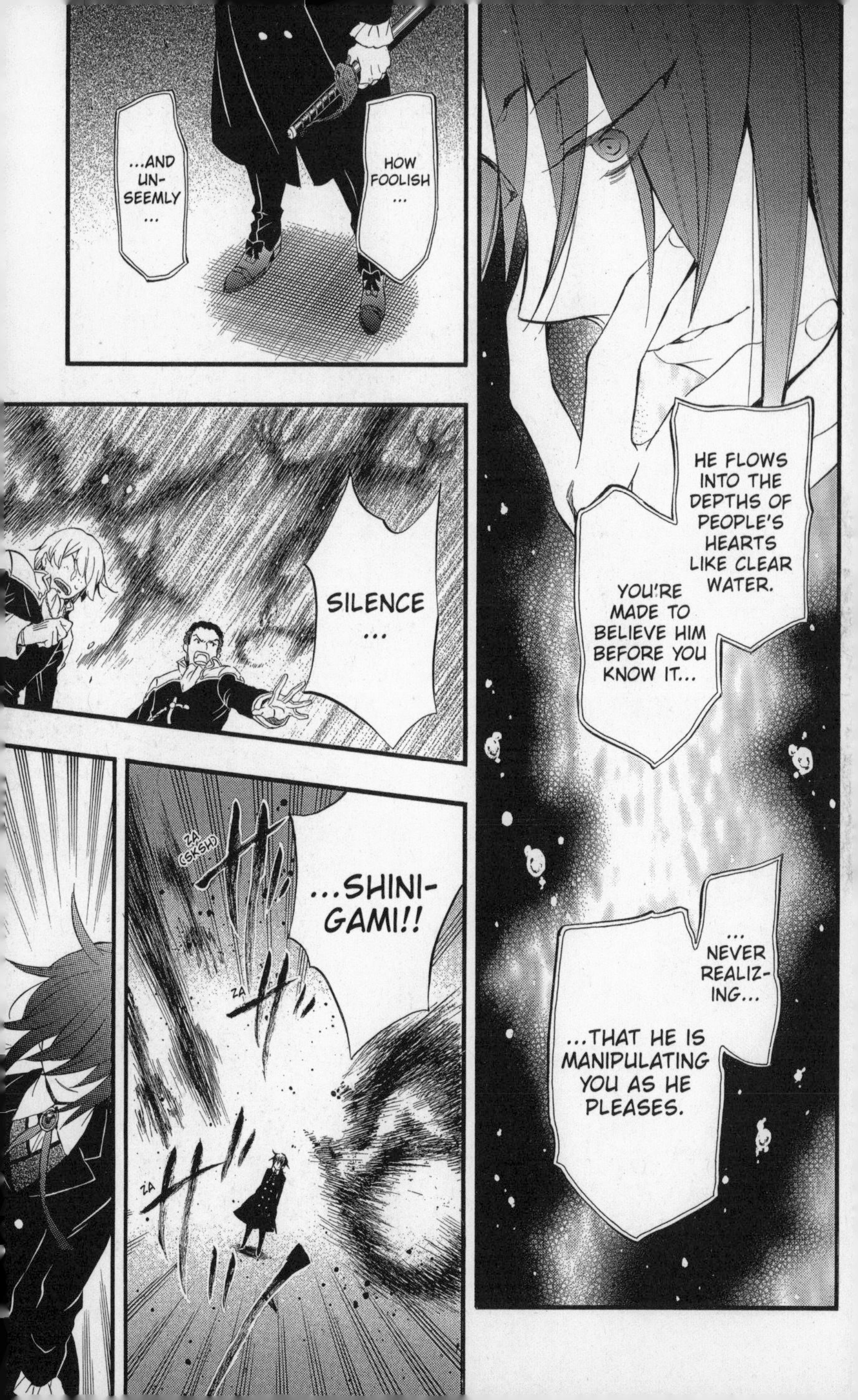
HE FLOWS INTO THE DEPTHS OF PEOPLE'S HEARTS LIKE CLEAR WATER.
YOU'RE MADE TO BELIEVE HIM BEFORE YOU KNOW IT...
...NEVER REALIZING...
...THAT HE IS MANIPULATING YOU AS HE PLEASES.
HOW FOOLISH...
...AND UN-SEEMLY...
SILENCE...
ZA (SKSH)
...SHINI-GAMI!!
ZA
ZA

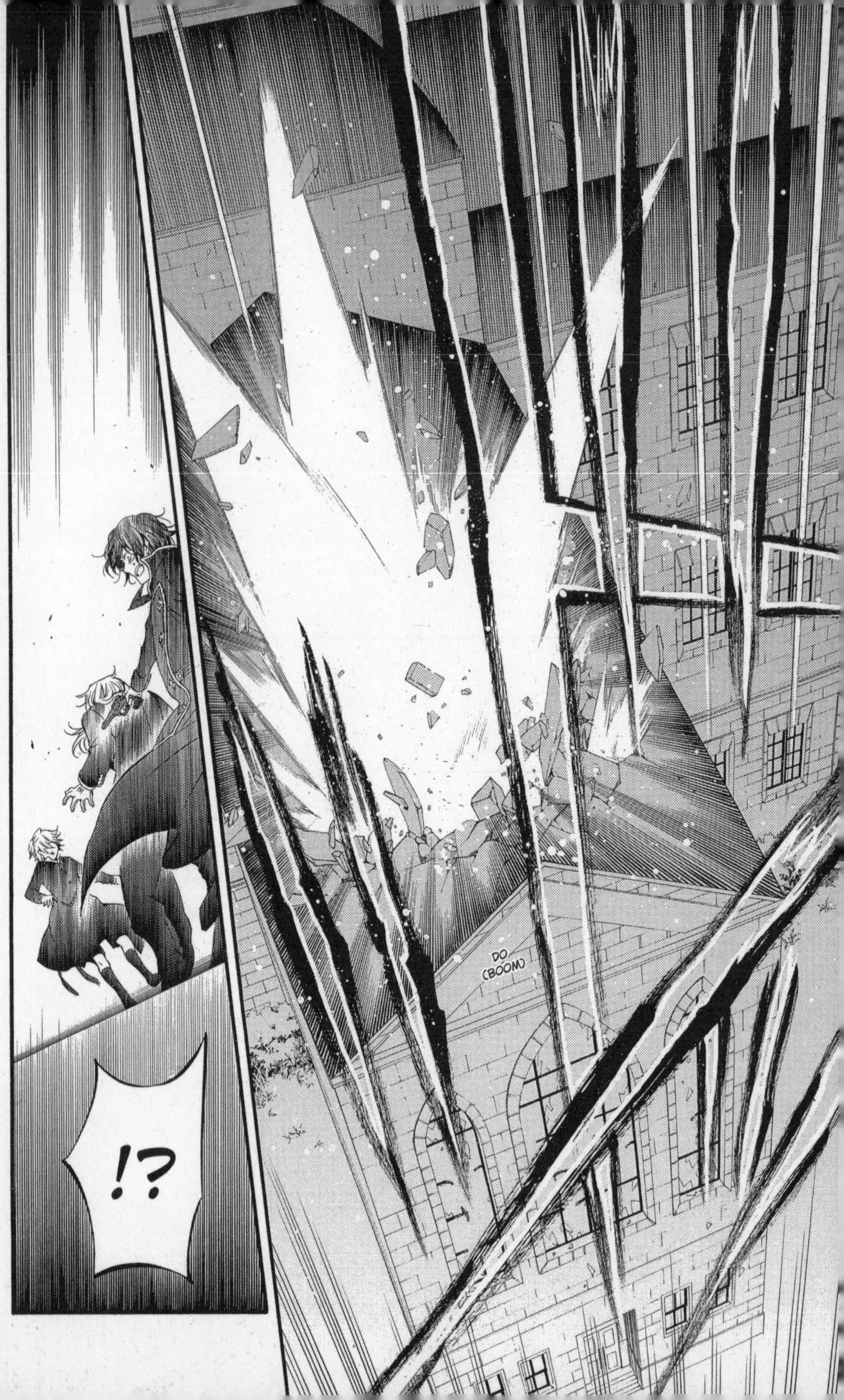
DO
(BOOM)
!?

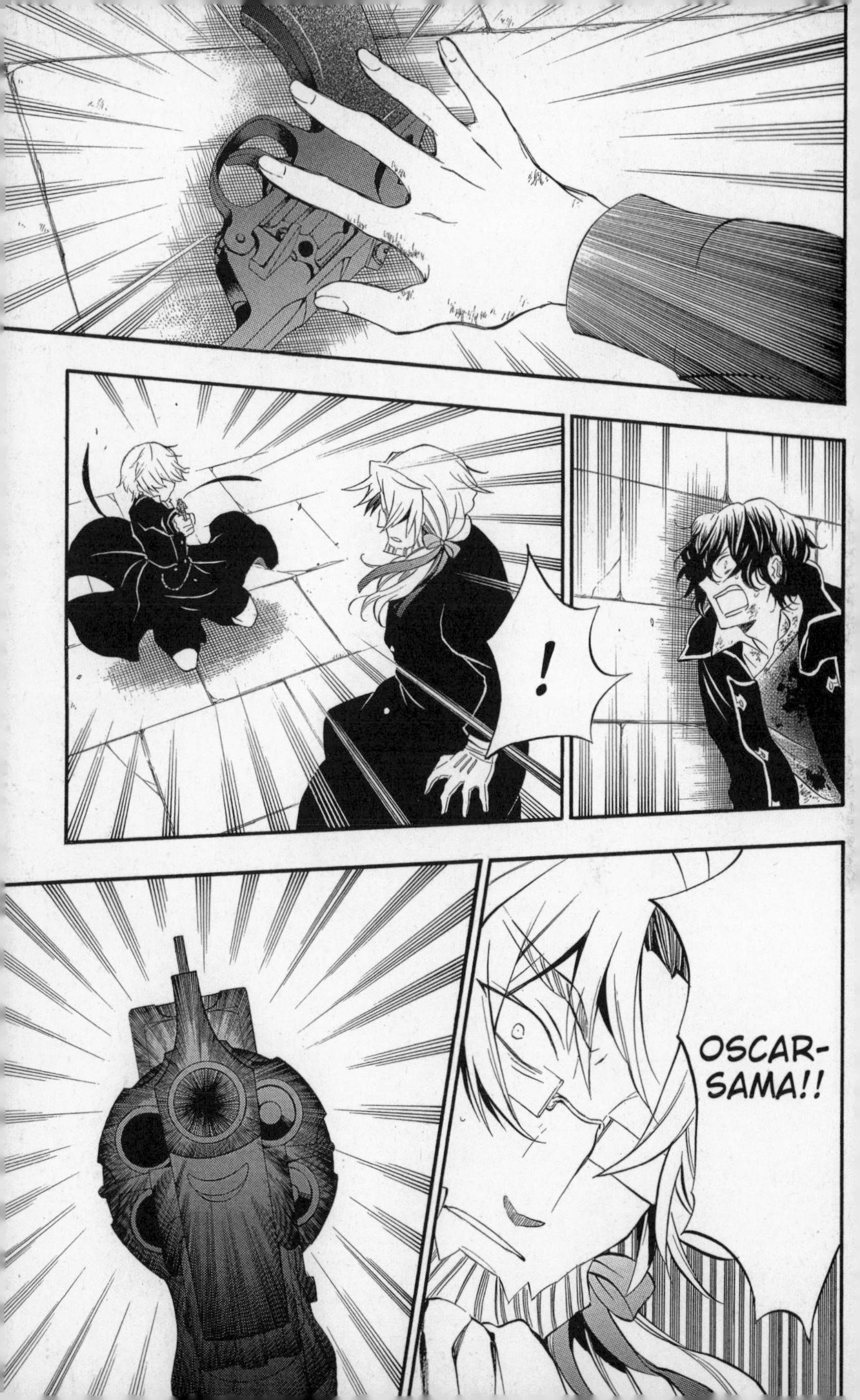
!
OSCAR-
SAMA!!

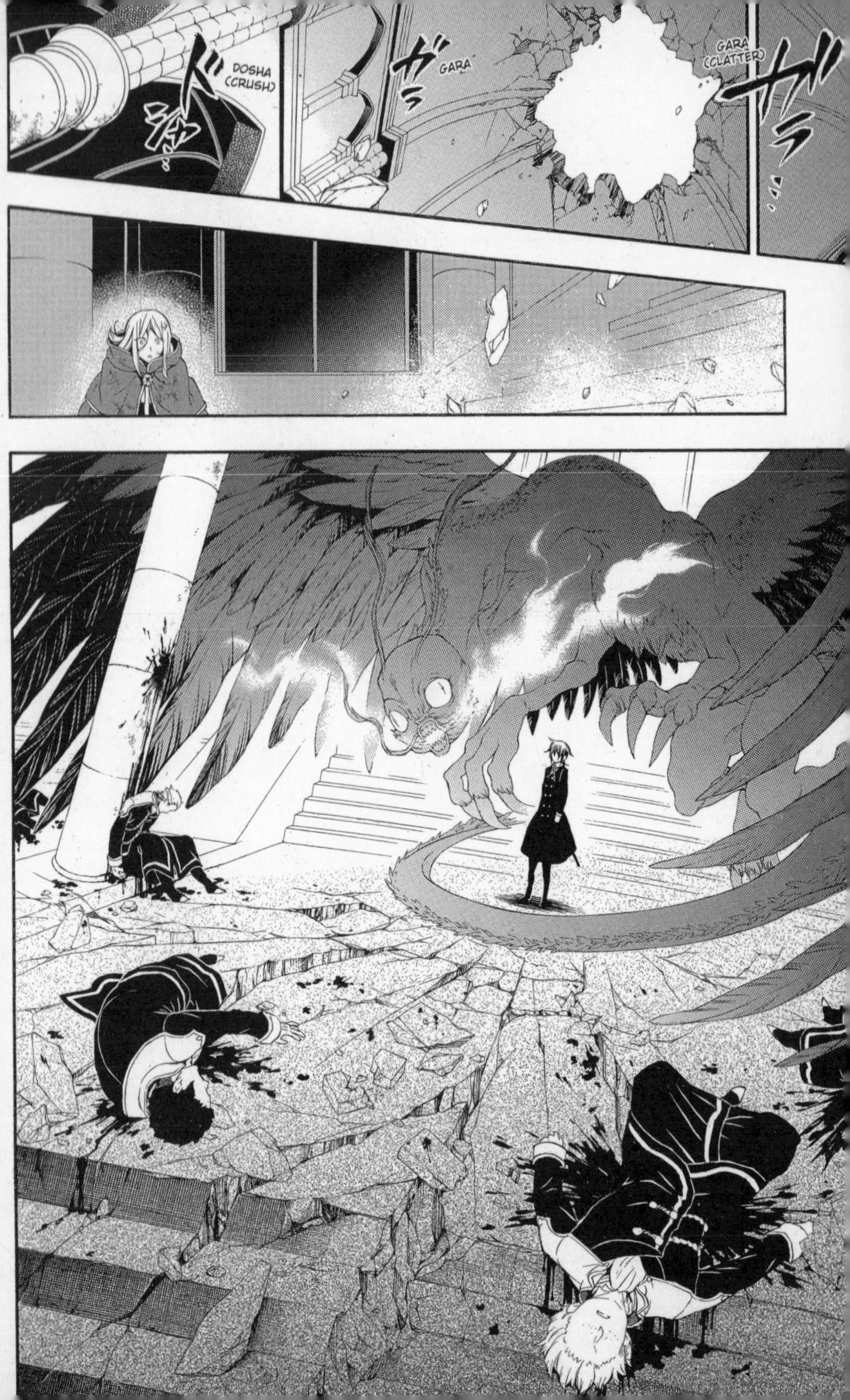
GARA (CLATTER)
GARA
DOSHA (CRUSH)

SA—

JA—

ti
ri
KATSU
(CLICK)

KATSU
ti
ri
...

UH
...

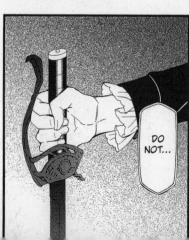

DO NOT...

DO
(STAB)

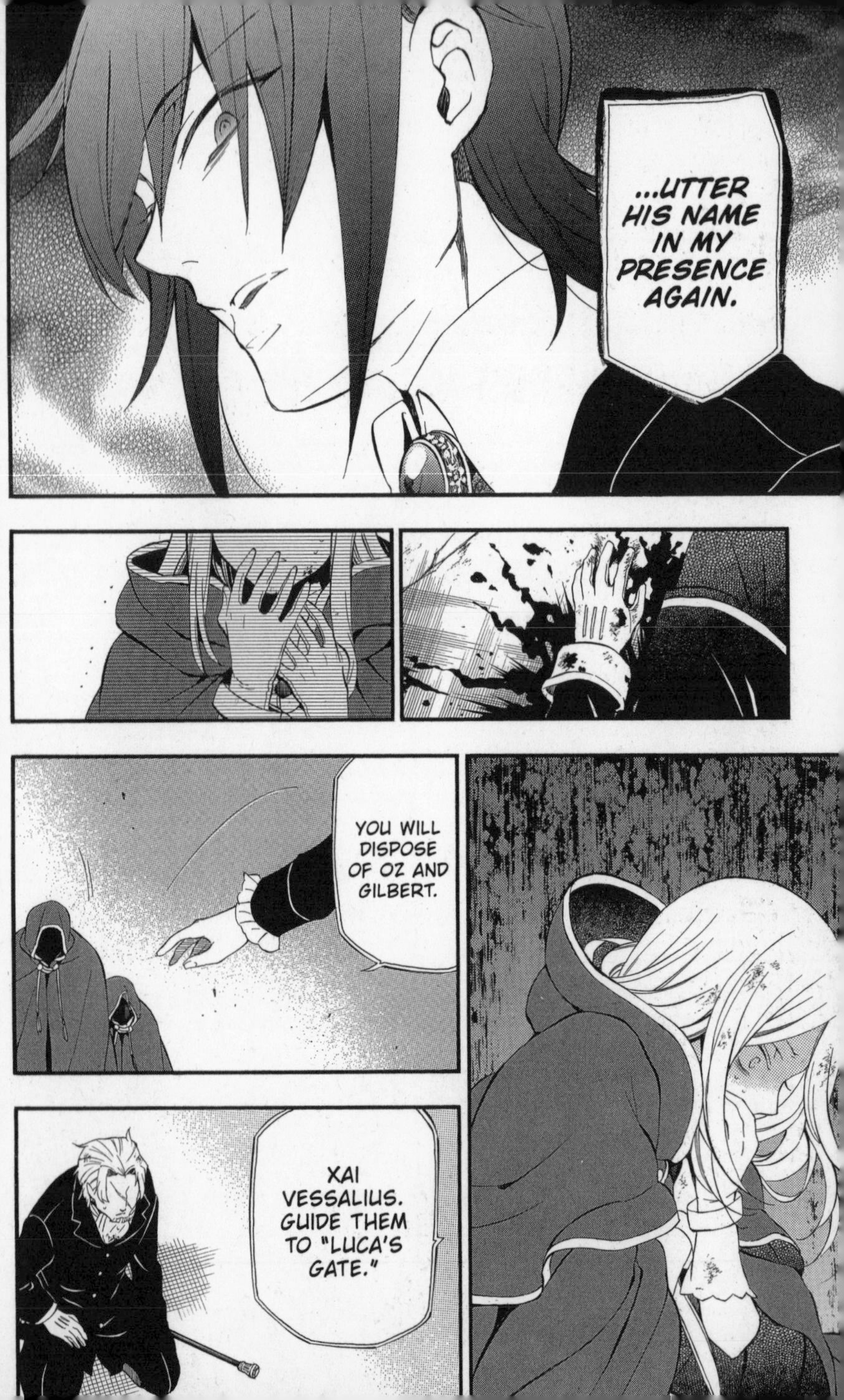
...UTTER HIS NAME IN MY PRESENCE AGAIN.
YOU WILL DISPOSE OF OZ AND GILBERT.
XAI VESSALIUS. GUIDE THEM TO "LUCA'S GATE."

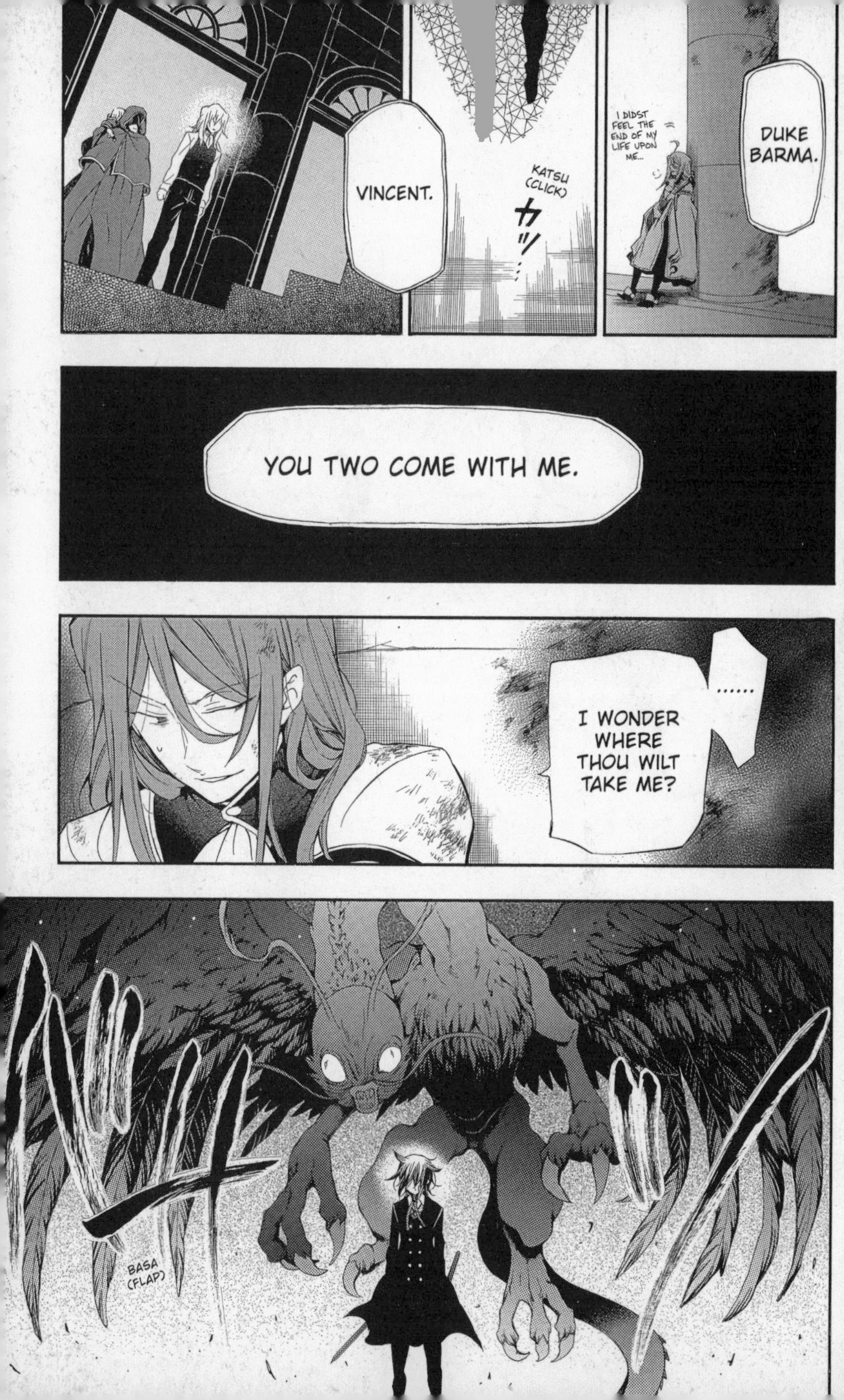
DUKE BARMA.
I DIDST FEEL THE END OF MY LIFE UPON ME...
KATSU (CLICK)
VINCENT.
YOU TWO COME WITH ME.
......
I WONDER WHERE THOU WILT TAKE ME?
BASA (FLAP)

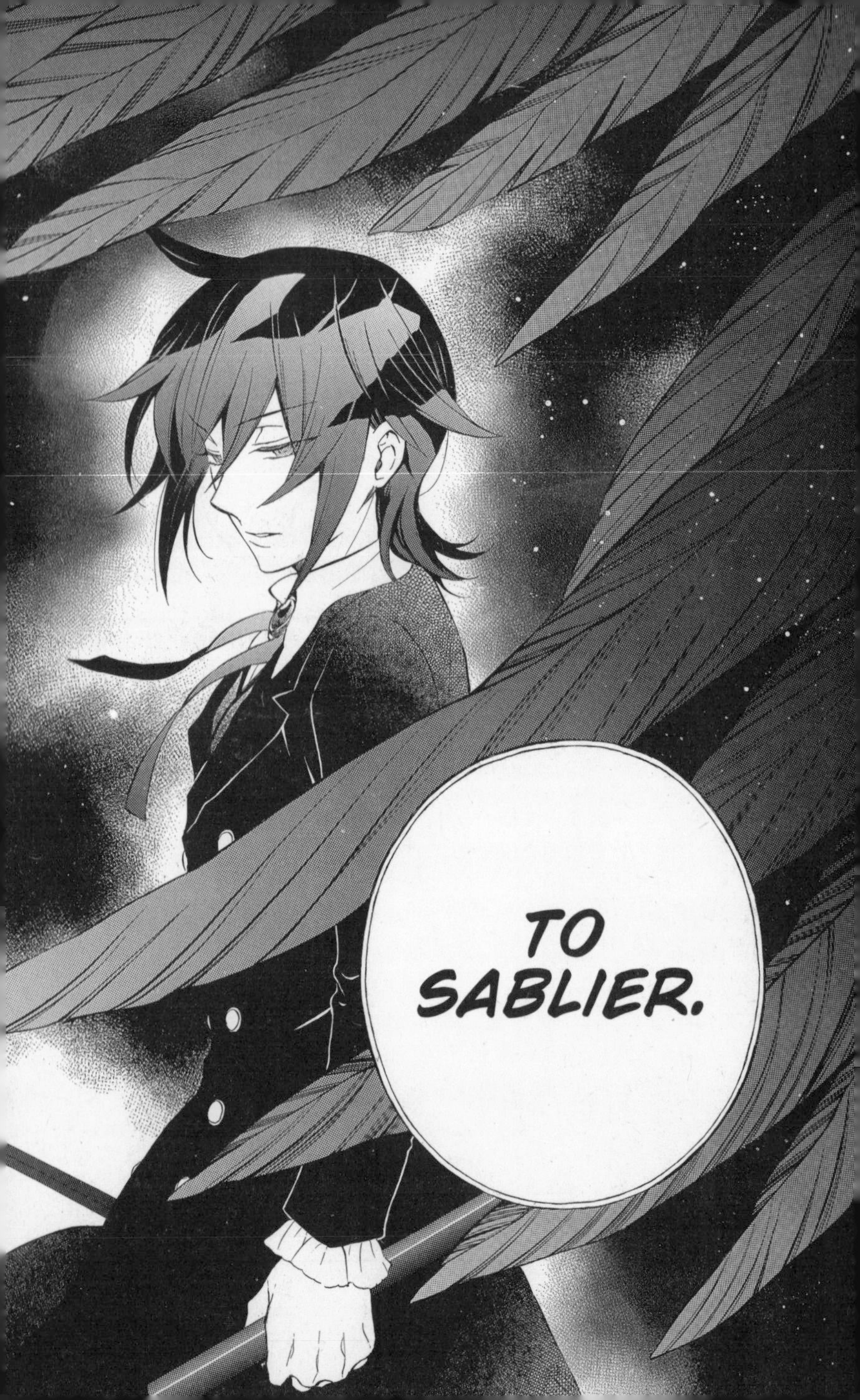
TO SABLIER.

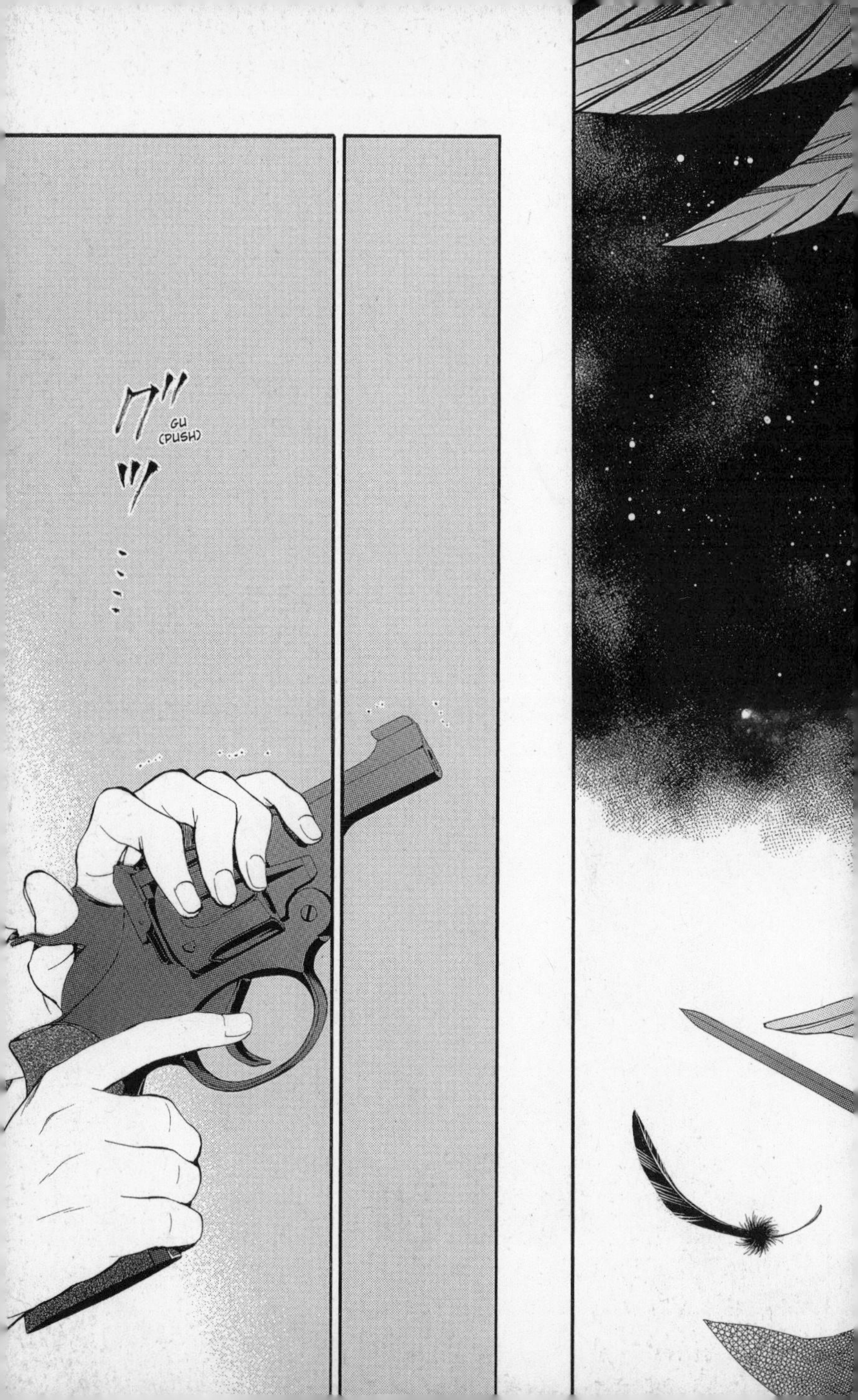
グッ
GU
(PUSH)

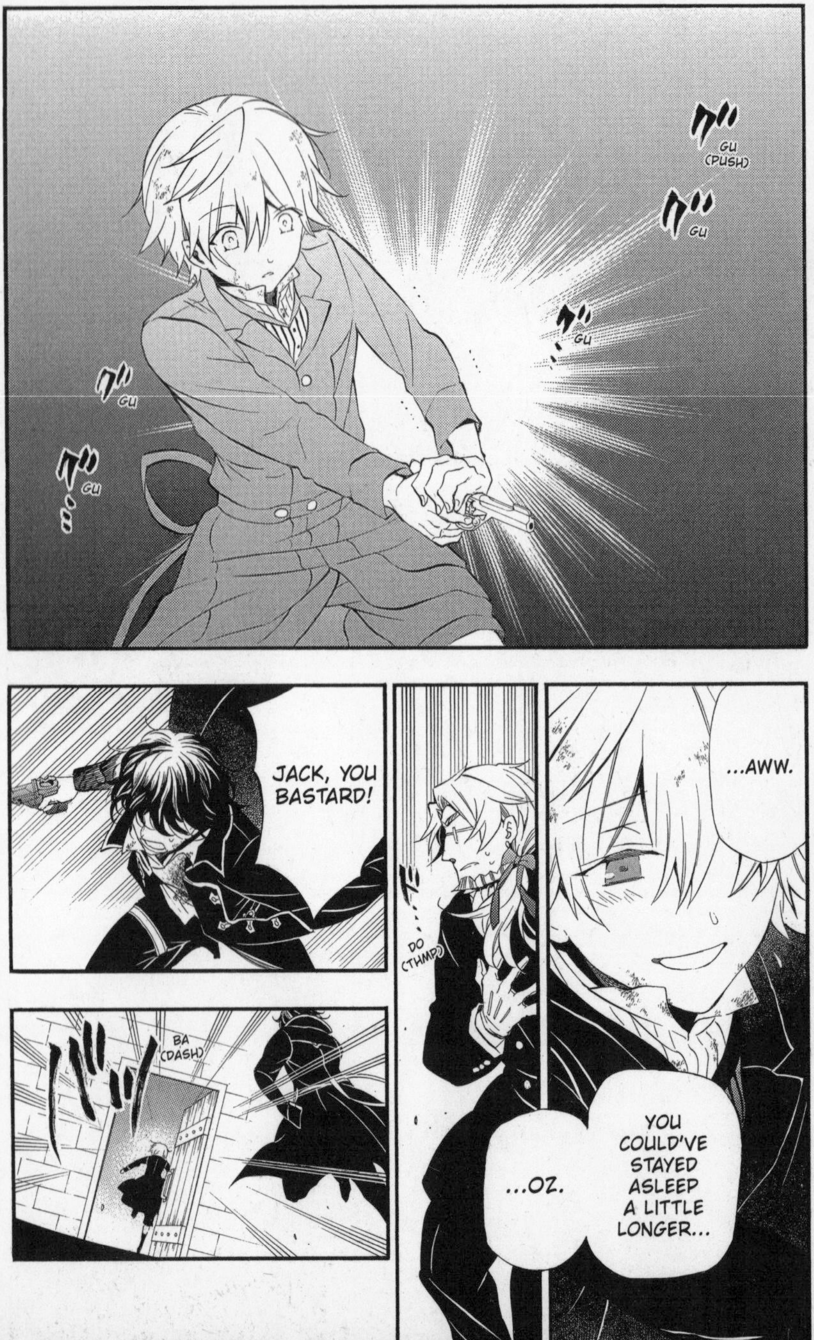
GU (PUSH)
GU
GU
GU
GU
...AWW.
YOU COULD'VE STAYED ASLEEP A LITTLE LONGER...
...OZ.
DO (THMP)
JACK, YOU BASTARD!
BA (DASH)

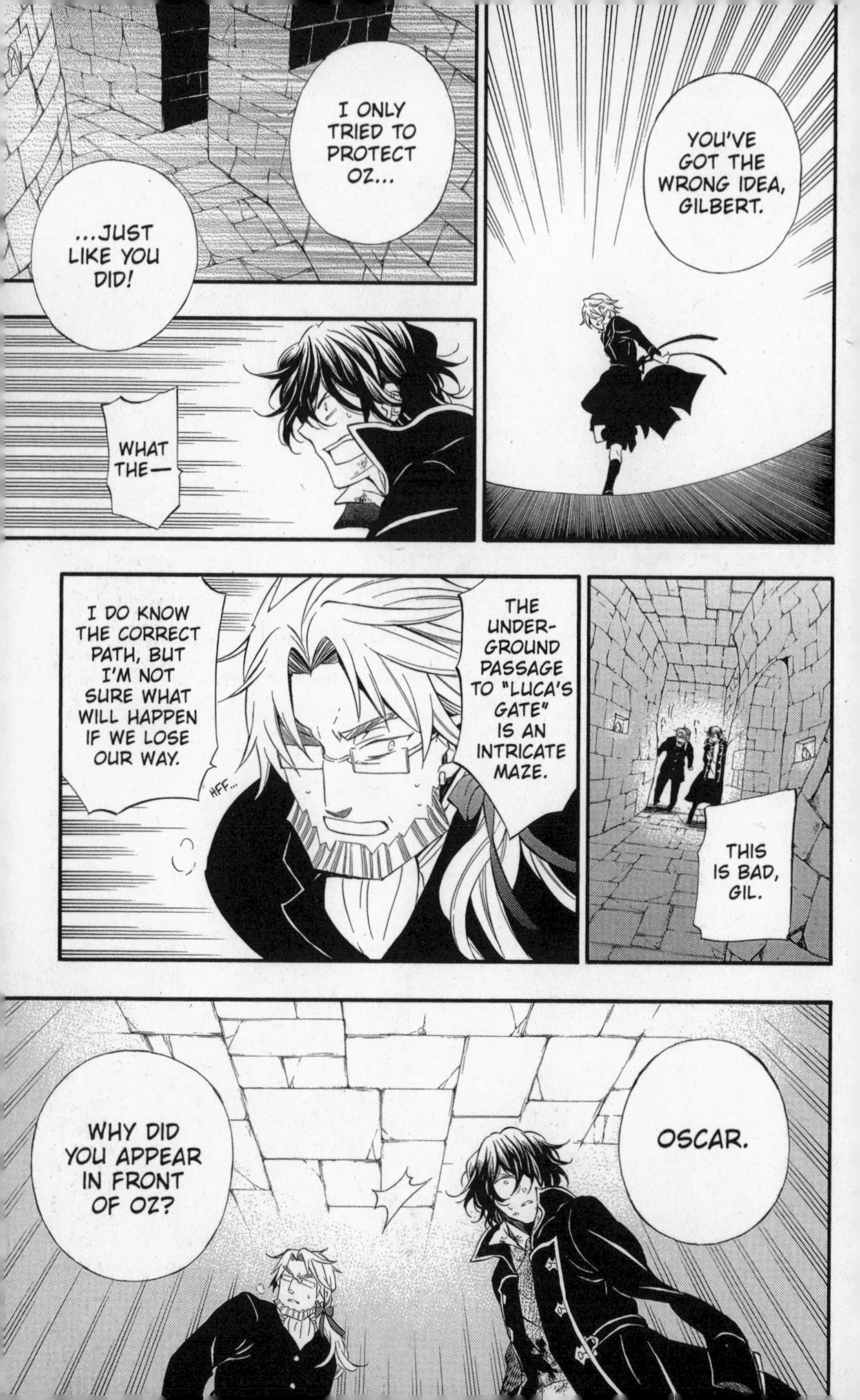
YOU'VE GOT THE WRONG IDEA, GILBERT.
I ONLY TRIED TO PROTECT OZ...
...JUST LIKE YOU DID!
WHAT THE—
THIS IS BAD, GIL.
THE UNDER-GROUND PASSAGE TO "LUCA'S GATE" IS AN INTRICATE MAZE.
I DO KNOW THE CORRECT PATH, BUT I'M NOT SURE WHAT WILL HAPPEN IF WE LOSE OUR WAY.
HFF...
OSCAR.
WHY DID YOU APPEAR IN FRONT OF OZ?

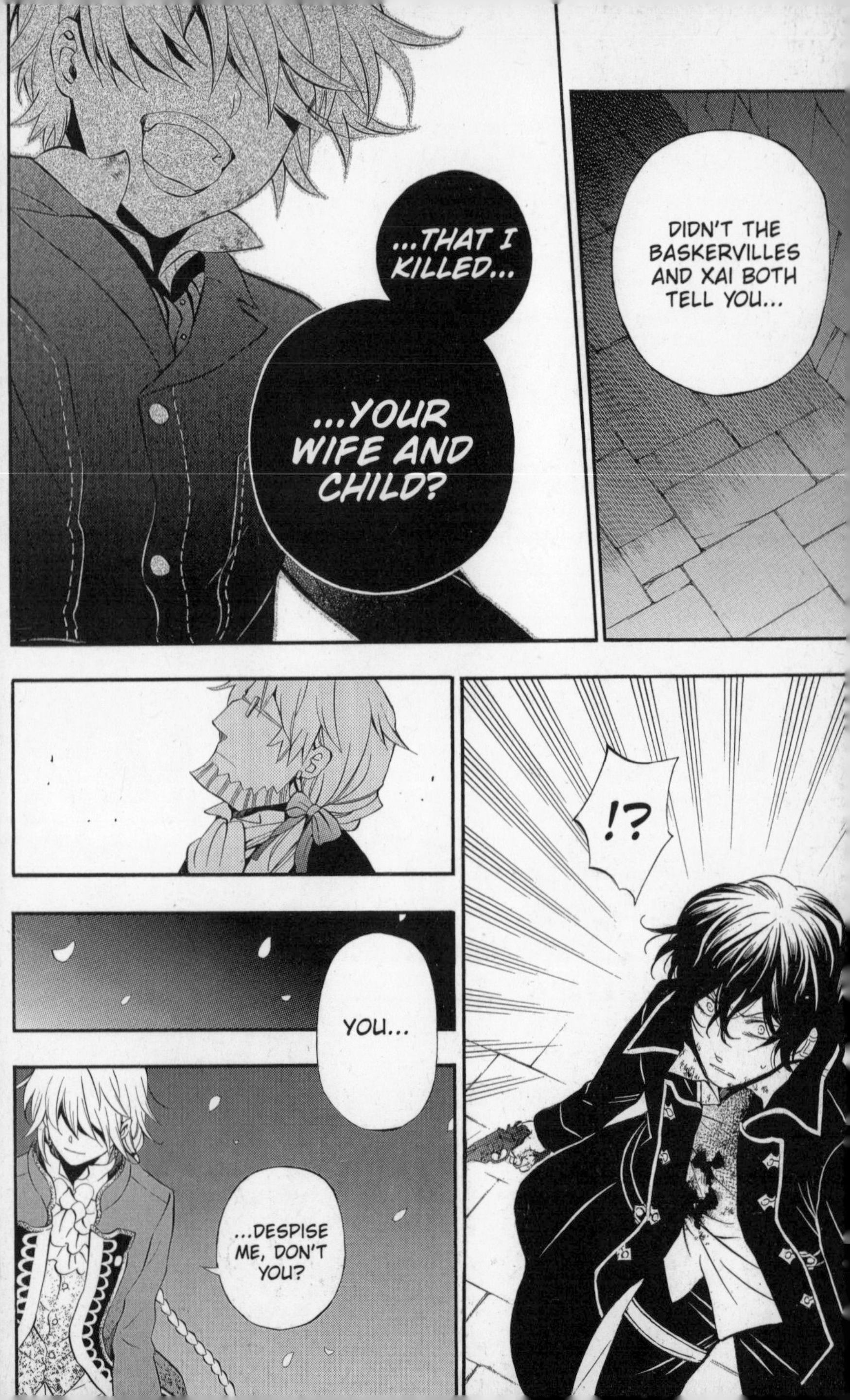
DIDN'T THE BASKERVILLES AND XAI BOTH TELL YOU...
...THAT I KILLED...
...YOUR WIFE AND CHILD?
!?
YOU...
...DESPISE ME, DON'T YOU?

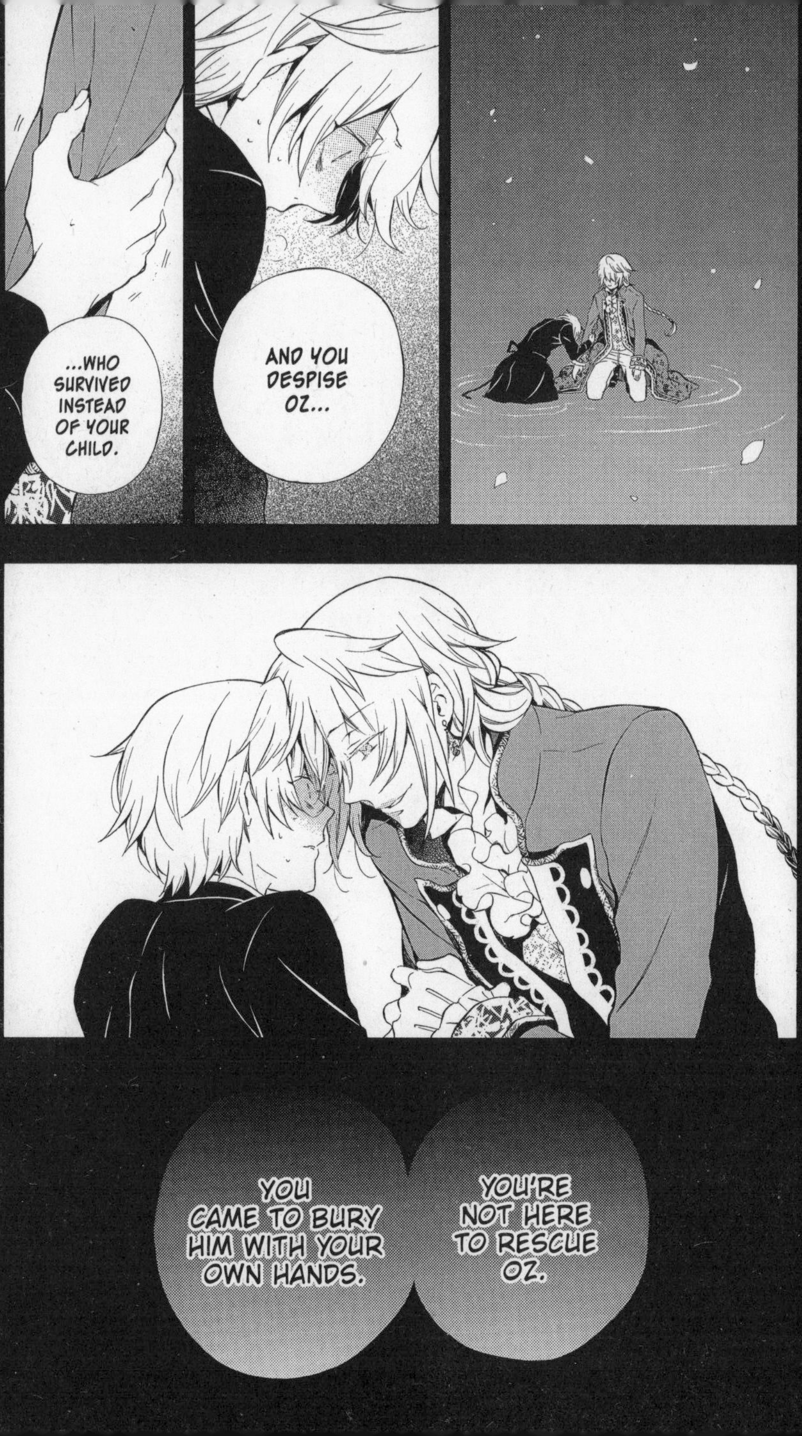
AND YOU DESPISE OZ...
...WHO SURVIVED INSTEAD OF YOUR CHILD.
YOU'RE NOT HERE TO RESCUE OZ.
YOU CAME TO BURY HIM WITH YOUR OWN HANDS.

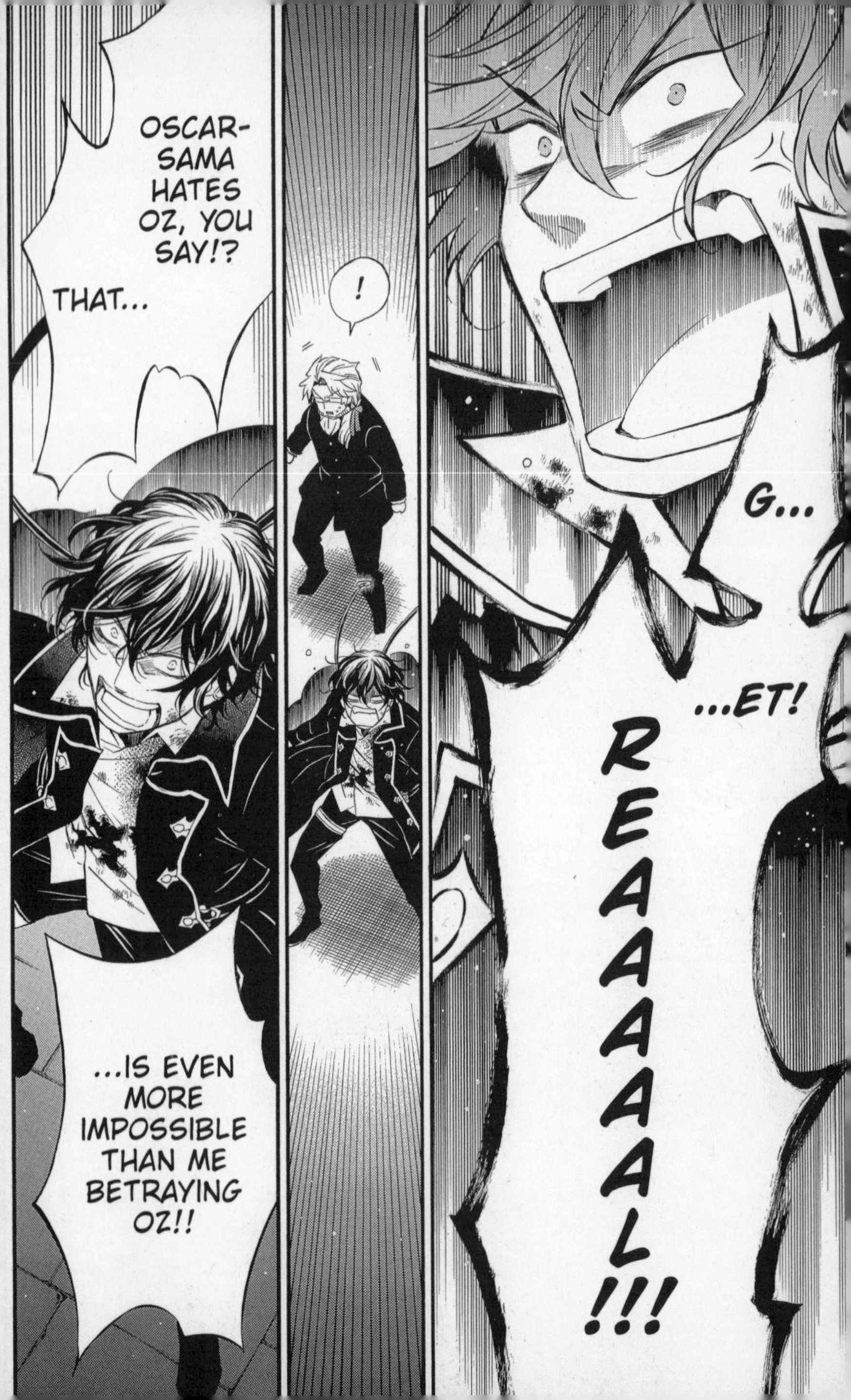
G...
...ET!
REAAAAAL!!!
!
OSCAR-SAMA HATES OZ, YOU SAY!?
THAT...
...IS EVEN MORE IMPOSSIBLE THAN ME BETRAYING OZ!!

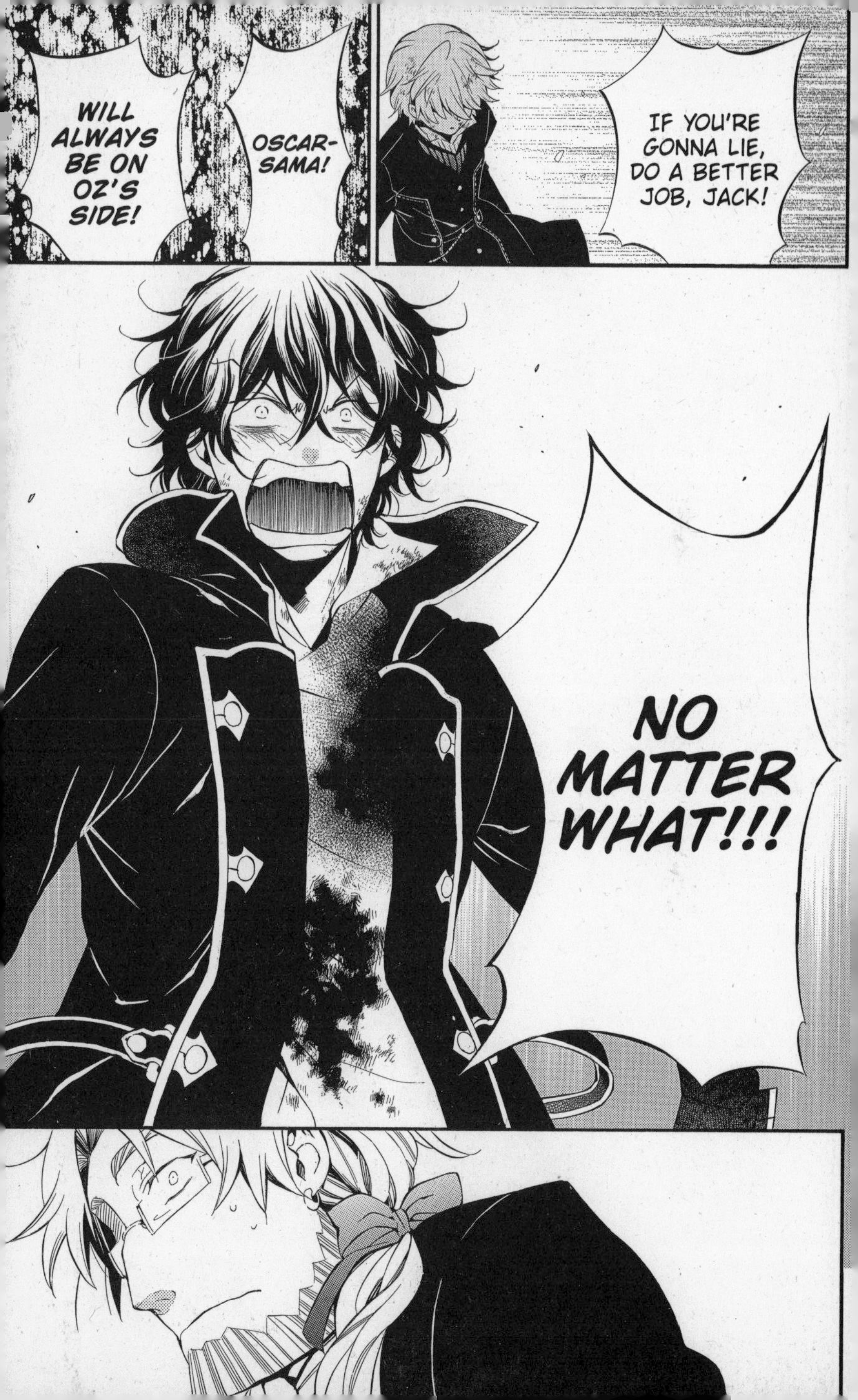
IF YOU'RE GONNA LIE, DO A BETTER JOB, JACK!
OSCAR-SAMA!
WILL ALWAYS BE ON OZ'S SIDE!
NO MATTER WHAT!!!

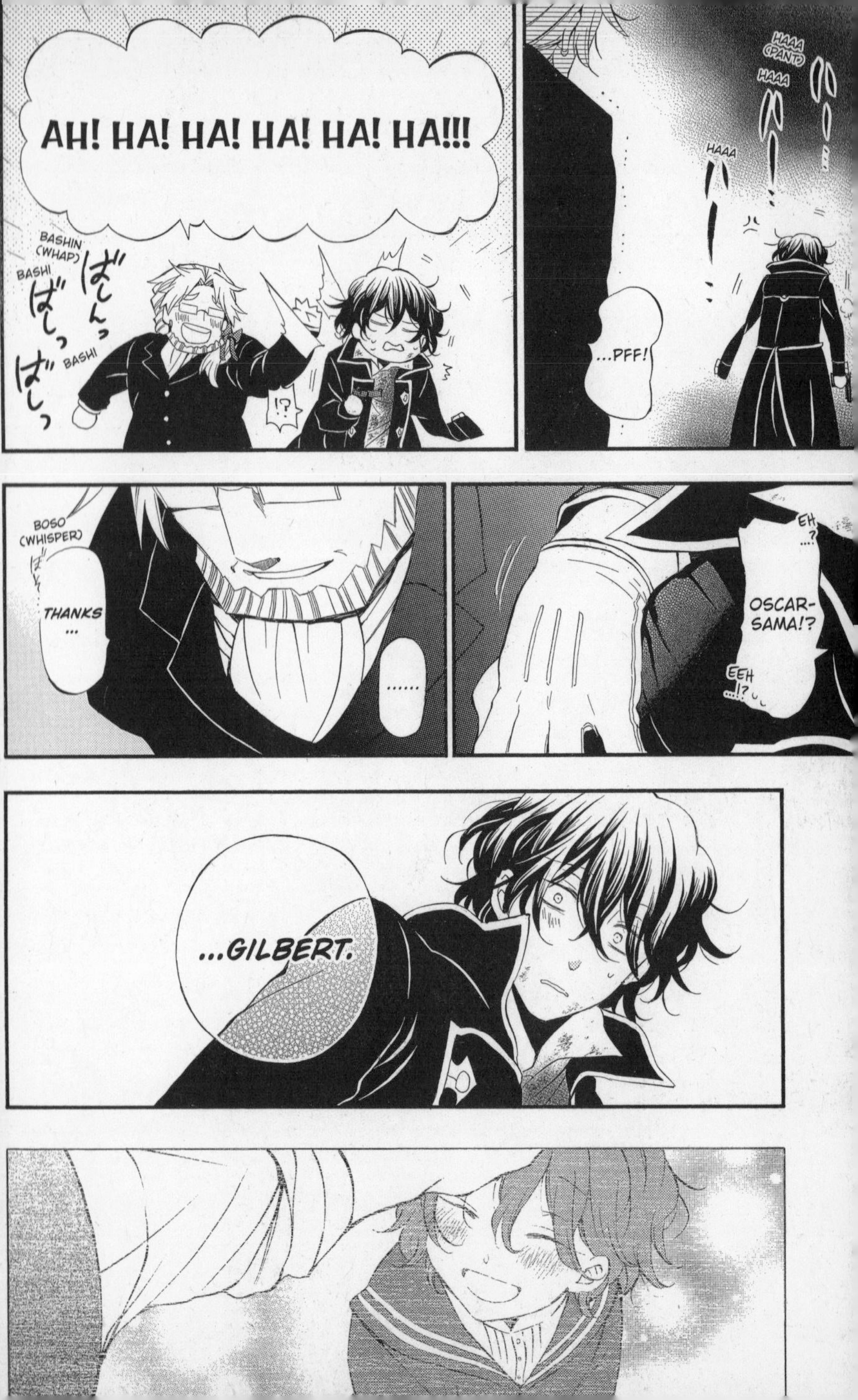
HAAA (PANT)
HAAA
HAAA
...PFF!
AH! HA! HA! HA! HA! HA!!!
BASHIN (WHAP)
ばしんっ
BASHI
ばしっ
BASHI
ばしっ
!?
EH ...?
OSCAR-SAMA!?
EEH ...!?
BOSO (WHISPER)
THANKS ...
......
...GILBERT.

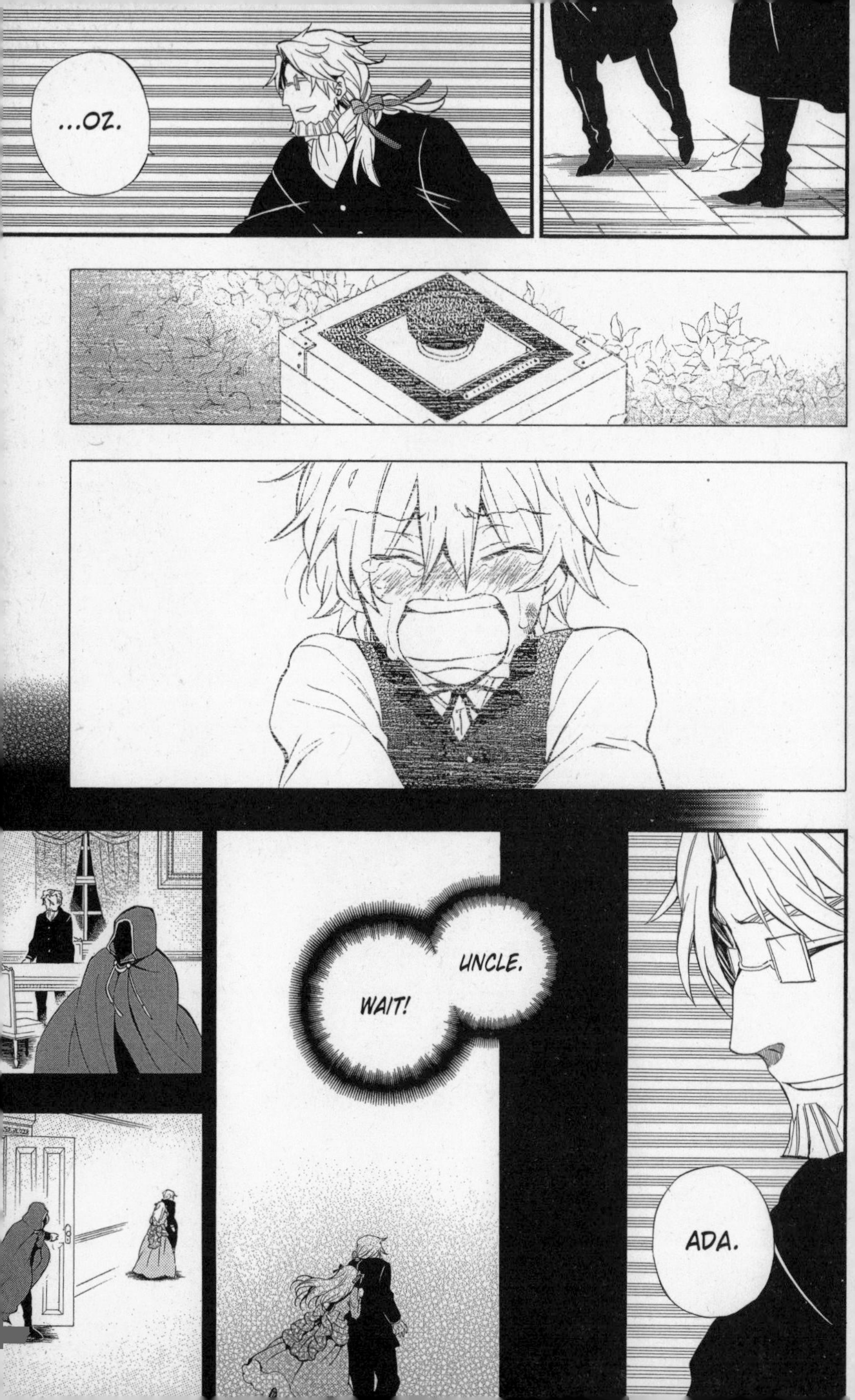
...OZ.
ADA.
UNCLE.
WAIT!

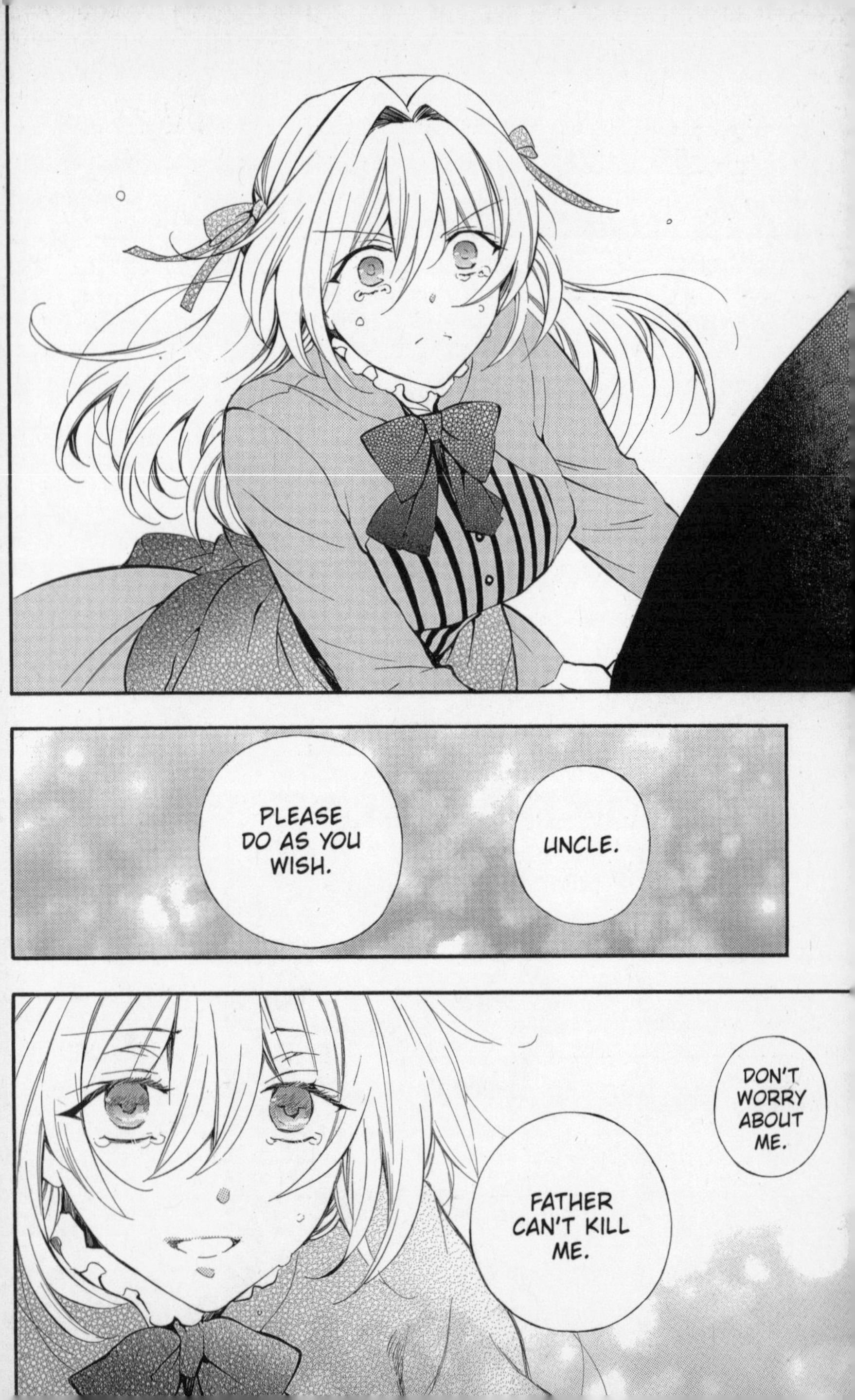
UNCLE.
PLEASE DO AS YOU WISH.
DON'T WORRY ABOUT ME.
FATHER CAN'T KILL ME.

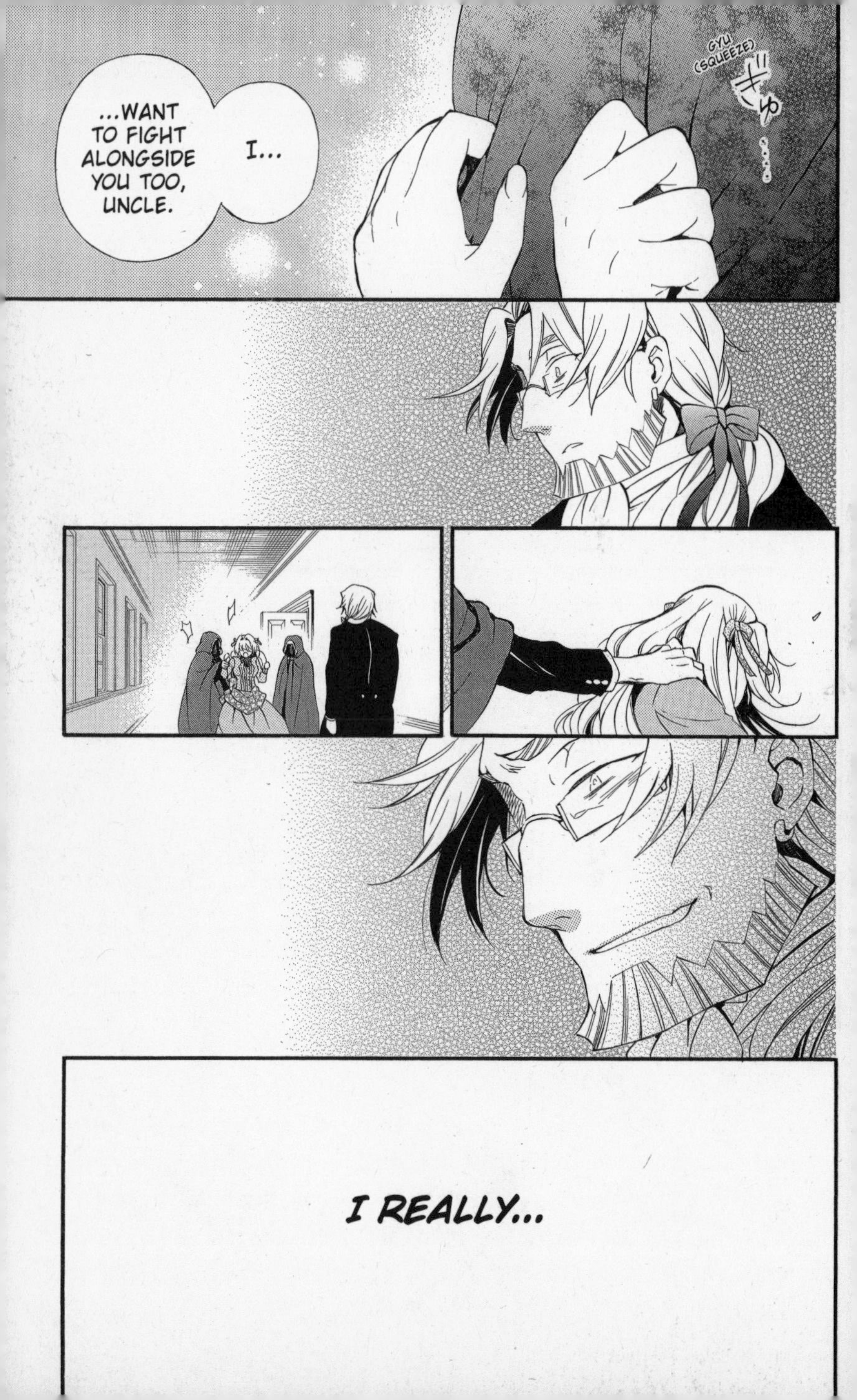
GYU (SQUEEZE)
ぎゅ…
I...
...WANT TO FIGHT ALONGSIDE YOU TOO, UNCLE.
I REALLY...

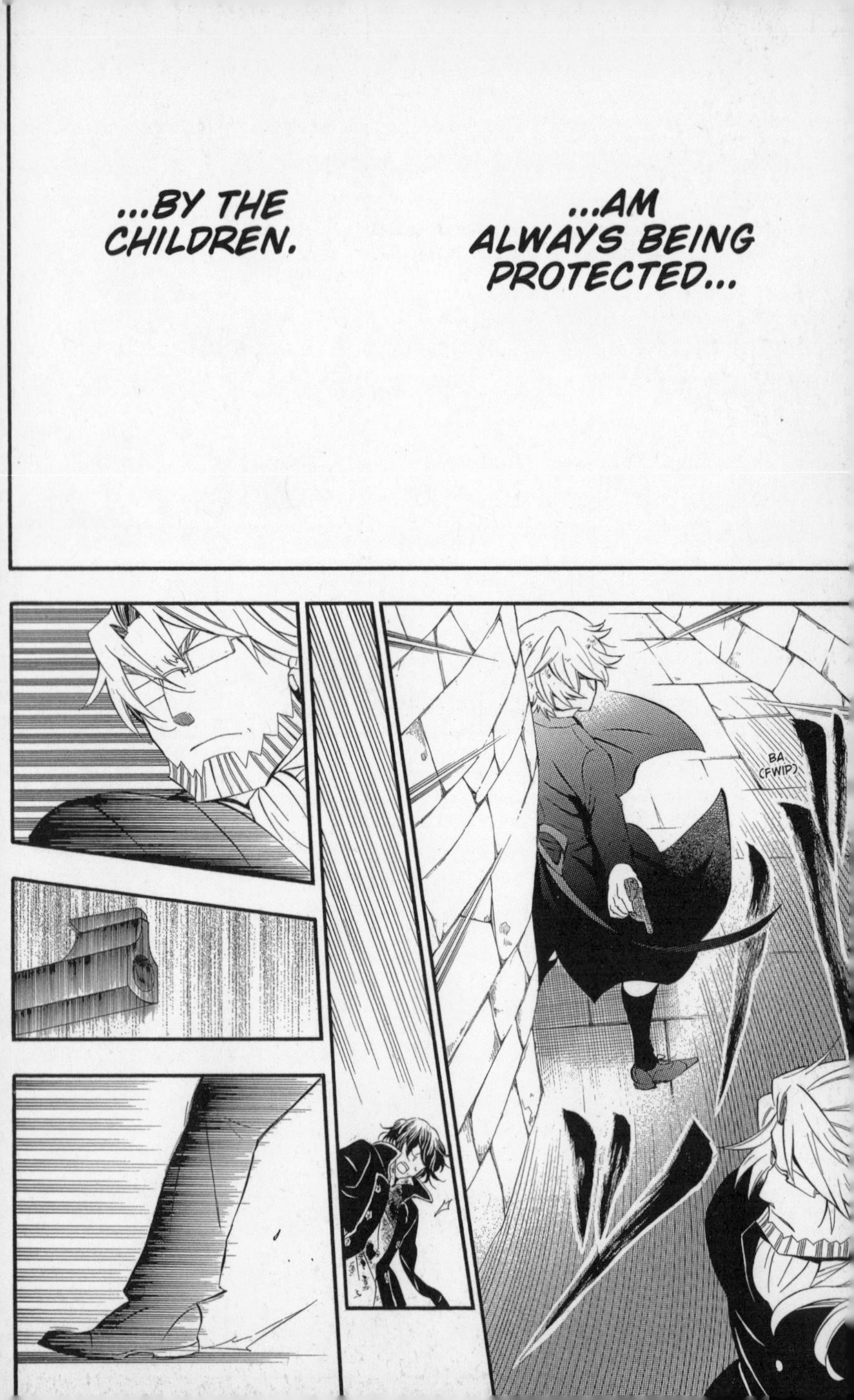
...AM ALWAYS BEING PROTECTED...
...BY THE CHILDREN.
BA (FWIP)

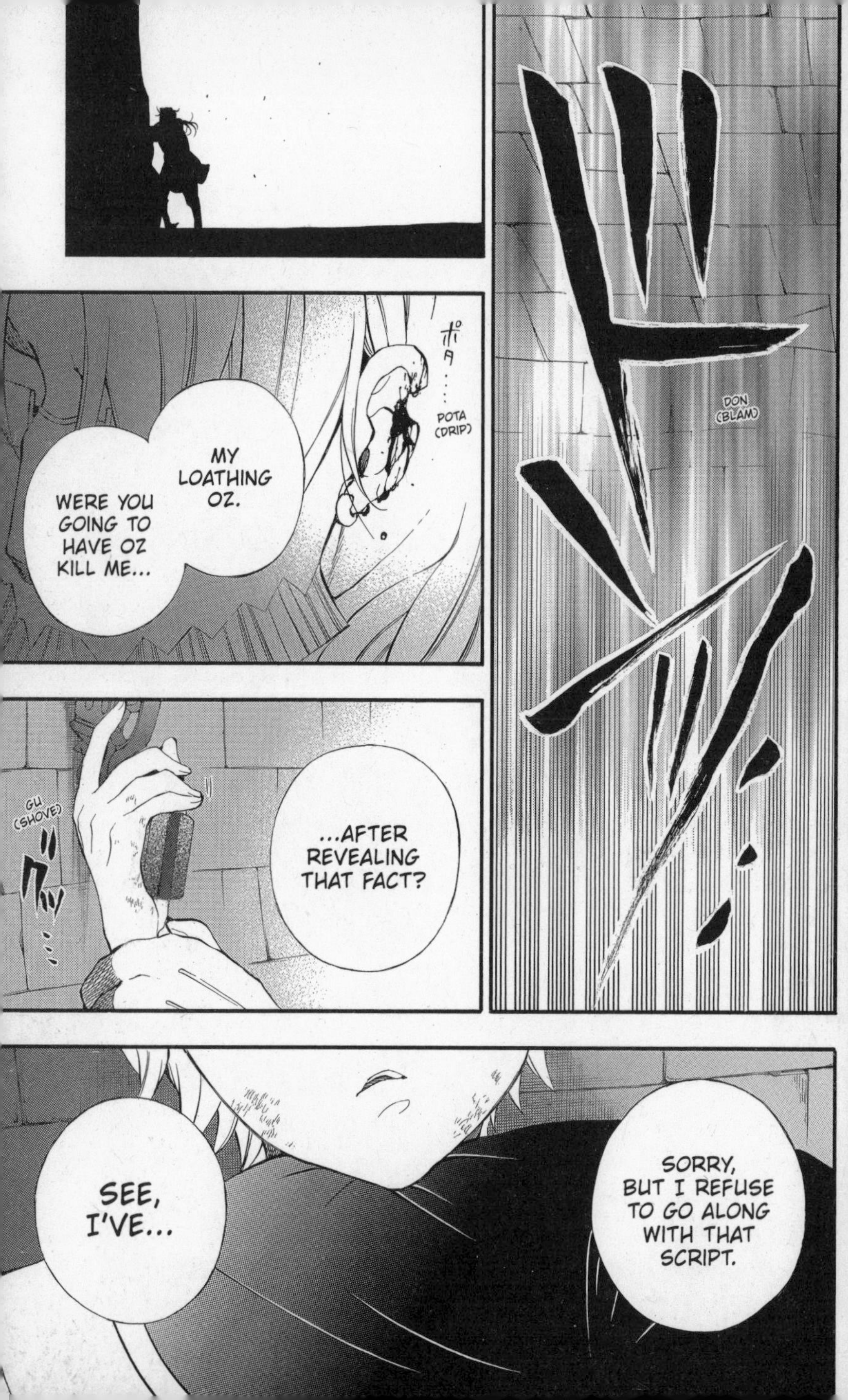
DON (BLAM)
ポタ…
POTA (DRIP)
MY LOATHING OZ.
WERE YOU GOING TO HAVE OZ KILL ME...
...AFTER REVEALING THAT FACT?
グッ…
GU (SHOVE)
SORRY, BUT I REFUSE TO GO ALONG WITH THAT SCRIPT.
SEE, I'VE...

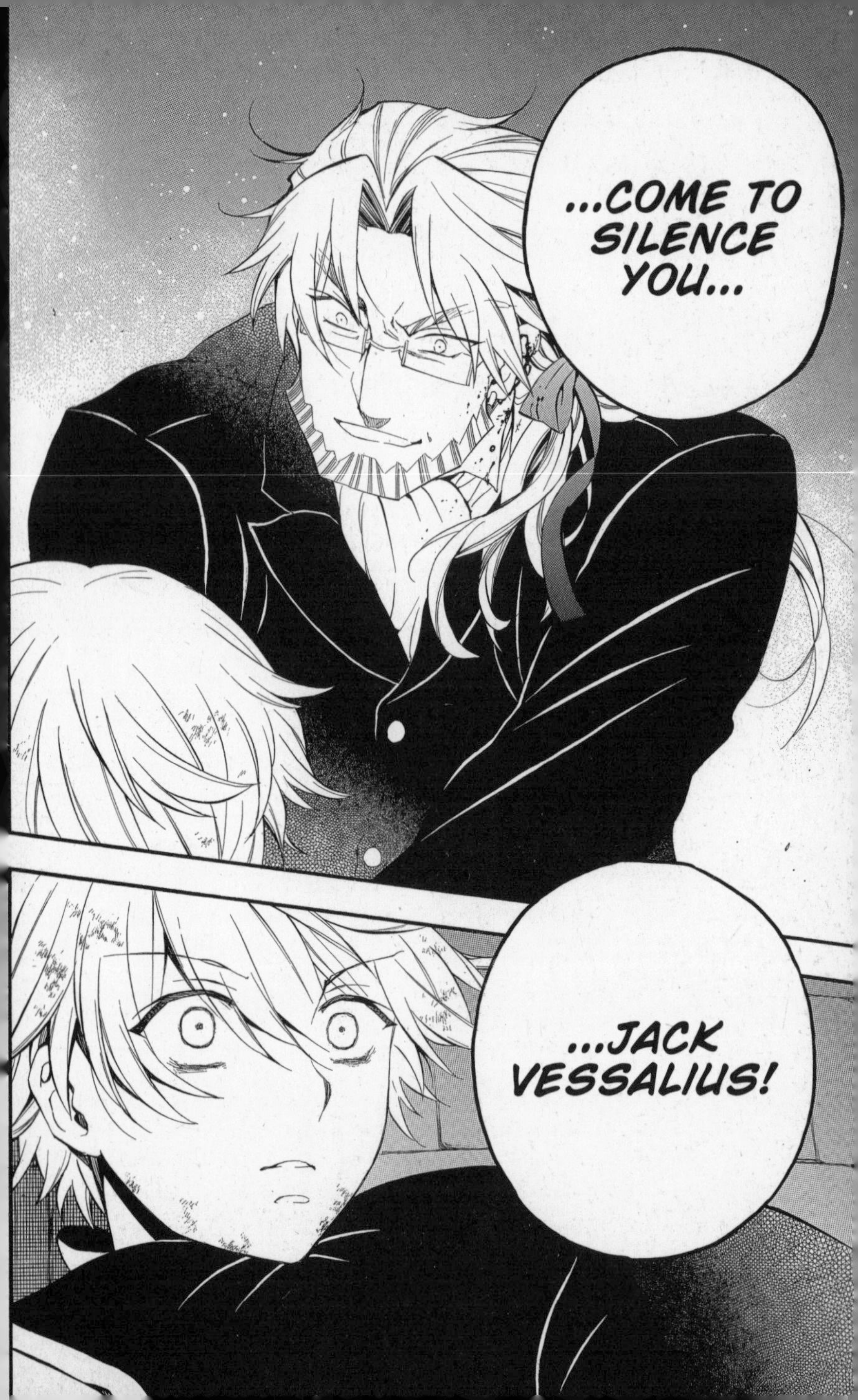
...COME TO SILENCE YOU...
...JACK VESSALIUS!

Retrace:LXXXI   Children

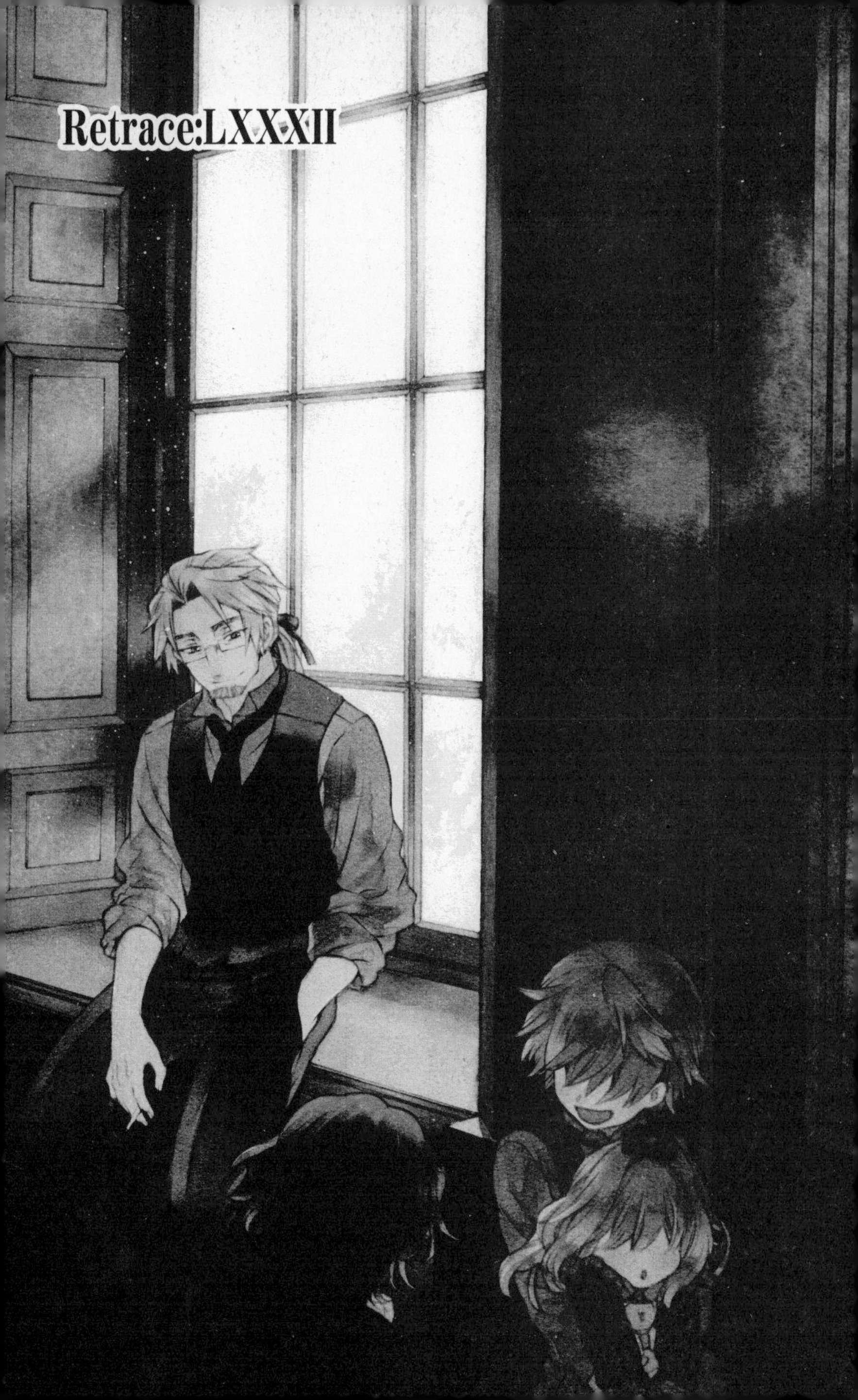
Retrace:LXXXII

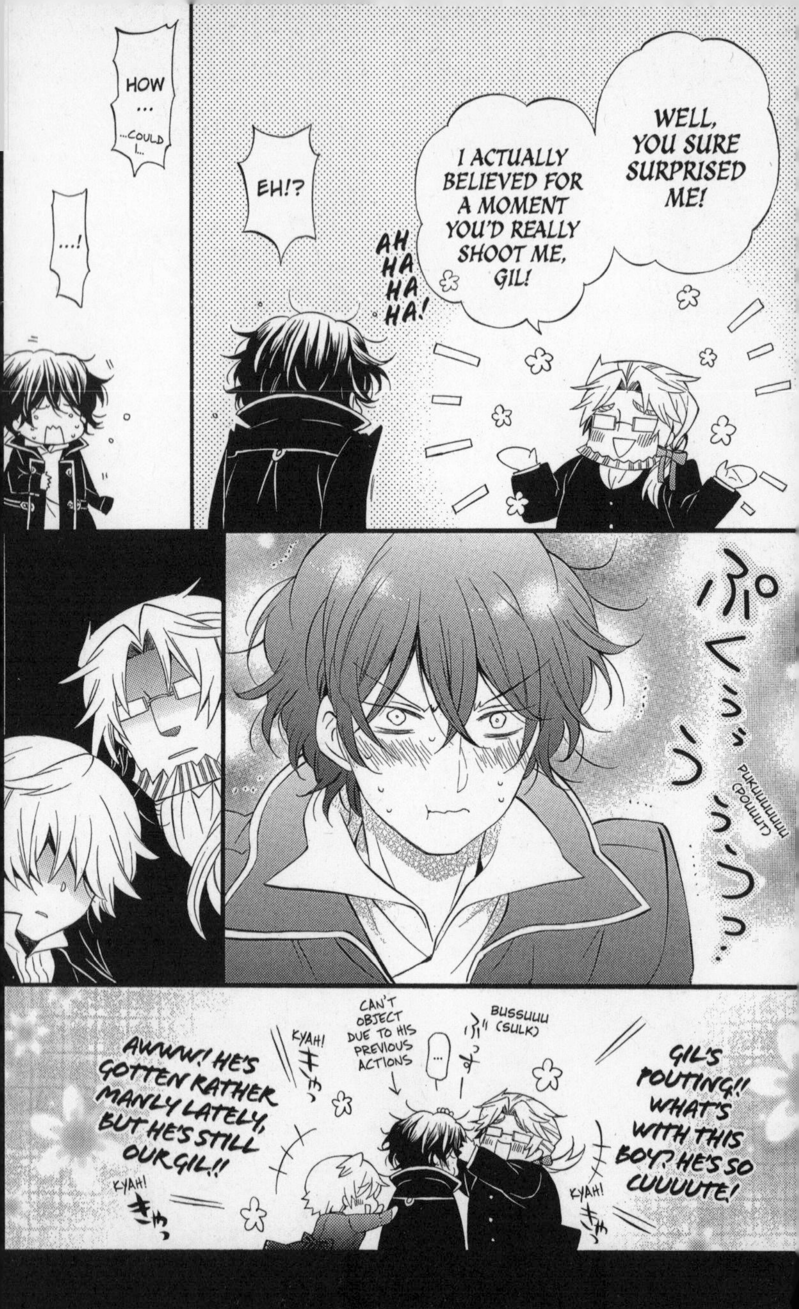

WELL, YOU SURE SURPRISED ME!
I ACTUALLY BELIEVED FOR A MOMENT YOU'D REALLY SHOOT ME, GIL!
AH HA HA HA!
EH!?
HOW... ...COULD I...
...!
PUKUUUUUUU (POUUUT)
GIL'S POUTING!! WHAT'S WITH THIS BOY? HE'S SO CUUUUTE!
KYAH!
BUSSUUU (SULK)
CAN'T OBJECT DUE TO HIS PREVIOUS ACTIONS
...
KYAH!
AWWW! HE'S GOTTEN RATHER MANLY LATELY, BUT HE'S STILL OUR GIL!!
KYAH!

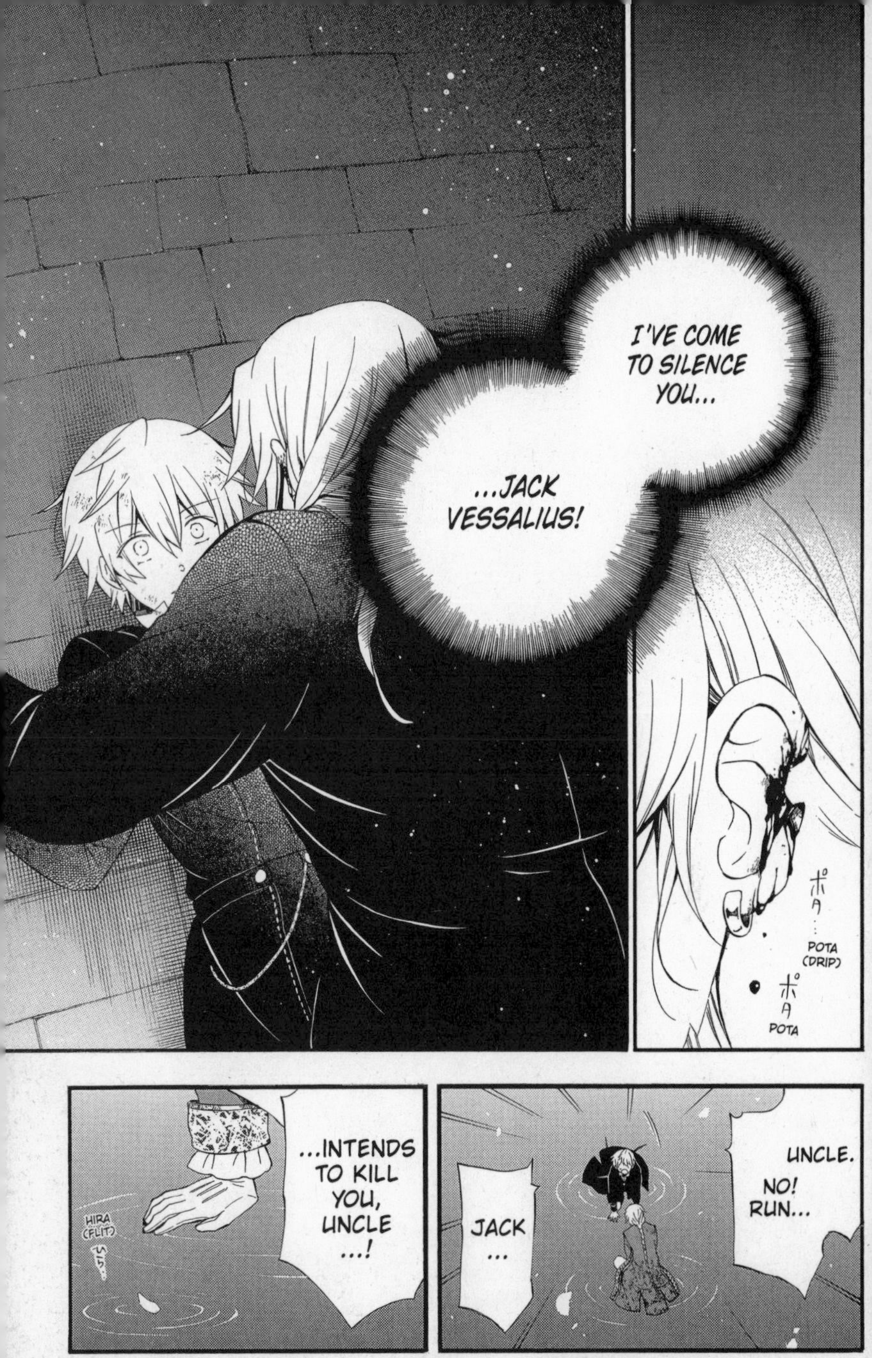
ポタ…
POTA (DRIP)
ポタ
POTA
I'VE COME TO SILENCE YOU...
...JACK VESSALIUS!
UNCLE.
NO! RUN...
JACK ...
...INTENDS TO KILL YOU, UNCLE ...!
HIRA (FLIT)
ひら…

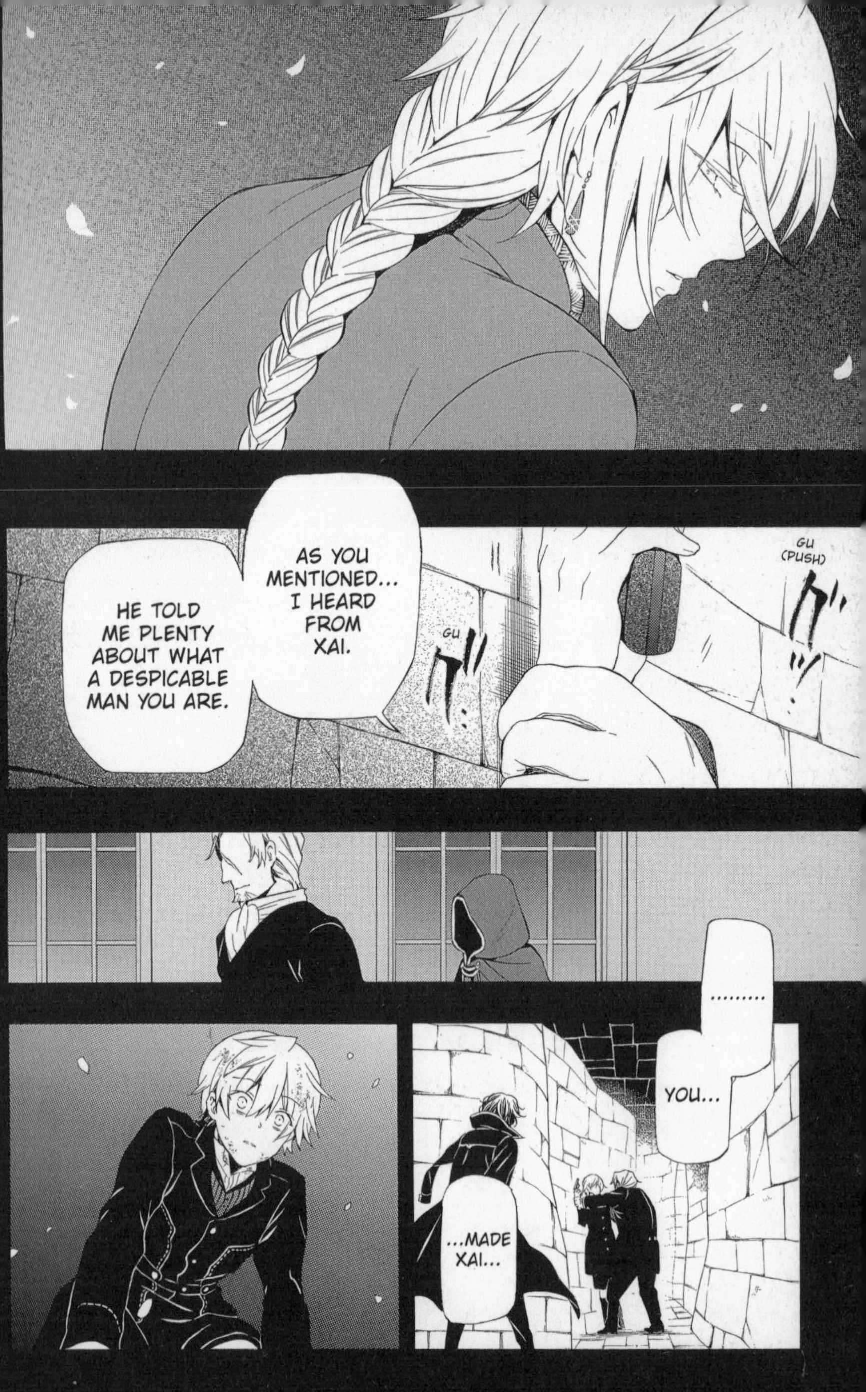

GU (PUSH)
AS YOU MENTIONED... I HEARD FROM XAI.
GU
HE TOLD ME PLENTY ABOUT WHAT A DESPICABLE MAN YOU ARE.
....
YOU...
...MADE XAI...

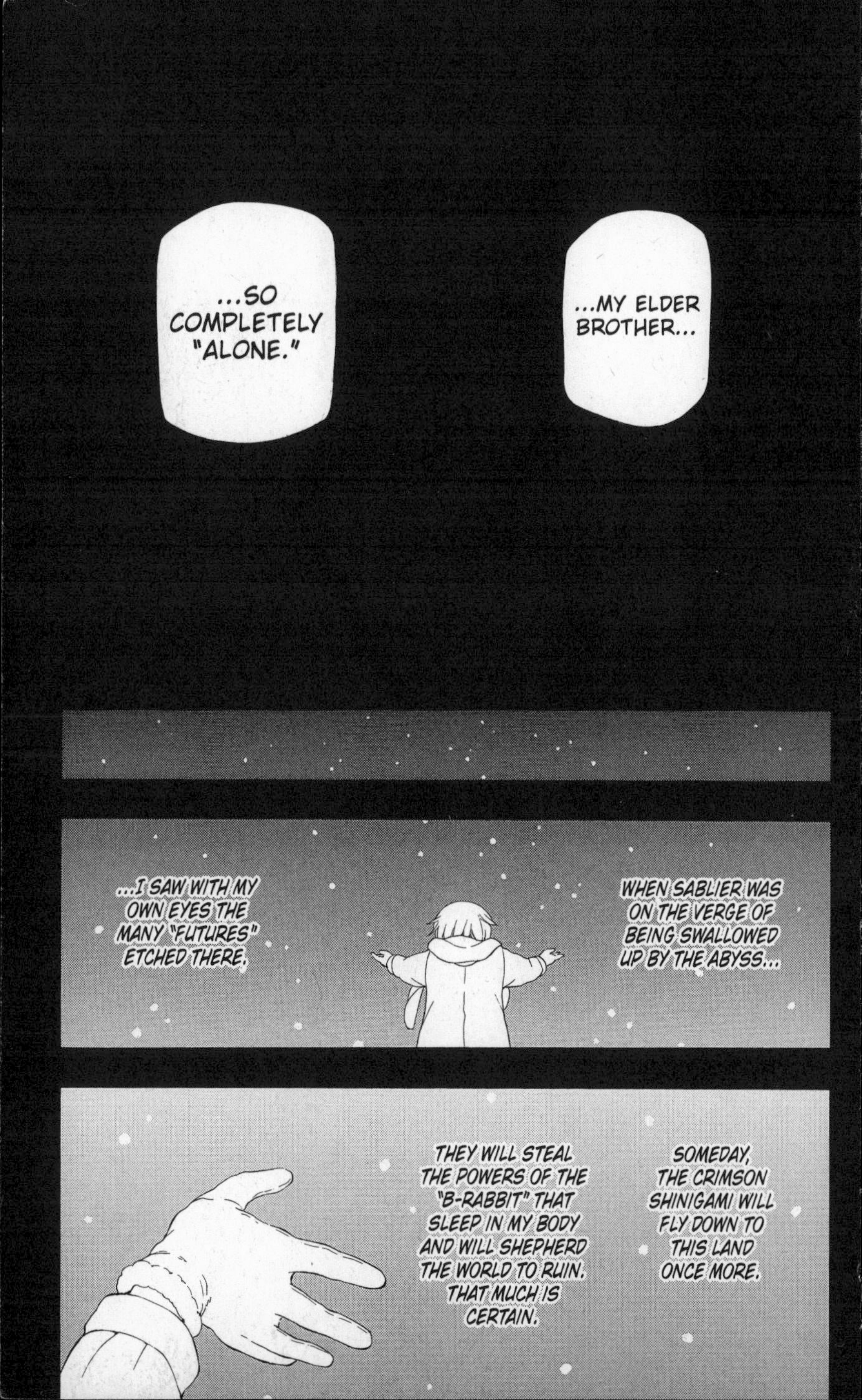
...MY ELDER BROTHER...
...SO COMPLETELY "ALONE."
WHEN SABLIER WAS ON THE VERGE OF BEING SWALLOWED UP BY THE ABYSS...
...I SAW WITH MY OWN EYES THE MANY "FUTURES" ETCHED THERE.
SOMEDAY, THE CRIMSON SHINIGAMI WILL FLY DOWN TO THIS LAND ONCE MORE.
THEY WILL STEAL THE POWERS OF THE "B-RABBIT" THAT SLEEP IN MY BODY AND WILL SHEPHERD THE WORLD TO RUIN. THAT MUCH IS CERTAIN.

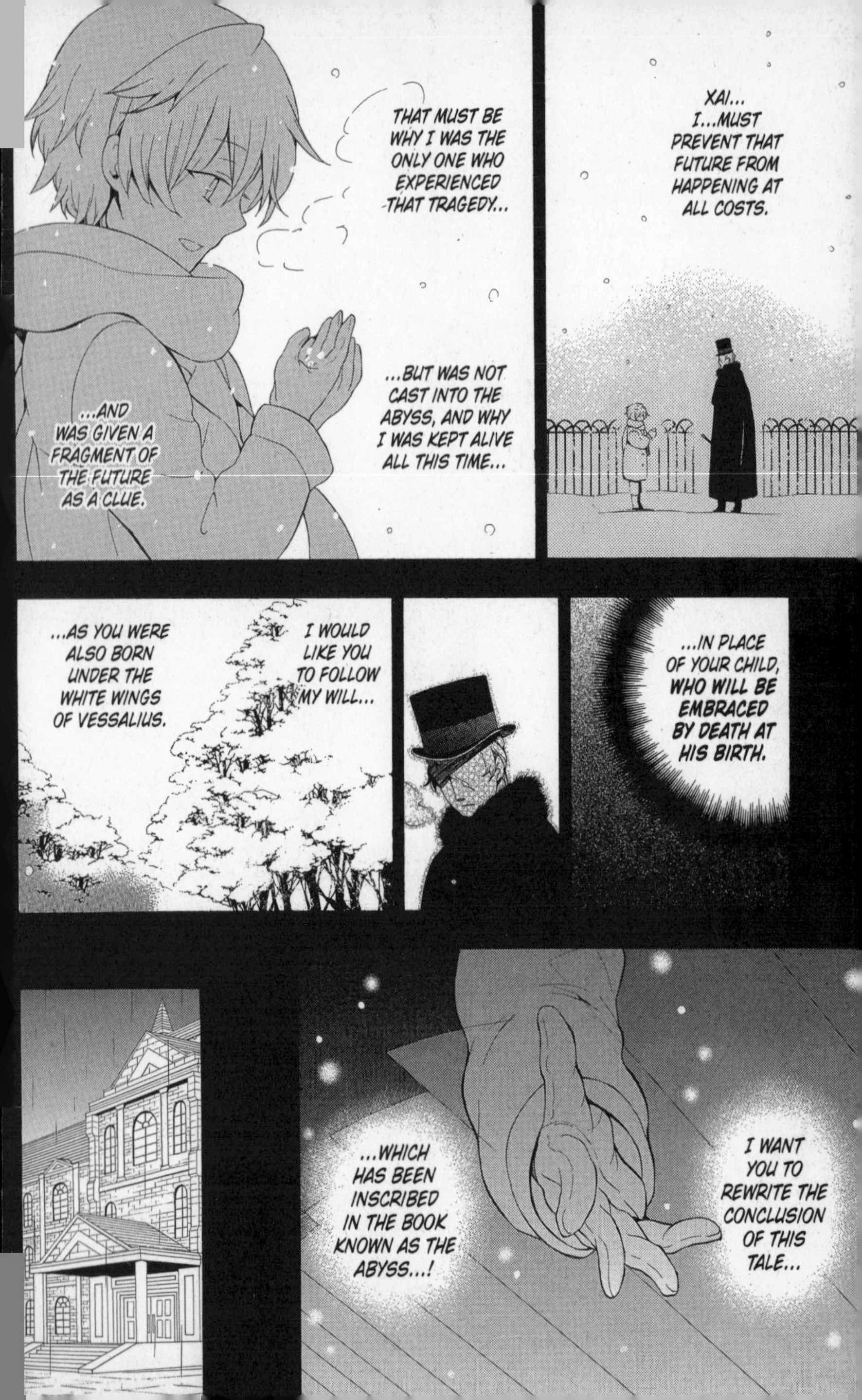
XAI... I...MUST PREVENT THAT FUTURE FROM HAPPENING AT ALL COSTS.
THAT MUST BE WHY I WAS THE ONLY ONE WHO EXPERIENCED THAT TRAGEDY...
...BUT WAS NOT CAST INTO THE ABYSS, AND WHY I WAS KEPT ALIVE ALL THIS TIME...
...AND WAS GIVEN A FRAGMENT OF THE FUTURE AS A CLUE.
...IN PLACE OF YOUR CHILD, WHO WILL BE EMBRACED BY DEATH AT HIS BIRTH.
I WOULD LIKE YOU TO FOLLOW MY WILL...
...AS YOU WERE ALSO BORN UNDER THE WHITE WINGS OF VESSALIUS.
I WANT YOU TO REWRITE THE CONCLUSION OF THIS TALE...
...WHICH HAS BEEN INSCRIBED IN THE BOOK KNOWN AS THE ABYSS...!

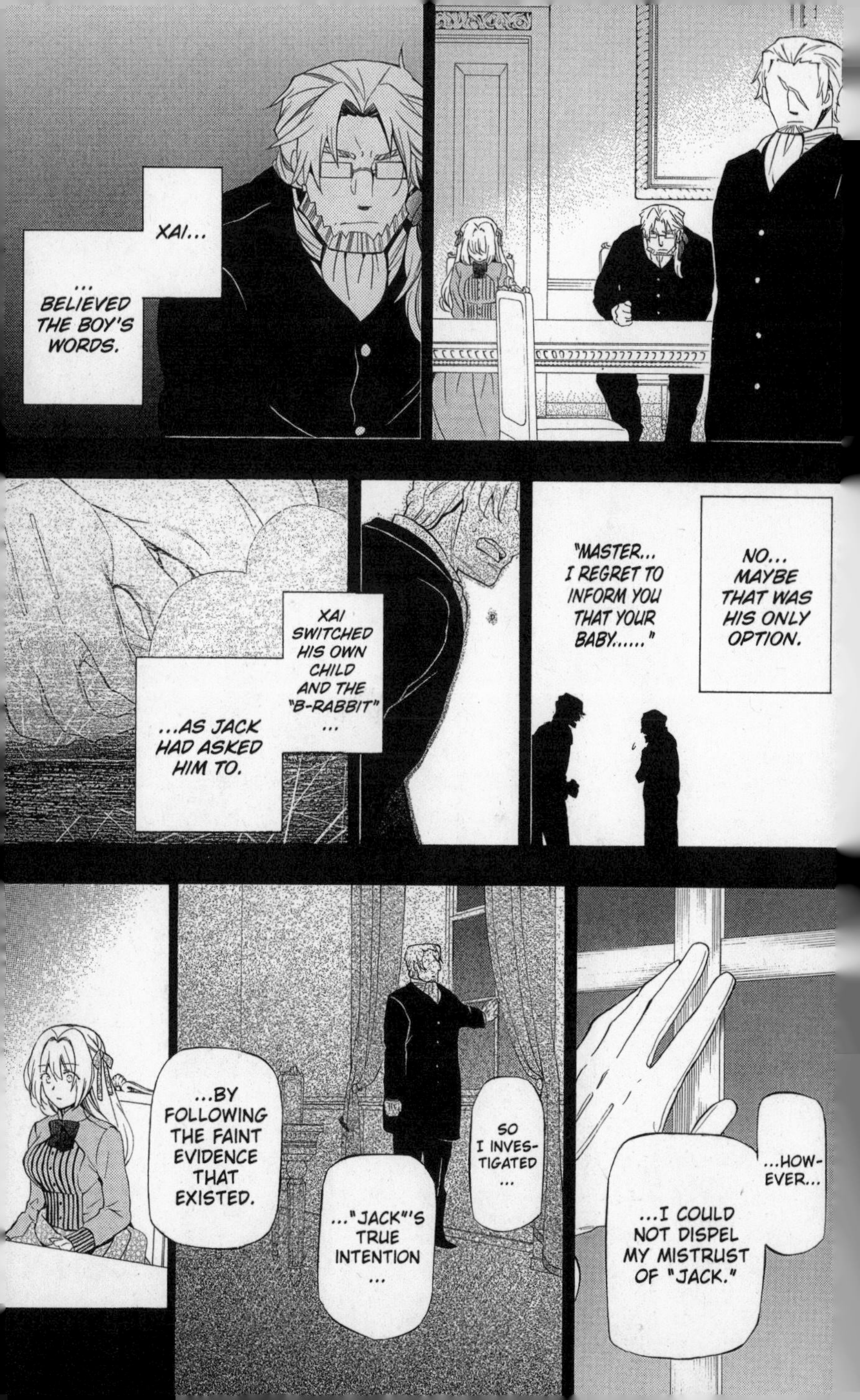
XAI...
...BELIEVED THE BOY'S WORDS.
NO... MAYBE THAT WAS HIS ONLY OPTION.
"MASTER... I REGRET TO INFORM YOU THAT YOUR BABY......"
XAI SWITCHED HIS OWN CHILD AND THE "B-RABBIT"...
...AS JACK HAD ASKED HIM TO.
...HOW-EVER...
...I COULD NOT DISPEL MY MISTRUST OF "JACK."
SO I INVES-TIGATED...
..."JACK"'S TRUE INTENTION...
...BY FOLLOWING THE FAINT EVIDENCE THAT EXISTED.

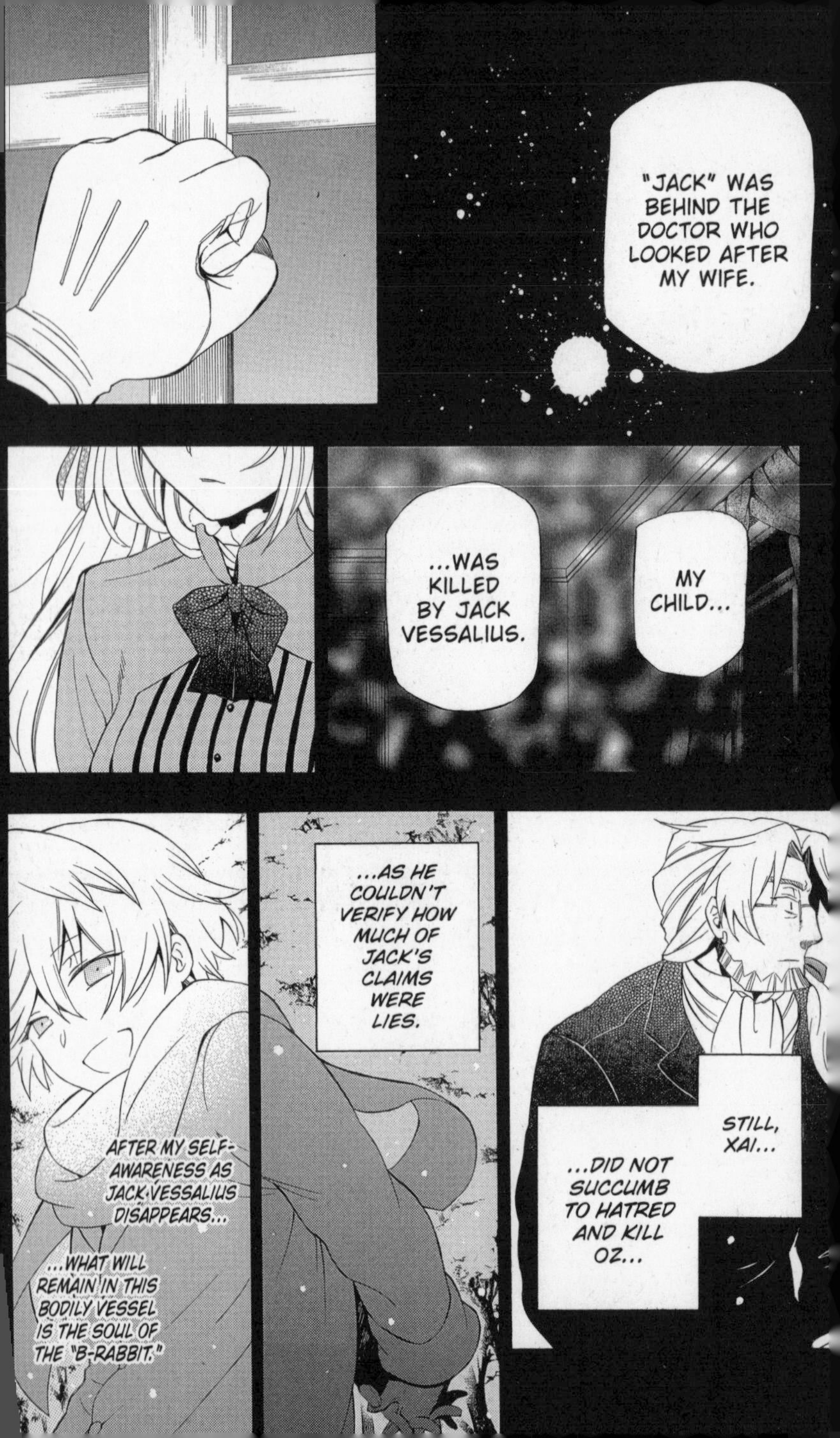
"JACK" WAS BEHIND THE DOCTOR WHO LOOKED AFTER MY WIFE.
MY CHILD...
...WAS KILLED BY JACK VESSALIUS.
STILL, XAI...
...DID NOT SUCCUMB TO HATRED AND KILL OZ...
...AS HE COULDN'T VERIFY HOW MUCH OF JACK'S CLAIMS WERE LIES.
AFTER MY SELF-AWARENESS AS JACK VESSALIUS DISAPPEARS...
...WHAT WILL REMAIN IN THIS BODILY VESSEL IS THE SOUL OF THE "B-RABBIT."

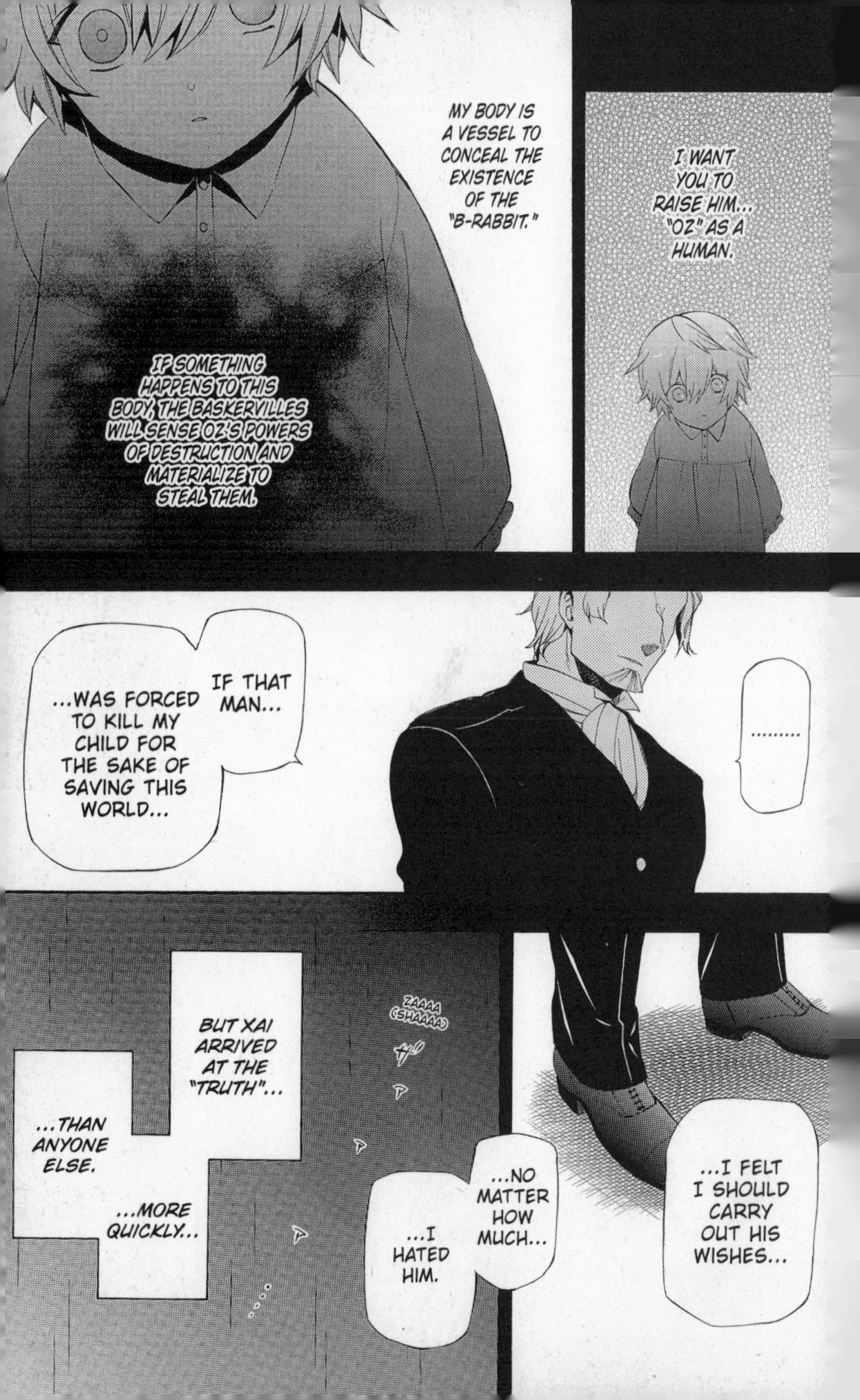
I WANT YOU TO RAISE HIM... "OZ" AS A HUMAN.
MY BODY IS A VESSEL TO CONCEAL THE EXISTENCE OF THE "B-RABBIT."
IF SOMETHING HAPPENS TO THIS BODY, THE BASKERVILLES WILL SENSE OZ'S POWERS OF DESTRUCTION AND MATERIALIZE TO STEAL THEM.
....
IF THAT MAN...
...WAS FORCED TO KILL MY CHILD FOR THE SAKE OF SAVING THIS WORLD...
...I FELT I SHOULD CARRY OUT HIS WISHES...
...NO MATTER HOW MUCH...
...I HATED HIM.
ZAAAA (SHAAAA)
BUT XAI ARRIVED AT THE "TRUTH"...
...THAN ANYONE ELSE.
...MORE QUICKLY...

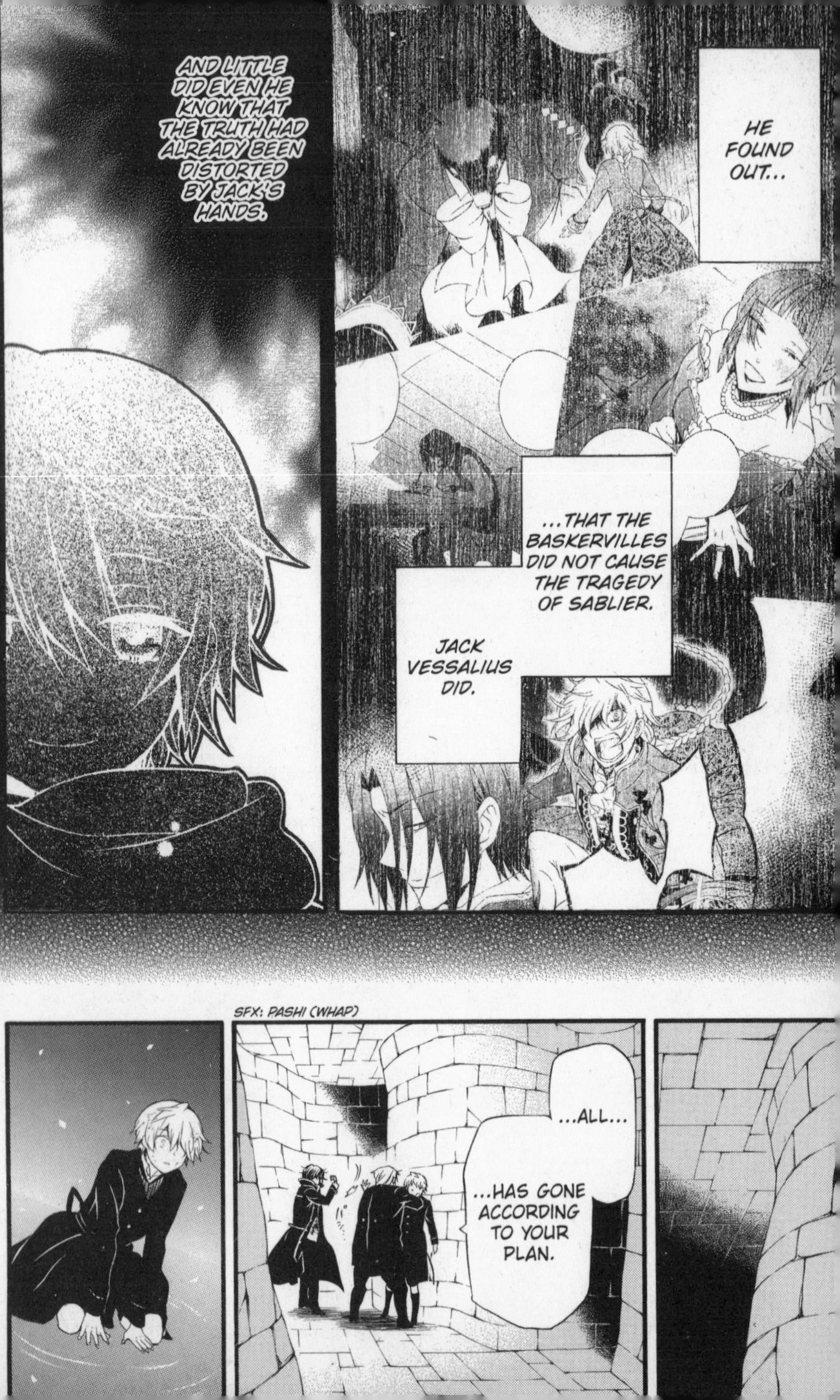
HE FOUND OUT...
...THAT THE BASKERVILLES DID NOT CAUSE THE TRAGEDY OF SABLIER.
JACK VESSALIUS DID.
AND LITTLE DID EVEN HE KNOW THAT THE TRUTH HAD ALREADY BEEN DISTORTED BY JACK'S HANDS.
SFX: PASHI (WHAP)
...ALL...
...HAS GONE ACCORDING TO YOUR PLAN.

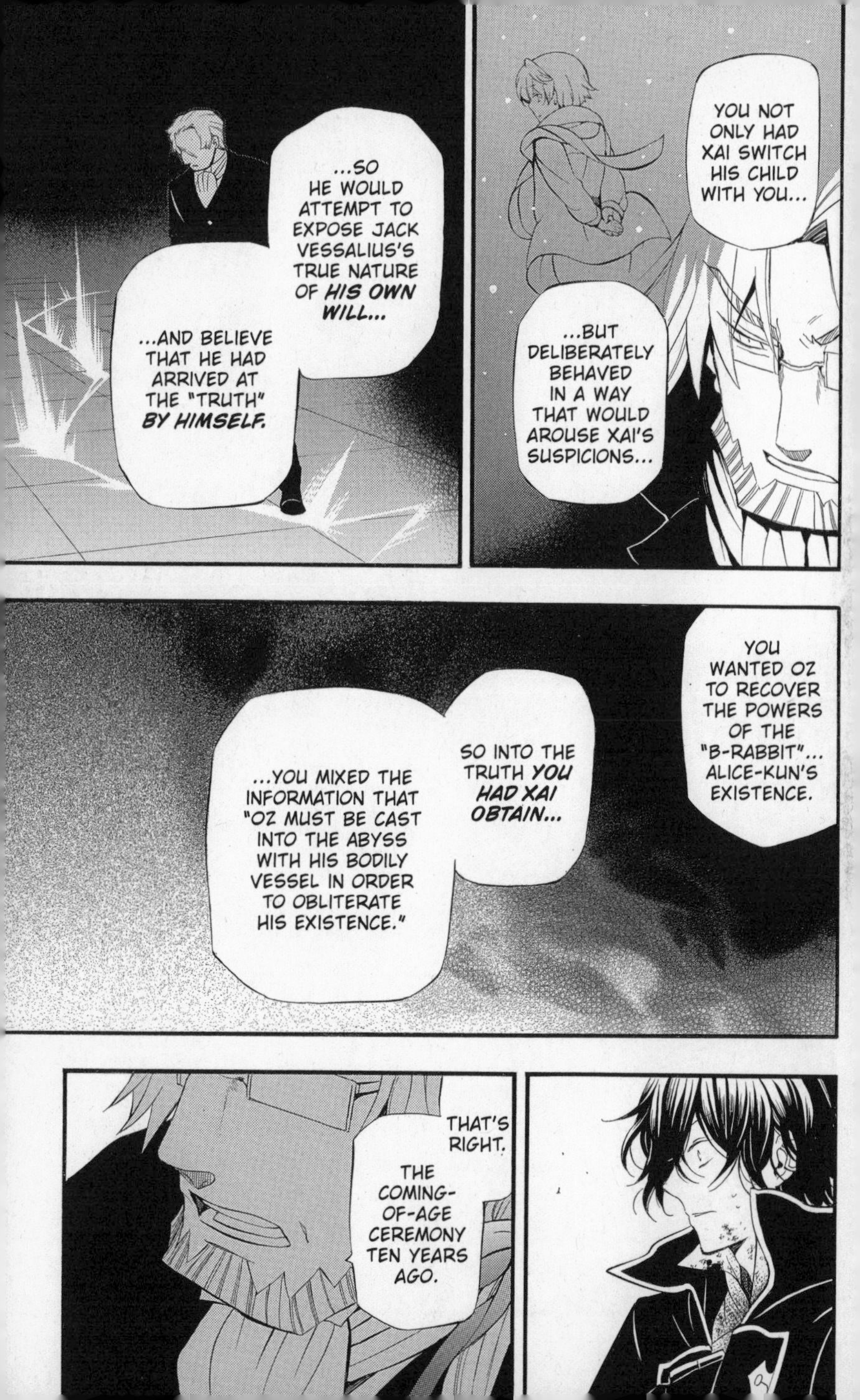
YOU NOT ONLY HAD XAI SWITCH HIS CHILD WITH YOU...
...BUT DELIBERATELY BEHAVED IN A WAY THAT WOULD AROUSE XAI'S SUSPICIONS...
...SO HE WOULD ATTEMPT TO EXPOSE JACK VESSALIUS'S TRUE NATURE OF *HIS OWN WILL...*
...AND BELIEVE THAT HE HAD ARRIVED AT THE "TRUTH" *BY HIMSELF.*
YOU WANTED OZ TO RECOVER THE POWERS OF THE "B-RABBIT"... ALICE-KUN'S EXISTENCE.
SO INTO THE TRUTH *YOU HAD XAI OBTAIN...*
...YOU MIXED THE INFORMATION THAT "OZ MUST BE CAST INTO THE ABYSS WITH HIS BODILY VESSEL IN ORDER TO OBLITERATE HIS EXISTENCE."
THAT'S RIGHT.
THE COMING-OF-AGE CEREMONY TEN YEARS AGO.

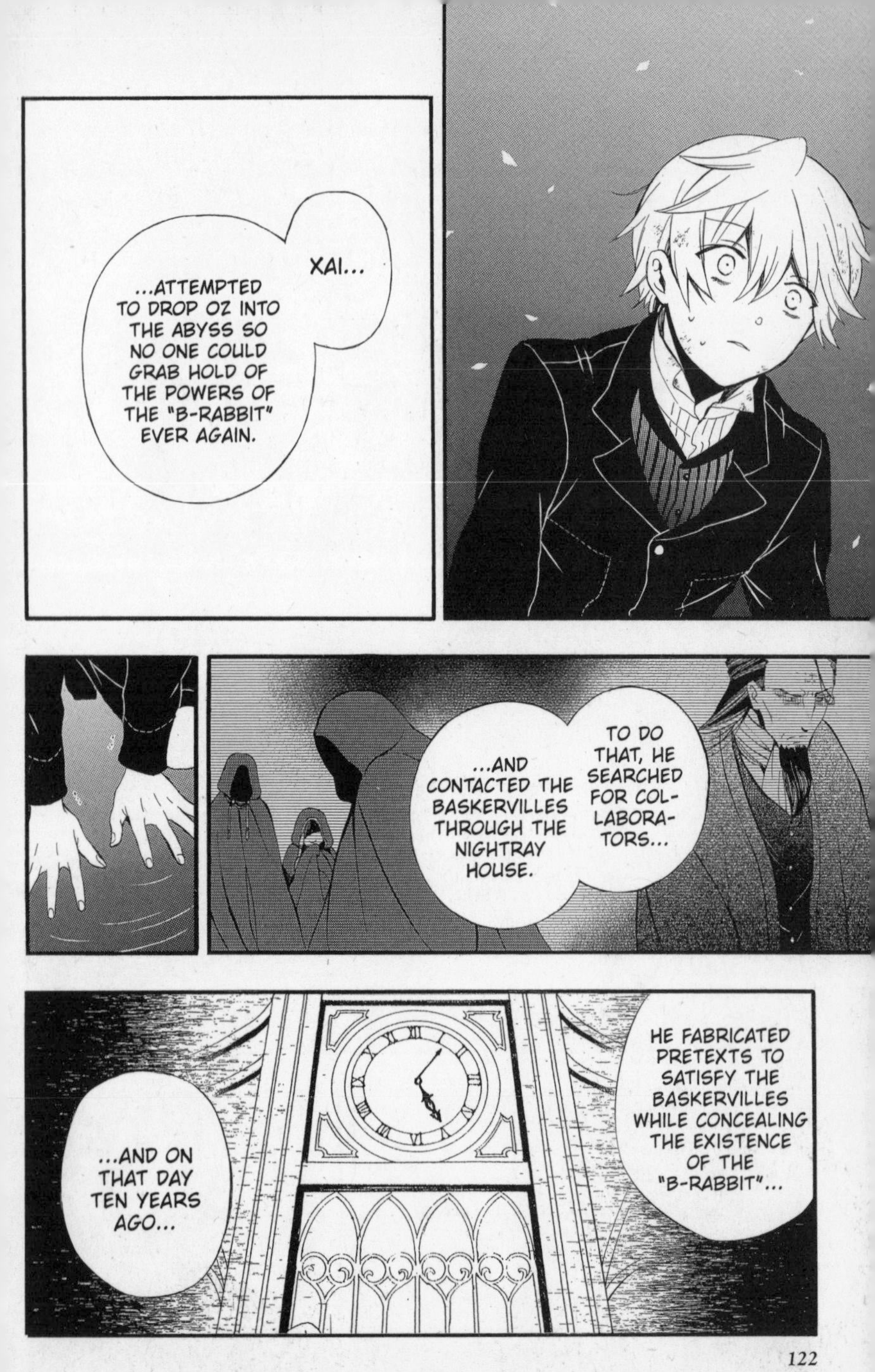
XAI...
...ATTEMPTED TO DROP OZ INTO THE ABYSS SO NO ONE COULD GRAB HOLD OF THE POWERS OF THE "B-RABBIT" EVER AGAIN.
TO DO THAT, HE SEARCHED FOR COL-LABORA-TORS...
...AND CONTACTED THE BASKERVILLES THROUGH THE NIGHTRAY HOUSE.
HE FABRICATED PRETEXTS TO SATISFY THE BASKERVILLES WHILE CONCEALING THE EXISTENCE OF THE "B-RABBIT"...
...AND ON THAT DAY TEN YEARS AGO...

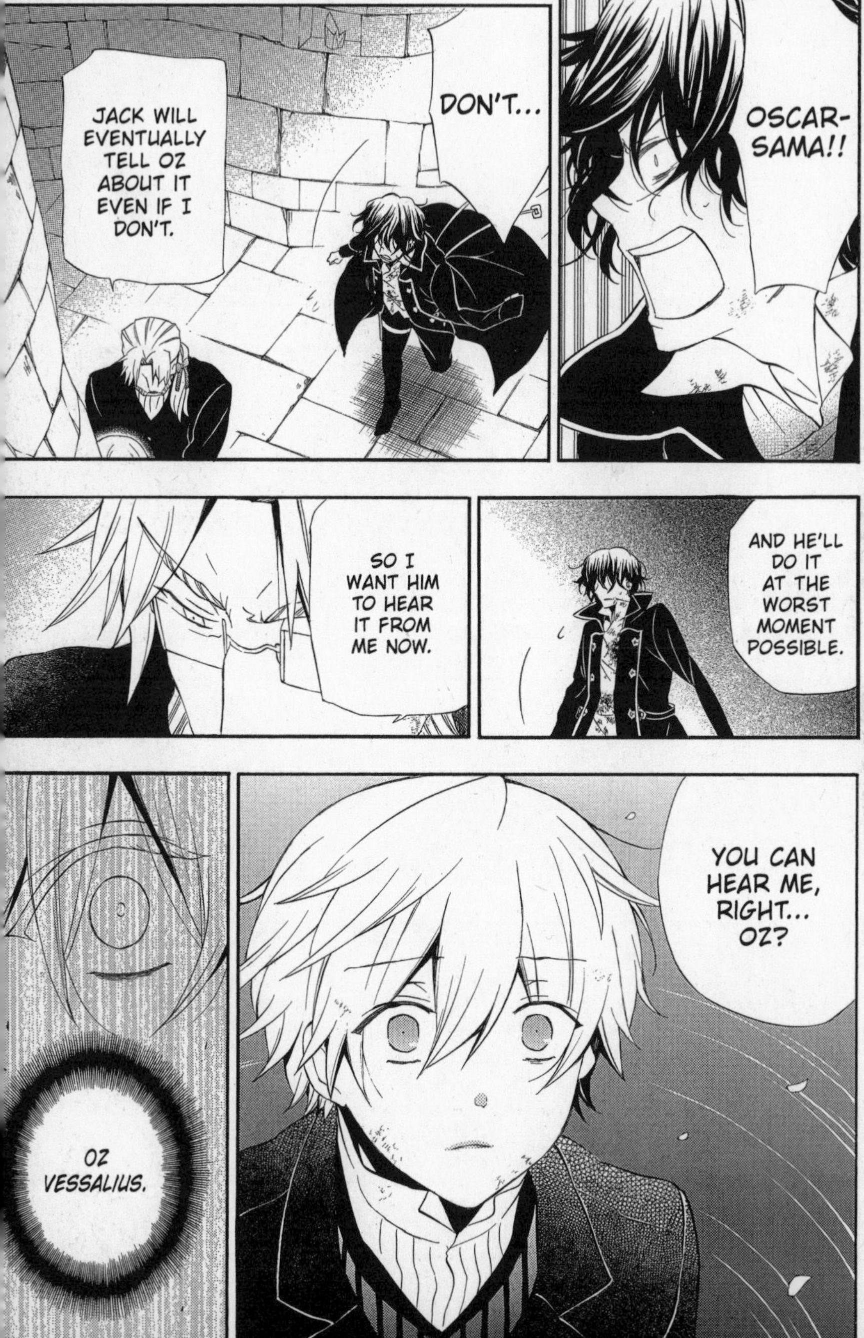
OSCAR-SAMA!!
DON'T...
JACK WILL EVENTUALLY TELL OZ ABOUT IT EVEN IF I DON'T.
AND HE'LL DO IT AT THE WORST MOMENT POSSIBLE.
SO I WANT HIM TO HEAR IT FROM ME NOW.
YOU CAN HEAR ME, RIGHT... OZ?
OZ VESSALIUS.

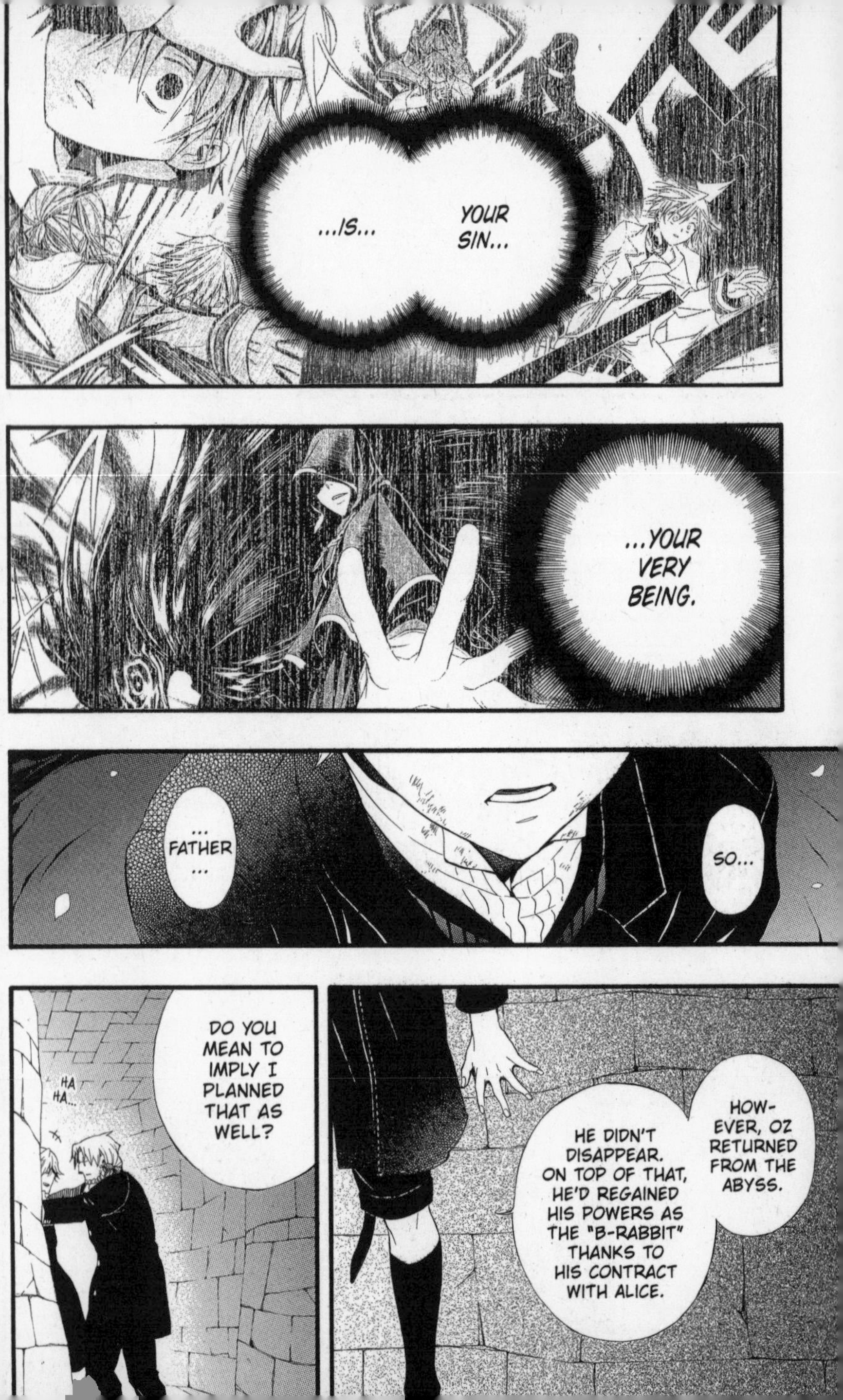
...IS... YOUR SIN...
...YOUR VERY BEING.
SO...
...FATHER...
HOW-EVER, OZ RETURNED FROM THE ABYSS.
HE DIDN'T DISAPPEAR. ON TOP OF THAT, HE'D REGAINED HIS POWERS AS THE "B-RABBIT" THANKS TO HIS CONTRACT WITH ALICE.
DO YOU MEAN TO IMPLY I PLANNED THAT AS WELL?
HA HA...

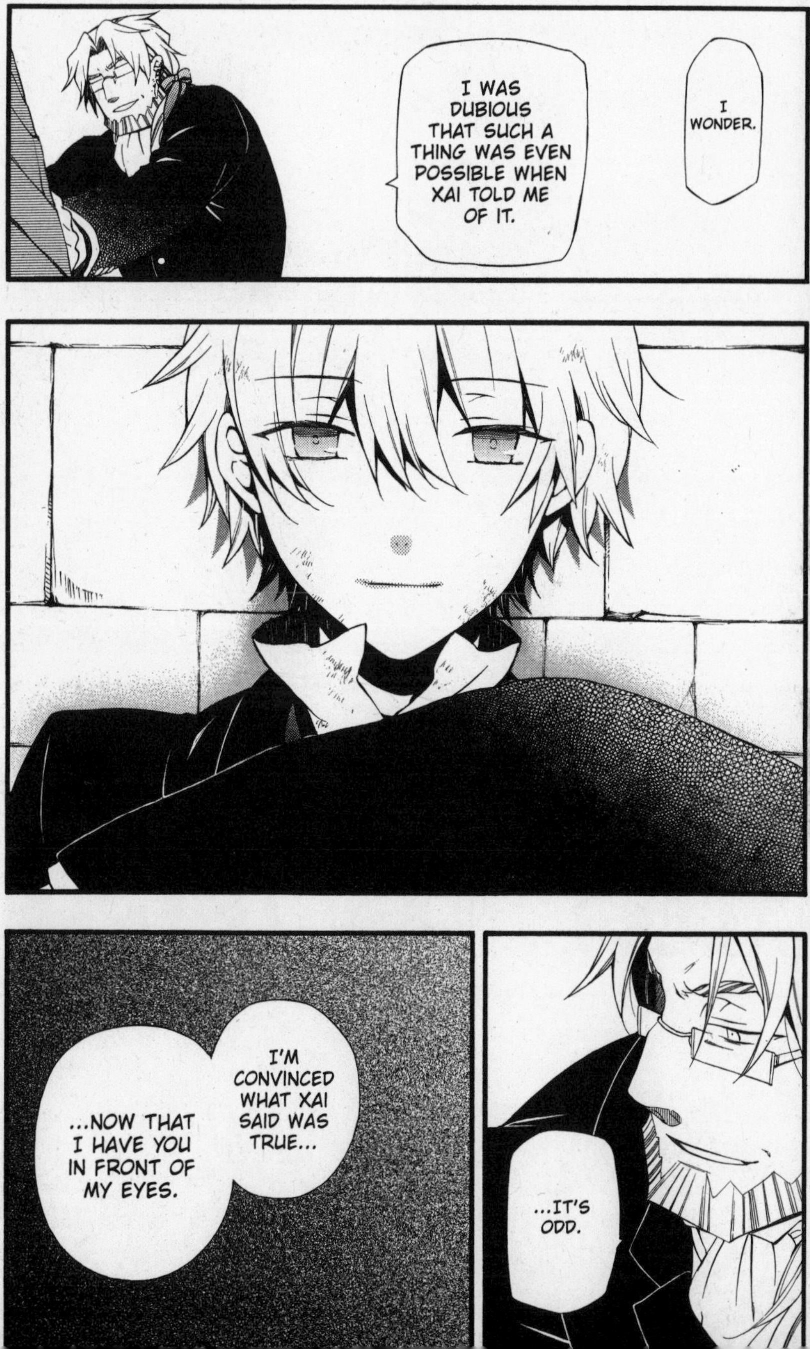
I WONDER.
I WAS DUBIOUS THAT SUCH A THING WAS EVEN POSSIBLE WHEN XAI TOLD ME OF IT.
...
...IT'S ODD.
I'M CONVINCED WHAT XAI SAID WAS TRUE...
...NOW THAT I HAVE YOU IN FRONT OF MY EYES.

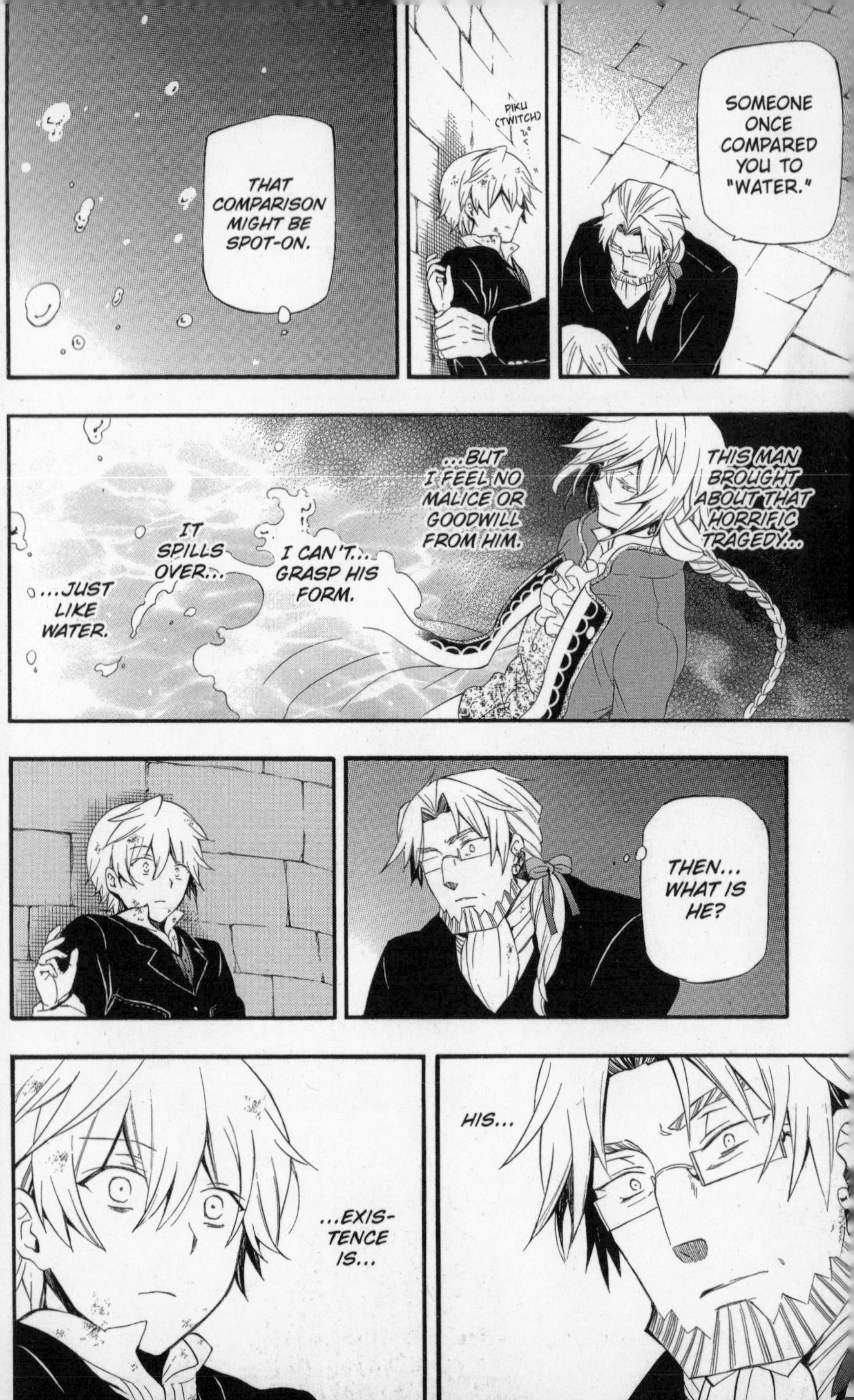
SOMEONE ONCE COMPARED YOU TO "WATER."
PIKU (TWITCH)
THAT COMPARISON MIGHT BE SPOT-ON.
THIS MAN BROUGHT ABOUT THAT HORRIFIC TRAGEDY...
...BUT I FEEL NO MALICE OR GOODWILL FROM HIM.
I CAN'T... GRASP HIS FORM.
IT SPILLS OVER...
...JUST LIKE WATER.
THEN... WHAT IS HE?
HIS...
...EXIS-TENCE IS...

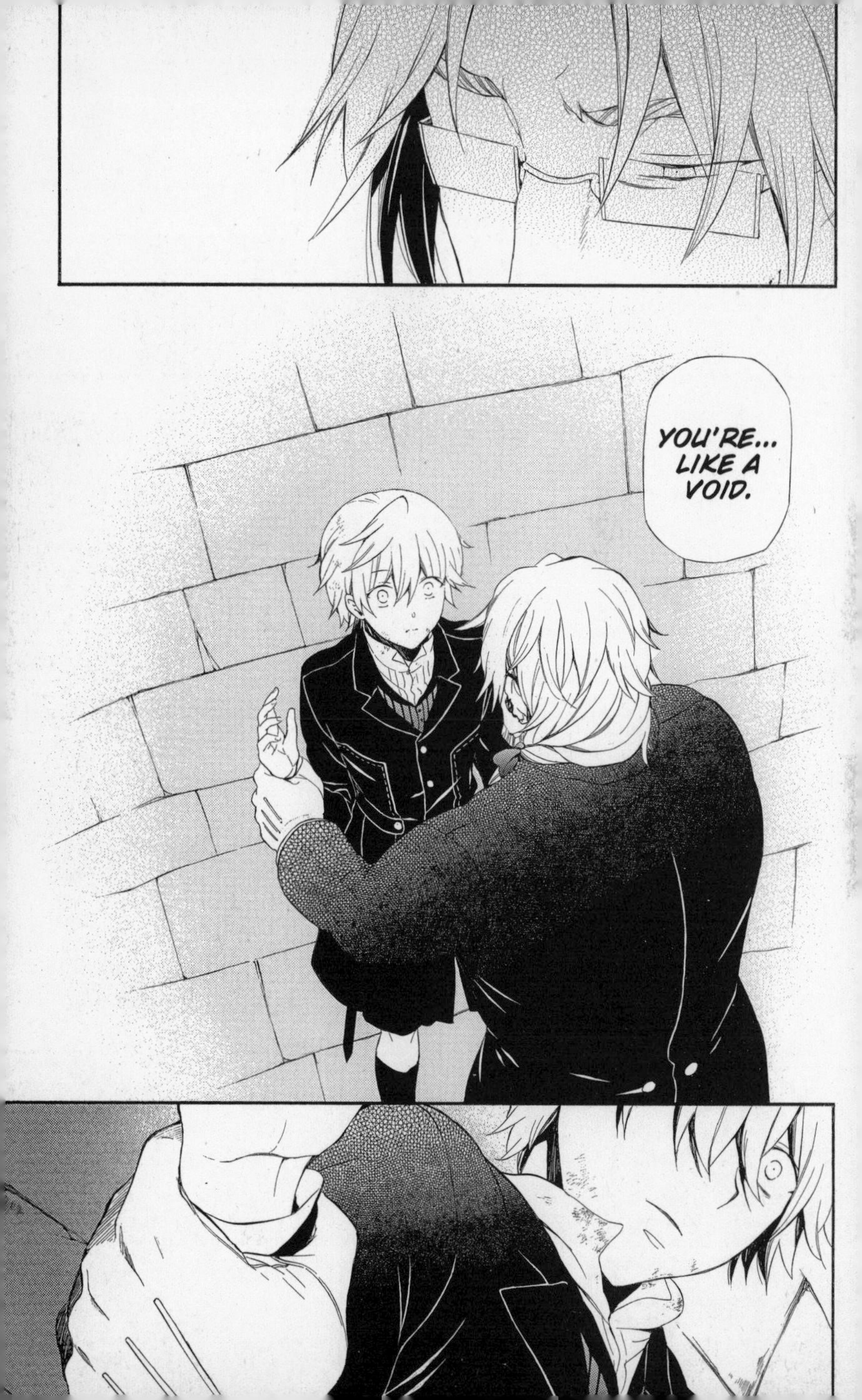
YOU'RE... LIKE A VOID.

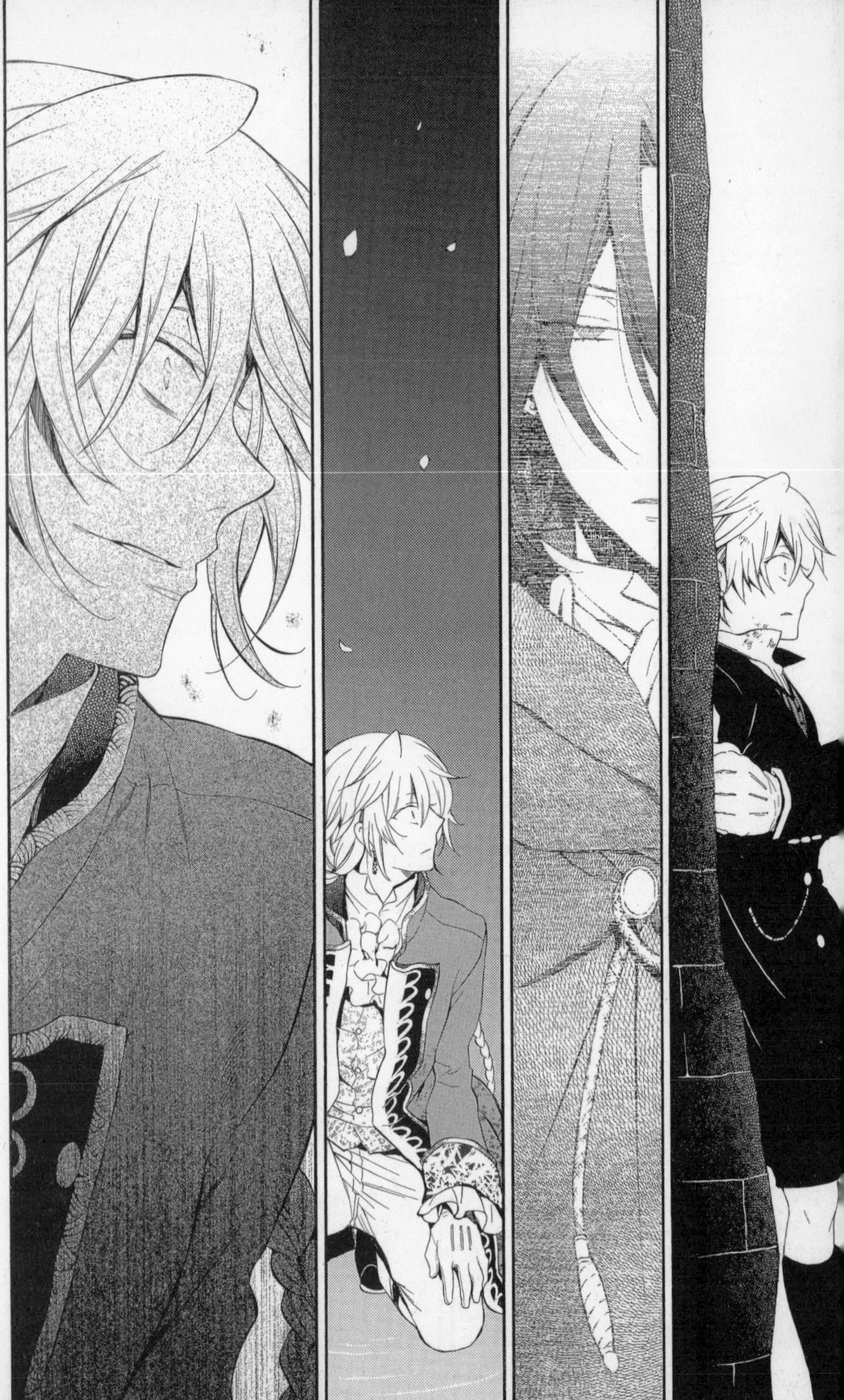

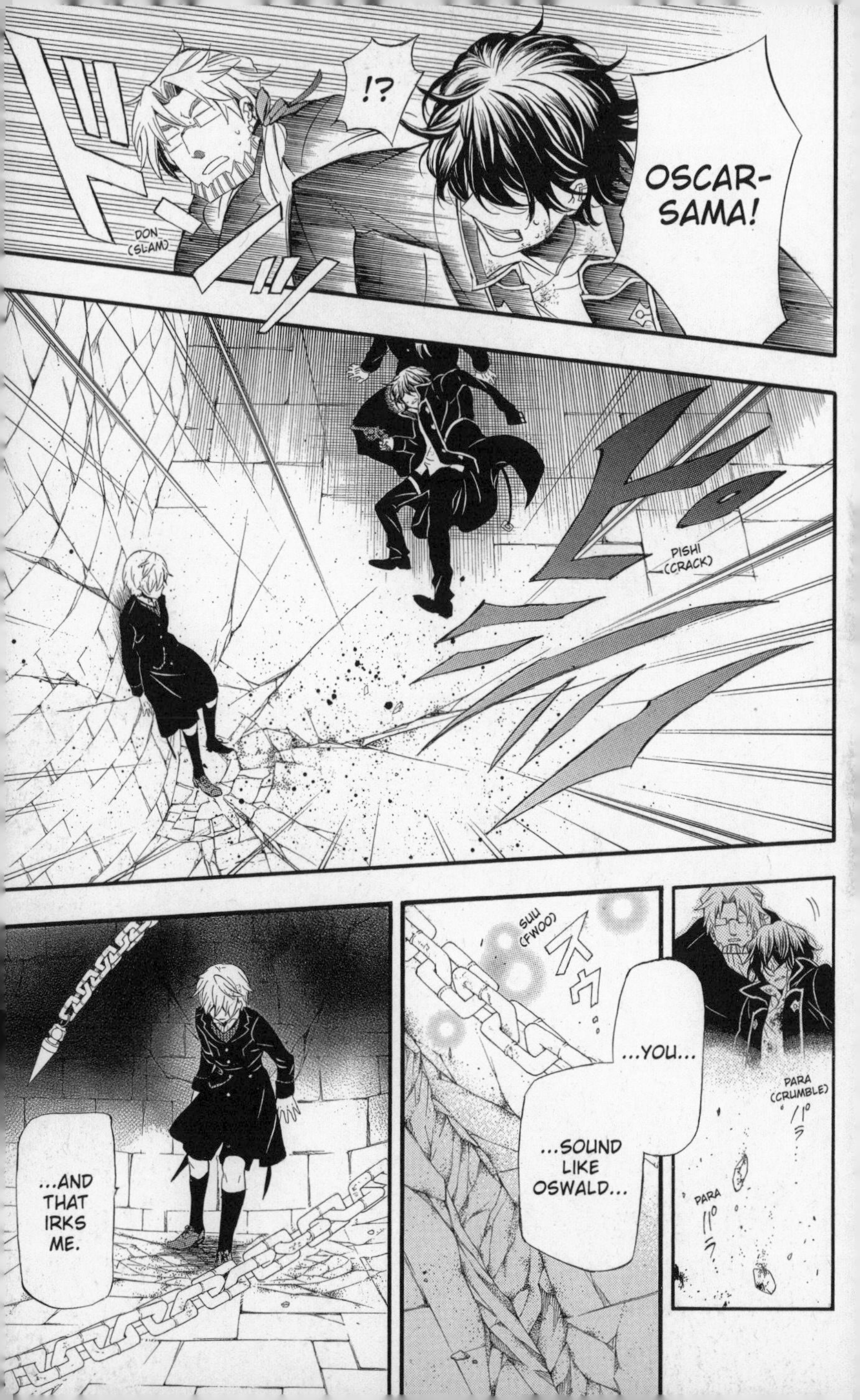

OSCAR-SAMA!
!?
DON (SLAM)
PISHI (CRACK)
PARA (CRUMBLE)
PARA
SUU (FWOO)
...YOU...
...SOUND LIKE OSWALD...
...AND THAT IRKS ME.

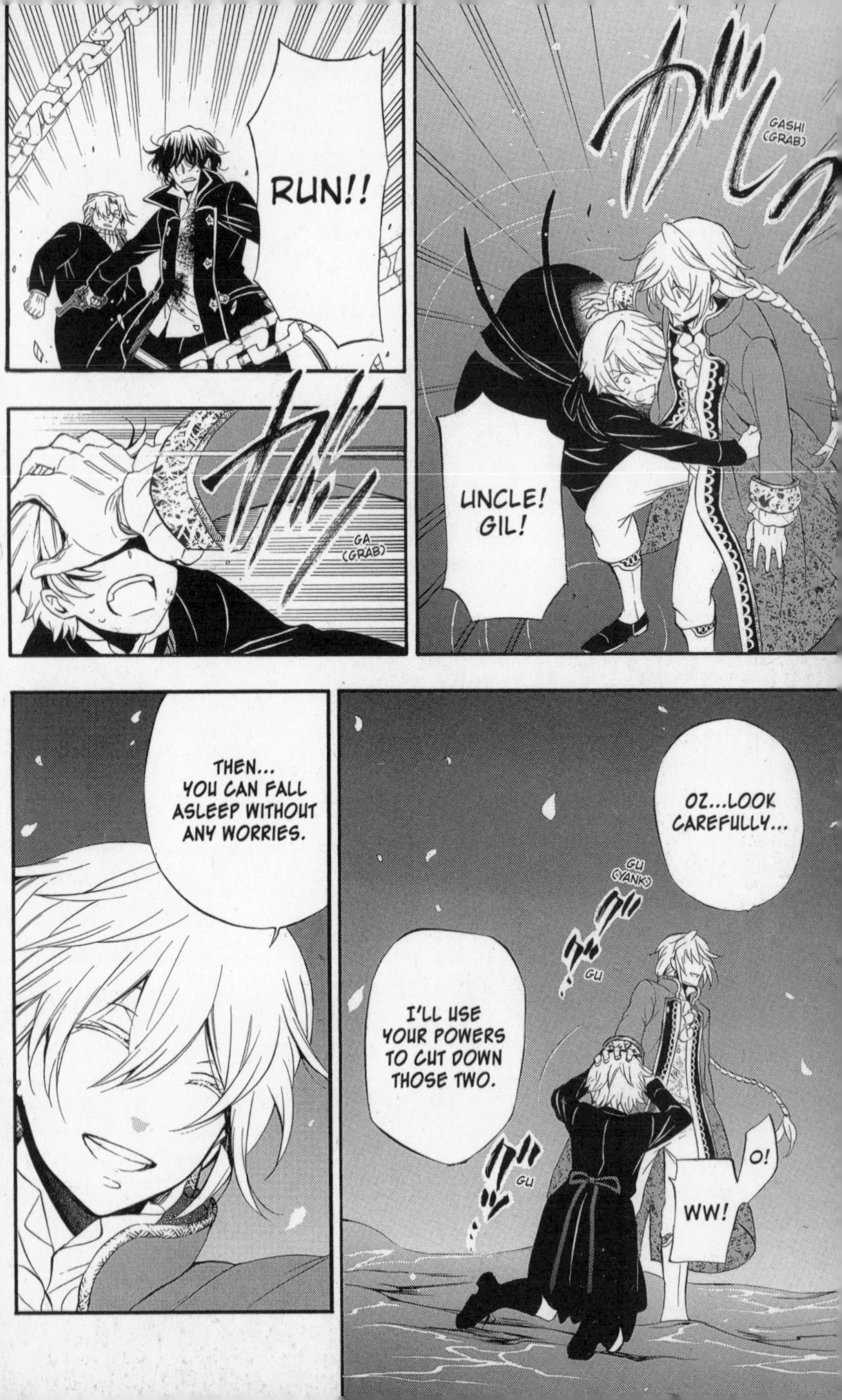
GASHI (GRAB)
UNCLE! GIL!
RUN!!
GA (GRAB)
OZ...LOOK CAREFULLY...
GU (YANK)
GU
I'LL USE YOUR POWERS TO CUT DOWN THOSE TWO.
GU
O!
WW!
THEN... YOU CAN FALL ASLEEP WITHOUT ANY WORRIES.

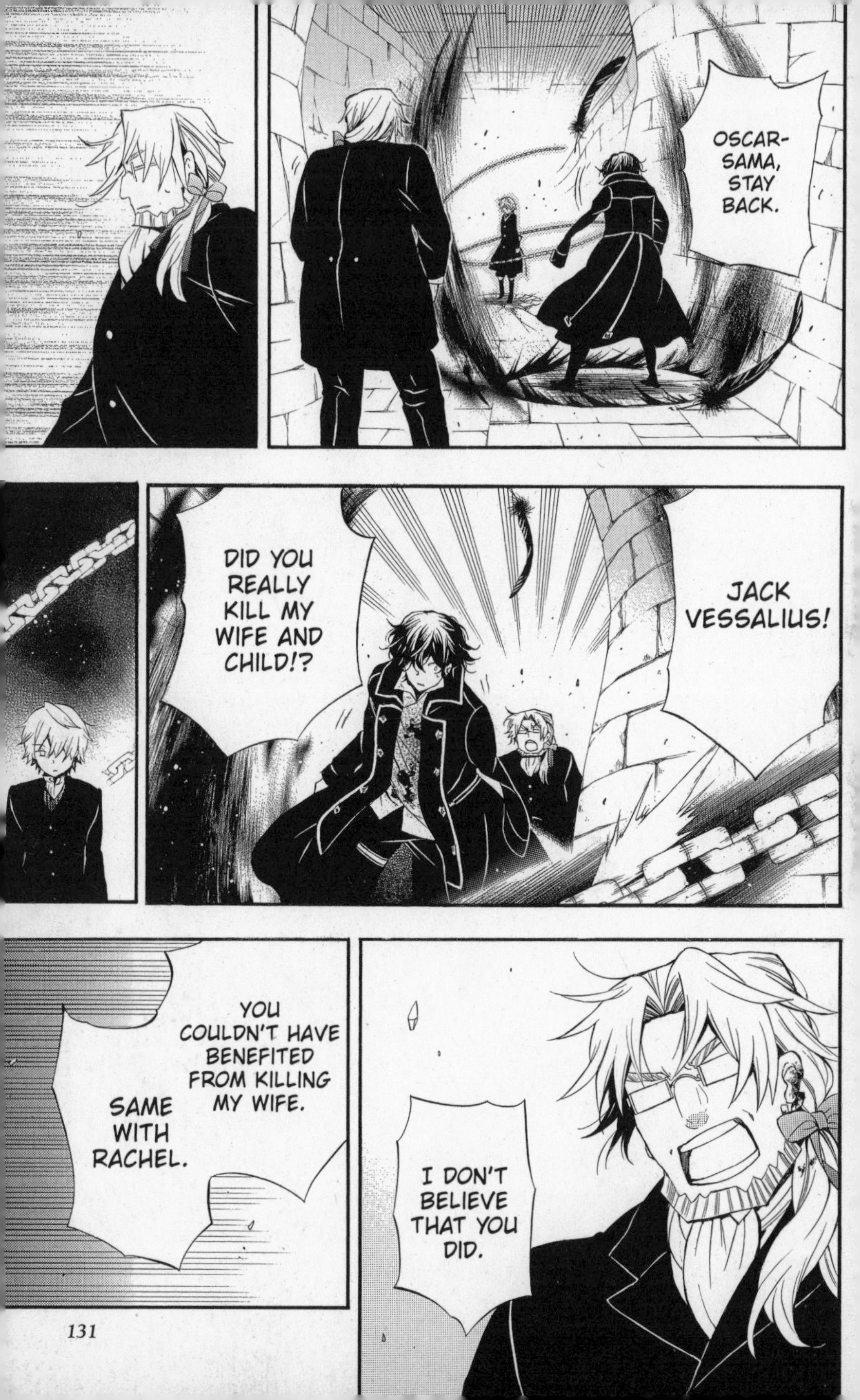
OSCAR-SAMA, STAY BACK.
JACK VESSALIUS!
DID YOU REALLY KILL MY WIFE AND CHILD!?
I DON'T BELIEVE THAT YOU DID.
YOU COULDN'T HAVE BENEFITED FROM KILLING MY WIFE.
SAME WITH RACHEL.

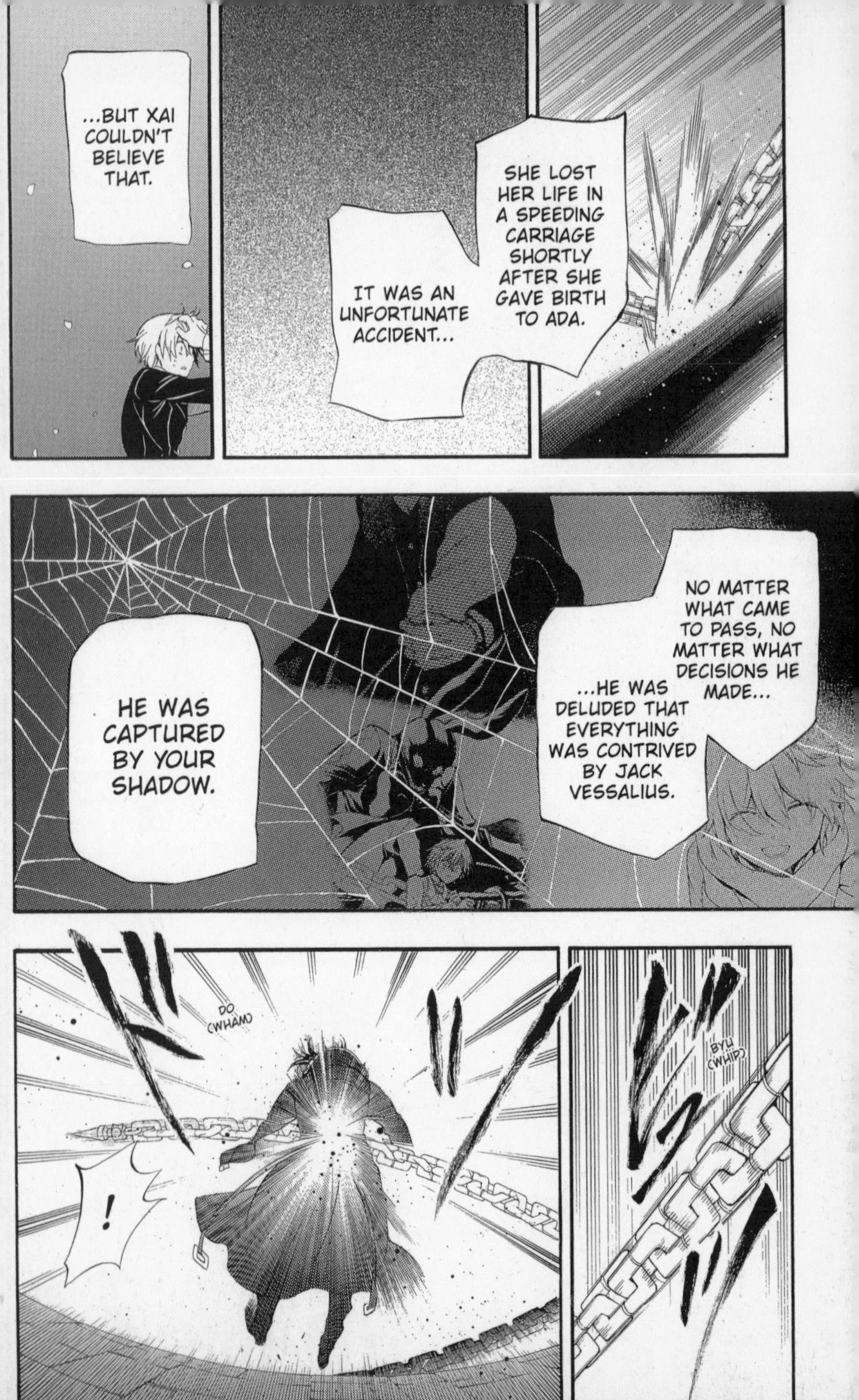
SHE LOST HER LIFE IN A SPEEDING CARRIAGE SHORTLY AFTER SHE GAVE BIRTH TO ADA.
IT WAS AN UNFORTUNATE ACCIDENT...
...BUT XAI COULDN'T BELIEVE THAT.
NO MATTER WHAT CAME TO PASS, NO MATTER WHAT DECISIONS HE MADE...
...HE WAS DELUDED THAT EVERYTHING WAS CONTRIVED BY JACK VESSALIUS.
HE WAS CAPTURED BY YOUR SHADOW.
BYU (WHIP)
DO (WHAM)
!

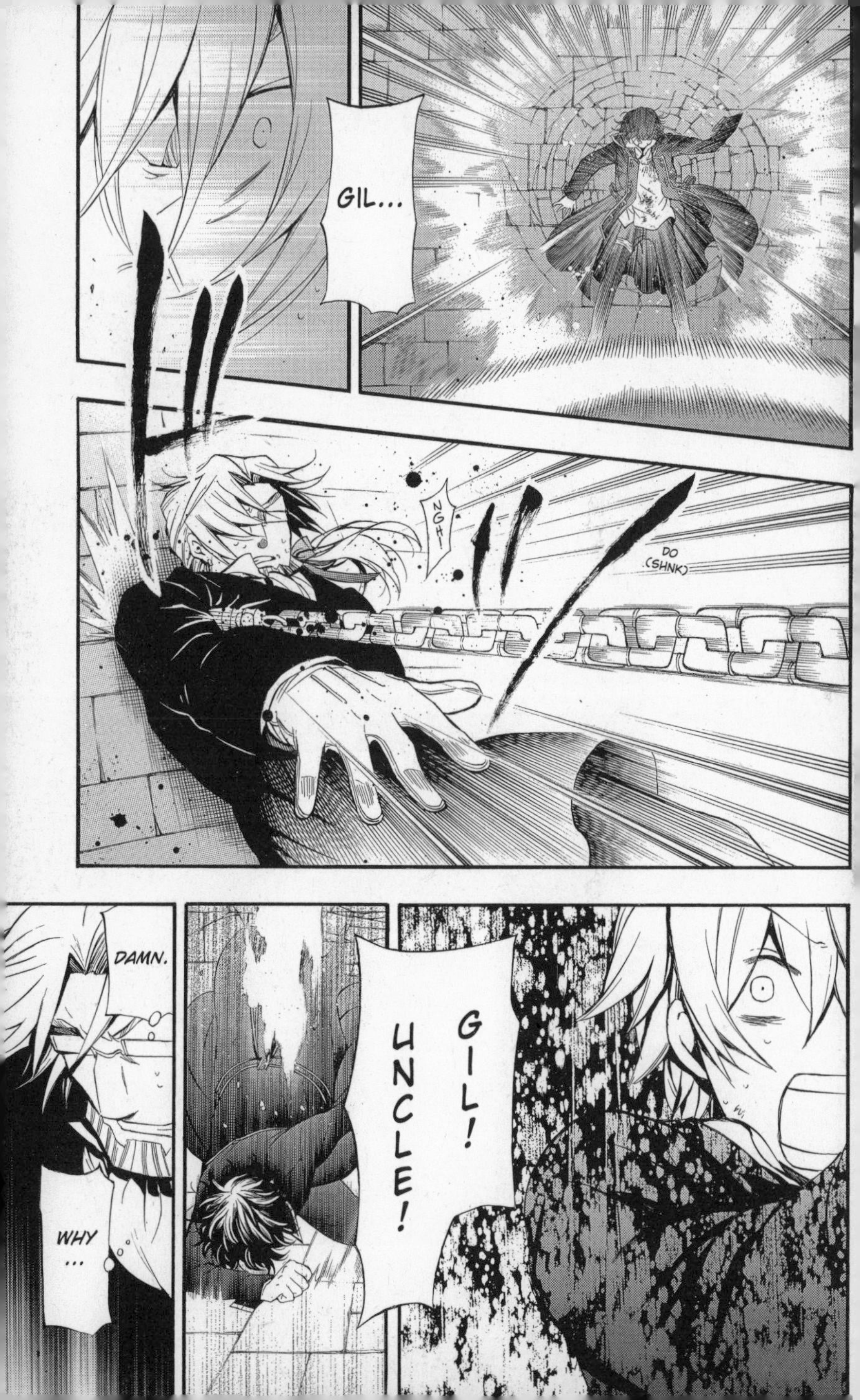
GIL...
NGH!
DO
(SHNK)
GIL! UNCLE!
DAMN.
WHY ...

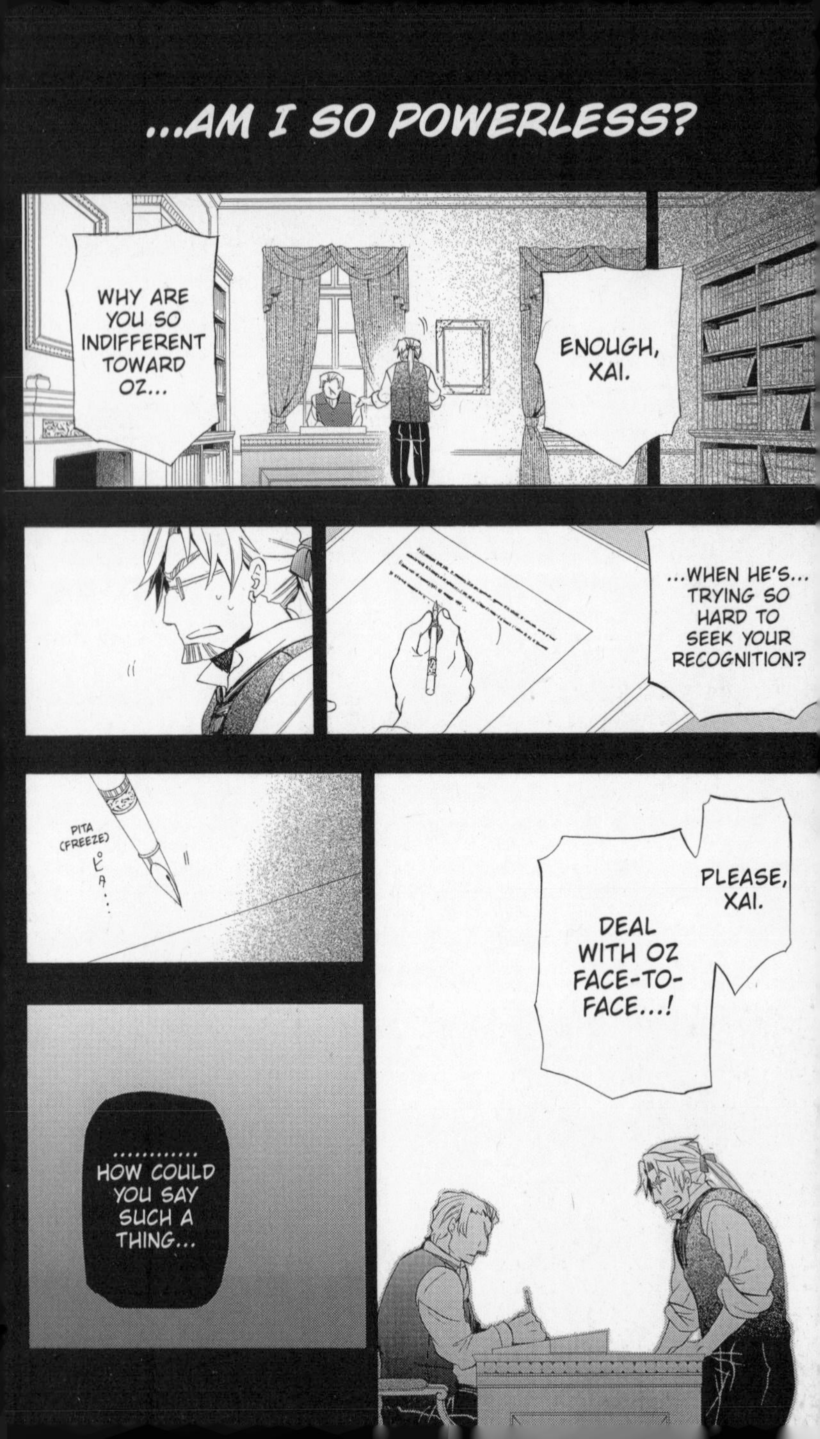
...AM I SO POWERLESS?
WHY ARE YOU SO INDIFFERENT TOWARD OZ...
ENOUGH, XAI.
...WHEN HE'S... TRYING SO HARD TO SEEK YOUR RECOGNITION?
PLEASE, XAI.
DEAL WITH OZ FACE-TO-FACE...!
PITA (FREEZE)
ピタ・・・
....
HOW COULD YOU SAY SUCH A THING...

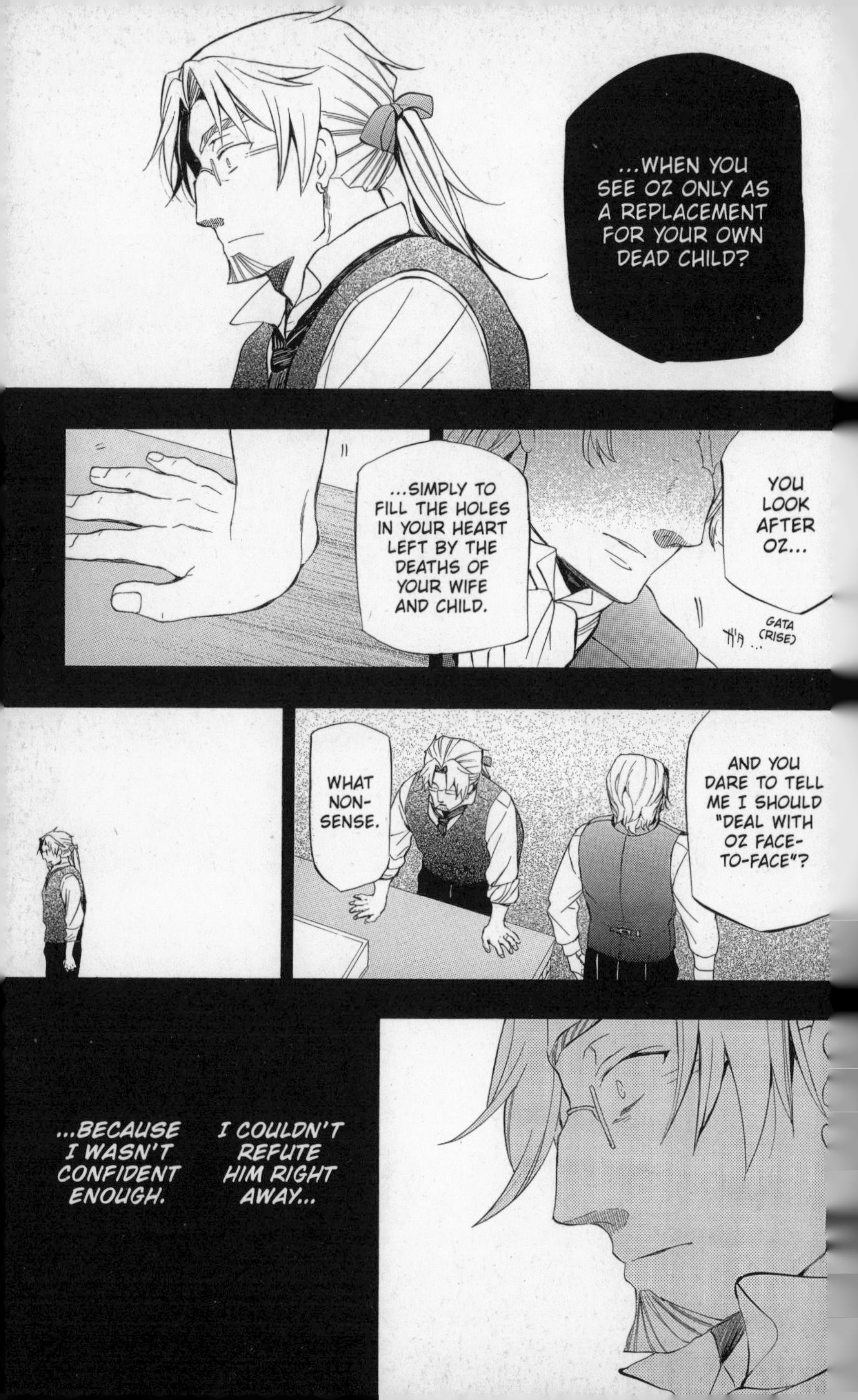
...WHEN YOU SEE OZ ONLY AS A REPLACEMENT FOR YOUR OWN DEAD CHILD?
YOU LOOK AFTER OZ...
...SIMPLY TO FILL THE HOLES IN YOUR HEART LEFT BY THE DEATHS OF YOUR WIFE AND CHILD.
GATA (RISE)
AND YOU DARE TO TELL ME I SHOULD "DEAL WITH OZ FACE-TO-FACE"?
WHAT NON-SENSE.
I COULDN'T REFUTE HIM RIGHT AWAY...
...BECAUSE I WASN'T CONFIDENT ENOUGH.

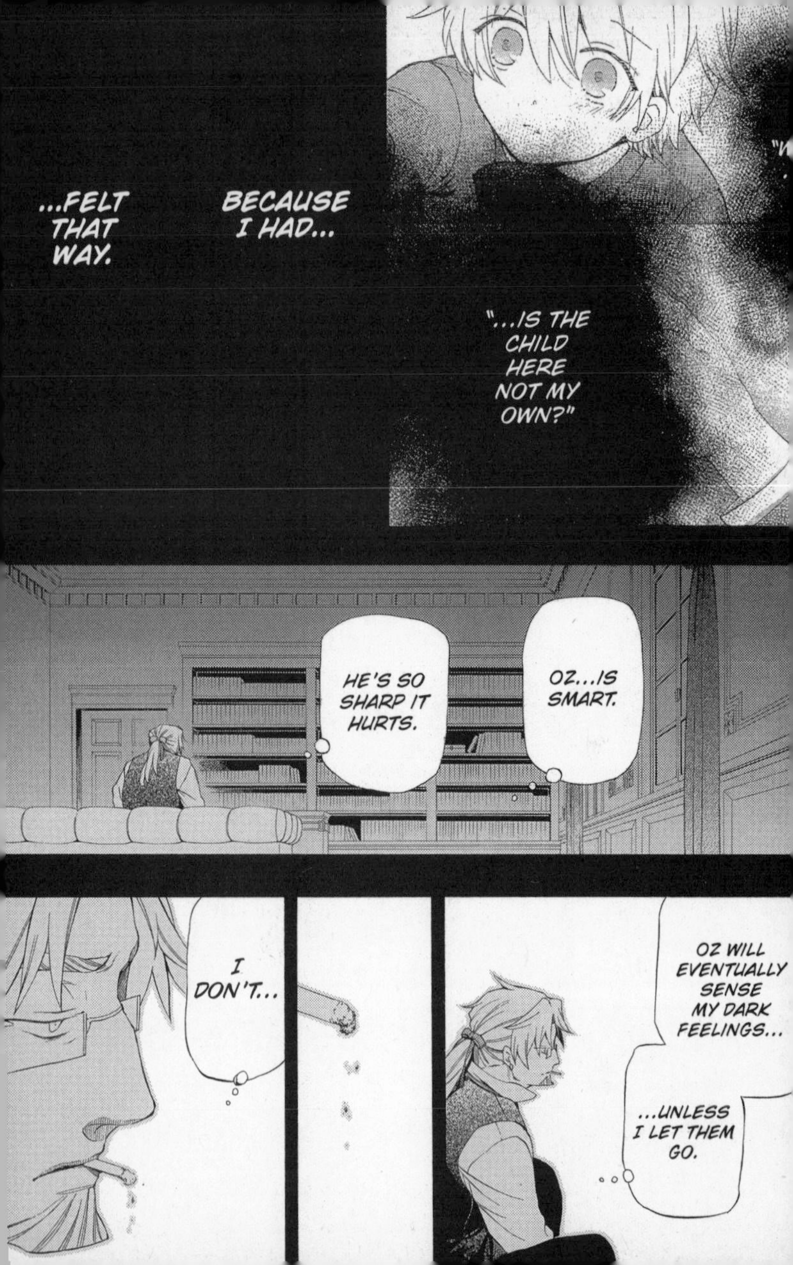
"...IS THE CHILD HERE NOT MY OWN?"
BECAUSE I HAD...
...FELT THAT WAY.
OZ...IS SMART.
HE'S SO SHARP IT HURTS.
OZ WILL EVENTUALLY SENSE MY DARK FEELINGS...
...UNLESS I LET THEM GO.
I DON'T...

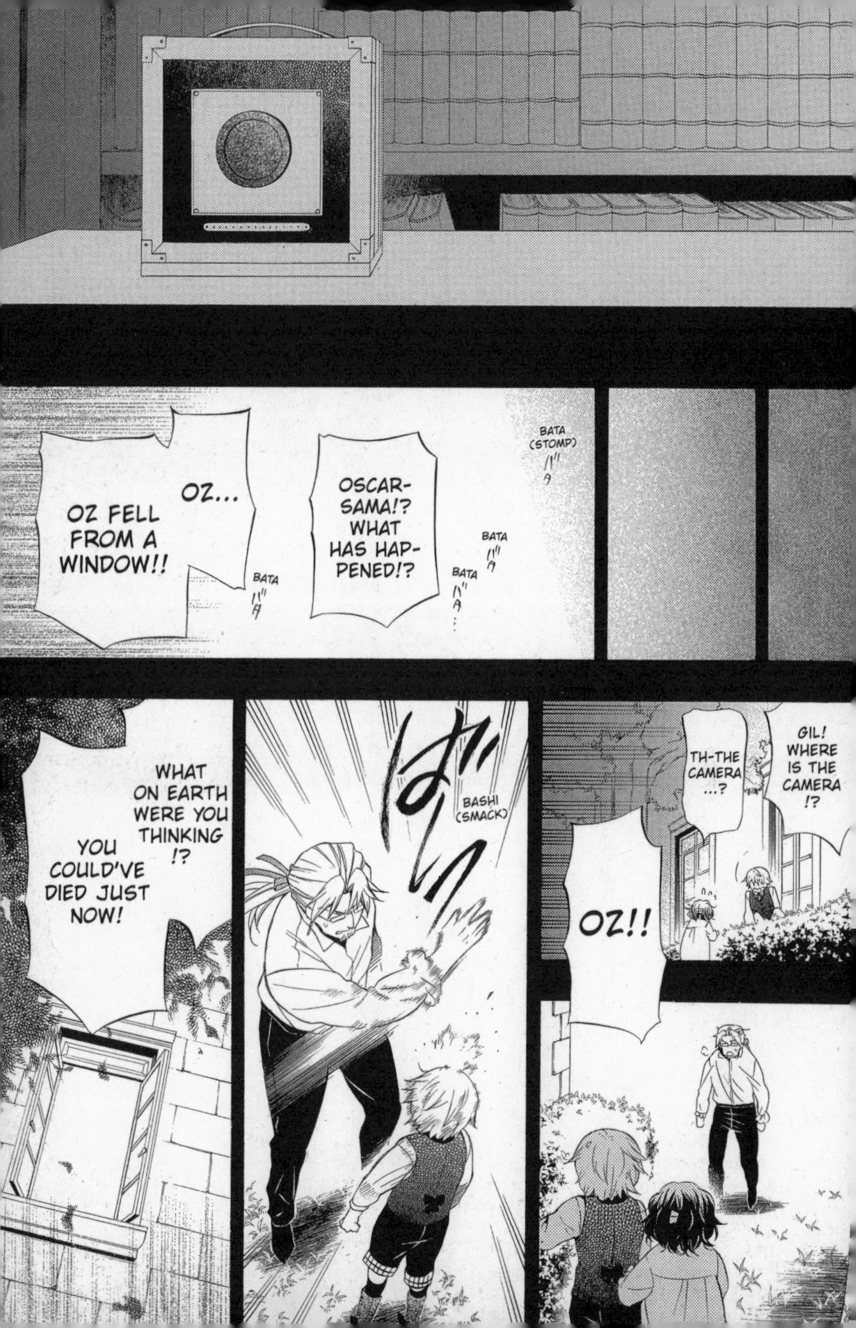
BATA (STOMP)
BATA
OSCAR-SAMA!? WHAT HAS HAPPENED!?
BATA
OZ...
OZ FELL FROM A WINDOW!!
BATA
GIL! WHERE IS THE CAMERA !?
TH-THE CAMERA ...?
OZ!!
BASHI (SMACK)
WHAT ON EARTH WERE YOU THINKING !?
YOU COULD'VE DIED JUST NOW!

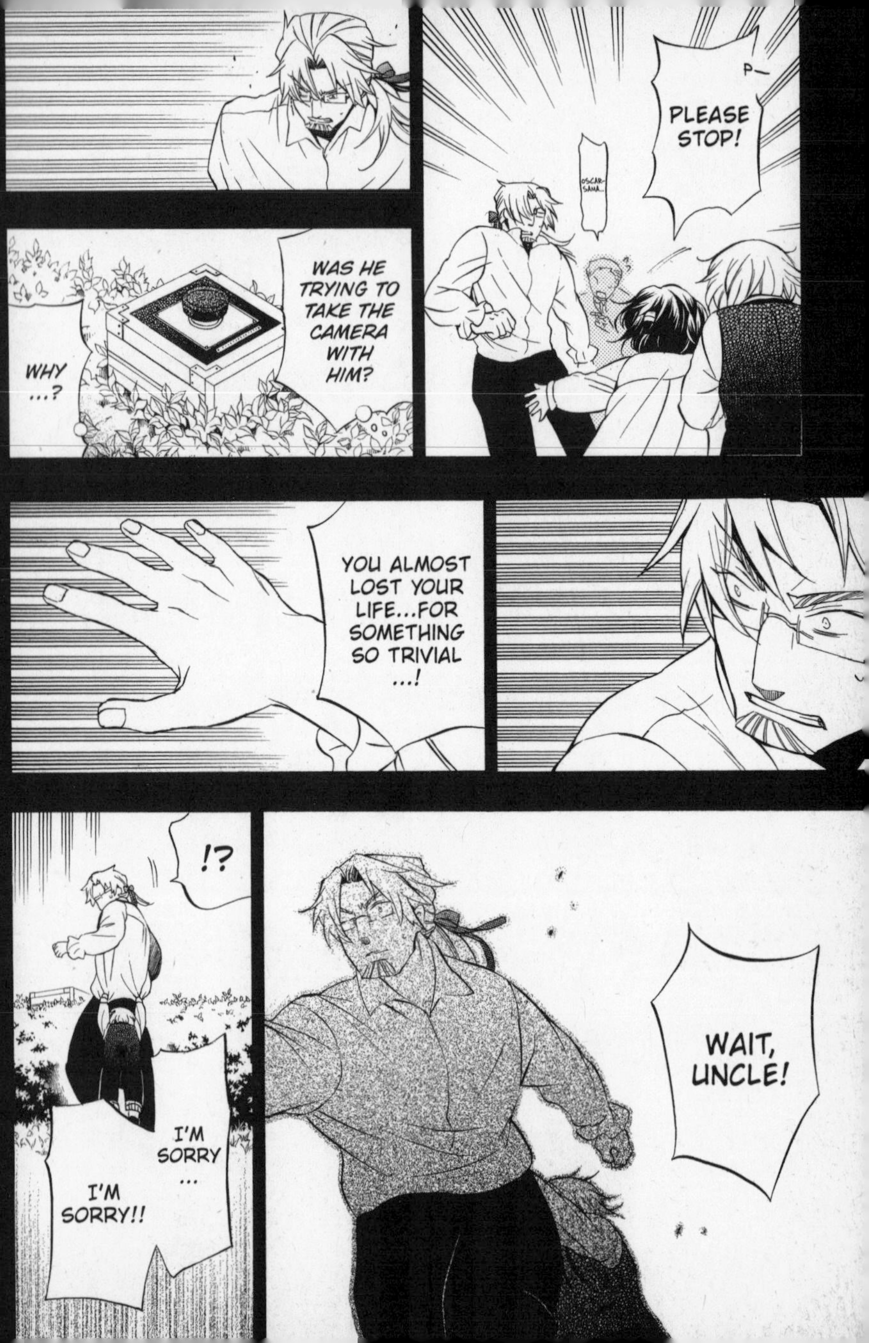
P—
PLEASE STOP!
OSCAR-SAMA...
WAS HE TRYING TO TAKE THE CAMERA WITH HIM?
WHY ...?
YOU ALMOST LOST YOUR LIFE...FOR SOMETHING SO TRIVIAL ...!
WAIT, UNCLE!
!?
I'M SORRY ...
I'M SORRY!!

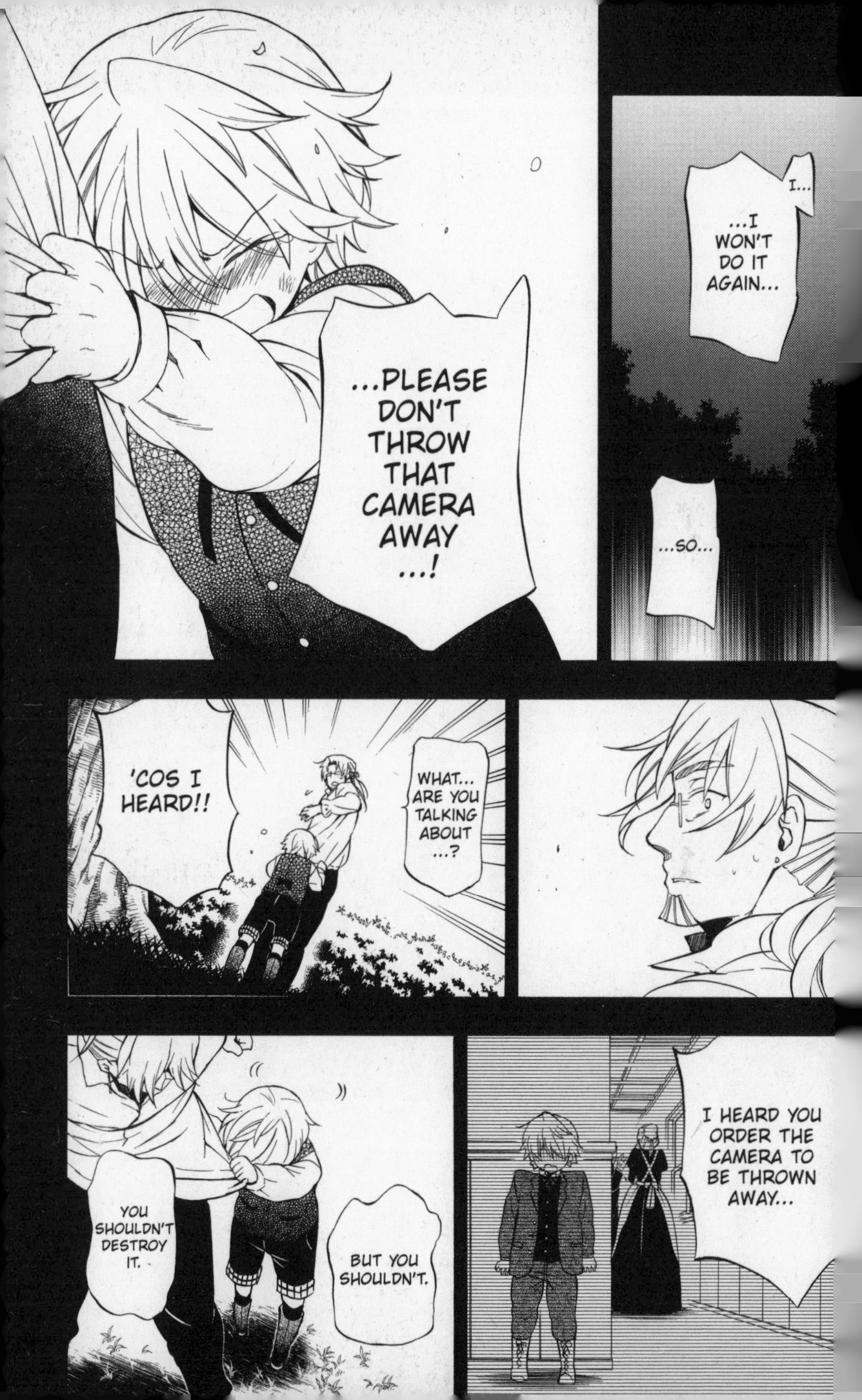
I...
...I WON'T DO IT AGAIN...
...SO...
...PLEASE DON'T THROW THAT CAMERA AWAY ...!
WHAT... ARE YOU TALKING ABOUT ...?
'COS I HEARD!!
I HEARD YOU ORDER THE CAMERA TO BE THROWN AWAY...
BUT YOU SHOULDN'T.
YOU SHOULDN'T DESTROY IT.

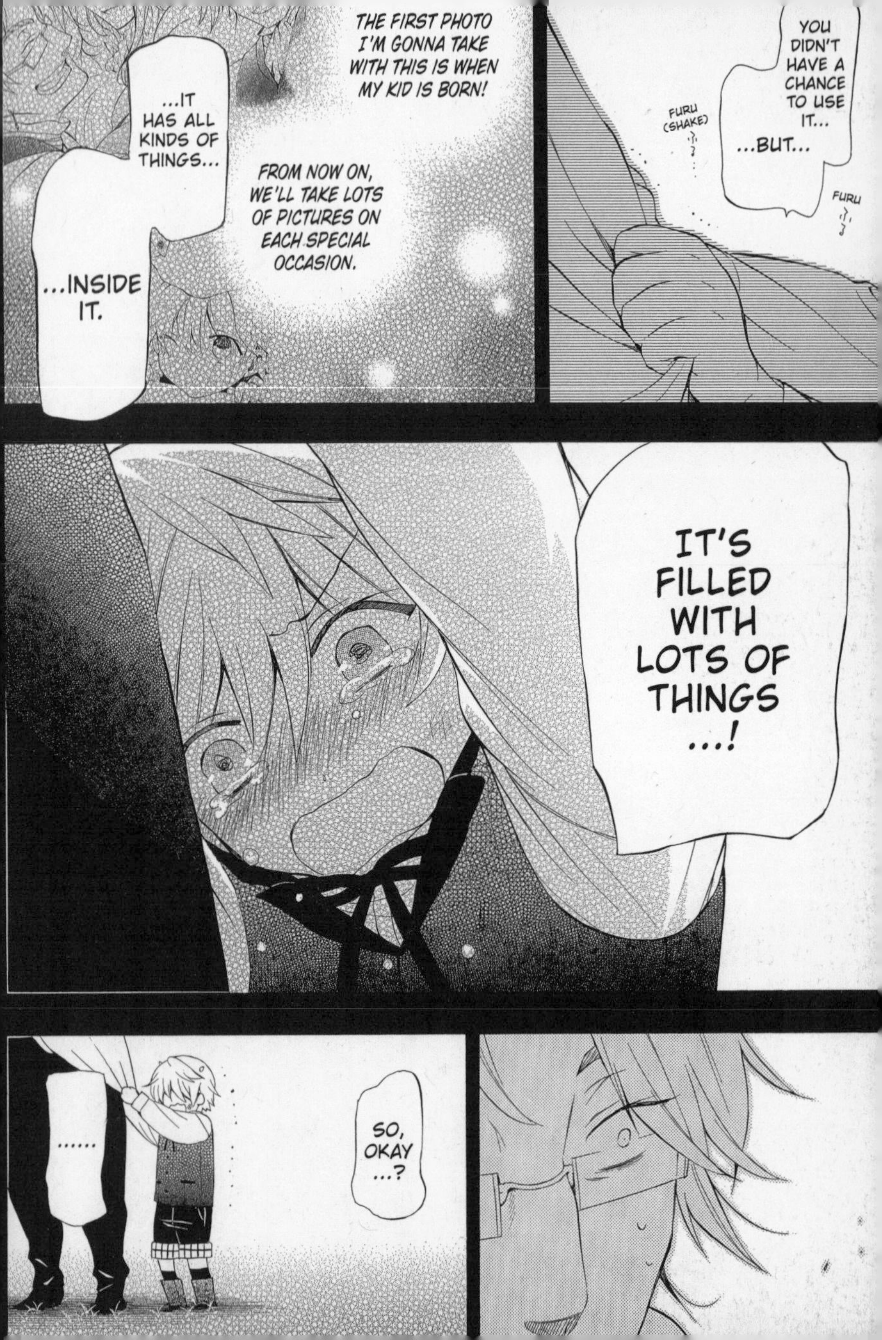
YOU DIDN'T HAVE A CHANCE TO USE IT...
...BUT...
FURU (SHAKE)
FURU
THE FIRST PHOTO I'M GONNA TAKE WITH THIS IS WHEN MY KID IS BORN!
...IT HAS ALL KINDS OF THINGS...
FROM NOW ON, WE'LL TAKE LOTS OF PICTURES ON EACH SPECIAL OCCASION.
...INSIDE IT.
IT'S FILLED WITH LOTS OF THINGS ...!
SO, OKAY ...?
......

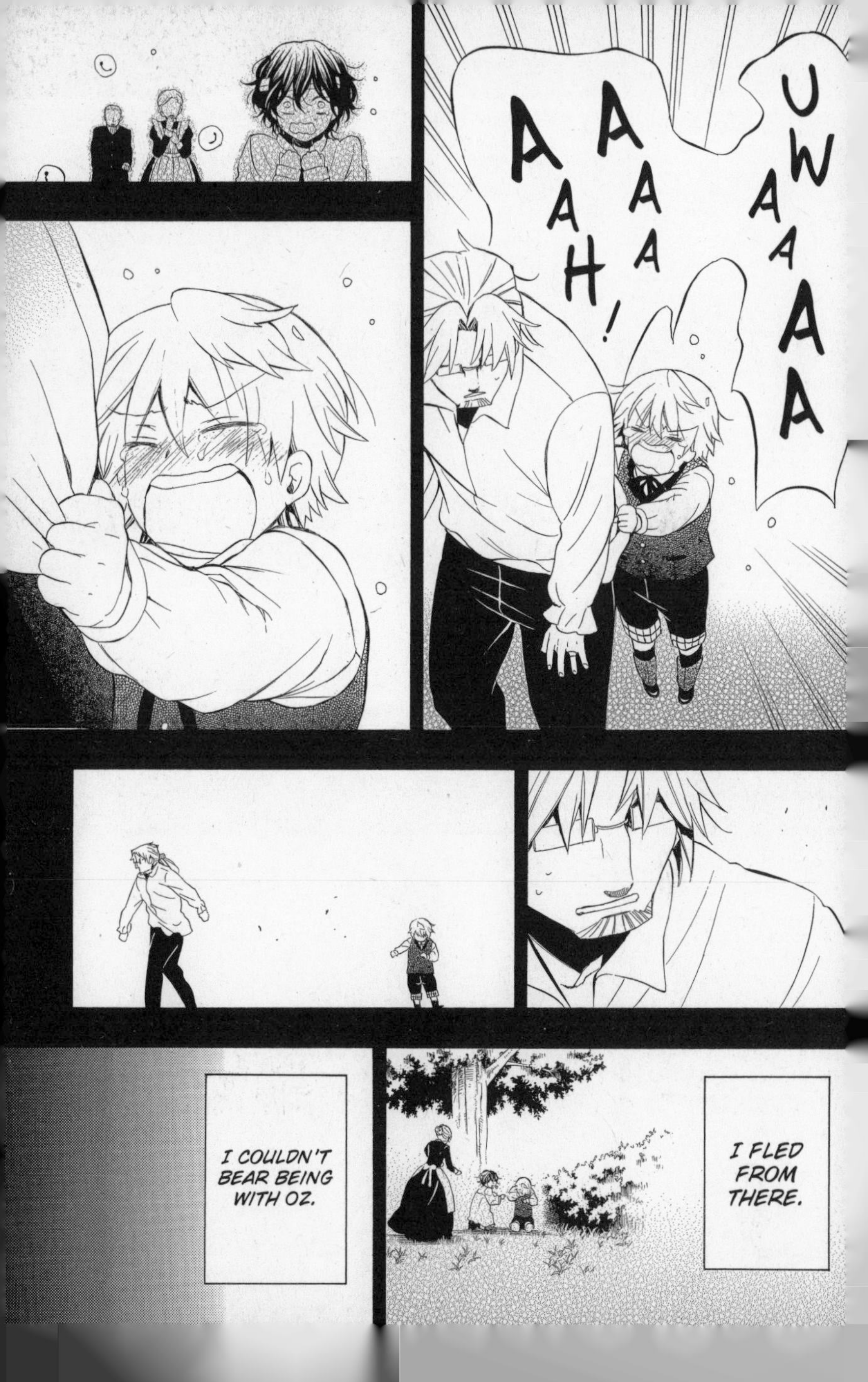
UWAAAAAA
AAAAH!
I FLED FROM THERE.
I COULDN'T BEAR BEING WITH OZ.

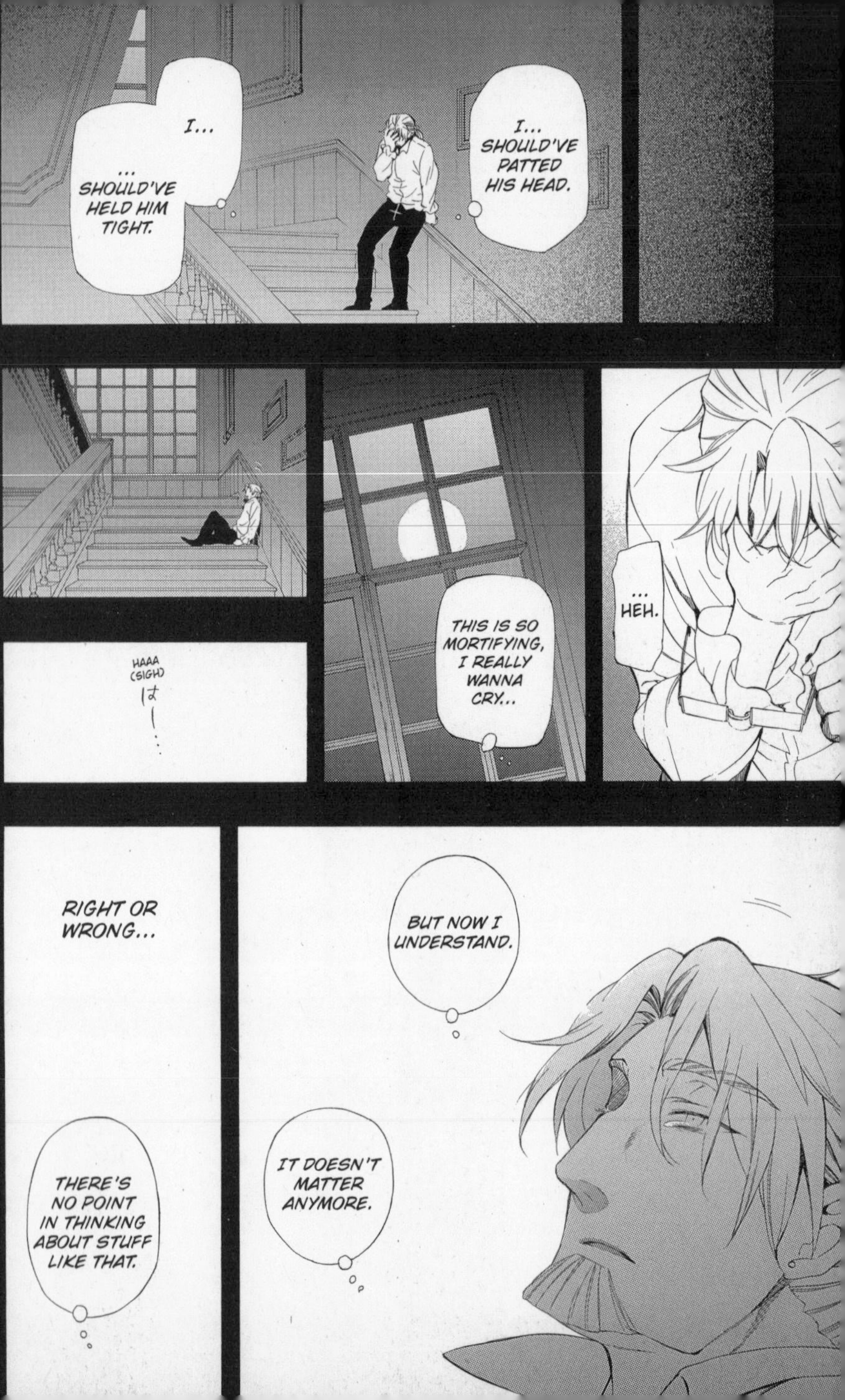
I... SHOULD'VE PATTED HIS HEAD.
I...
... SHOULD'VE HELD HIM TIGHT.
... HEH.
THIS IS SO MORTIFYING, I REALLY WANNA CRY...
HAAA (SIGH)
はー…
BUT NOW I UNDERSTAND.
IT DOESN'T MATTER ANYMORE.
RIGHT OR WRONG...
THERE'S NO POINT IN THINKING ABOUT STUFF LIKE THAT.

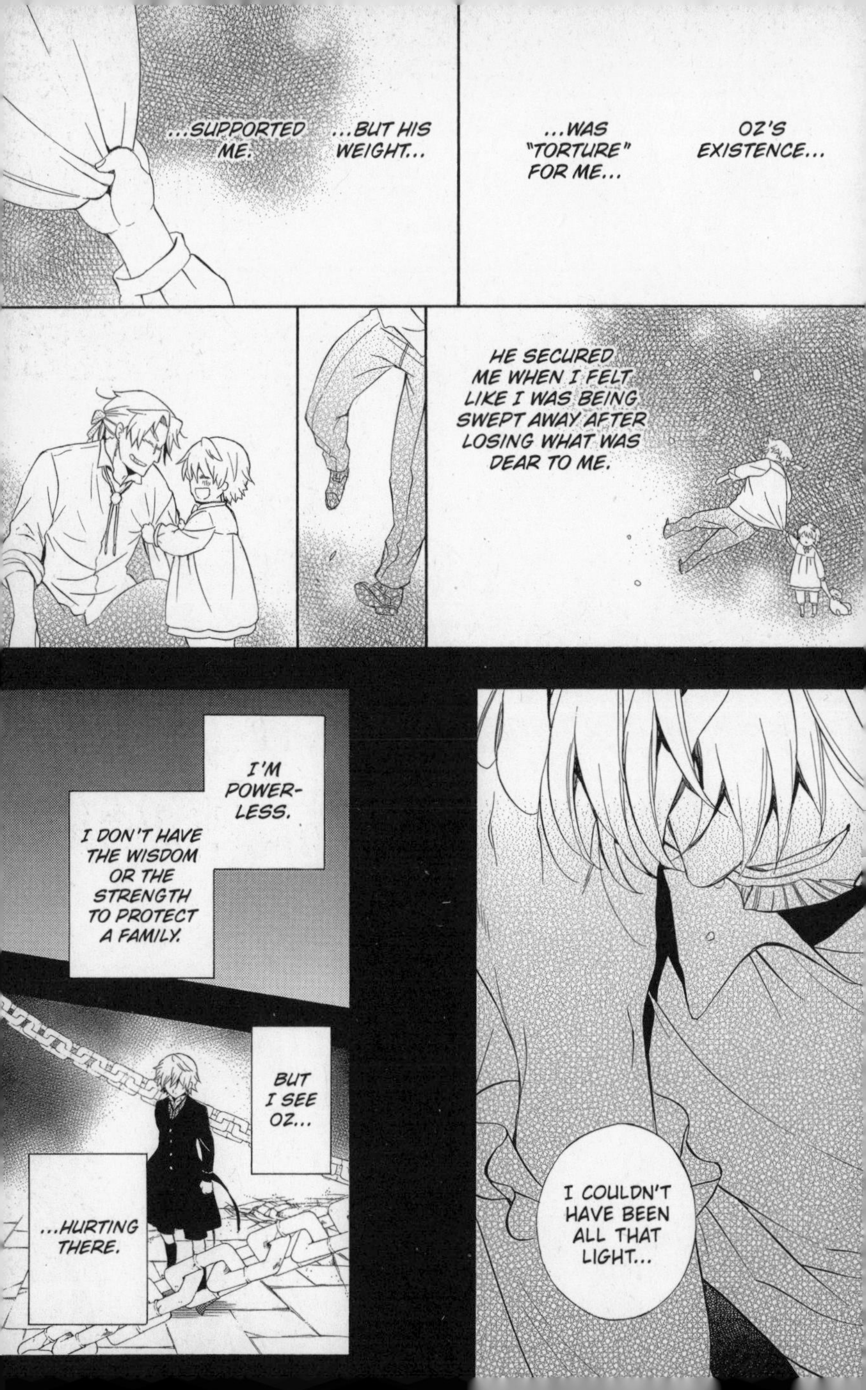
OZ'S EXISTENCE...
...WAS "TORTURE" FOR ME...
...BUT HIS WEIGHT...
...SUPPORTED ME.
HE SECURED ME WHEN I FELT LIKE I WAS BEING SWEPT AWAY AFTER LOSING WHAT WAS DEAR TO ME.
I COULDN'T HAVE BEEN ALL THAT LIGHT...
I'M POWER-LESS.
I DON'T HAVE THE WISDOM OR THE STRENGTH TO PROTECT A FAMILY.
BUT I SEE OZ...
...HURTING THERE.

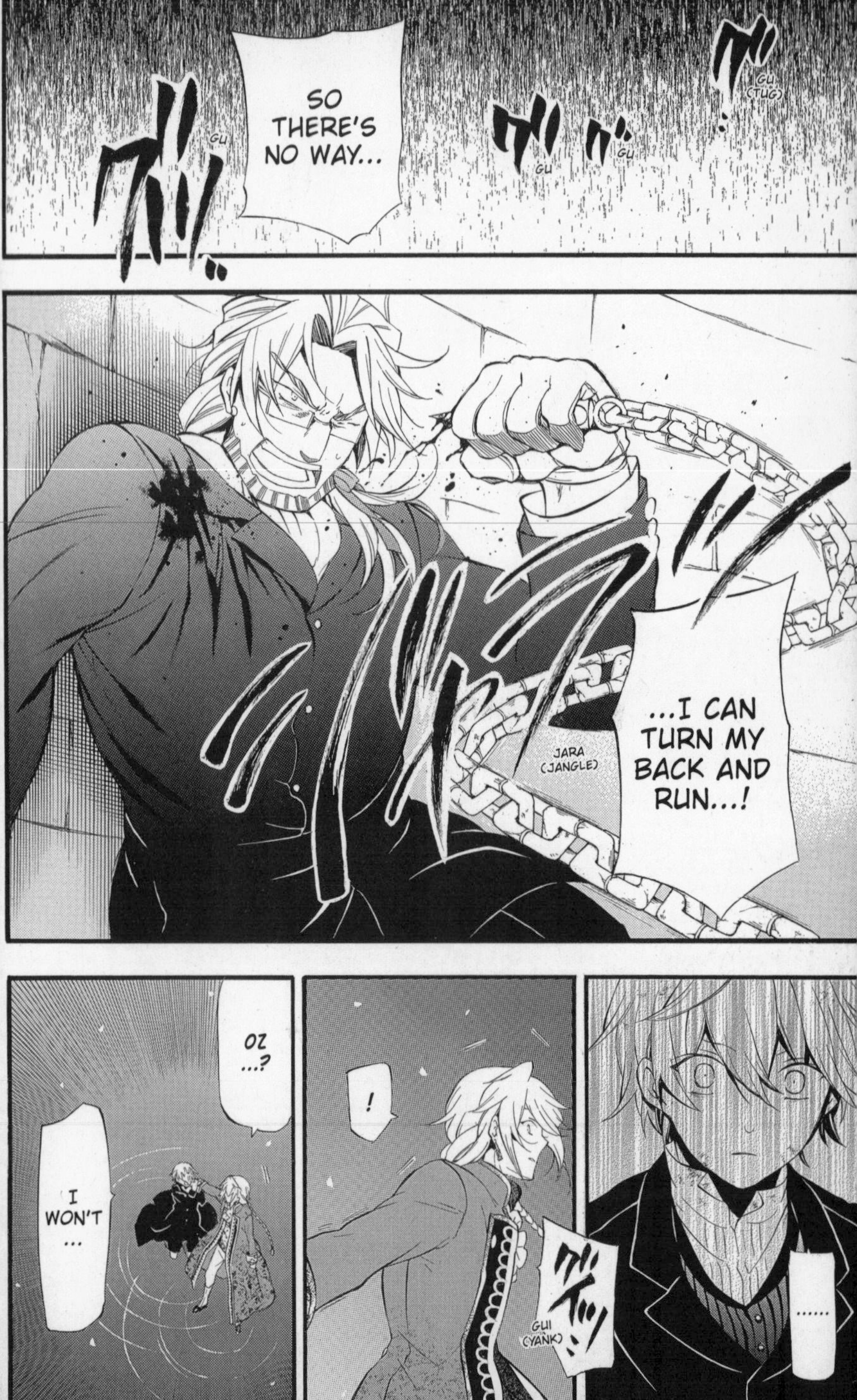
GU (TUG)
GU
GU
SO THERE'S NO WAY...
GU
...I CAN TURN MY BACK AND RUN...!
JARA (JANGLE)
......
!
GUI (YANK)
OZ ...?
I WON'T ...

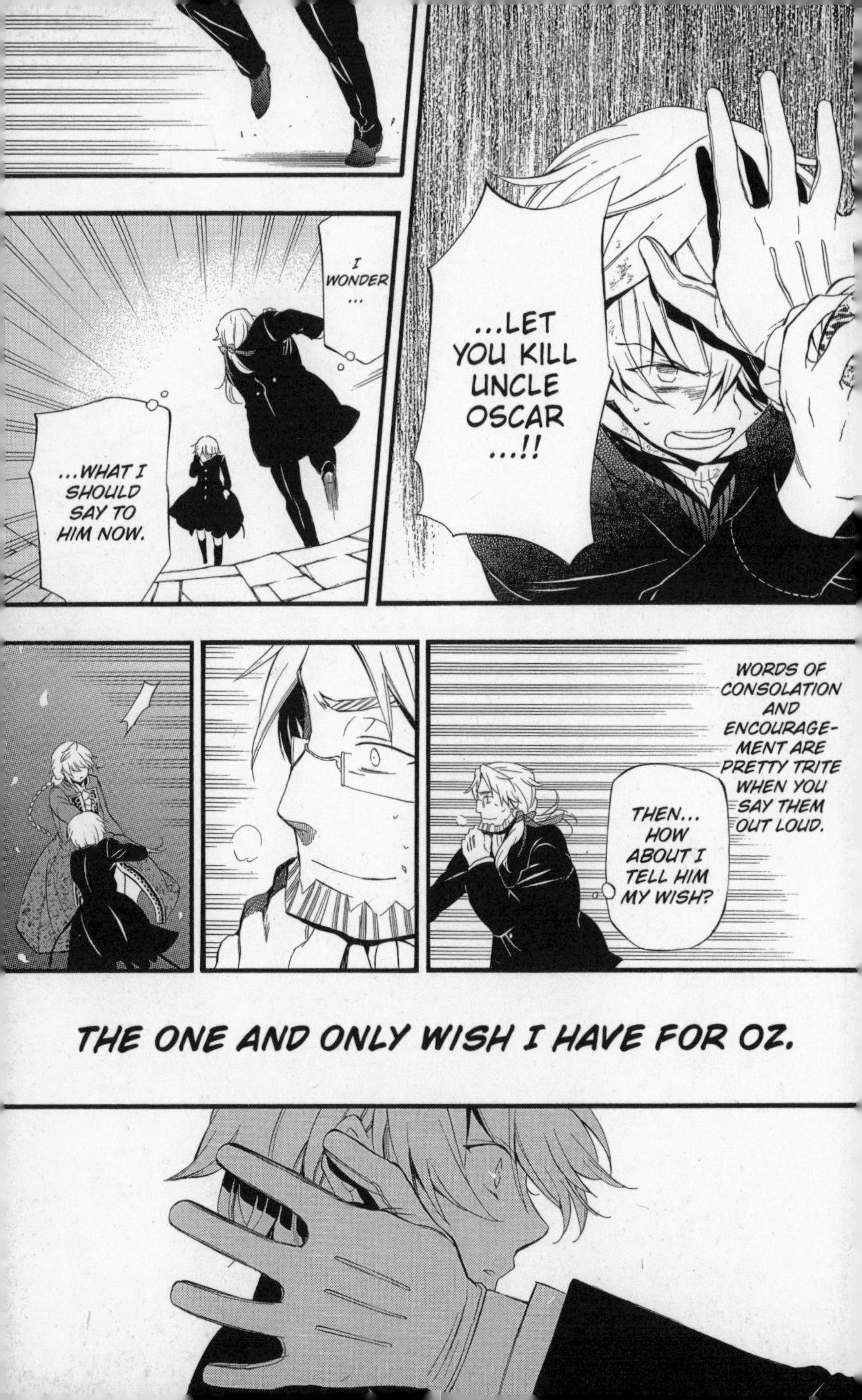
...LET YOU KILL UNCLE OSCAR...!!
I WONDER...
...WHAT I SHOULD SAY TO HIM NOW.
WORDS OF CONSOLATION AND ENCOURAGE-MENT ARE PRETTY TRITE WHEN YOU SAY THEM OUT LOUD.
THEN... HOW ABOUT I TELL HIM MY WISH?
THE ONE AND ONLY WISH I HAVE FOR OZ.

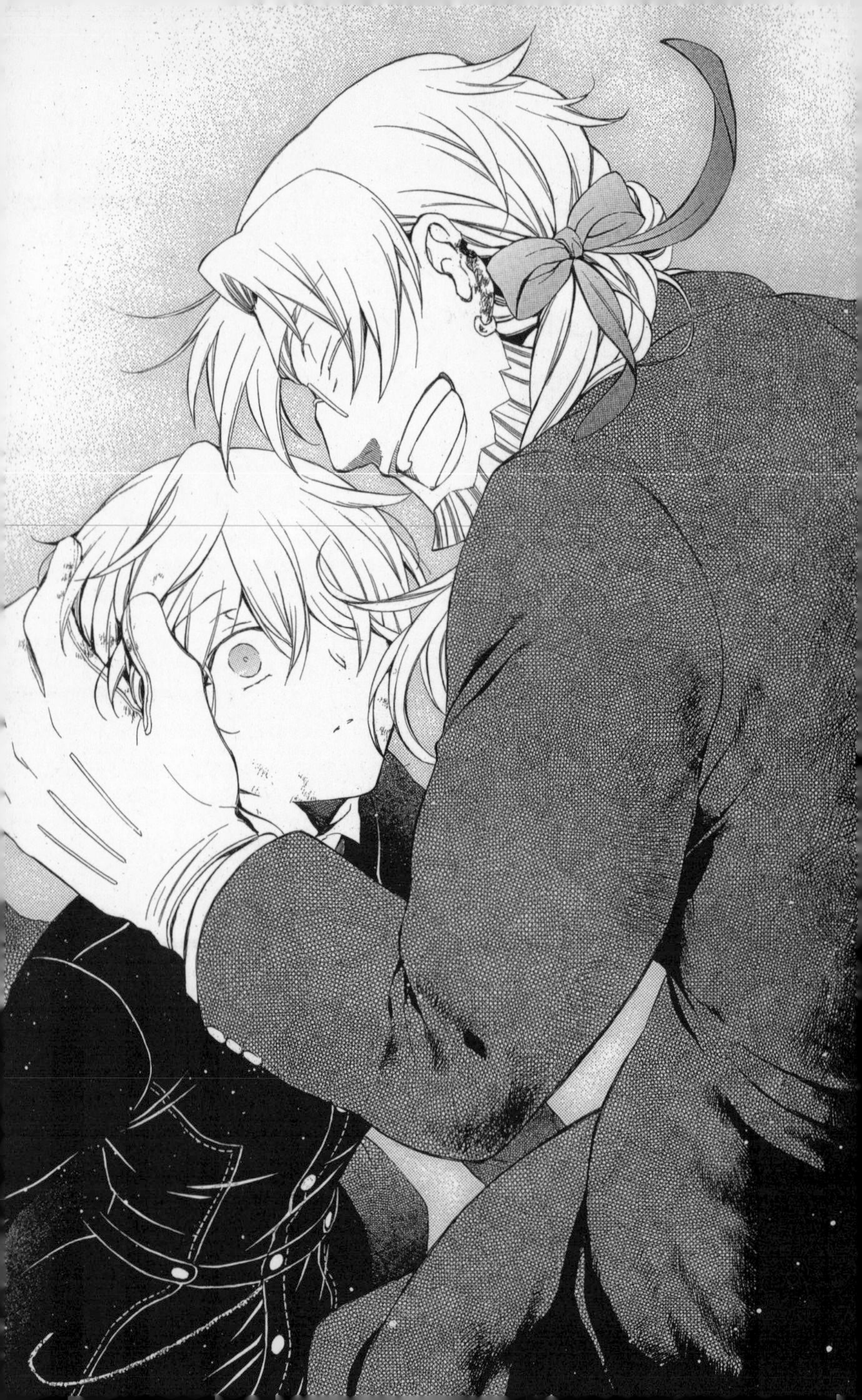

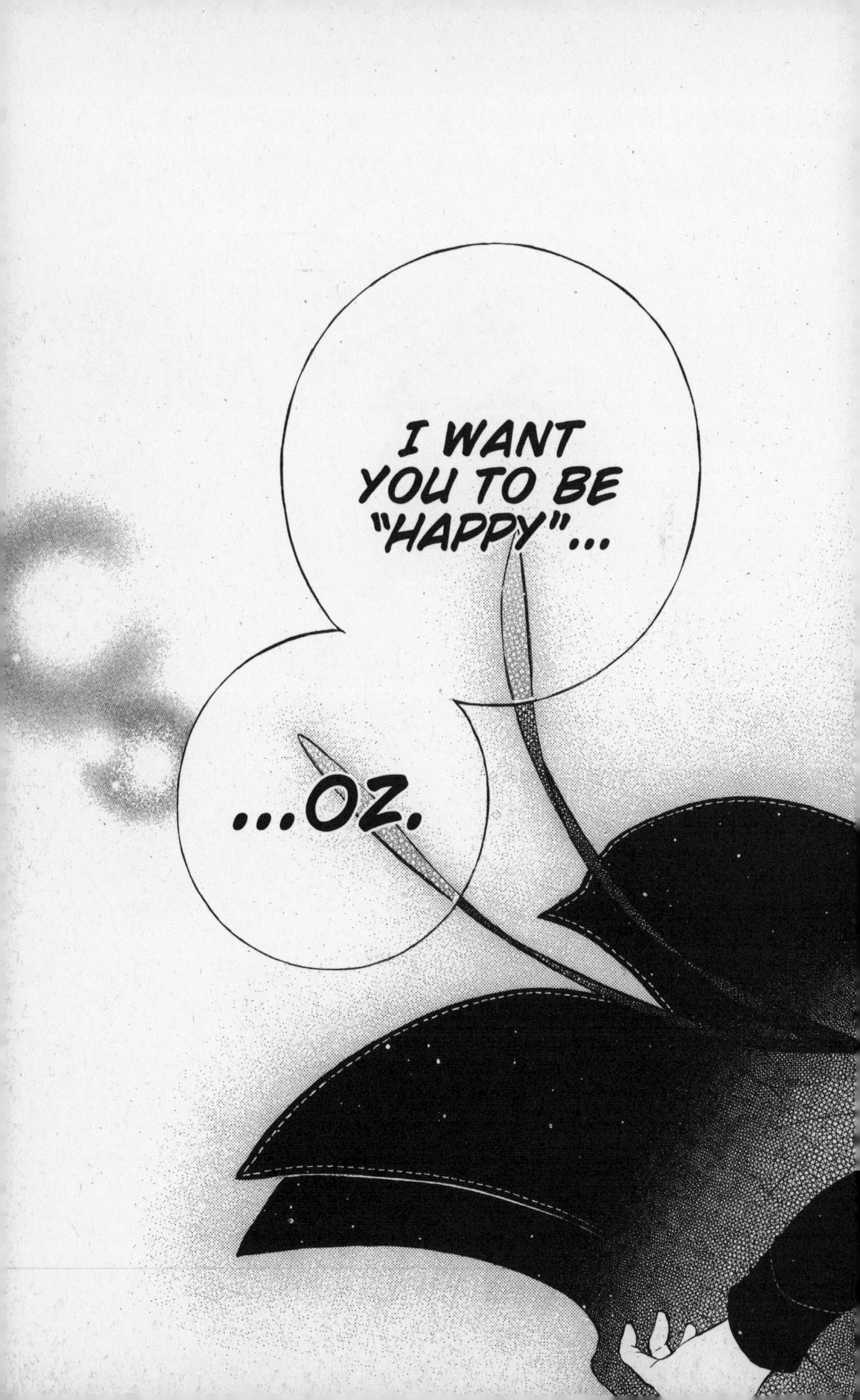
I WANT YOU TO BE "HAPPY"...
...OZ.

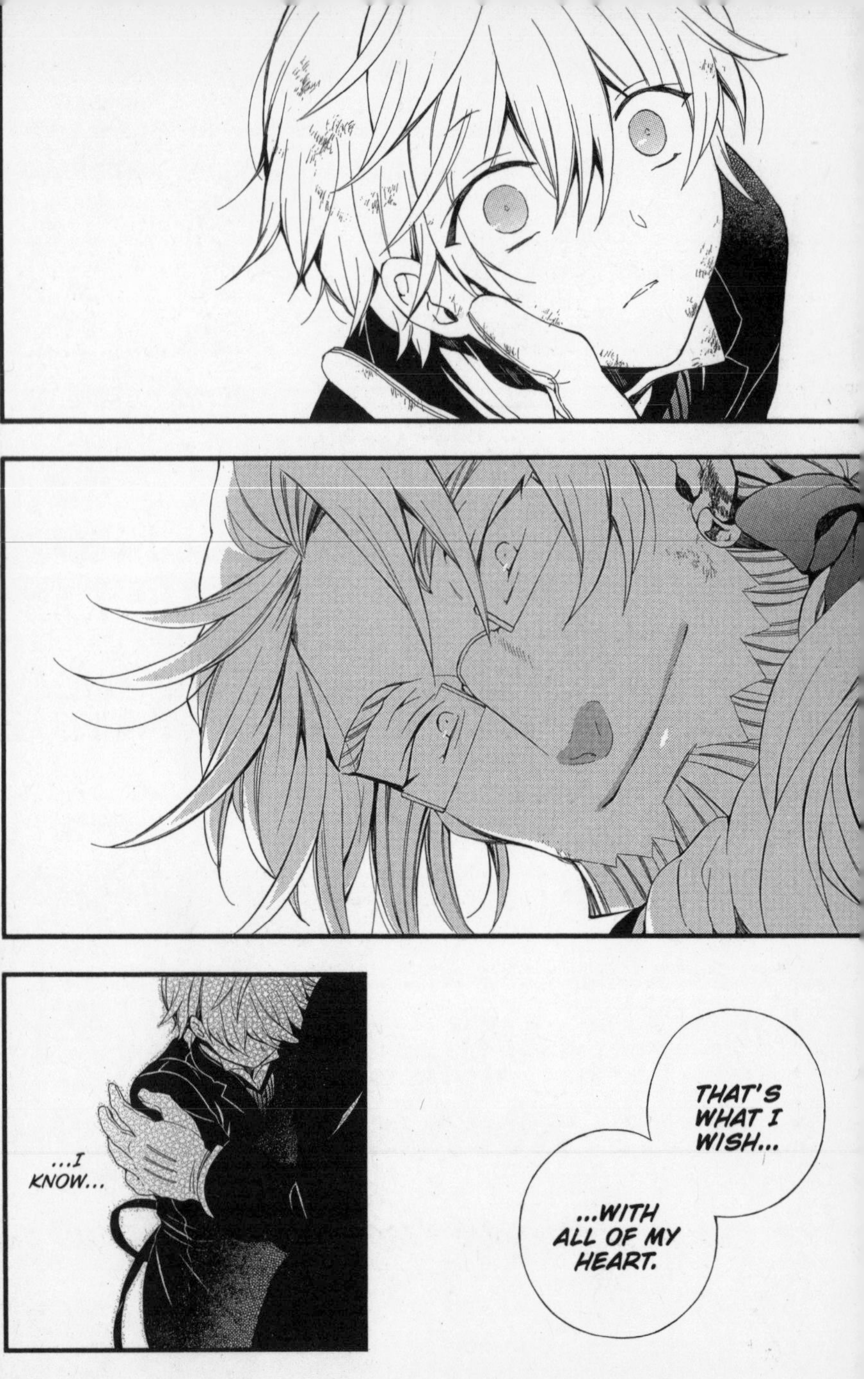
THAT'S WHAT I WISH...
...WITH ALL OF MY HEART.
...I KNOW...

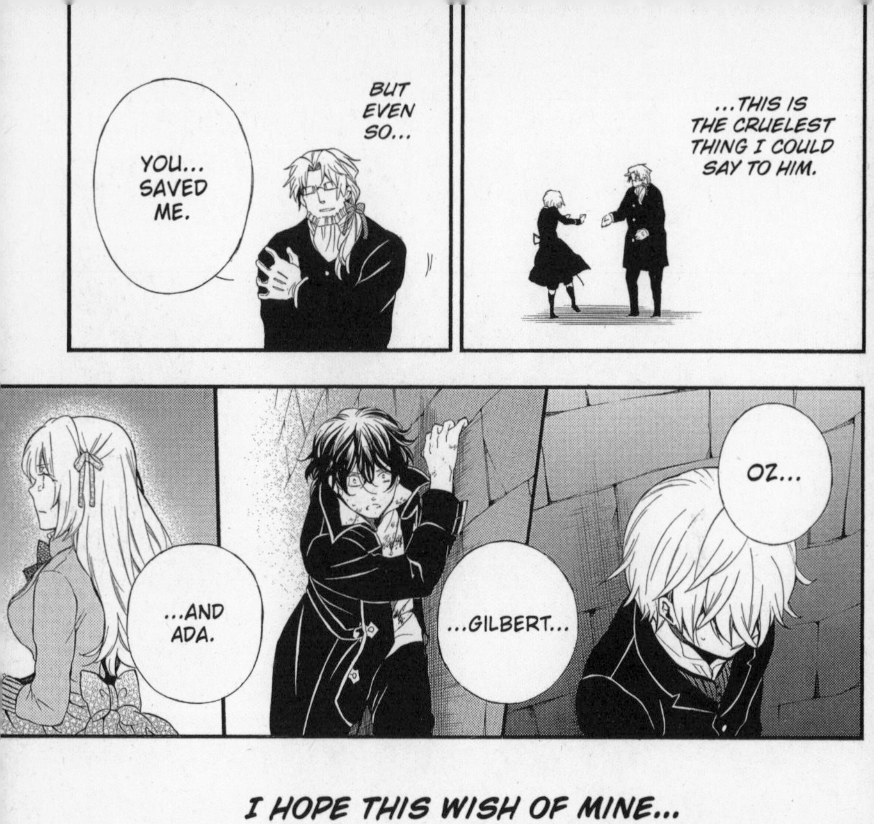
...THIS IS THE CRUELEST THING I COULD SAY TO HIM.
BUT EVEN SO...
YOU... SAVED ME.
OZ...
...GILBERT...
...AND ADA.

I HOPE THIS WISH OF MINE...

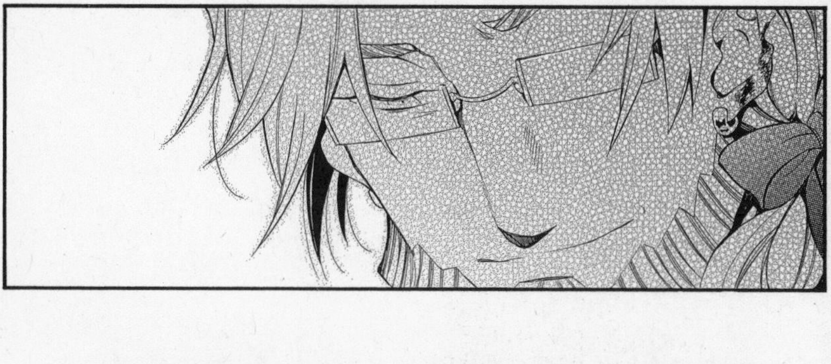

...DOES NOT BECOME A "CURSE" THAT BINDS YOU.

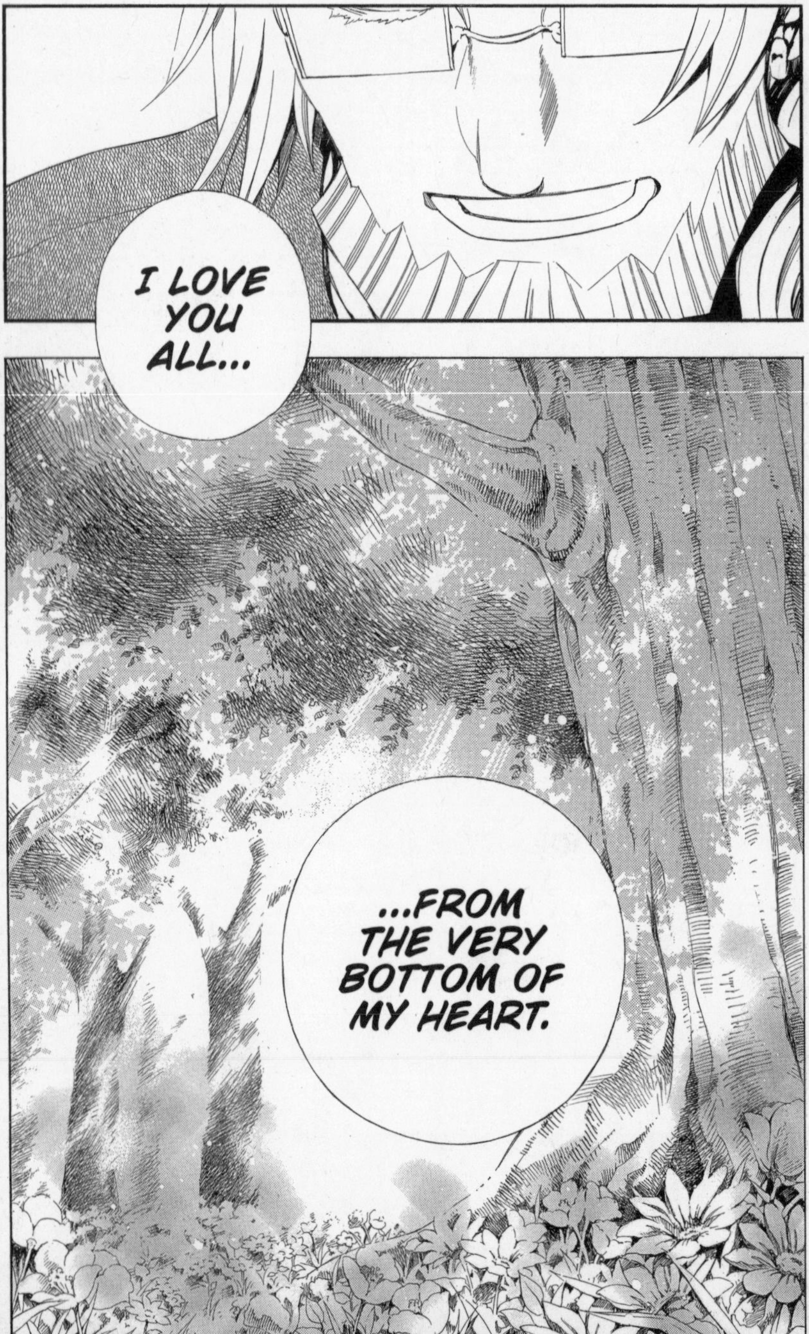
I LOVE YOU ALL...
...FROM THE VERY BOTTOM OF MY HEART.

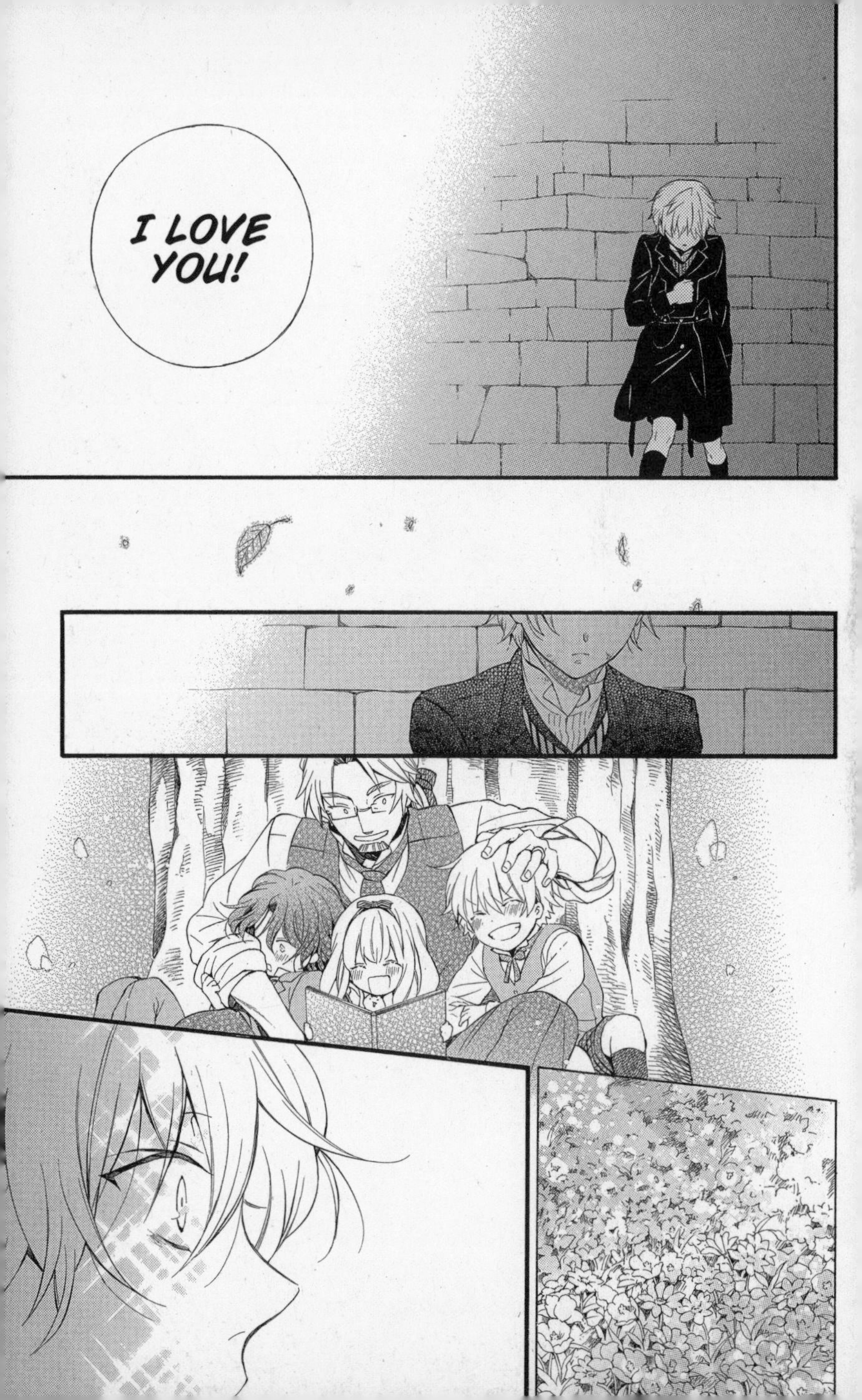
I LOVE YOU!

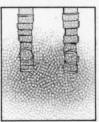

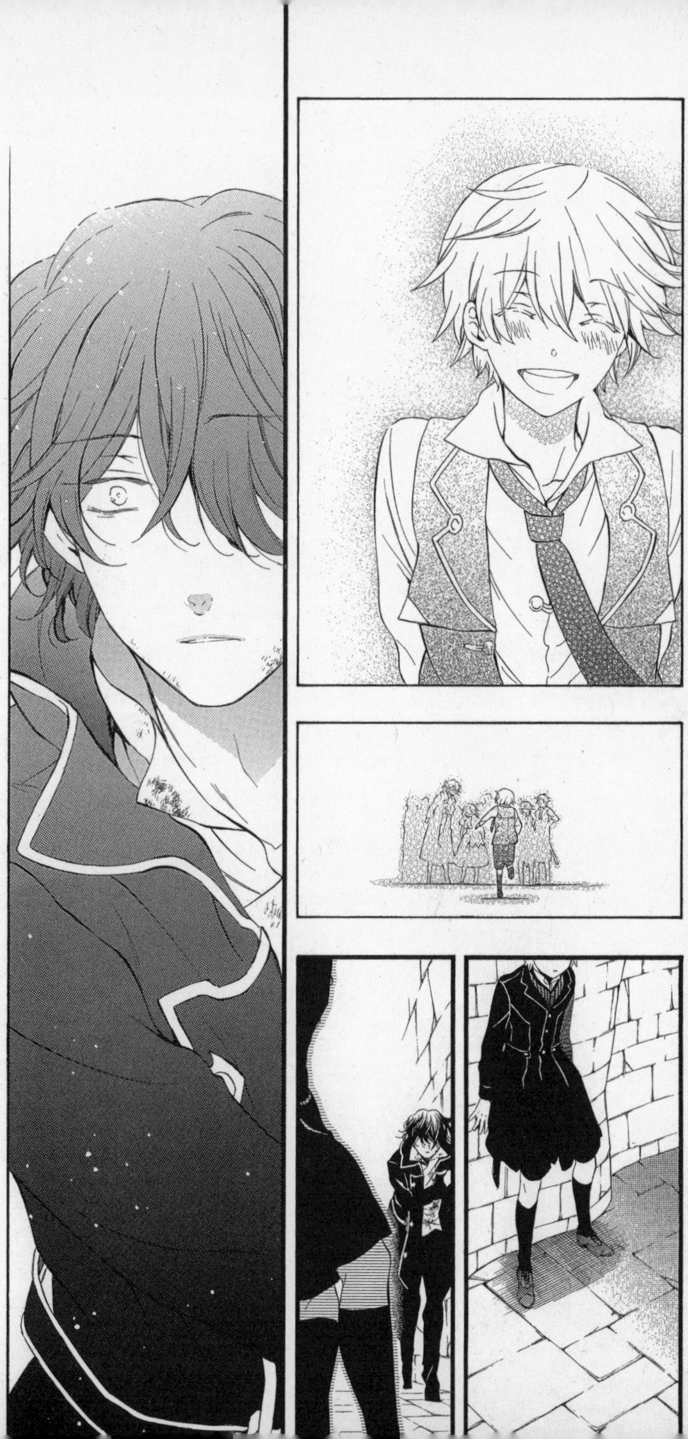

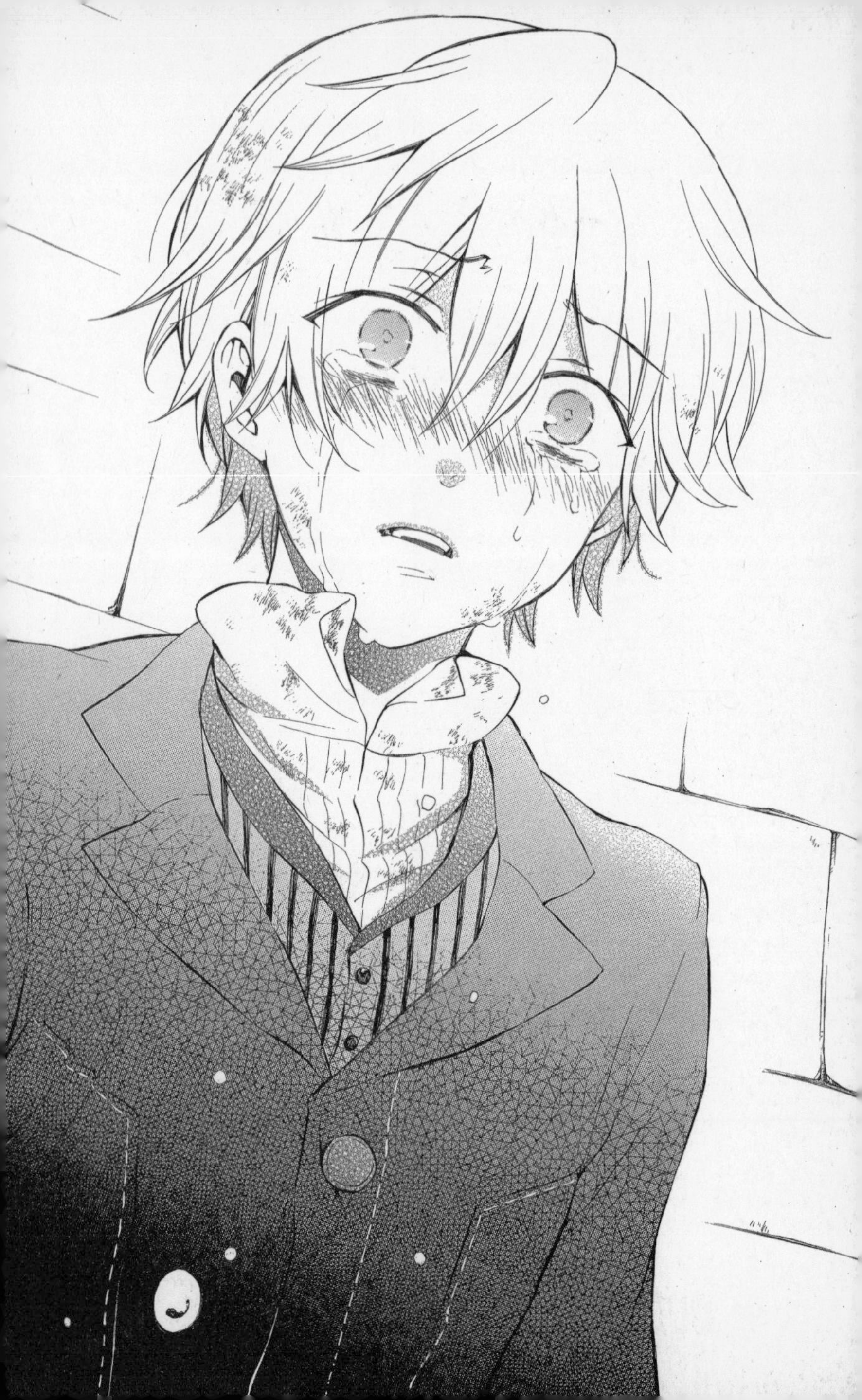

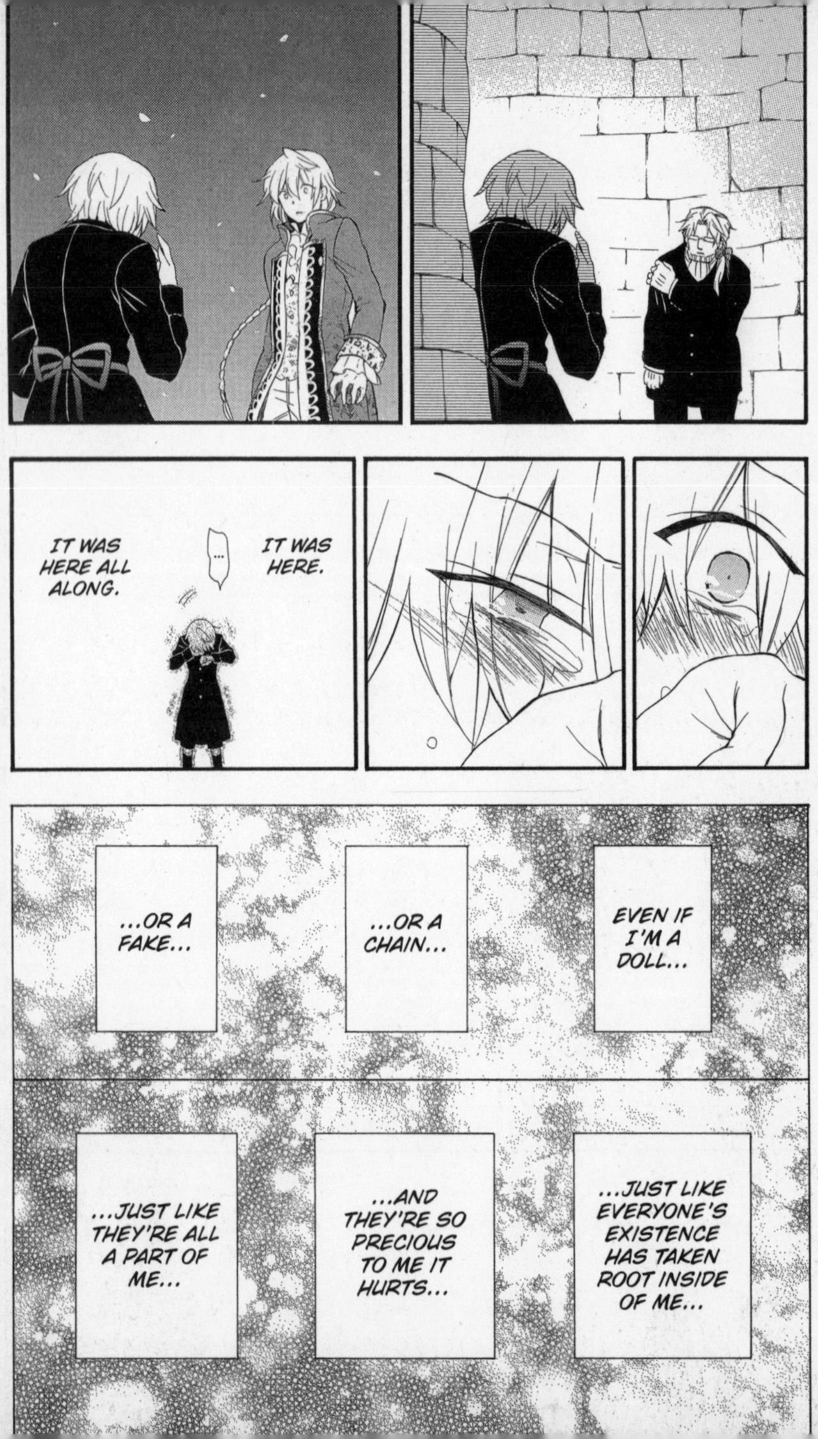
IT WAS HERE.
...
IT WAS HERE ALL ALONG.
EVEN IF I'M A DOLL...
...OR A CHAIN...
...OR A FAKE...
...JUST LIKE EVERYONE'S EXISTENCE HAS TAKEN ROOT INSIDE OF ME...
...AND THEY'RE SO PRECIOUS TO ME IT HURTS...
...JUST LIKE THEY'RE ALL A PART OF ME...

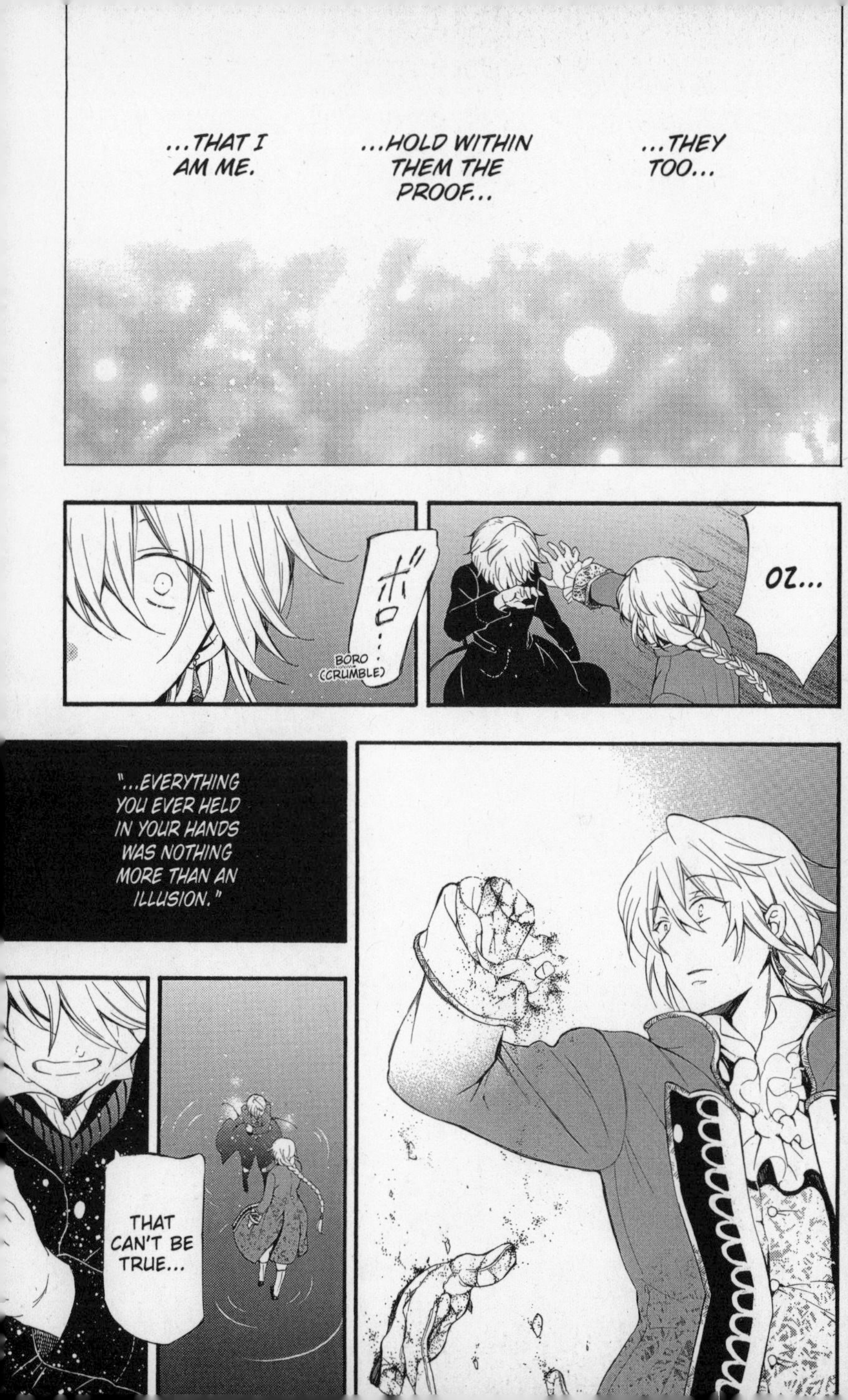
...THEY TOO...
...HOLD WITHIN THEM THE PROOF...
...THAT I AM ME.
OZ...
ボロ…
BORO (CRUMBLE)
"...EVERYTHING YOU EVER HELD IN YOUR HANDS WAS NOTHING MORE THAN AN ILLUSION."
THAT CAN'T BE TRUE...

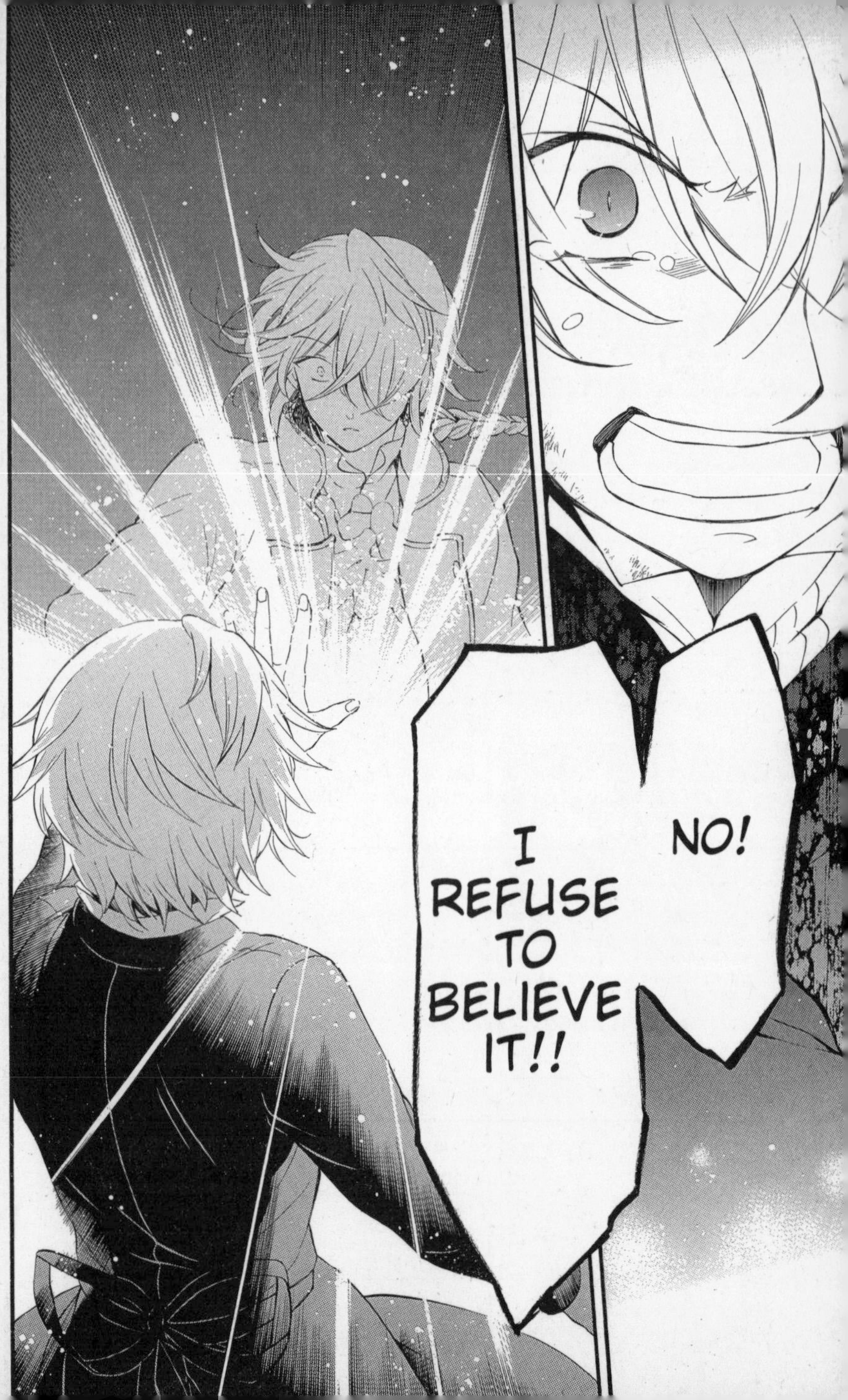
NO!
I REFUSE TO BELIEVE IT!!

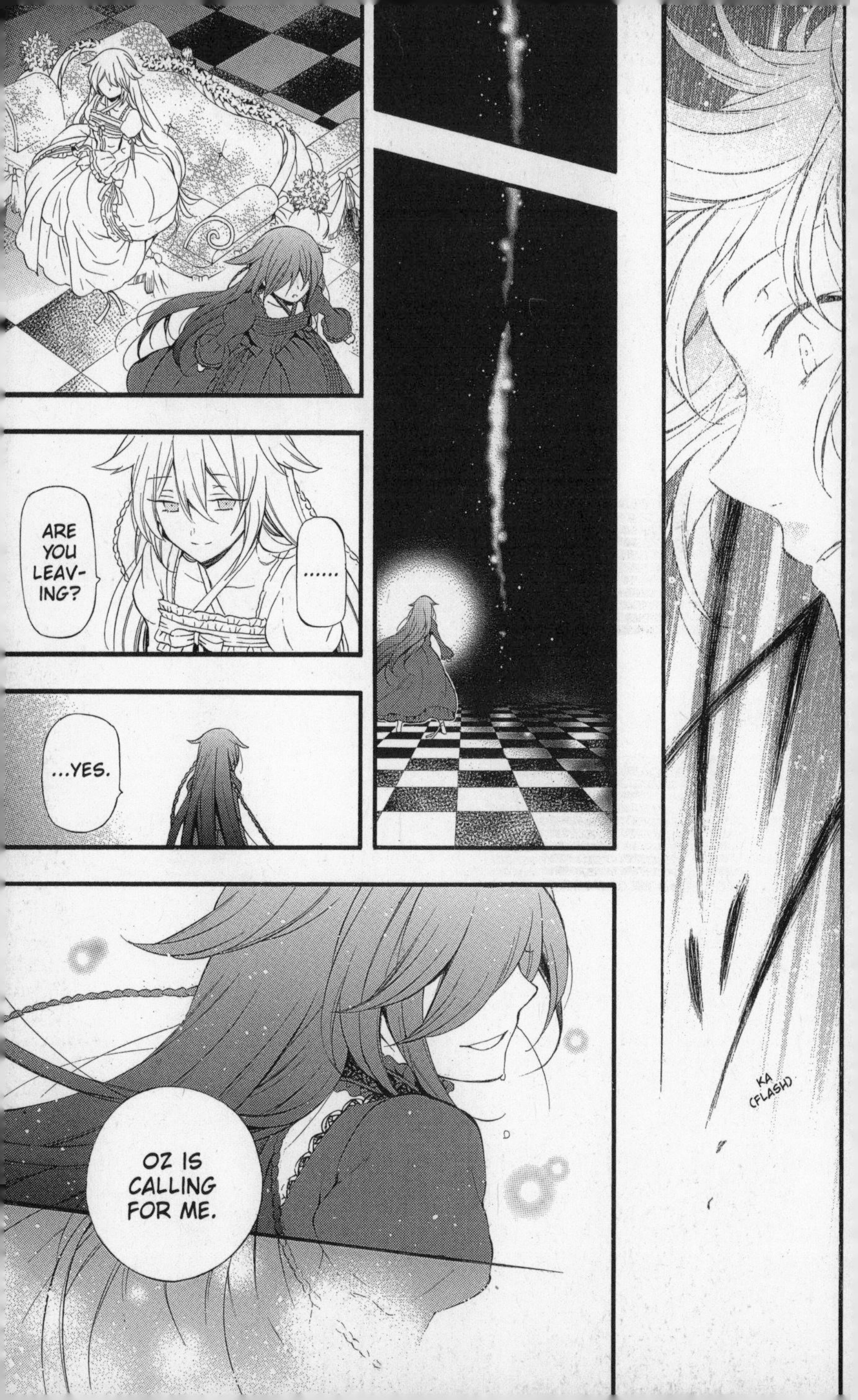
KA (FLASH)
ARE YOU LEAV-ING?
......
...YES.
OZ IS CALLING FOR ME.

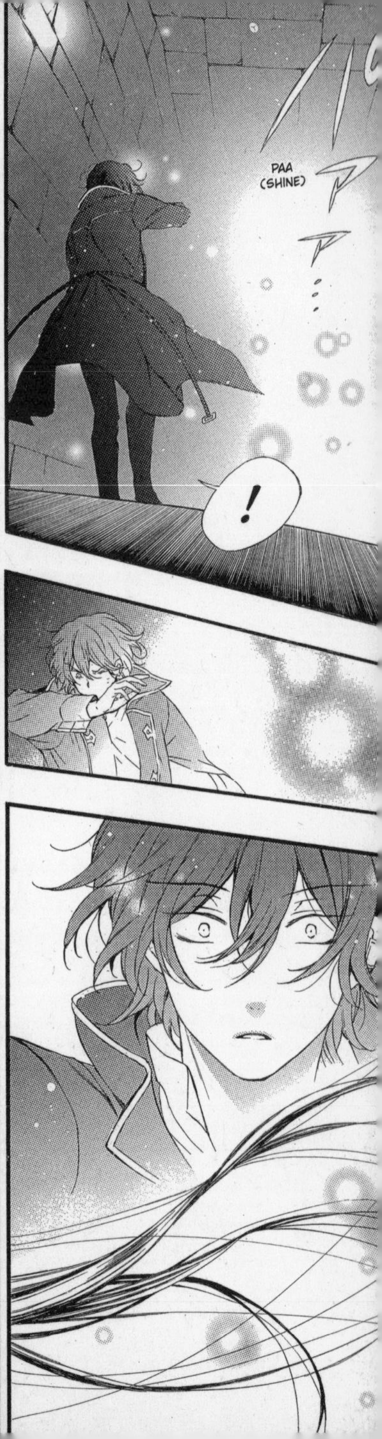
PAA
(SHINE)
!
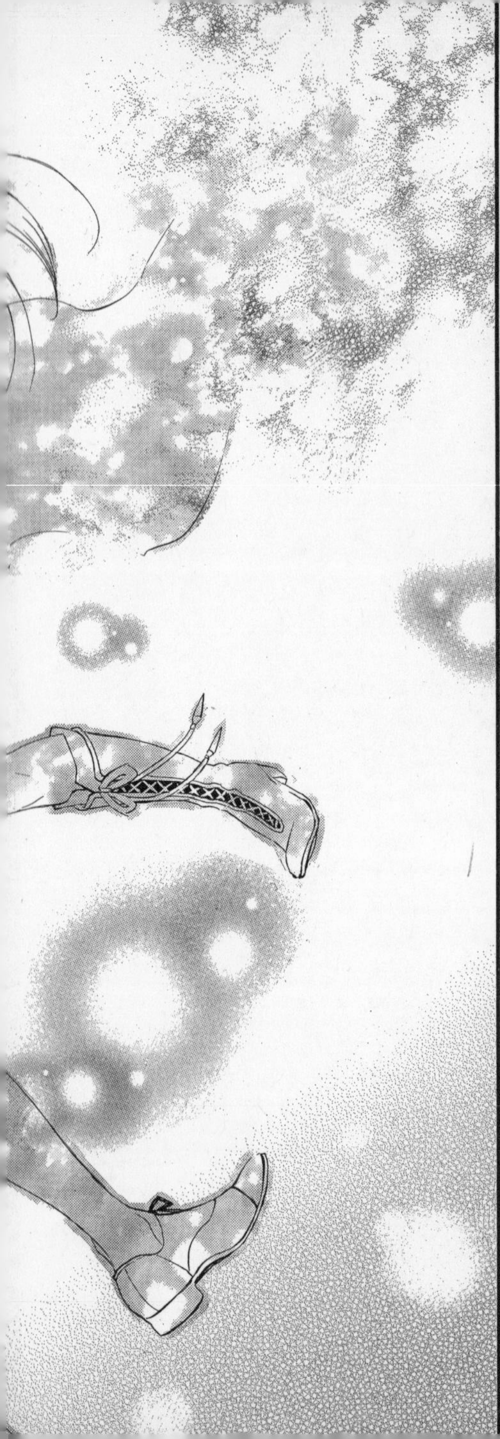

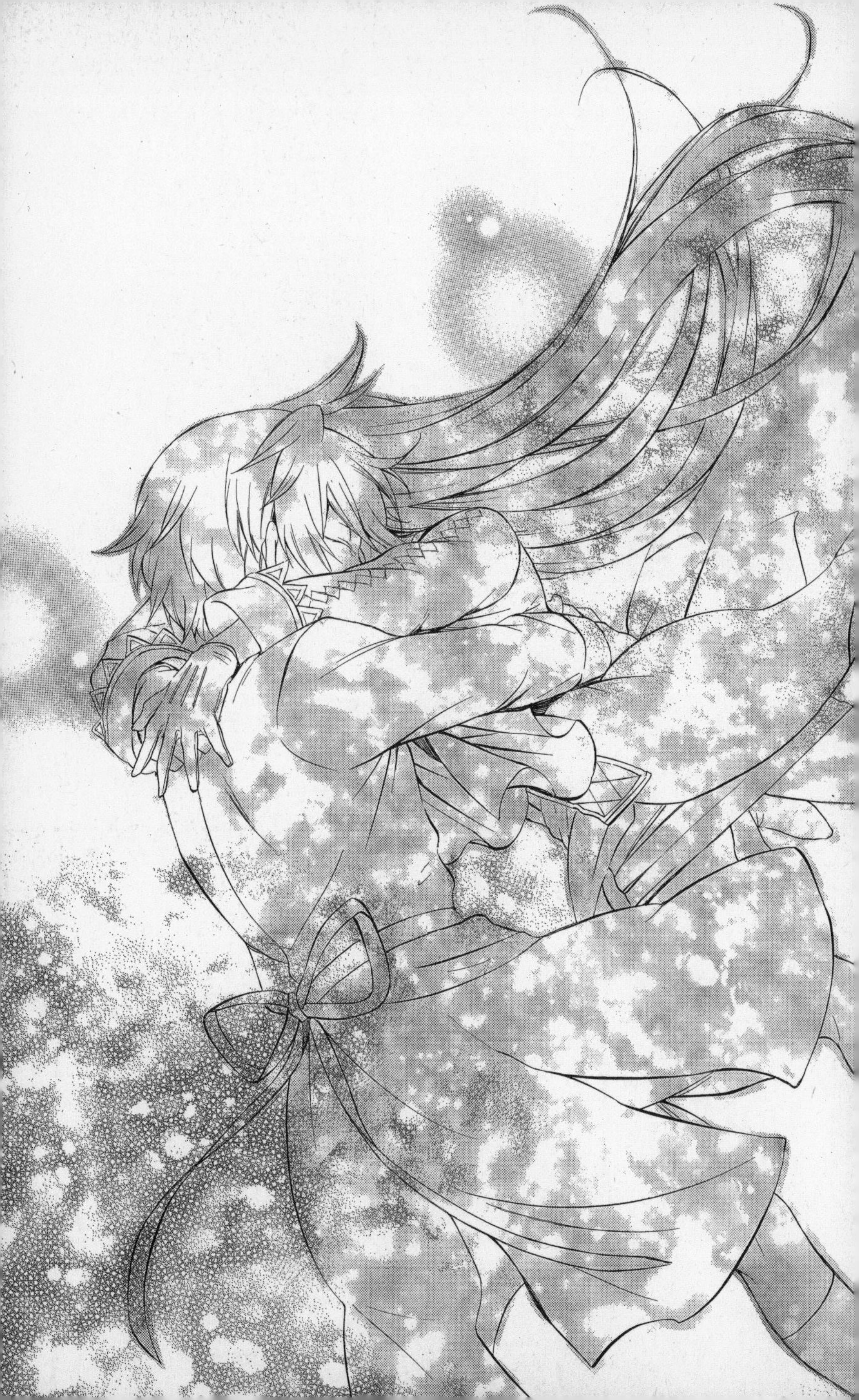

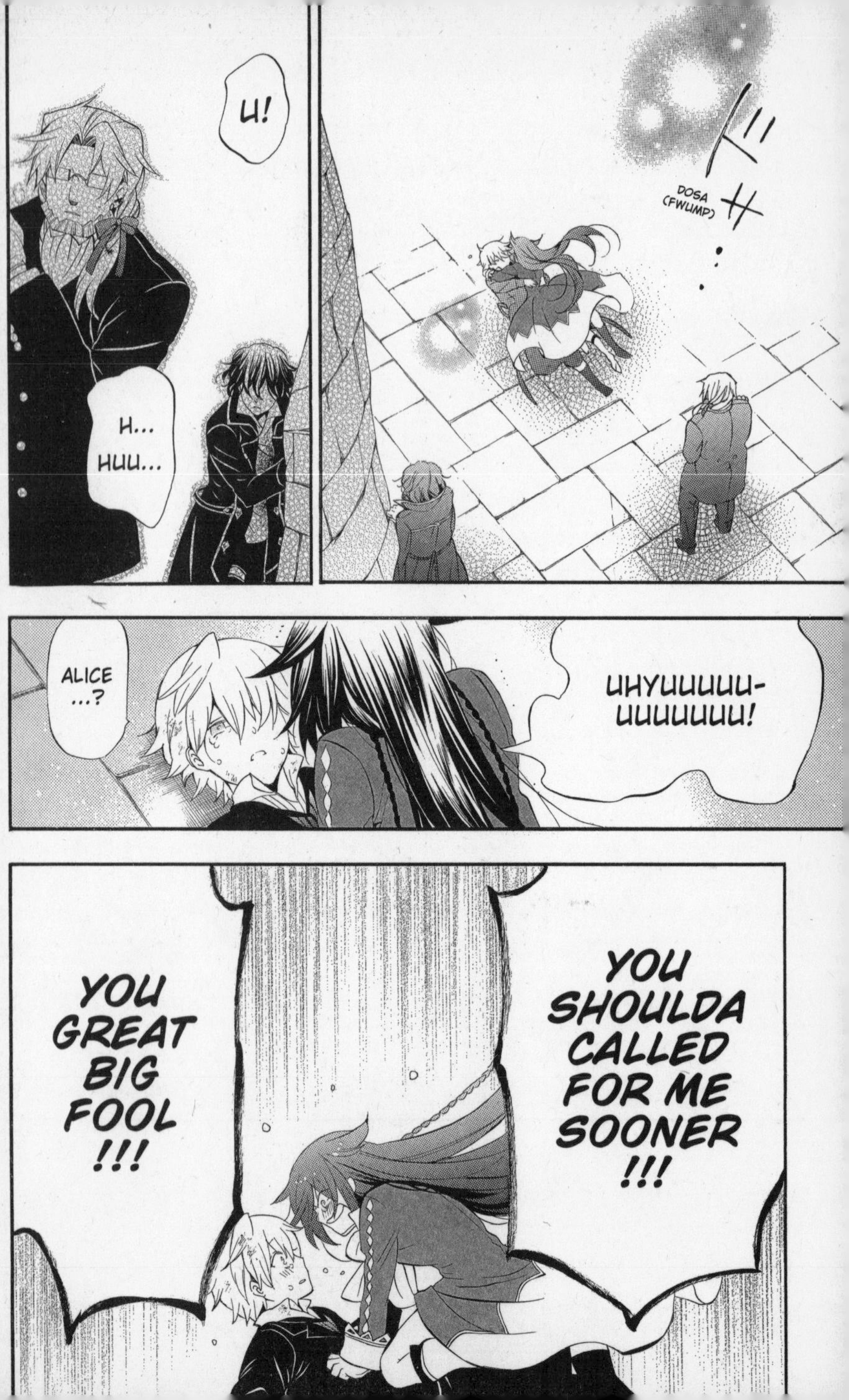
DOSA (FWUMP)
U!
H... HUU...
UHYUUUUU-UUUUUUU!
ALICE ...?
YOU SHOULDA CALLED FOR ME SOONER !!!
YOU GREAT BIG FOOL !!!

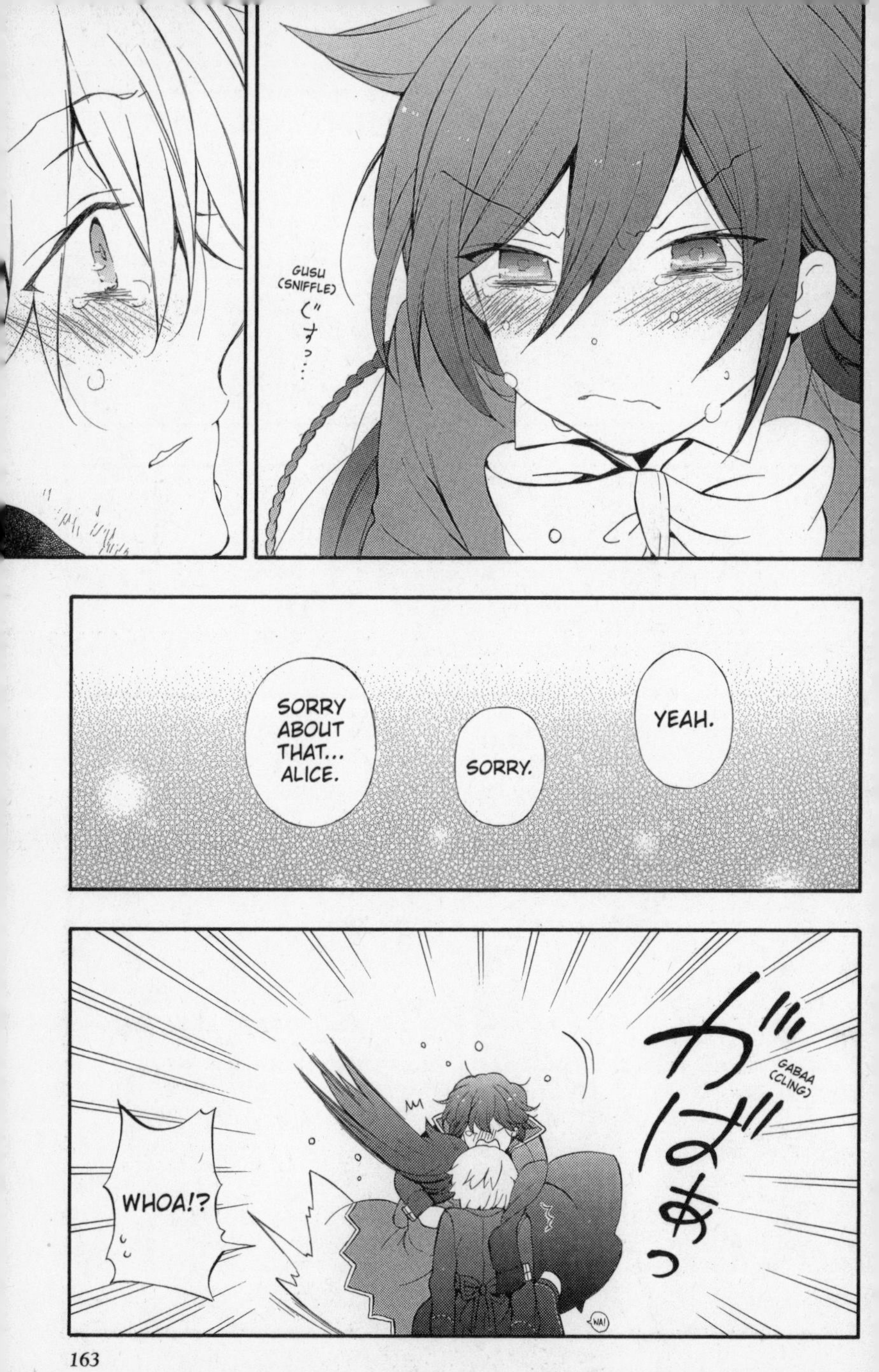
GUSU (SNIFFLE)
ぐすっ…
YEAH.
SORRY.
SORRY ABOUT THAT… ALICE.
がばぁっ
GABAA (CLING)
WA!
WHOA!?

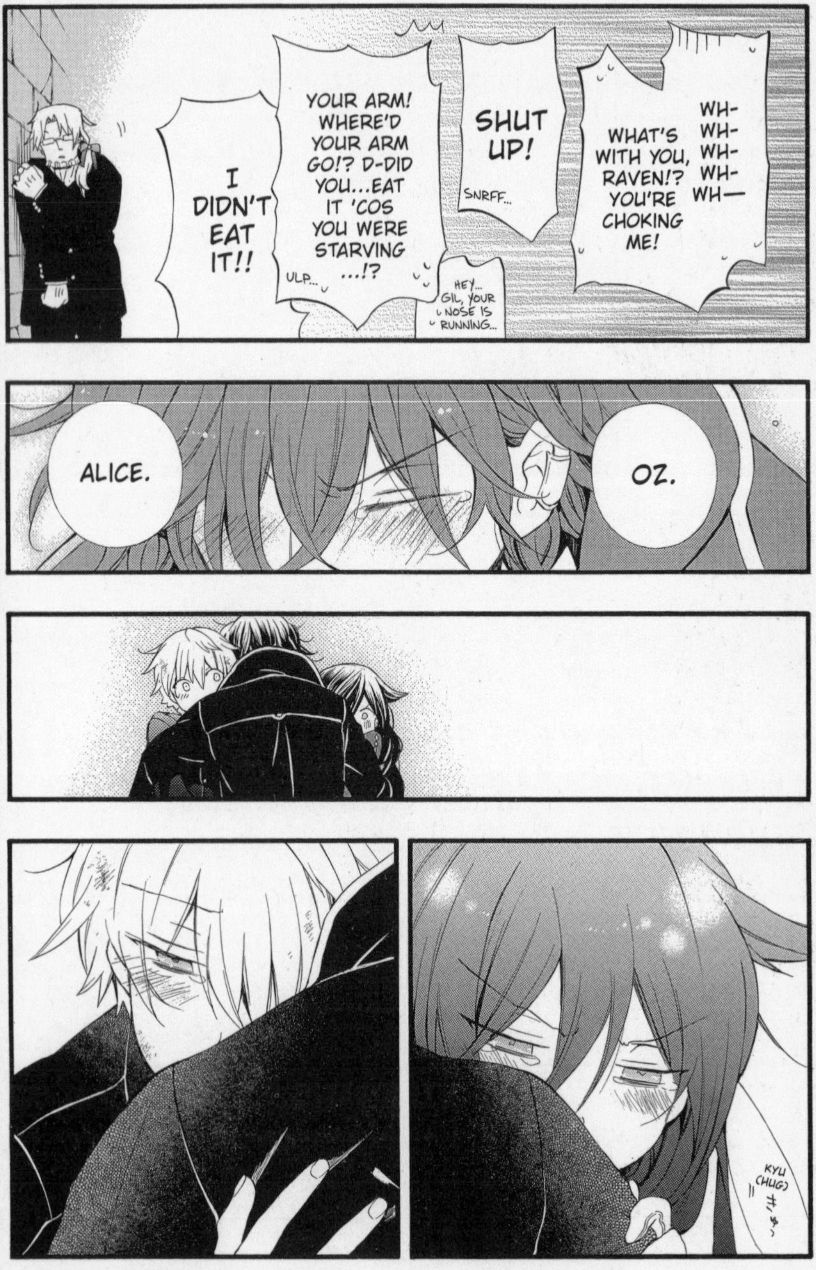
WH- WH- WH- WH- WH—
WHAT'S WITH YOU, RAVEN!? YOU'RE CHOKING ME!
SHUT UP!
SNRFF...
HEY... GIL, YOUR NOSE IS RUNNING...
YOUR ARM! WHERE'D YOUR ARM GO!? D-DID YOU...EAT IT 'COS YOU WERE STARVING ...!?
ULP...
I DIDN'T EAT IT!!
OZ.
ALICE.
KYU (HUG)

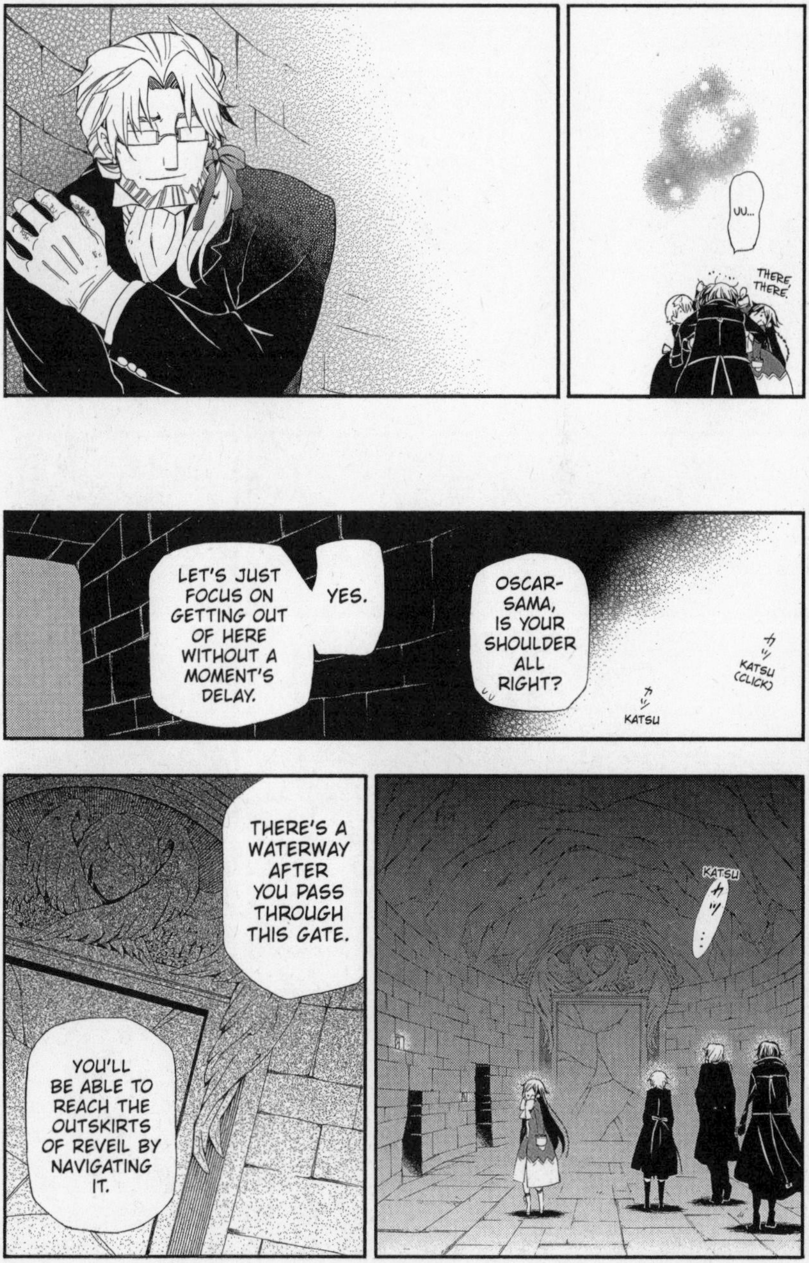
UU...
THERE, THERE.
KATSU (CLICK)
KATSU
OSCAR-SAMA, IS YOUR SHOULDER ALL RIGHT?
YES.
LET'S JUST FOCUS ON GETTING OUT OF HERE WITHOUT A MOMENT'S DELAY.
KATSU
THERE'S A WATERWAY AFTER YOU PASS THROUGH THIS GATE.
YOU'LL BE ABLE TO REACH THE OUTSKIRTS OF REVEIL BY NAVIGATING IT.

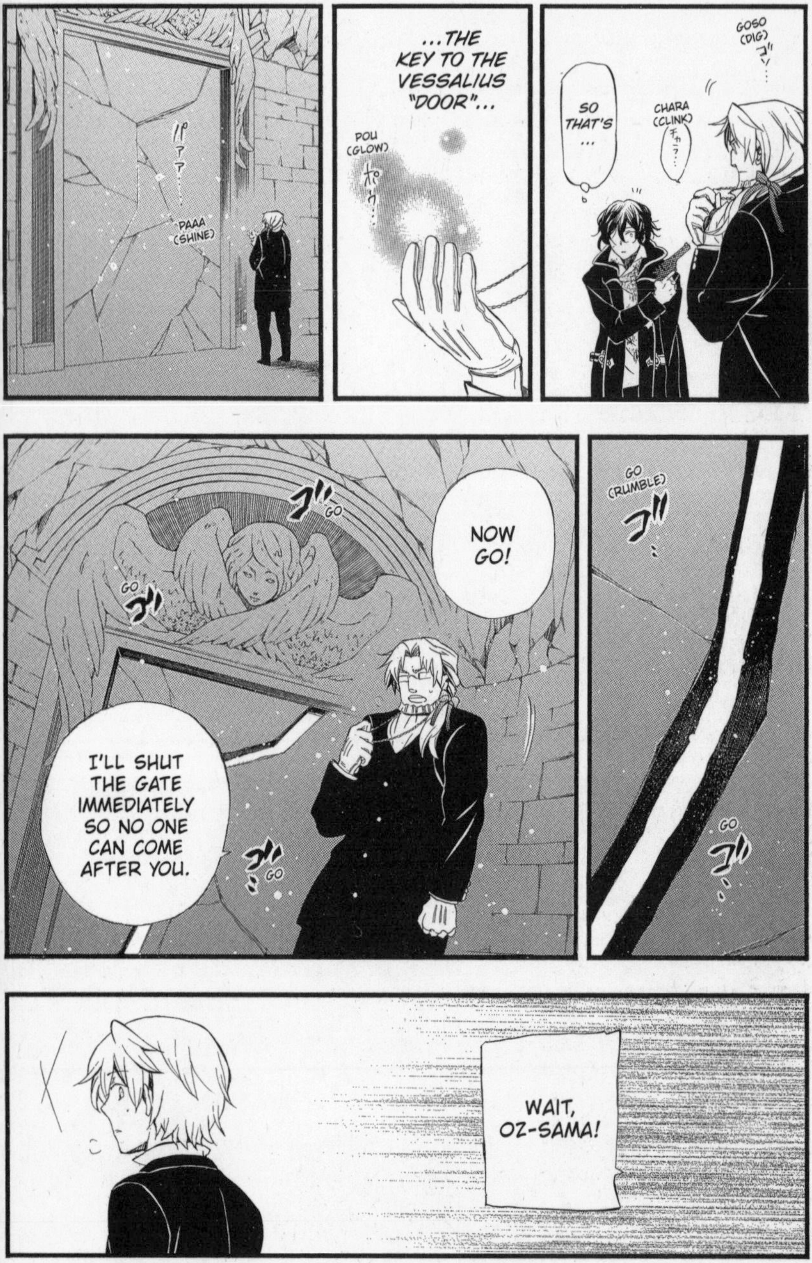
GOSO (DIG)
SO THAT'S ...
CHARA (CLINK)
...THE KEY TO THE VESSALIUS "DOOR"...
POU (GLOW)
PAAA (SHINE)
GO (RUMBLE)
GO
NOW GO!
GO
GO
I'LL SHUT THE GATE IMMEDIATELY SO NO ONE CAN COME AFTER YOU.
GO
WAIT, OZ-SAMA!

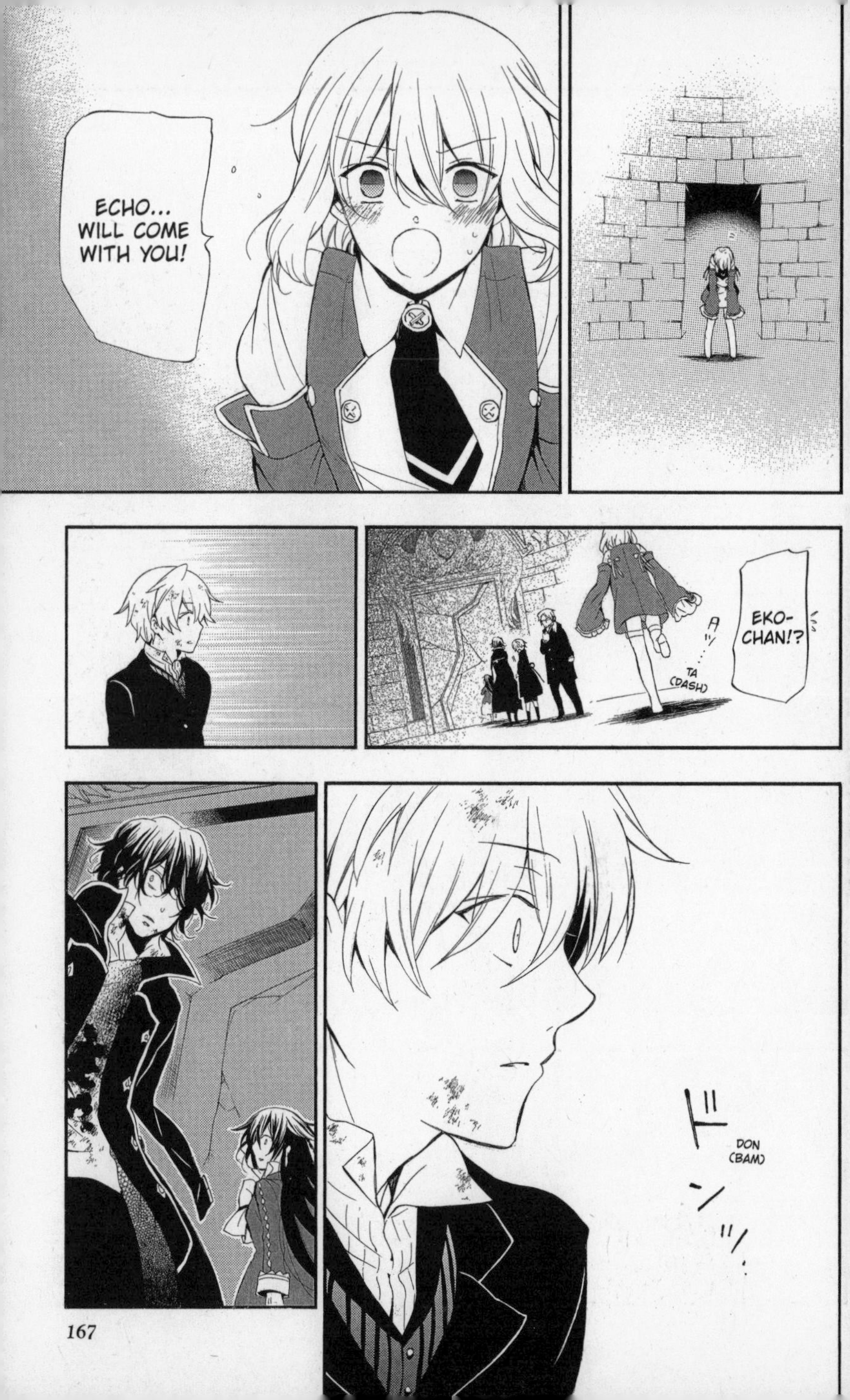
ECHO... WILL COME WITH YOU!
EKO-CHAN!?
A
TA (DASH)
DON (BAM)

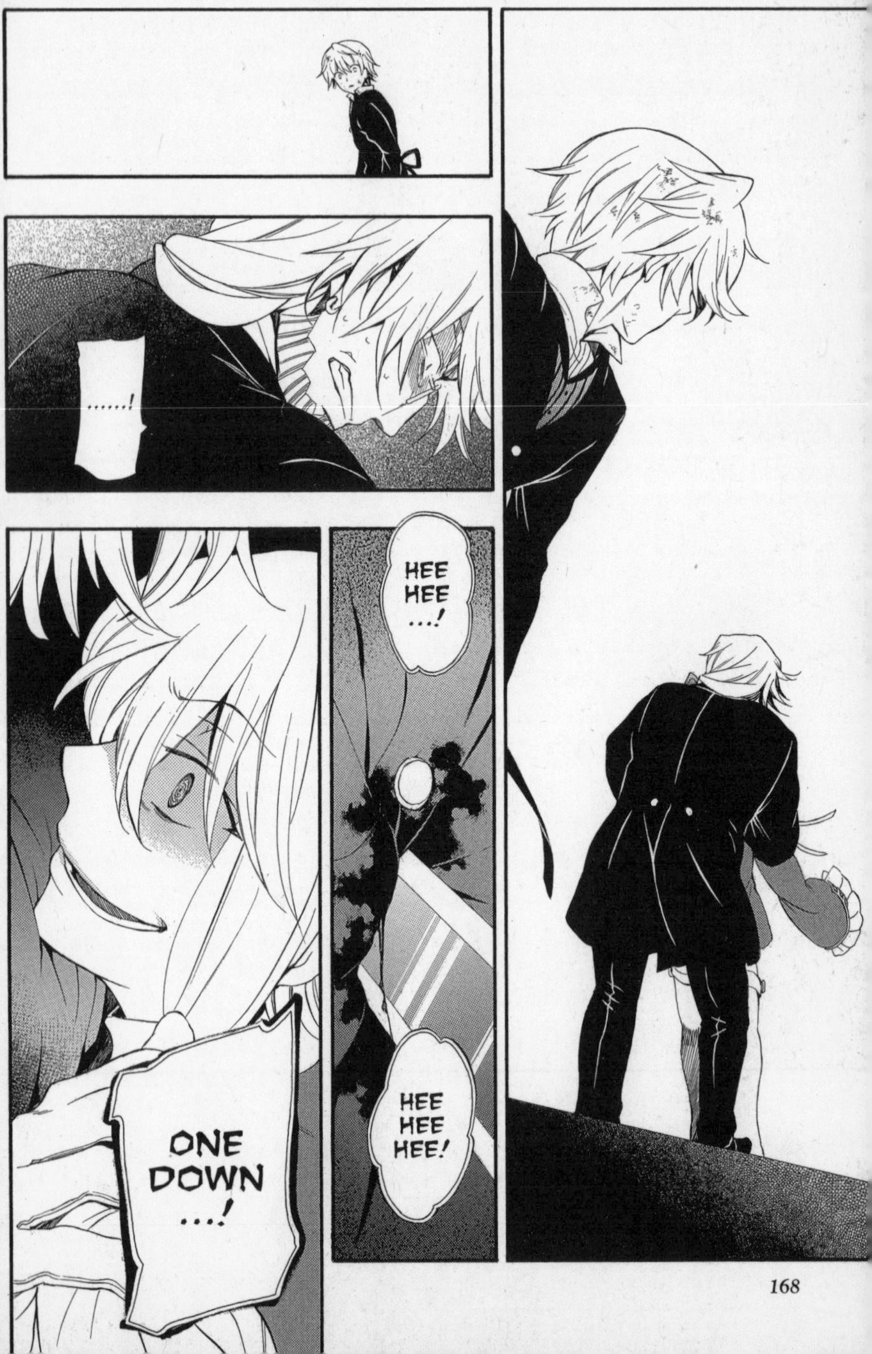
......!
HEE HEE ...!
HEE HEE HEE!
ONE DOWN ...!

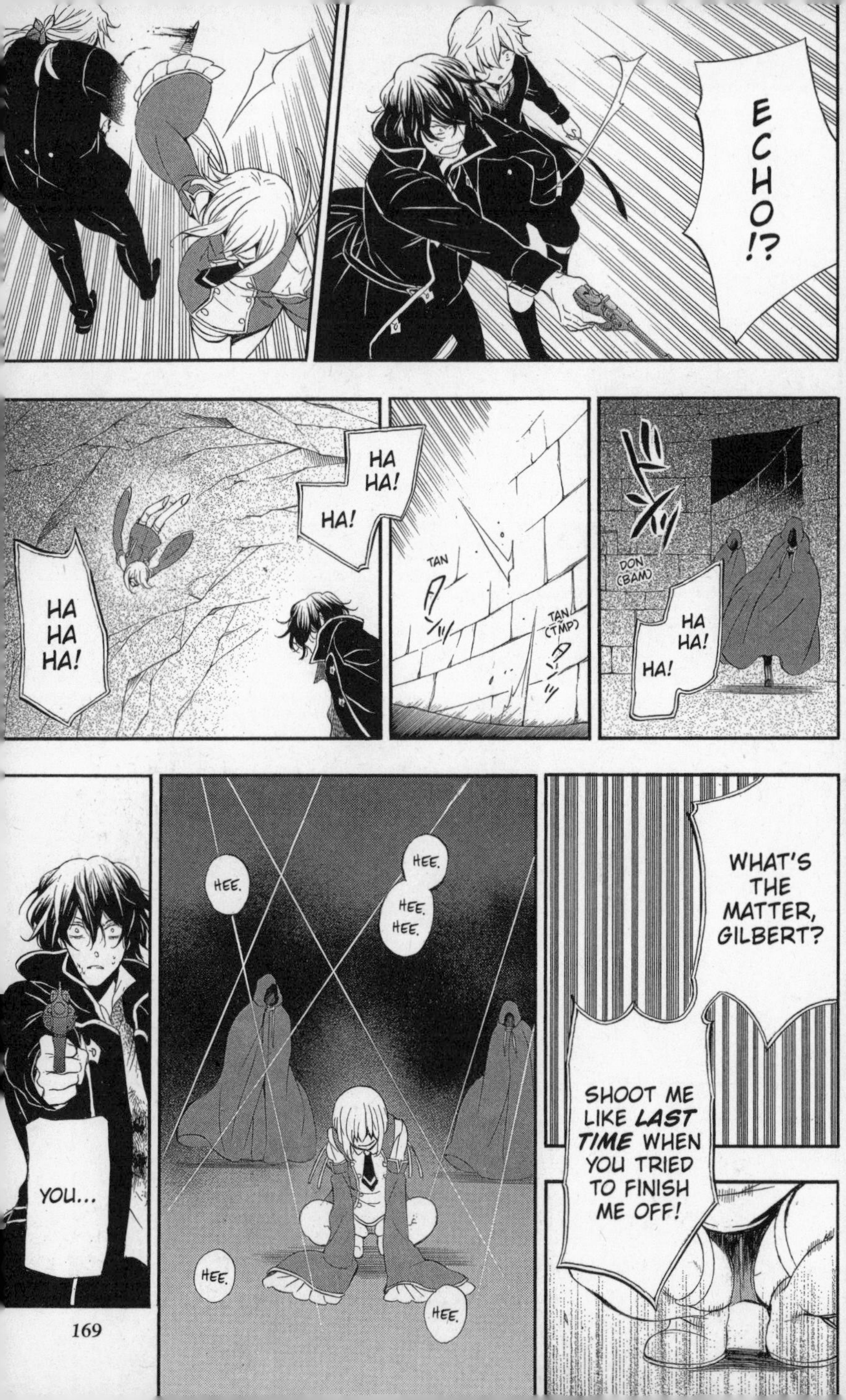
ECHO!?
DON (BAM)
HA HA! HA!
TAN
TAN (TMP)
HA HA! HA!
HA HA HA!
WHAT'S THE MATTER, GILBERT?
SHOOT ME LIKE *LAST TIME* WHEN YOU TRIED TO FINISH ME OFF!
HEE.
HEE.
HEE. HEE.
HEE.
HEE.
YOU...

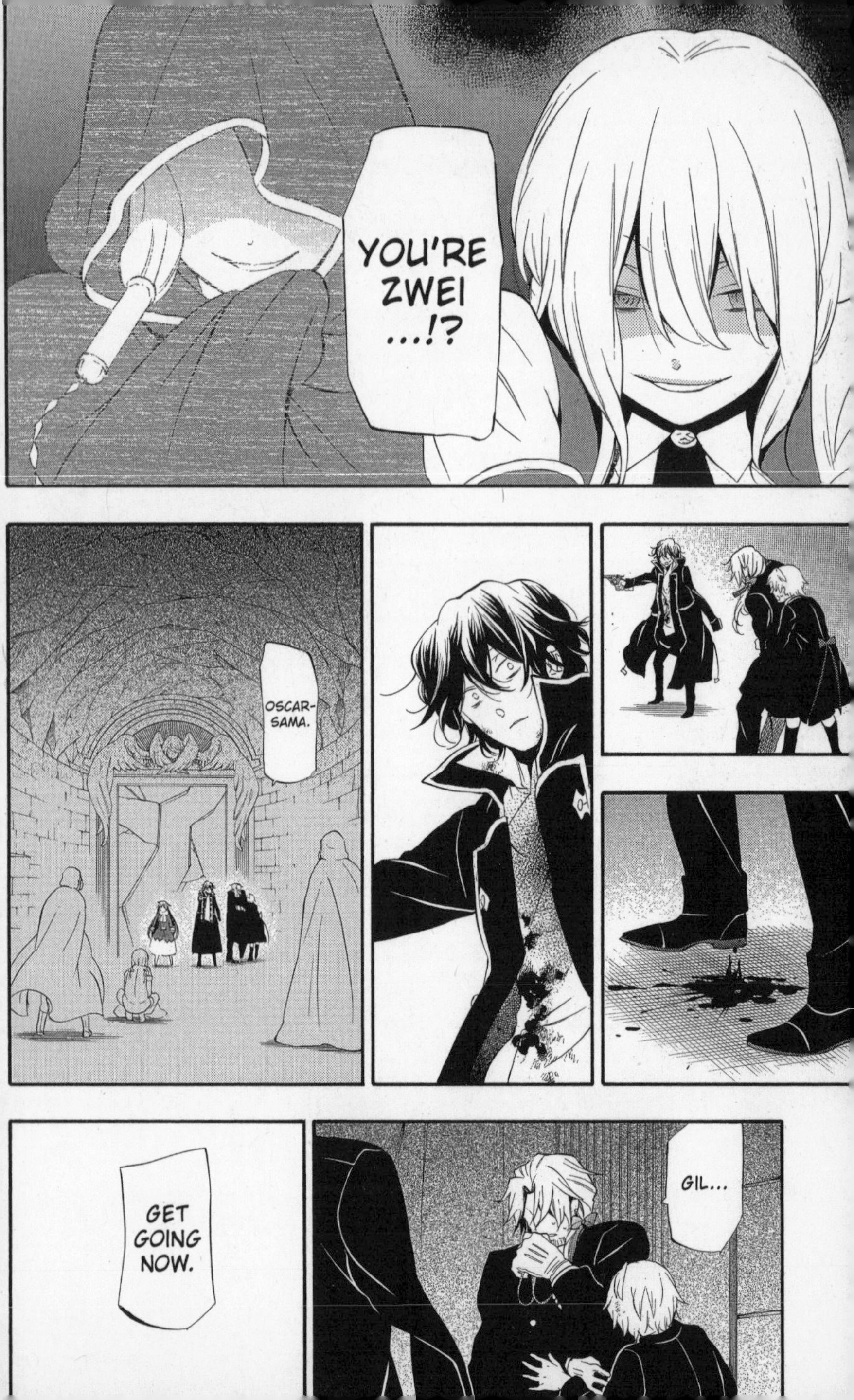
YOU'RE ZWEI ...!?
OSCAR-SAMA.
GIL...
GET GOING NOW.

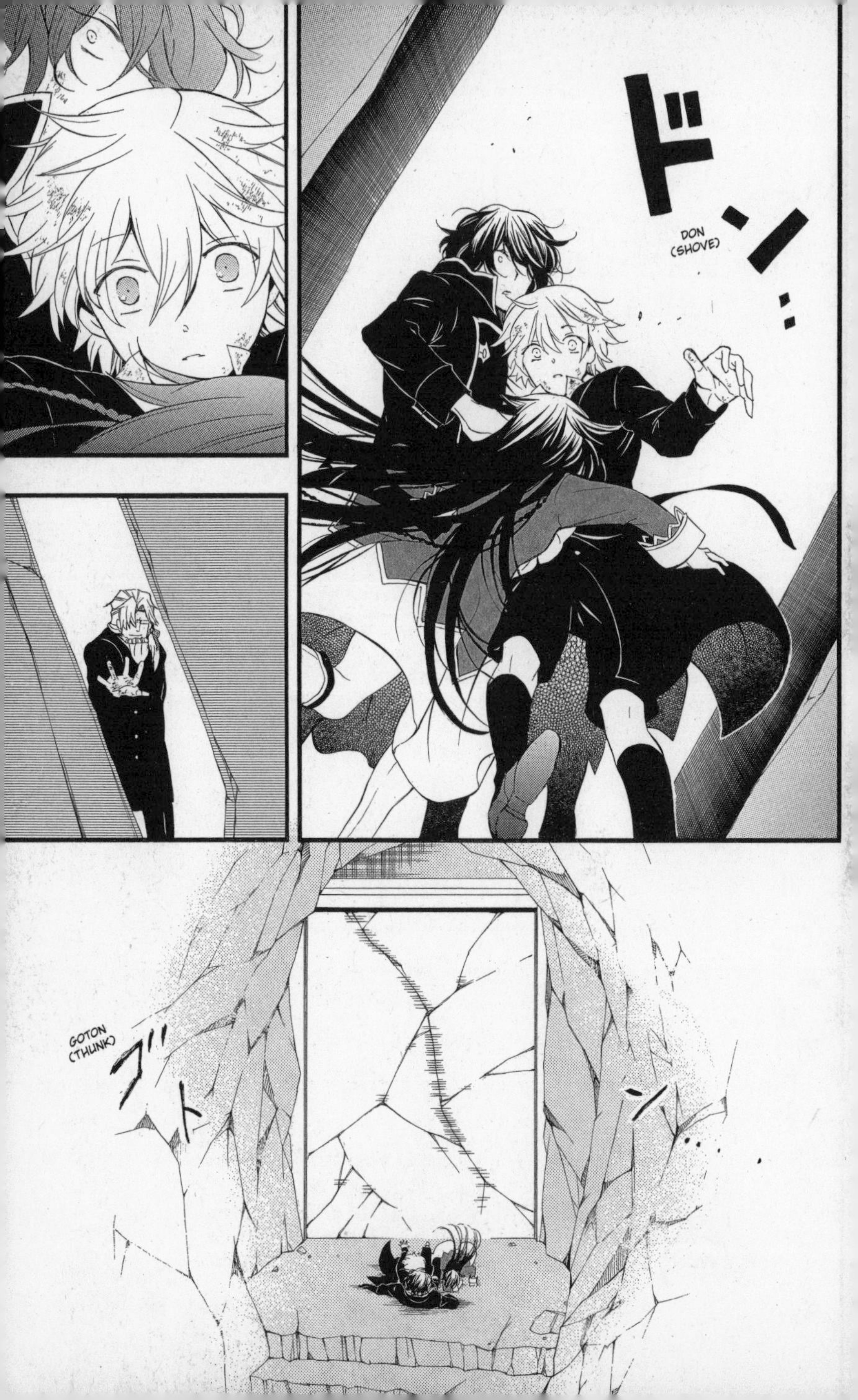
ドン…
DON (SHOVE)
ゴトン…
GOTON (THUNK)

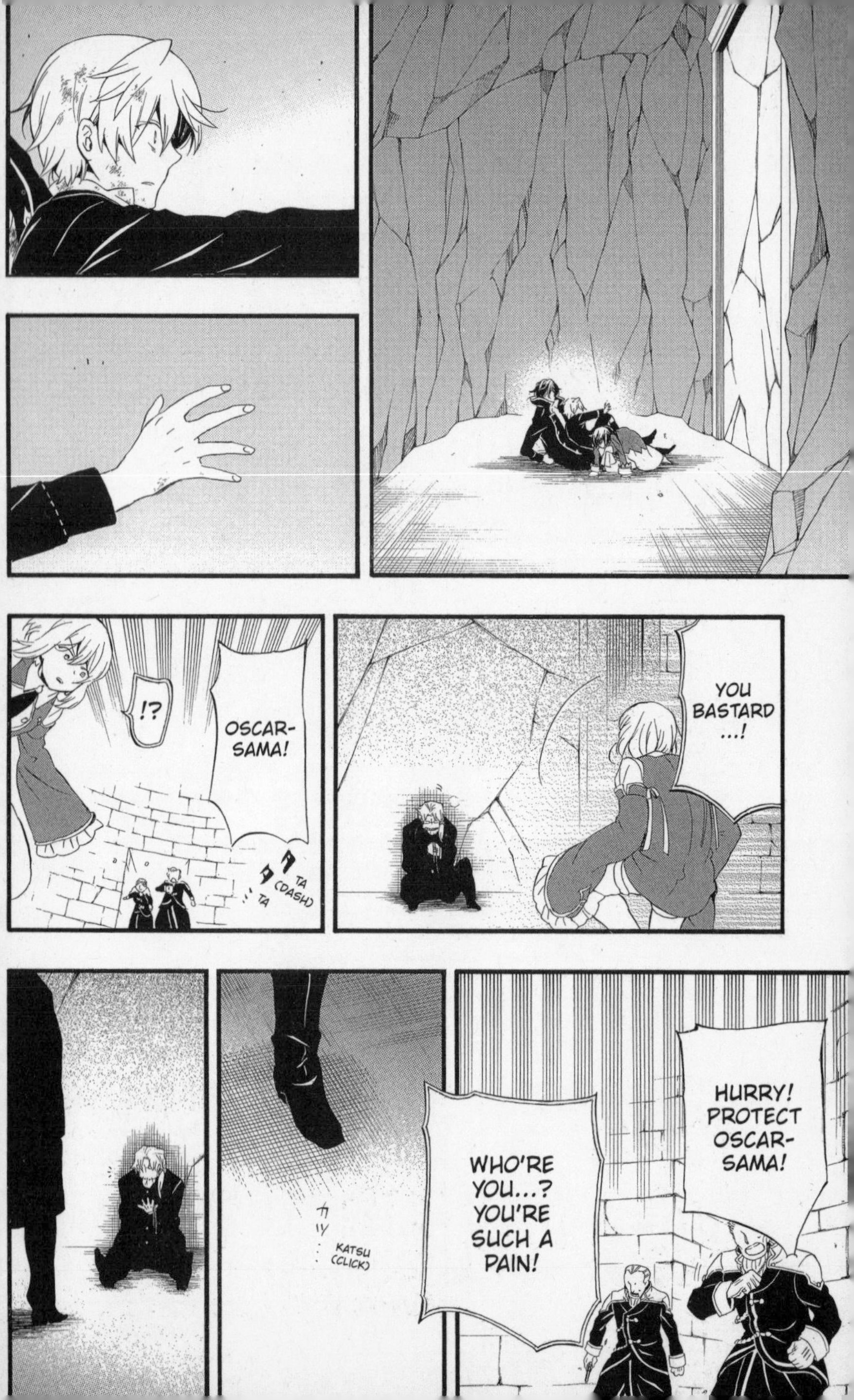
YOU BASTARD ...!
OSCAR-SAMA!
!?
TA (DASH)
TA
HURRY! PROTECT OSCAR-SAMA!
WHO'RE YOU...? YOU'RE SUCH A PAIN!
カツ…
KATSU (CLICK)

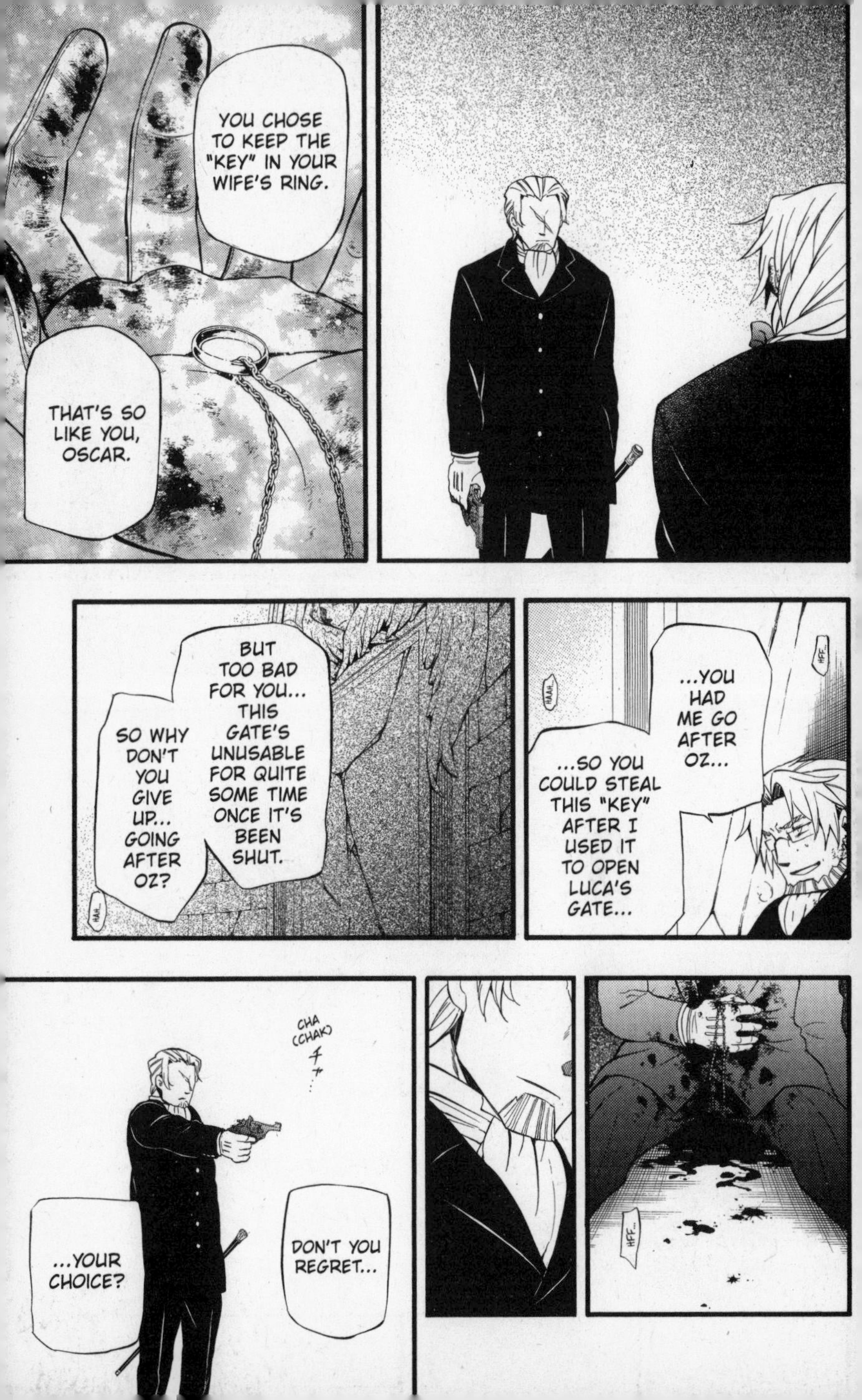
YOU CHOSE TO KEEP THE "KEY" IN YOUR WIFE'S RING.
THAT'S SO LIKE YOU, OSCAR.
HFF...
...YOU HAD ME GO AFTER OZ...
...SO YOU COULD STEAL THIS "KEY" AFTER I USED IT TO OPEN LUCA'S GATE...
HAAH...
BUT TOO BAD FOR YOU... THIS GATE'S UNUSABLE FOR QUITE SOME TIME ONCE IT'S BEEN SHUT.
SO WHY DON'T YOU GIVE UP... GOING AFTER OZ?
HAH...
HFF...
CHA (CHAK)
DON'T YOU REGRET...
...YOUR CHOICE?

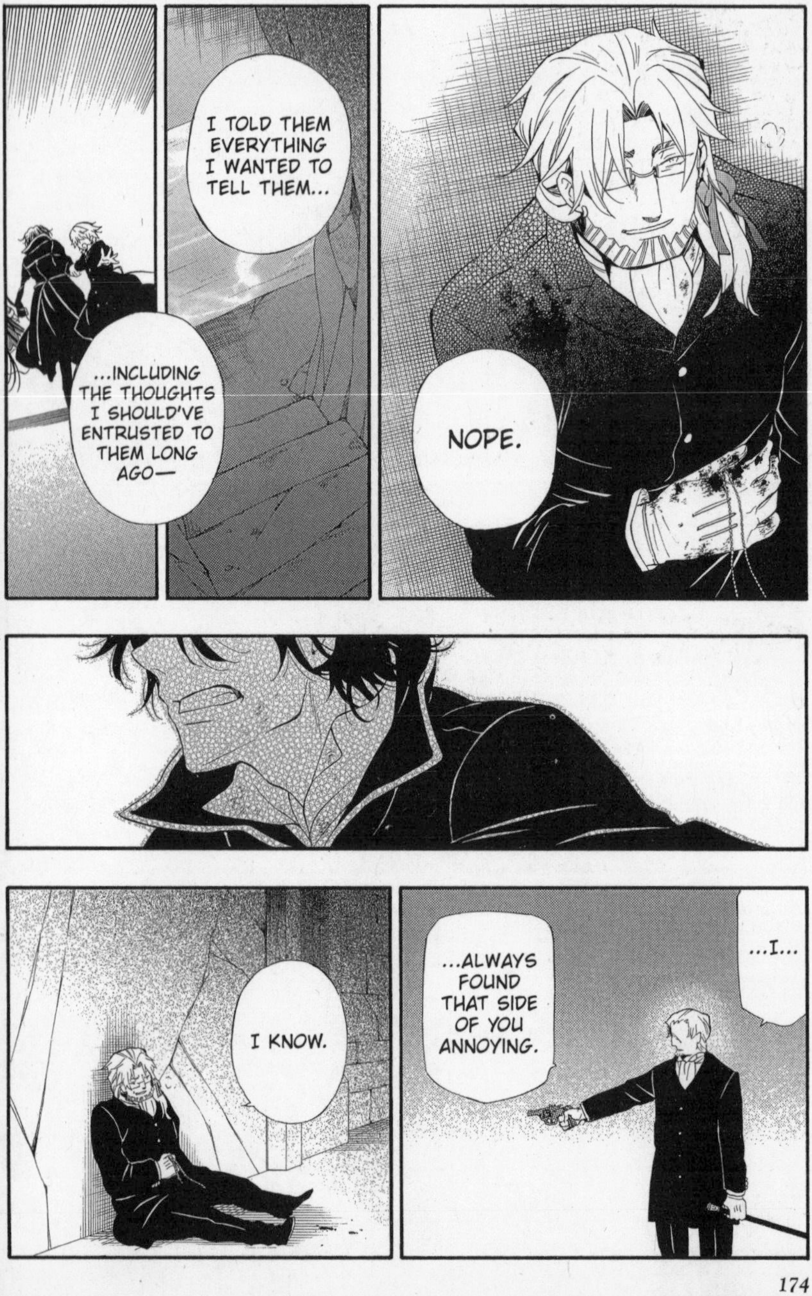
NOPE.
I TOLD THEM EVERYTHING I WANTED TO TELL THEM...
...INCLUDING THE THOUGHTS I SHOULD'VE ENTRUSTED TO THEM LONG AGO—
...I...
...ALWAYS FOUND THAT SIDE OF YOU ANNOYING.
I KNOW.

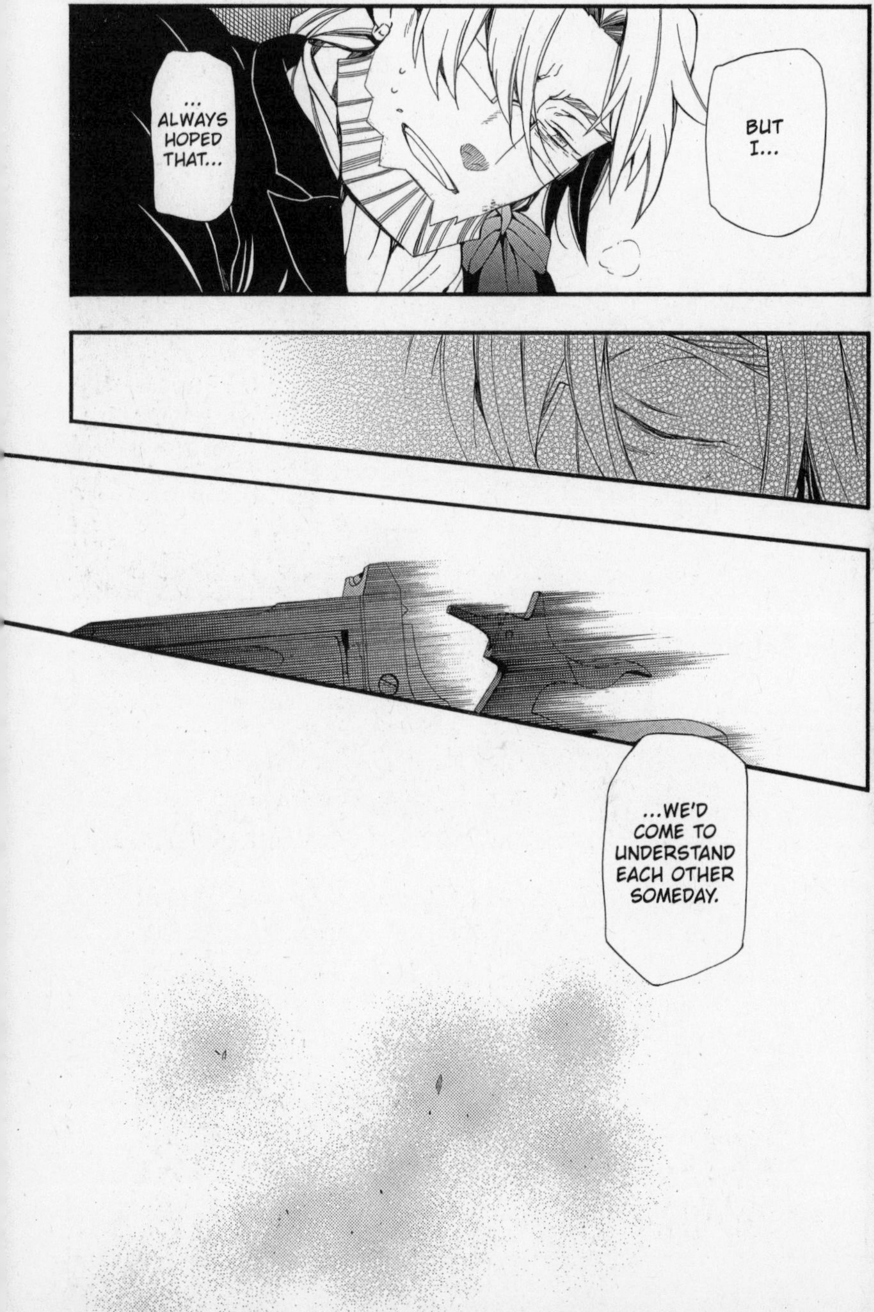
BUT I...
...ALWAYS HOPED THAT...
...WE'D COME TO UNDERSTAND EACH OTHER SOMEDAY.

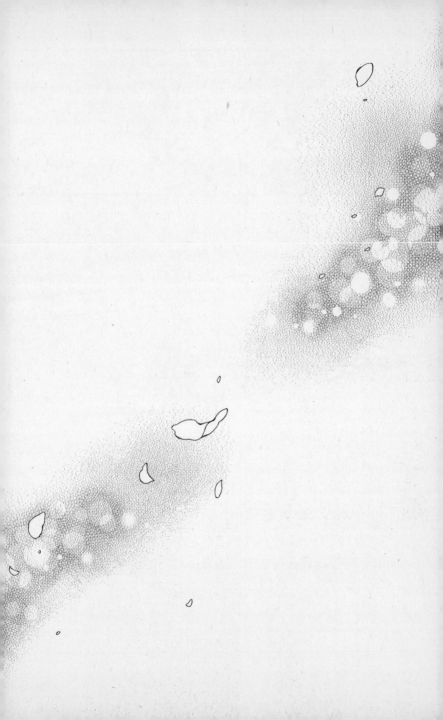

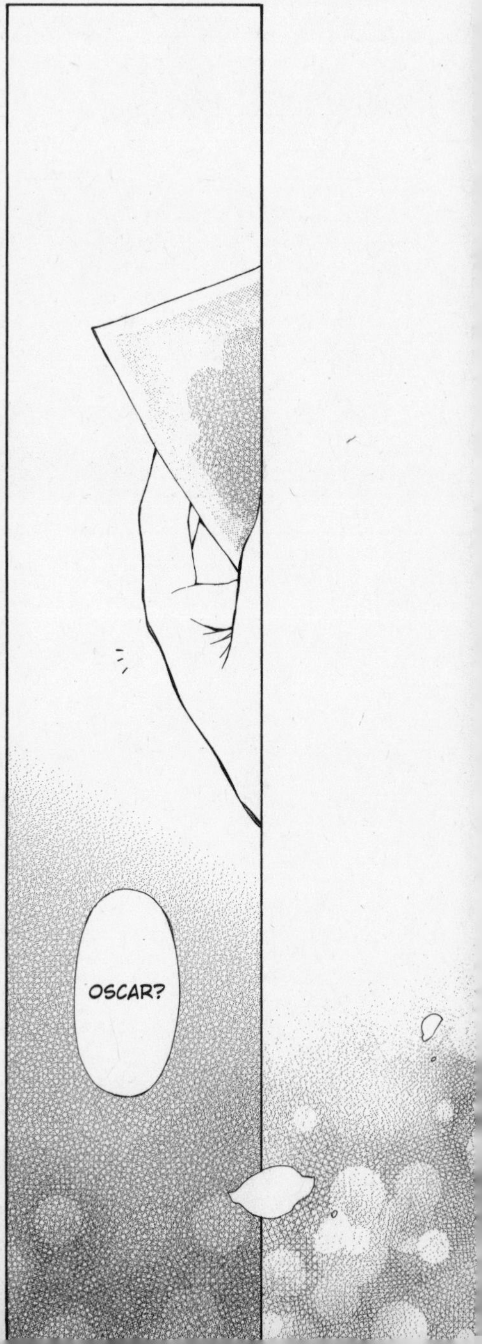
OSCAR?

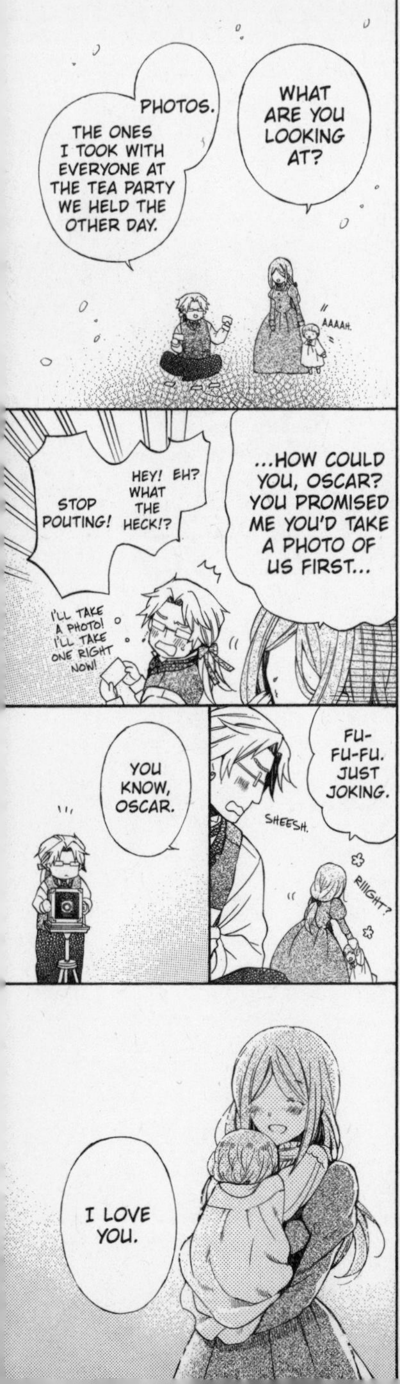
WHAT ARE YOU LOOKING AT?
PHOTOS. THE ONES I TOOK WITH EVERYONE AT THE TEA PARTY WE HELD THE OTHER DAY.
AAAAH.
...HOW COULD YOU, OSCAR? YOU PROMISED ME YOU'D TAKE A PHOTO OF US FIRST...
HEY! EH? WHAT THE HECK!?
STOP POUTING!
I'LL TAKE A PHOTO! I'LL TAKE ONE RIGHT NOW!
FU-FU-FU. JUST JOKING.
SHEESH.
RIIIGHT?
YOU KNOW, OSCAR.
I LOVE YOU.

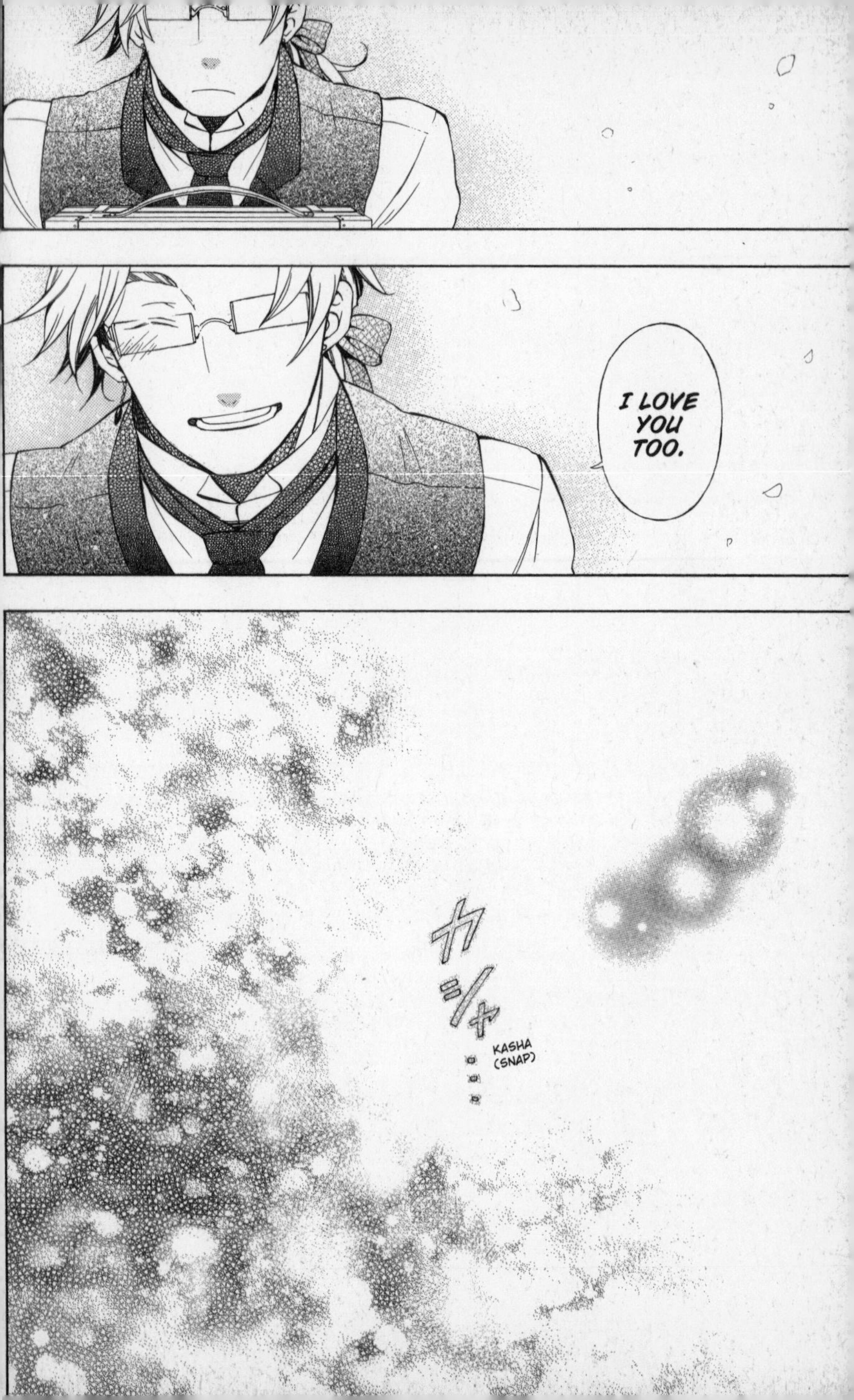
I LOVE YOU TOO.
カシャ
KASHA (SNAP)
...

Retrace:LXXXII Wish

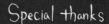
Special thanks

FUMITO YAMAZAKI
WEAR A PINK MOHICAN!!!

SAEKO TAKIGAWA-SAN
DON'T DROOL IN THE CAR!!

KANATA MINAZUKI-SAN
YOU GET IT!? YOU GET IT NOW!!??

YUKINO-SAN
I LOVE YOUR RUDE ATTITUDE TOWARD TADUU.

RYO-CHAN
COME BY MY SIDE AGAIN... (IN A SICKLY WAY)

MIZU KING-SAN
LOVE THAT T-SHIRT!!

TADUU-SAN
TADUU? NOERU?? WHICH!?

YAJI
GIMME SOME FURNITURE ADVIIICE!!

AYAHAM SAYA
A GIRL WHO LEAPT THROUGH TIME. I WONDER
ABOUT THE YEAR WE SPENT TOGETHER...

MY FAMILY. THANK YOU FOR ALWAYS
TAKING CARE OF TIME.

MY EDITOR TAKEGASA-SAN
I WANT TO KNOCK YOU DOWN. YAAY.

AND YOU..!!

REIM JUST
WOKE UP.

← A SIDE STORY
BEGINS NEXT.

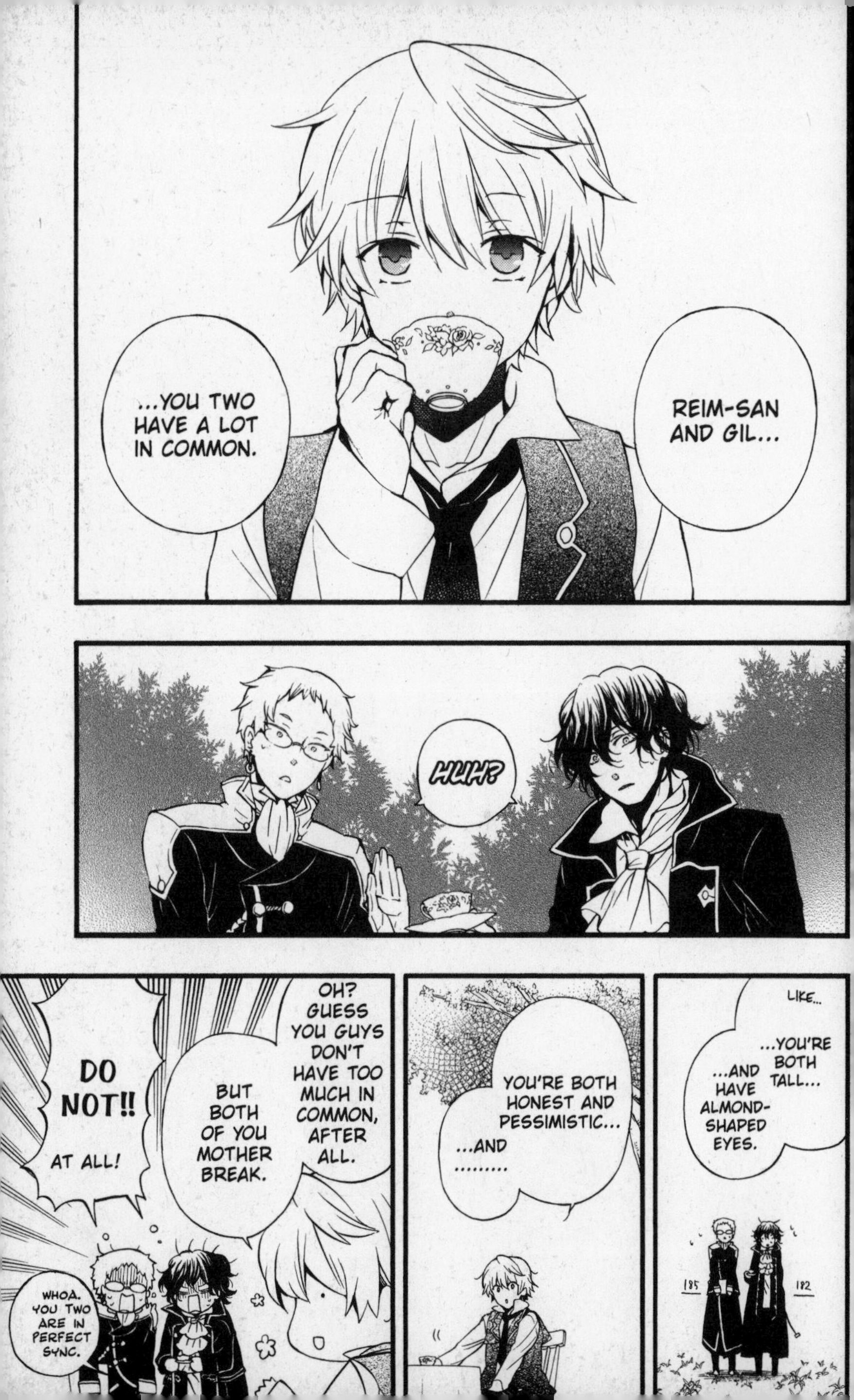
REIM-SAN AND GIL...
...YOU TWO HAVE A LOT IN COMMON.
HUH?
LIKE...
...YOU'RE BOTH TALL...
...AND HAVE ALMOND-SHAPED EYES.
185
182
YOU'RE BOTH HONEST AND PESSIMISTIC...
...AND ....
OH? GUESS YOU GUYS DON'T HAVE TOO MUCH IN COMMON, AFTER ALL.
BUT BOTH OF YOU MOTHER BREAK.
DO NOT!!
AT ALL!
WHOA. YOU TWO ARE IN PERFECT SYNC.

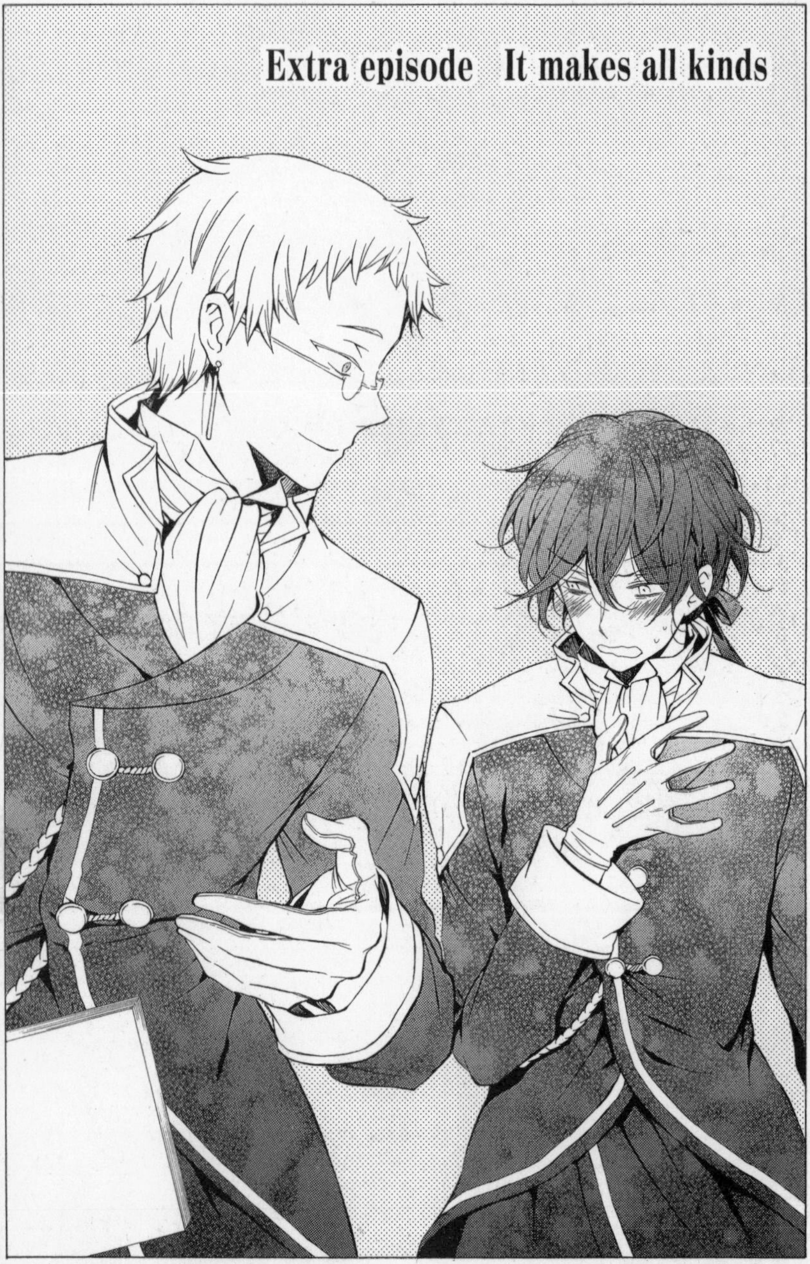
Extra episode It makes all kinds

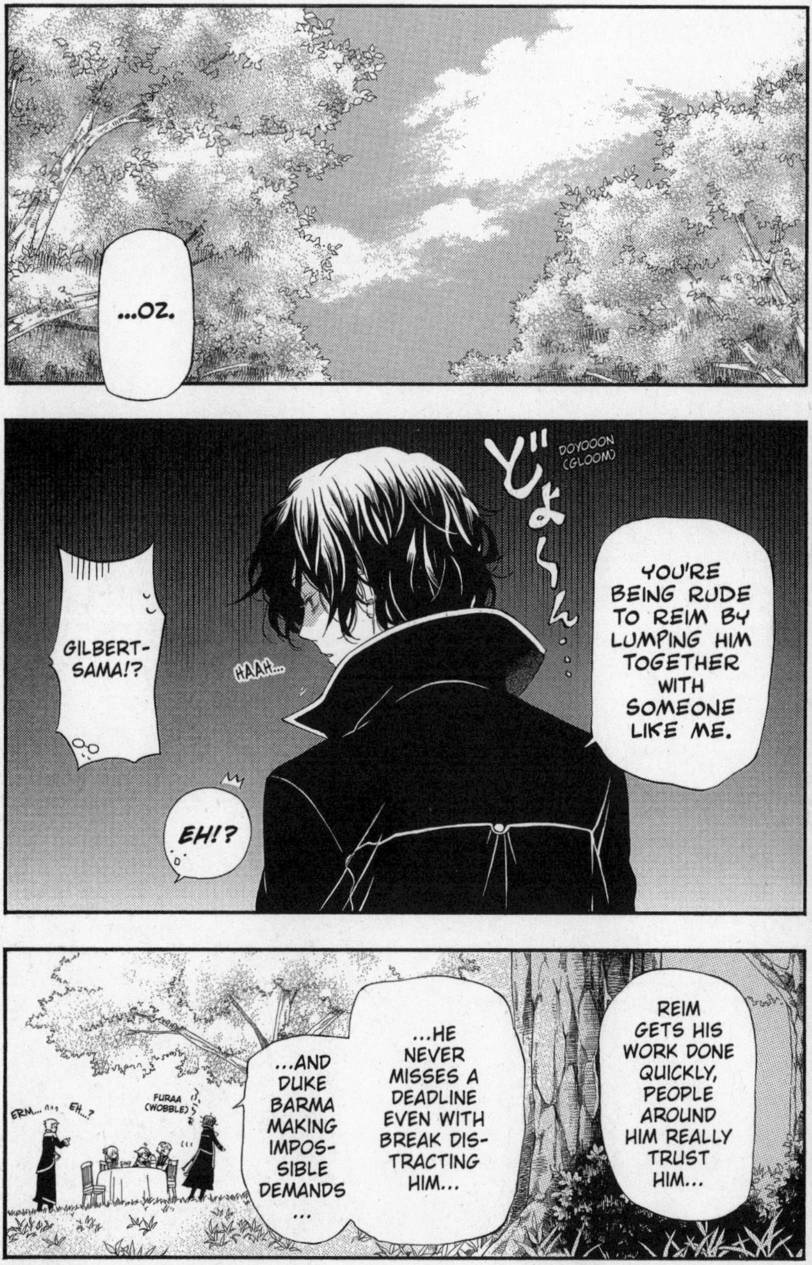
...OZ.
DOYOOON (GLOOM)
YOU'RE BEING RUDE TO REIM BY LUMPING HIM TOGETHER WITH SOMEONE LIKE ME.
GILBERT-SAMA!?
HAAH...
EH!?
REIM GETS HIS WORK DONE QUICKLY, PEOPLE AROUND HIM REALLY TRUST HIM...
...HE NEVER MISSES A DEADLINE EVEN WITH BREAK DISTRACTING HIM...
...AND DUKE BARMA MAKING IMPOSSIBLE DEMANDS...
FURAA (WOBBLE)
ERM... EH...?

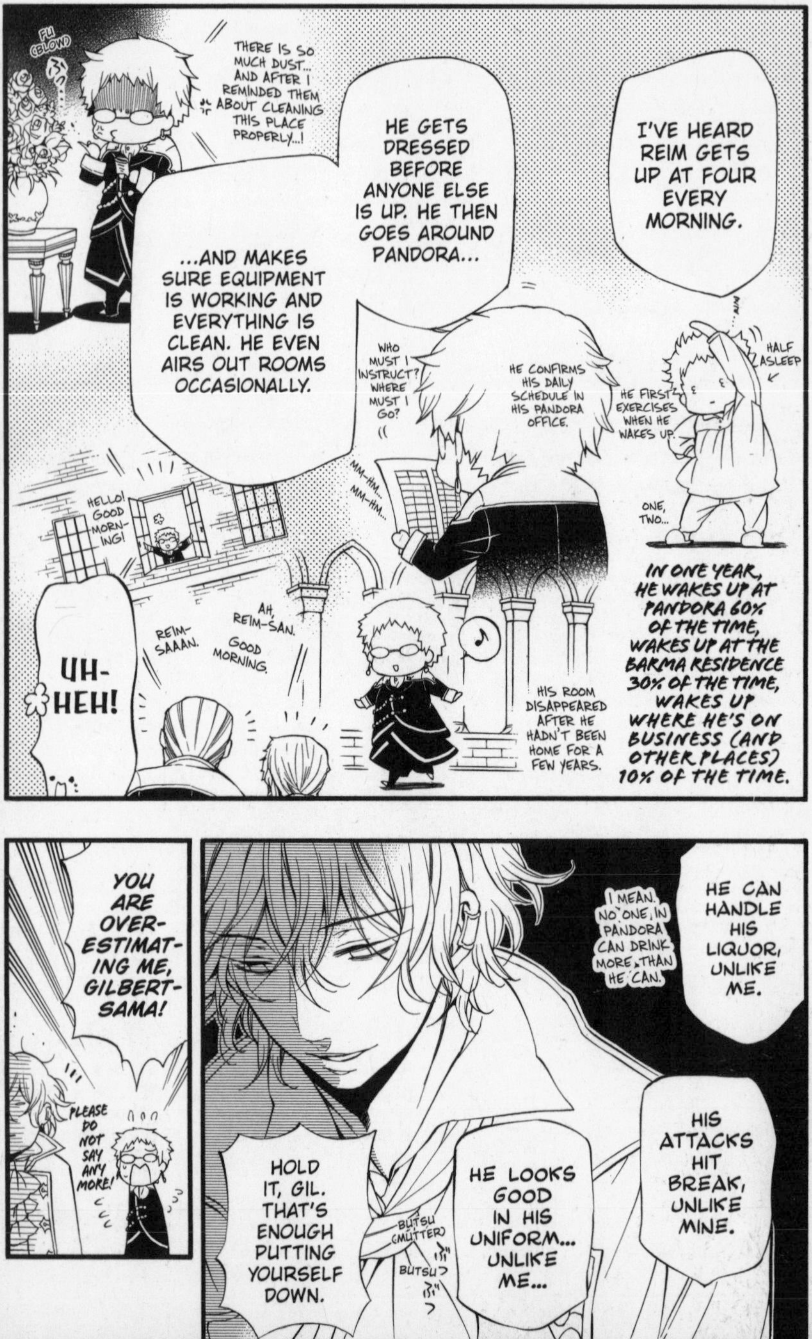
I'VE HEARD REIM GETS UP AT FOUR EVERY MORNING.
HALF ASLEEP
HE FIRST EXERCISES WHEN HE WAKES UP.
ONE, TWO...
HE GETS DRESSED BEFORE ANYONE ELSE IS UP. HE THEN GOES AROUND PANDORA...
HE CONFIRMS HIS DAILY SCHEDULE IN HIS PANDORA OFFICE.
WHO MUST I INSTRUCT? WHERE MUST I GO?
MM-HM. MM-HM...
...AND MAKES SURE EQUIPMENT IS WORKING AND EVERYTHING IS CLEAN. HE EVEN AIRS OUT ROOMS OCCASIONALLY.
THERE IS SO MUCH DUST... AND AFTER I REMINDED THEM ABOUT CLEANING THIS PLACE PROPERLY...!
FU (BLOW)
HELLO! GOOD MORNING!
IN ONE YEAR, HE WAKES UP AT PANDORA 60% OF THE TIME, WAKES UP AT THE BARMA RESIDENCE 30% OF THE TIME, WAKES UP WHERE HE'S ON BUSINESS (AND OTHER PLACES) 10% OF THE TIME.
HIS ROOM DISAPPEARED AFTER HE HADN'T BEEN HOME FOR A FEW YEARS.
AH, REIM-SAN.
GOOD MORNING.
REIM-SAAAN.
UH-HEH!
HE CAN HANDLE HIS LIQUOR, UNLIKE ME.
I MEAN, NO ONE IN PANDORA CAN DRINK MORE THAN HE CAN.
HIS ATTACKS HIT BREAK, UNLIKE MINE.
HE LOOKS GOOD IN HIS UNIFORM... UNLIKE ME...
BUTSU (MUTTER)
BUTSU
HOLD IT, GIL. THAT'S ENOUGH PUTTING YOURSELF DOWN.
YOU ARE OVER-ESTIMATING ME, GILBERT-SAMA!
PLEASE DO NOT SAY ANY MORE!

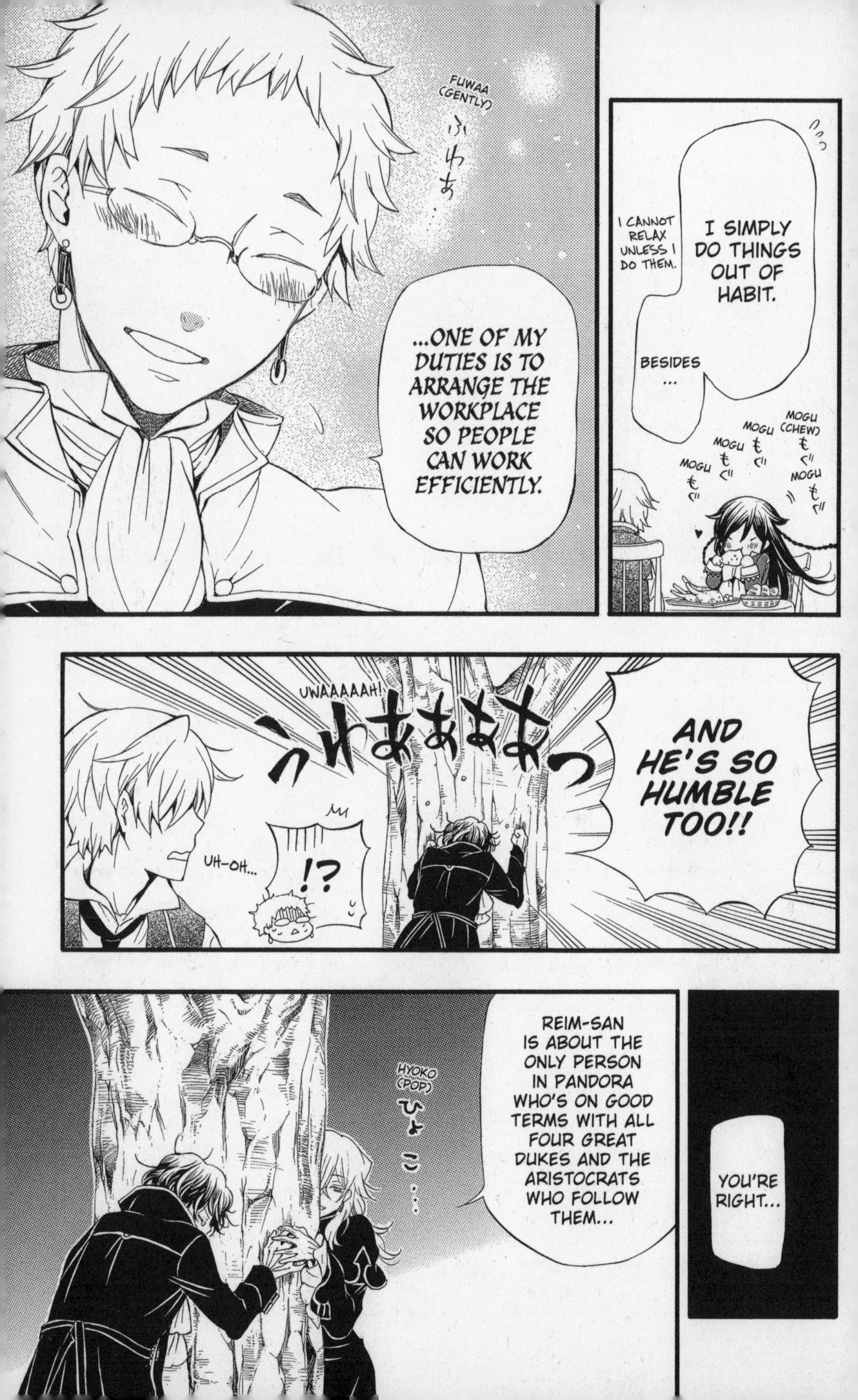

I SIMPLY DO THINGS OUT OF HABIT.
I CANNOT RELAX UNLESS I DO THEM.
BESIDES...
MOGU (CHEW) もぐ
MOGU もぐ
MOGU もぐ
MOGU もぐ
MOGU もぐ
FUWAA (GENTLY) ふわぁ...
...ONE OF MY DUTIES IS TO ARRANGE THE WORKPLACE SO PEOPLE CAN WORK EFFICIENTLY.
AND HE'S SO HUMBLE TOO!!
UWAAAAAH! うわあああっ
!?
UH-OH...
YOU'RE RIGHT...
REIM-SAN IS ABOUT THE ONLY PERSON IN PANDORA WHO'S ON GOOD TERMS WITH ALL FOUR GREAT DUKES AND THE ARISTOCRATS WHO FOLLOW THEM...
HYOKO (POP) ひょこ...

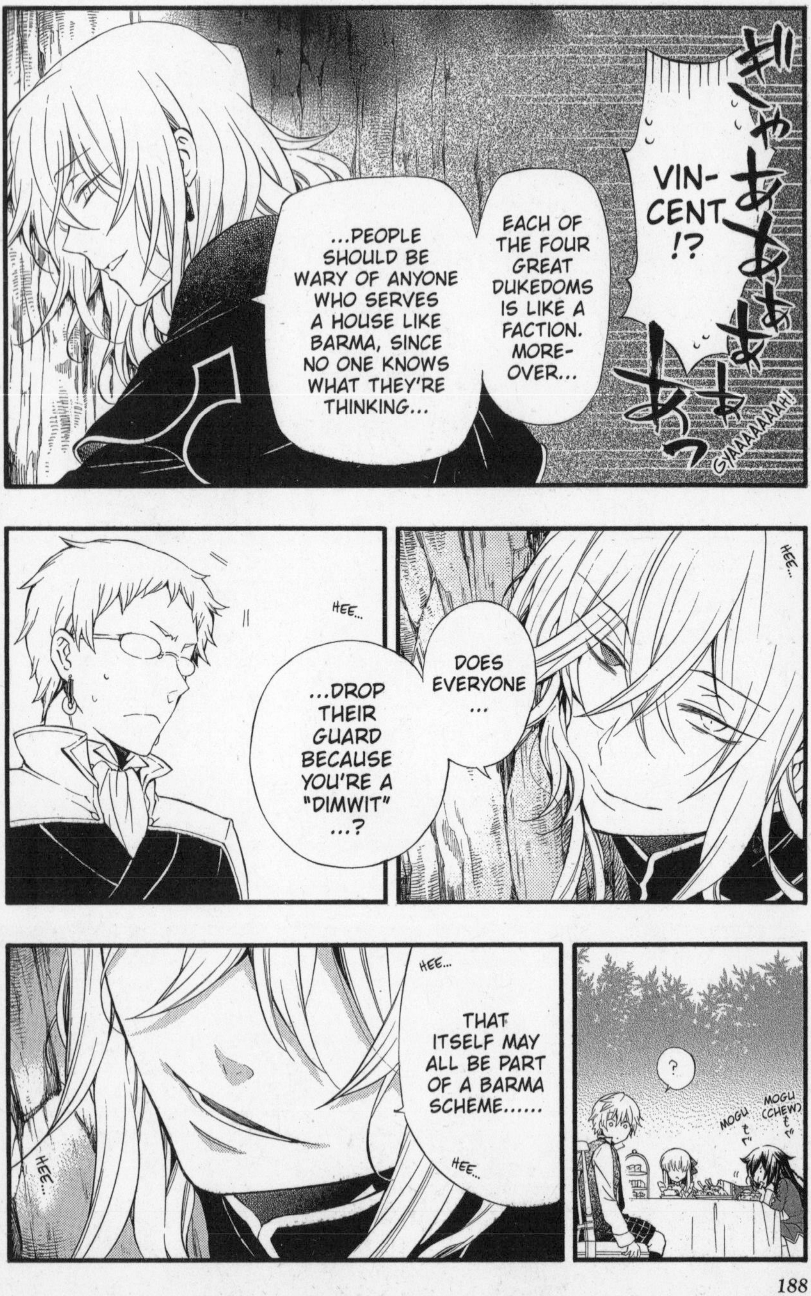
ぎゃあああああっ
GYAAAAAAAH!
VIN-CENT !?
EACH OF THE FOUR GREAT DUKEDOMS IS LIKE A FACTION. MORE-OVER...
...PEOPLE SHOULD BE WARY OF ANYONE WHO SERVES A HOUSE LIKE BARMA, SINCE NO ONE KNOWS WHAT THEY'RE THINKING...
HEE...
DOES EVERYONE...
...DROP THEIR GUARD BECAUSE YOU'RE A "DIMWIT" ...?
HEE...
?
MOGU (CHEW)
もぐ
MOGU
もぐ
HEE...
THAT ITSELF MAY ALL BE PART OF A BARMA SCHEME......
HEE...
HEE...

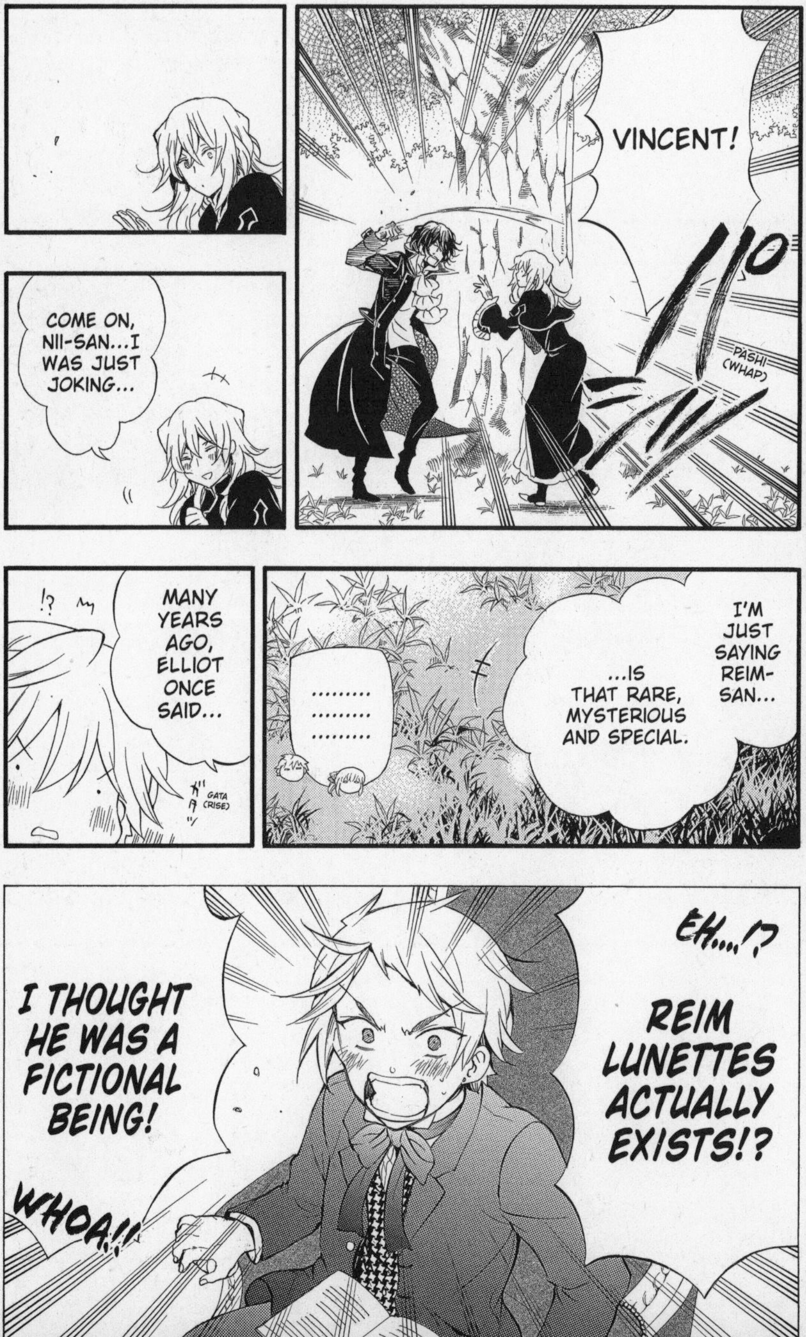
VINCENT!
PASHI (WHAP)
COME ON, NII-SAN...I WAS JUST JOKING...
I'M JUST SAYING REIM-SAN...
...IS THAT RARE, MYSTERIOUS AND SPECIAL.
....
....
....
MANY YEARS AGO, ELLIOT ONCE SAID...
!?
GATA (RISE)
EH...!?
REIM LUNETTES ACTUALLY EXISTS!?
I THOUGHT HE WAS A FICTIONAL BEING!
WHOA!!

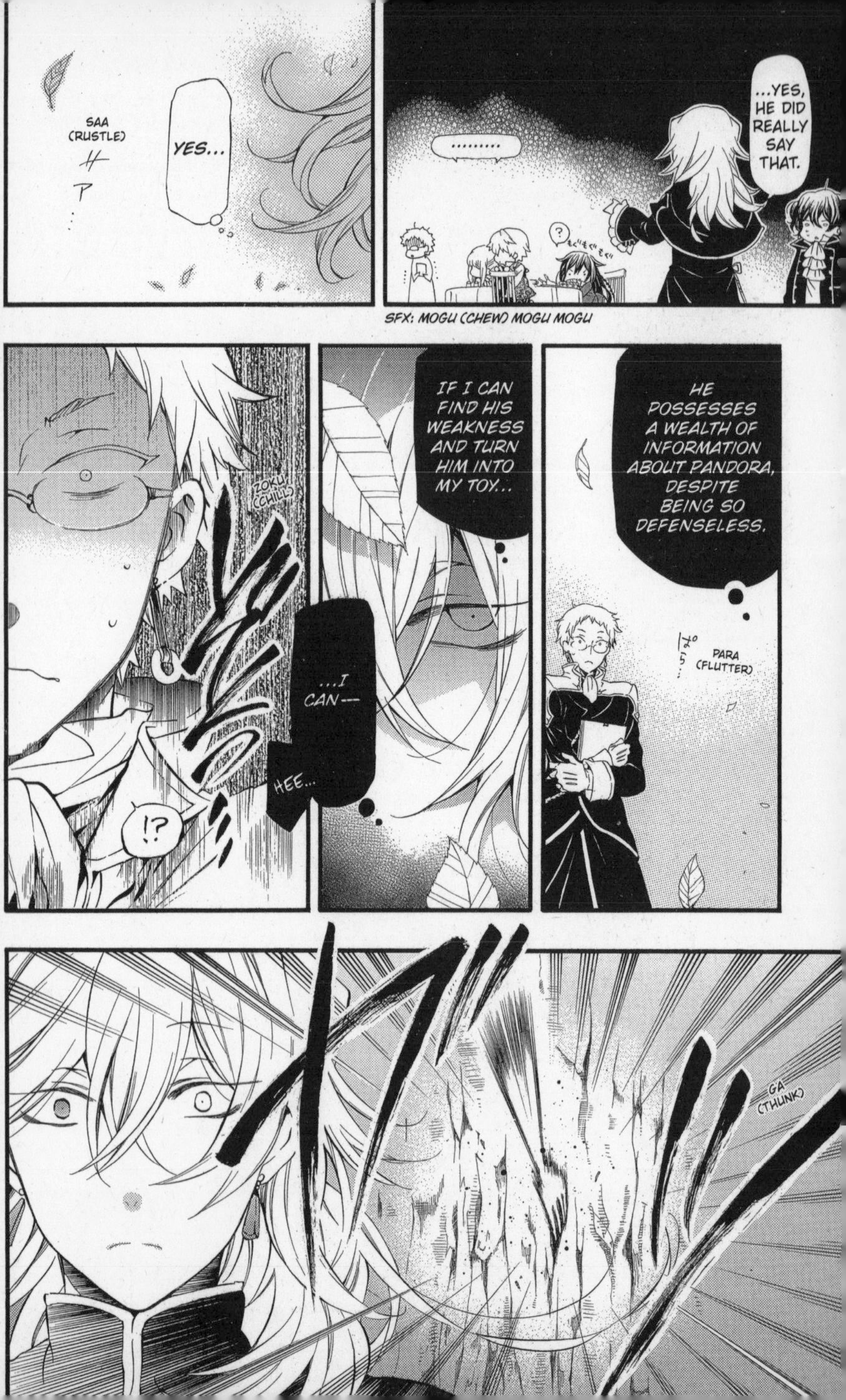
...YES, HE DID REALLY SAY THAT.
....
YES...
SAA (RUSTLE)
SFX: MOGU (CHEW) MOGU MOGU
HE POSSESSES A WEALTH OF INFORMATION ABOUT PANDORA, DESPITE BEING SO DEFENSELESS.
PARA (FLUTTER)
IF I CAN FIND HIS WEAKNESS AND TURN HIM INTO MY TOY...
...I CAN—
HEE...
ZOKU (CHILL)
!?
GA (THUNK)

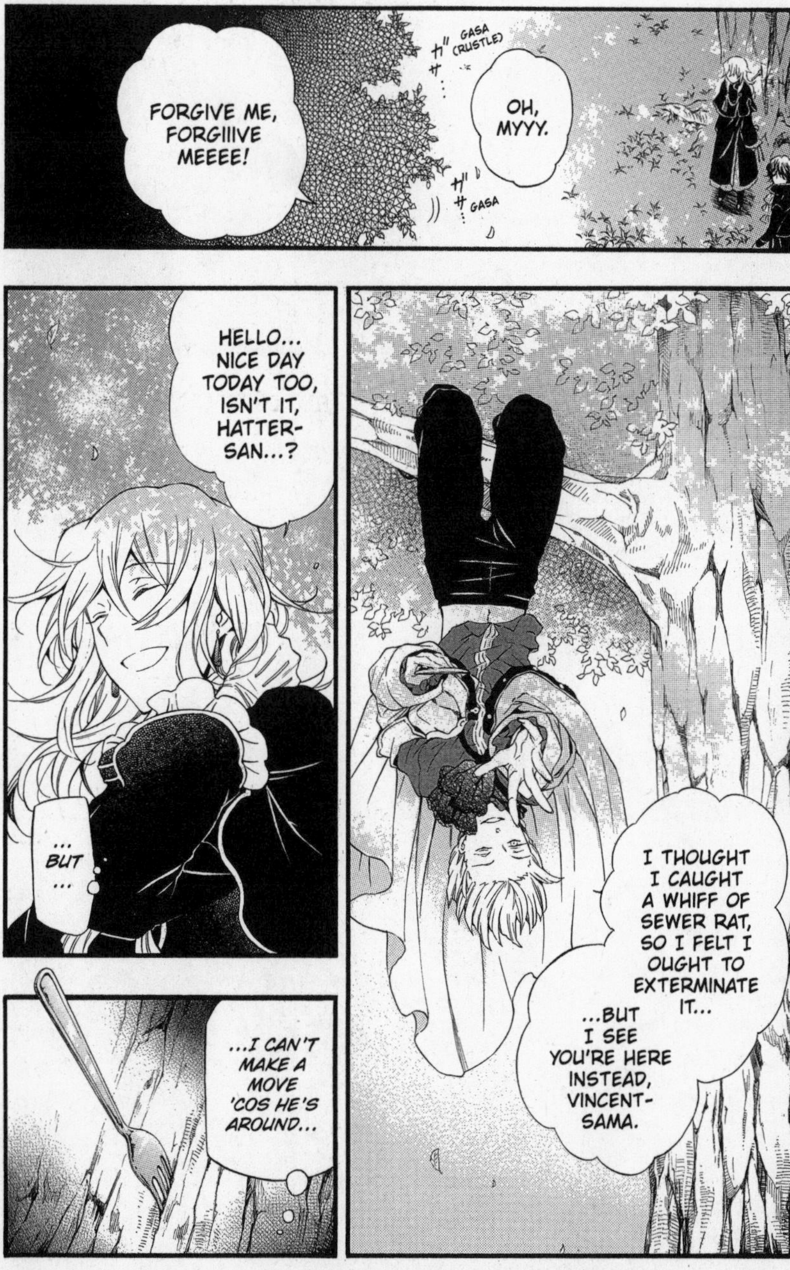

ガサ… GASA (RUSTLE)
OH, MYYY.
ガサ… GASA
FORGIVE ME, FORGIIIVE MEEEE!
I THOUGHT I CAUGHT A WHIFF OF SEWER RAT, SO I FELT I OUGHT TO EXTERMINATE IT...
...BUT I SEE YOU'RE HERE INSTEAD, VINCENT-SAMA.
HELLO... NICE DAY TODAY TOO, ISN'T IT, HATTER-SAN...?
...BUT...
...I CAN'T MAKE A MOVE 'COS HE'S AROUND...

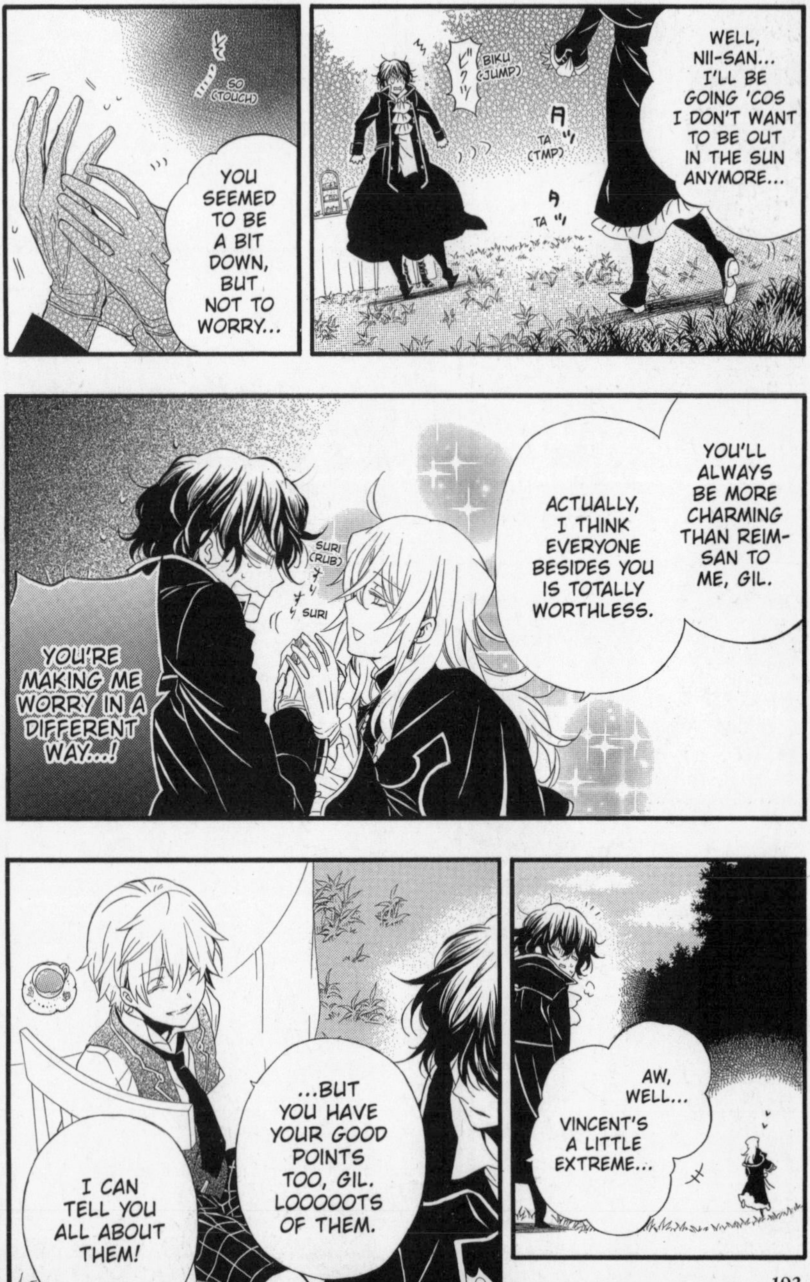
WELL, NII-SAN... I'LL BE GOING 'COS I DON'T WANT TO BE OUT IN THE SUN ANYMORE...
BIKU (JUMP)
TA (TMP)
TA
SO (TOUCH)
YOU SEEMED TO BE A BIT DOWN, BUT NOT TO WORRY...
YOU'LL ALWAYS BE MORE CHARMING THAN REIM-SAN TO ME, GIL.
ACTUALLY, I THINK EVERYONE BESIDES YOU IS TOTALLY WORTHLESS.
SURI (RUB)
SURI
YOU'RE MAKING ME WORRY IN A DIFFERENT WAY...!
AW, WELL... VINCENT'S A LITTLE EXTREME...
...BUT YOU HAVE YOUR GOOD POINTS TOO, GIL. LOOOOOTS OF THEM.
I CAN TELL YOU ALL ABOUT THEM!

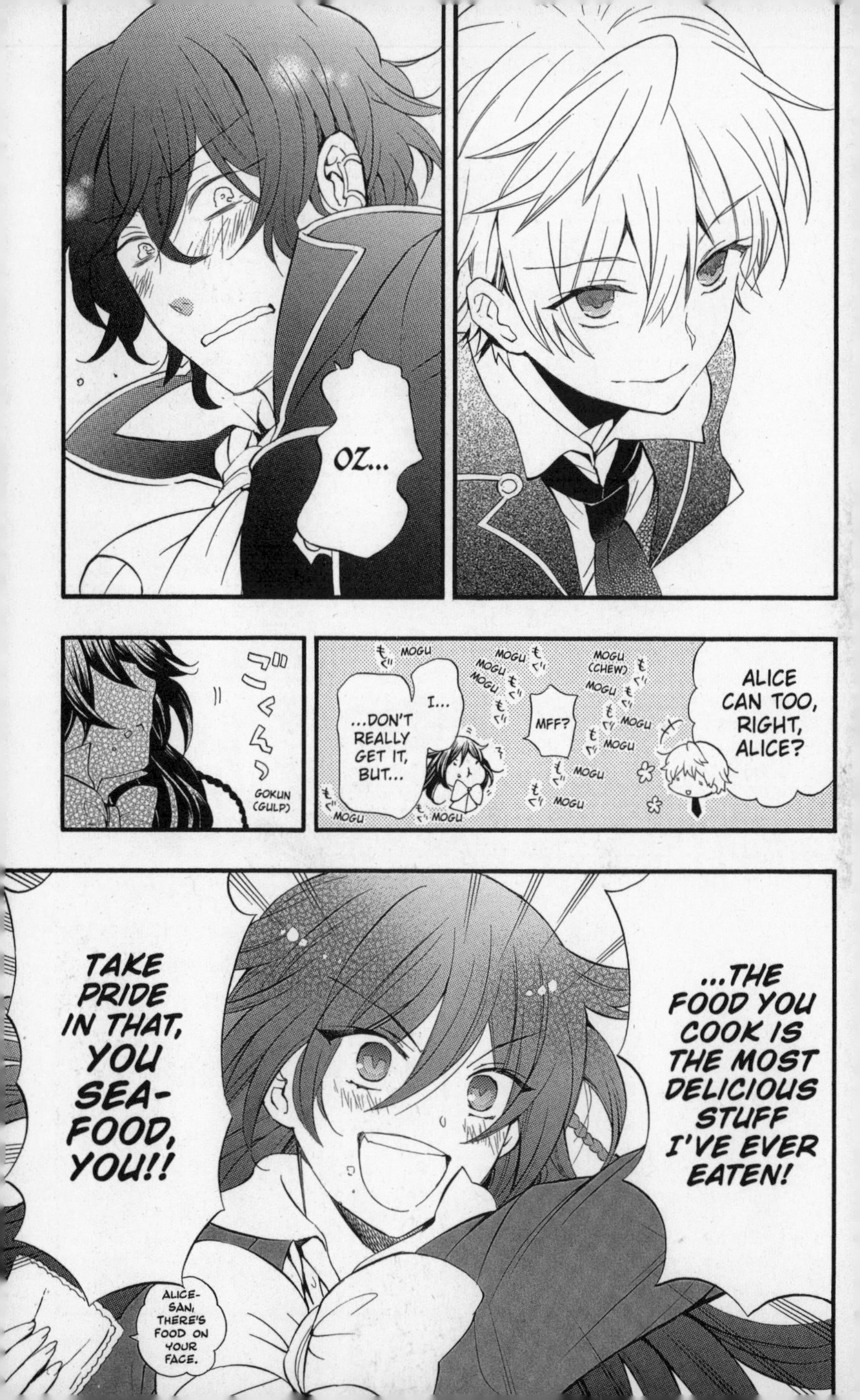
OZ...
ALICE CAN TOO, RIGHT, ALICE?
もぐ MOGU (CHEW)
もぐ MOGU
もぐ MOGU
もぐ MOGU
もぐ MOGU
もぐ MOGU
MFF?
もぐ MOGU
もぐ MOGU
もぐ MOGU
もぐ MOGU
I...
...DON'T REALLY GET IT, BUT...
もぐ MOGU
もぐ MOGU
ゴクン
GOKUN (GULP)
...THE FOOD YOU COOK IS THE MOST DELICIOUS STUFF I'VE EVER EATEN!
TAKE PRIDE IN THAT, YOU SEA-FOOD, YOU!!
ALICE-SAN, THERE'S FOOD ON YOUR FACE.

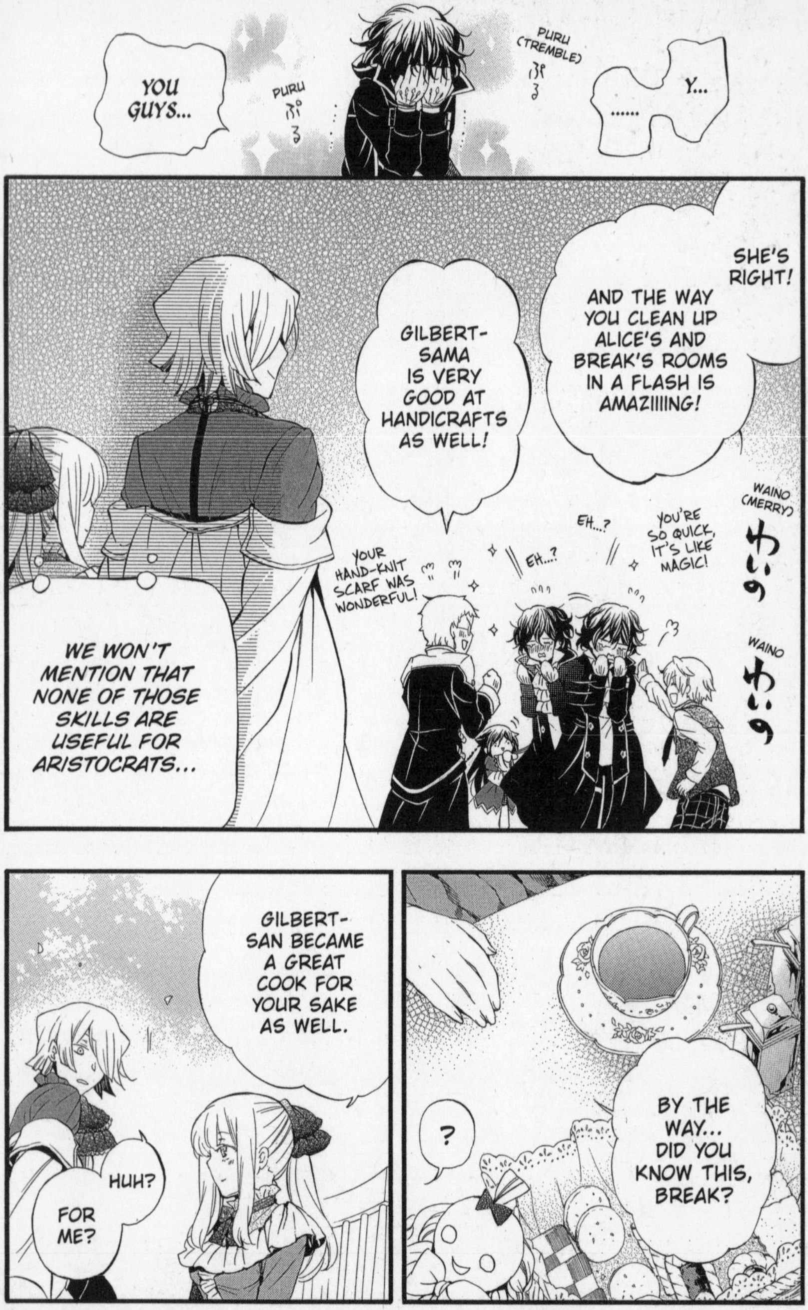
Y...
......
PURU (TREMBLE)
ぷる
PURU
ぷる
YOU GUYS...
SHE'S RIGHT!
AND THE WAY YOU CLEAN UP ALICE'S AND BREAK'S ROOMS IN A FLASH IS AMAZIIIING!
GILBERT-SAMA IS VERY GOOD AT HANDICRAFTS AS WELL!
WAINO (MERRY)
わいの
YOU'RE SO QUICK, IT'S LIKE MAGIC!
EH...?
EH...?
YOUR HAND-KNIT SCARF WAS WONDERFUL!
WAINO
わいの
WE WON'T MENTION THAT NONE OF THOSE SKILLS ARE USEFUL FOR ARISTOCRATS...
BY THE WAY... DID YOU KNOW THIS, BREAK?
?
GILBERT-SAN BECAME A GREAT COOK FOR YOUR SAKE AS WELL.
HUH?
FOR ME?

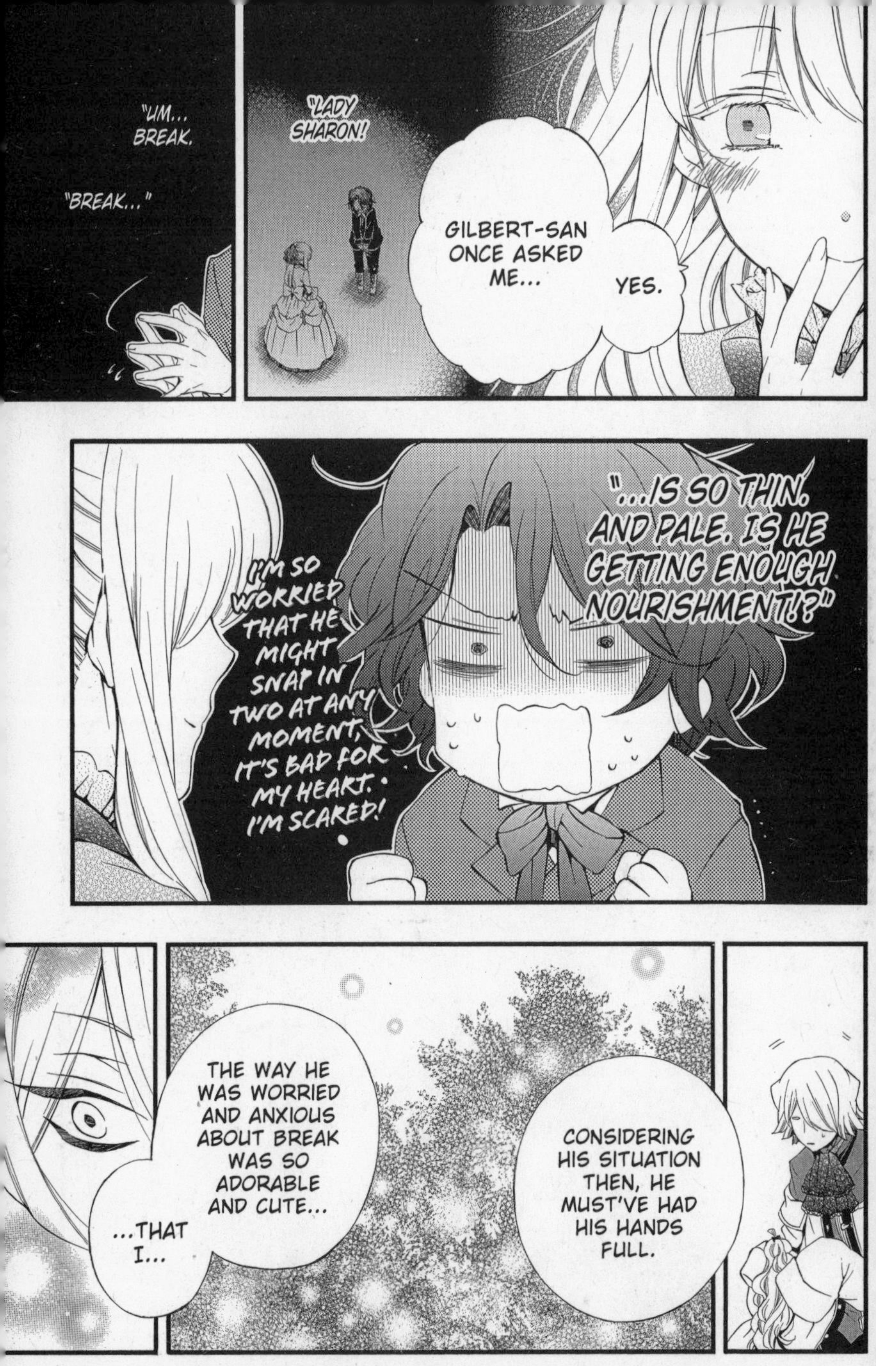
"LADY SHARON!
YES.
GILBERT-SAN ONCE ASKED ME...
"UM... BREAK.
"BREAK..."
"...IS SO THIN. AND PALE. IS HE GETTING ENOUGH NOURISHMENT!?"
I'M SO WORRIED THAT HE MIGHT SNAP IN TWO AT ANY MOMENT, IT'S BAD FOR MY HEART. I'M SCARED!
CONSIDERING HIS SITUATION THEN, HE MUST'VE HAD HIS HANDS FULL.
THE WAY HE WAS WORRIED AND ANXIOUS ABOUT BREAK WAS SO ADORABLE AND CUTE...
...THAT I...

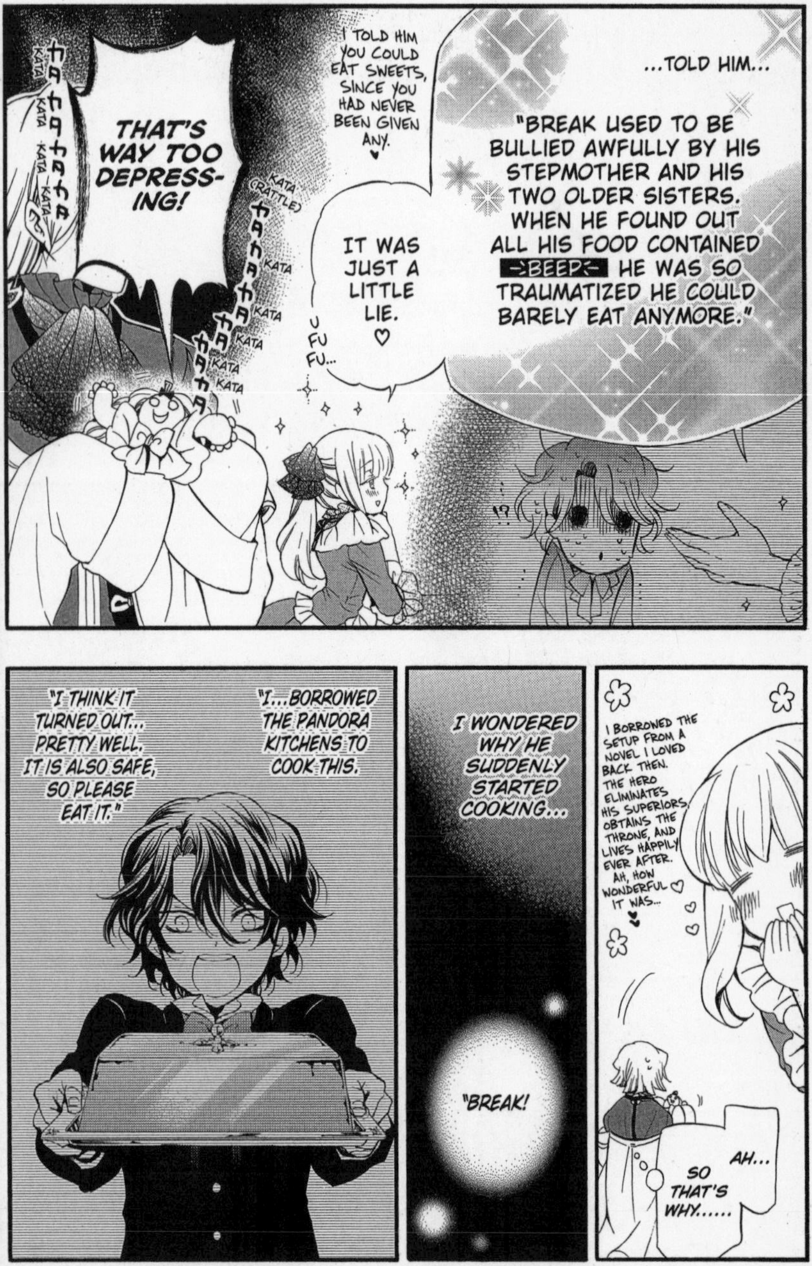
...TOLD HIM...
"BREAK USED TO BE BULLIED AWFULLY BY HIS STEPMOTHER AND HIS TWO OLDER SISTERS. WHEN HE FOUND OUT ALL HIS FOOD CONTAINED BEEP HE WAS SO TRAUMATIZED HE COULD BARELY EAT ANYMORE."
I TOLD HIM YOU COULD EAT SWEETS, SINCE YOU HAD NEVER BEEN GIVEN ANY.
IT WAS JUST A LITTLE LIE.
UFUFU...
KATA (RATTLE) KATA KATA KATA KATA KATA
THAT'S WAY TOO DEPRESSING!
KATA KATA KATA KATA
I BORROWED THE SETUP FROM A NOVEL I LOVED BACK THEN. THE HERO ELIMINATES HIS SUPERIORS, OBTAINS THE THRONE, AND LIVES HAPPILY EVER AFTER. AH, HOW WONDERFUL IT WAS...
AH... SO THAT'S WHY......
I WONDERED WHY HE SUDDENLY STARTED COOKING...
"BREAK!
"I... BORROWED THE PANDORA KITCHENS TO COOK THIS.
"I THINK IT TURNED OUT... PRETTY WELL. IT IS ALSO SAFE, SO PLEASE EAT IT."

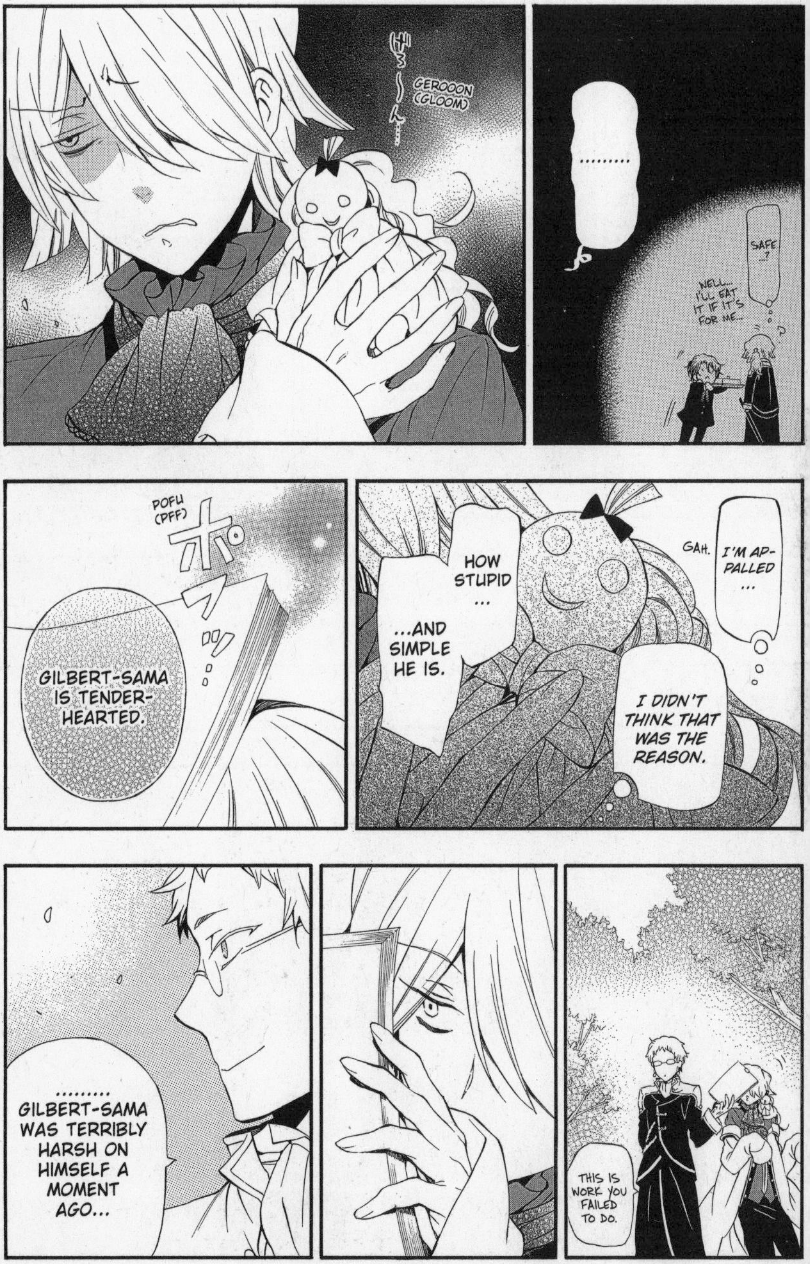
....
SAFE ...?
WELL... I'LL EAT IT IF IT'S FOR ME...
げろ～ん…
GEROOON (GLOOM)
I'M AP-PALLED ...
GAH.
HOW STUPID ...
I DIDN'T THINK THAT WAS THE REASON.
...AND SIMPLE HE IS.
POFU (PFF)
ポフッ
GILBERT-SAMA IS TENDER-HEARTED.
THIS IS WORK YOU FAILED TO DO.
.........GILBERT-SAMA WAS TERRIBLY HARSH ON HIMSELF A MOMENT AGO...

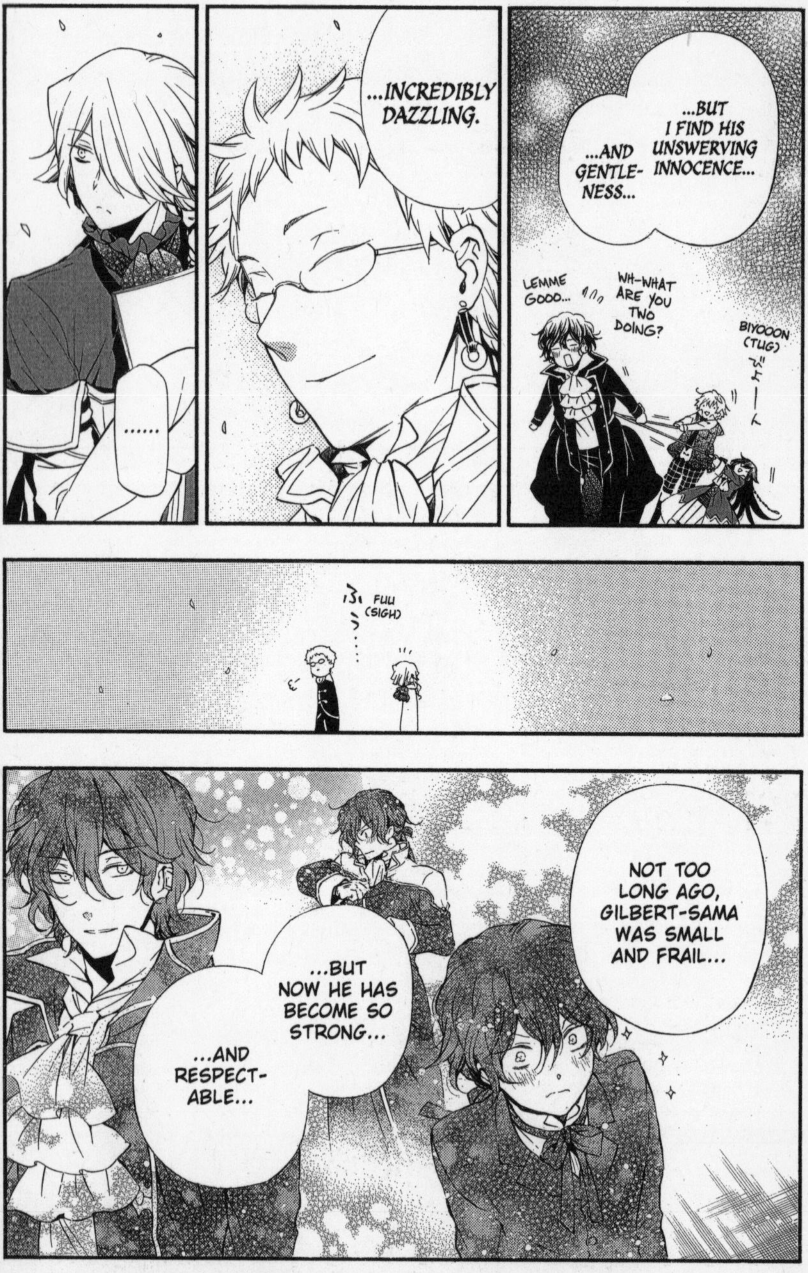
...BUT I FIND HIS UNSWERVING INNOCENCE...
...AND GENTLE-NESS...
BIYOOON (TUG)
WH-WHAT ARE YOU TWO DOING?
LEMME GOOO...
...INCREDIBLY DAZZLING.
......
FUU (SIGH)
NOT TOO LONG AGO, GILBERT-SAMA WAS SMALL AND FRAIL...
...BUT NOW HE HAS BECOME SO STRONG...
...AND RESPECT-ABLE...

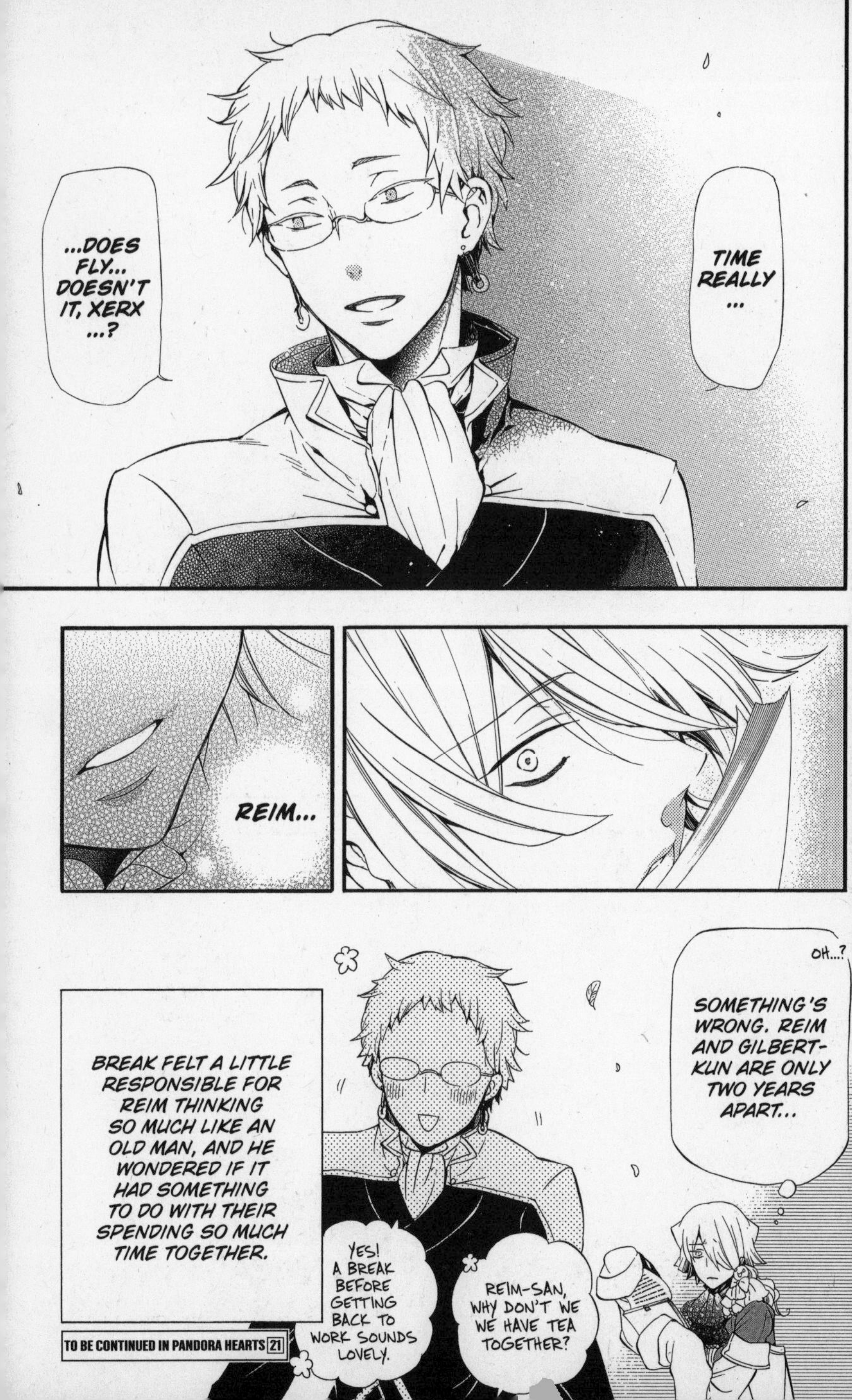
TIME REALLY ...
...DOES FLY... DOESN'T IT, XERX ...?
REIM...
OH...?
SOMETHING'S WRONG. REIM AND GILBERT-KUN ARE ONLY TWO YEARS APART...
REIM-SAN, WHY DON'T WE WE HAVE TEA TOGETHER?
YES! A BREAK BEFORE GETTING BACK TO WORK SOUNDS LOVELY.
BREAK FELT A LITTLE RESPONSIBLE FOR REIM THINKING SO MUCH LIKE AN OLD MAN, AND HE WONDERED IF IT HAD SOMETHING TO DO WITH THEIR SPENDING SO MUCH TIME TOGETHER.
TO BE CONTINUED IN PANDORA HEARTS 21

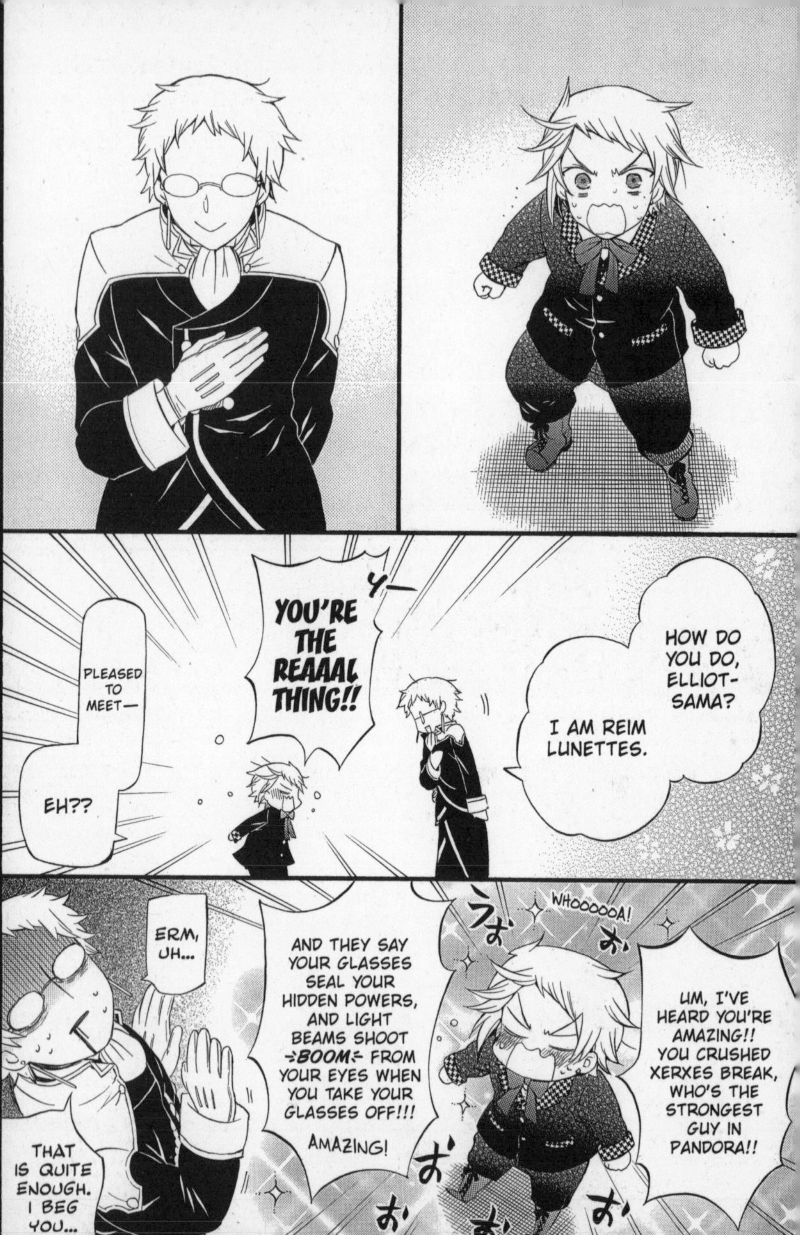
HOW DO YOU DO, ELLIOT-SAMA?
I AM REIM LUNETTES.
Y—
YOU'RE THE REAAAL THING!!
PLEASED TO MEET—
EH??
WHOOOOOA!
UM, I'VE HEARD YOU'RE AMAZING!! YOU CRUSHED XERXES BREAK, WHO'S THE STRONGEST GUY IN PANDORA!!
AND THEY SAY YOUR GLASSES SEAL YOUR HIDDEN POWERS, AND LIGHT BEAMS SHOOT *BOOM* FROM YOUR EYES WHEN YOU TAKE YOUR GLASSES OFF!!!
AMAZING!
ERM, UH...
THAT IS QUITE ENOUGH. I BEG YOU...

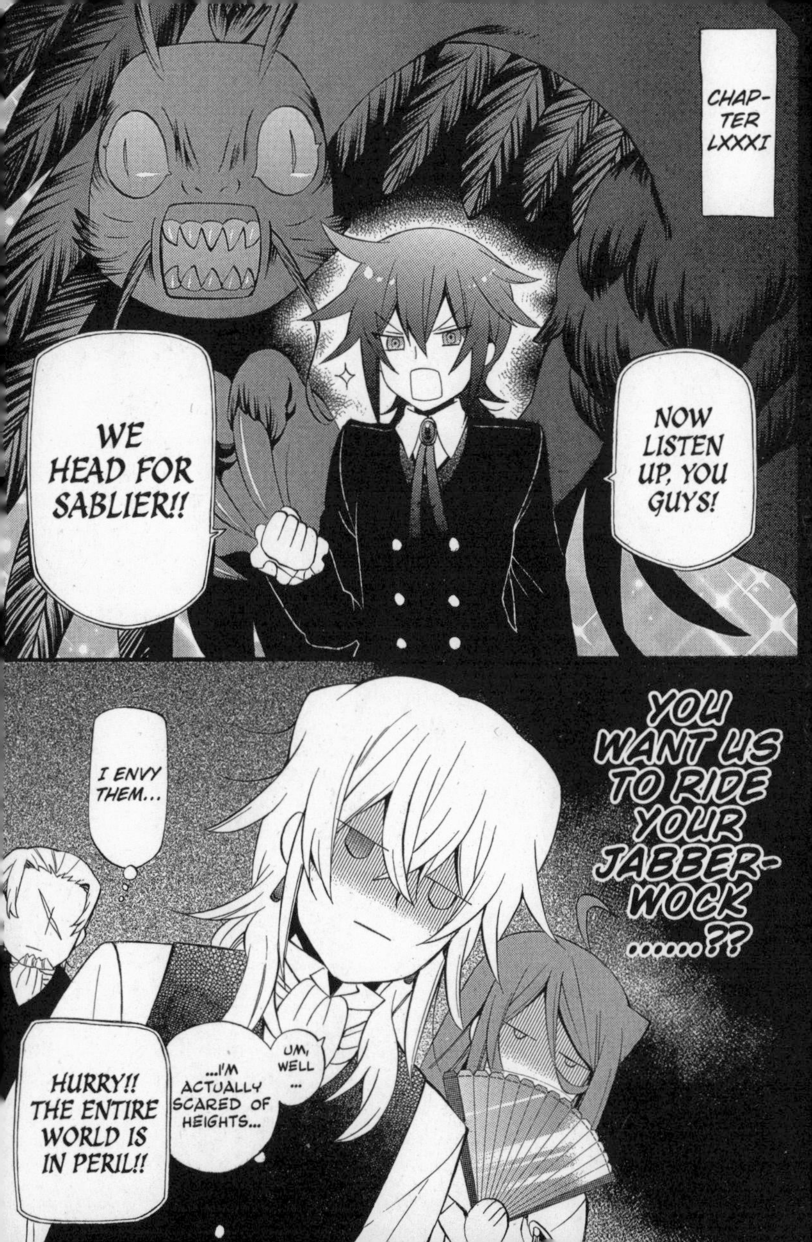
CHAPTER LXXXI
NOW LISTEN UP, YOU GUYS!
WE HEAD FOR SABLIER!!
YOU WANT US TO RIDE YOUR JABBERWOCK ......??
I ENVY THEM...
UM, WELL ...
...I'M ACTUALLY SCARED OF HEIGHTS...
HURRY!! THE ENTIRE WORLD IS IN PERIL!!

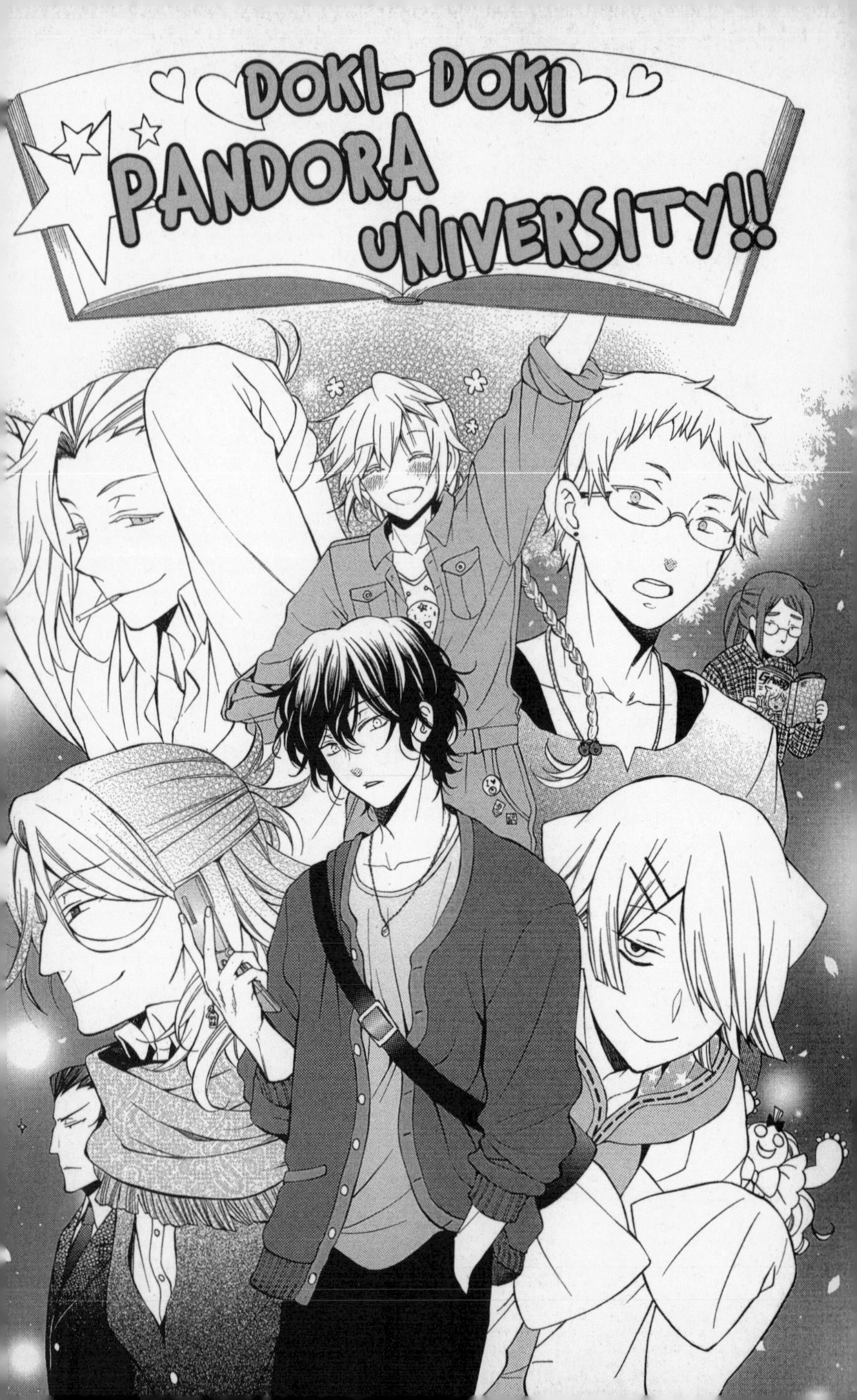
DOKI-DOKI
PANDORA
UNIVERSITY!!

THE PREQUEL TO "DOKI-DOKI PANDORA ACADEMY!!" IS FINALLY AVAILABLE ON MOBILE......!!

GILBERT, A JAPANESE TEACHER IN THE PREVIOUS GAME, AND REIM BOTH APPEAR AS NEW AND SHINY COLLEGE FIRST-YEARS! FOR SOME REASON, BREAK IS IN A LAB INSTEAD OF THE INFIRMARY!? YOU'LL MEET JACK BEFORE PANDORA ACADEMY BEGAN TAKING CARE OF HIM! NOW THEIR HIDDEN PASTS WILL BE REVEALED! LET'S GO NOW AND SEE THEM ENJOYING THEIR COLLEGE LIVES IN REAL TIME! (FREE-TO-PLAY)

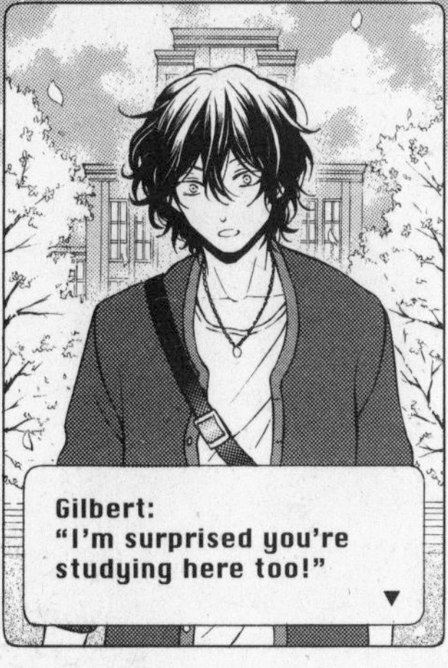
Gilbert:
"I'm surprised you're studying here too!"

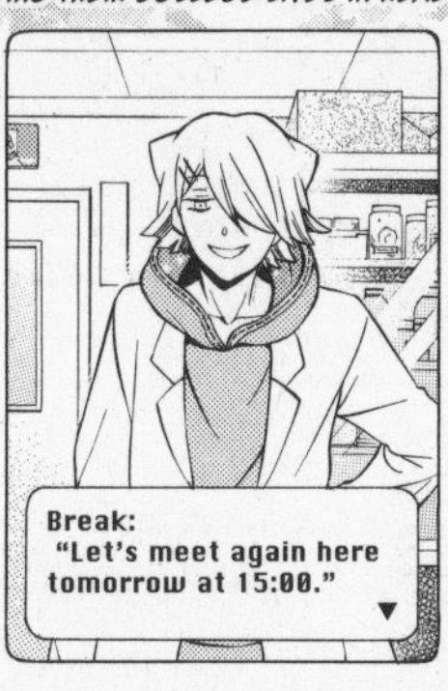
Break:
"Let's meet again here tomorrow at 15:00."

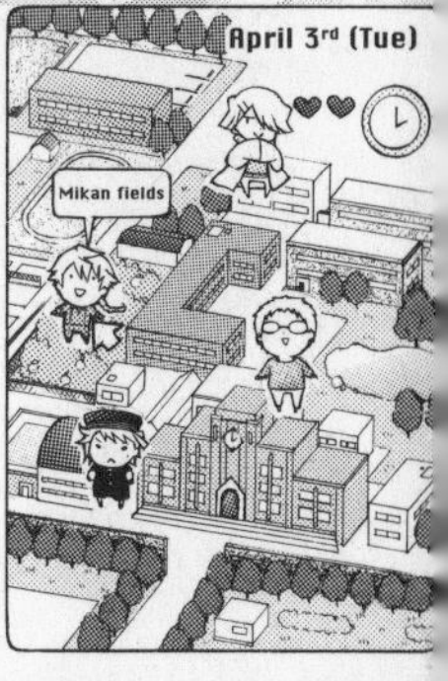
April 3rd (Tue)
Mikan fields

FOUR YEARS OF HEART-THUMPING COLLEGE LIFE. (CAN TAKE UP TO EIGHT YEARS)

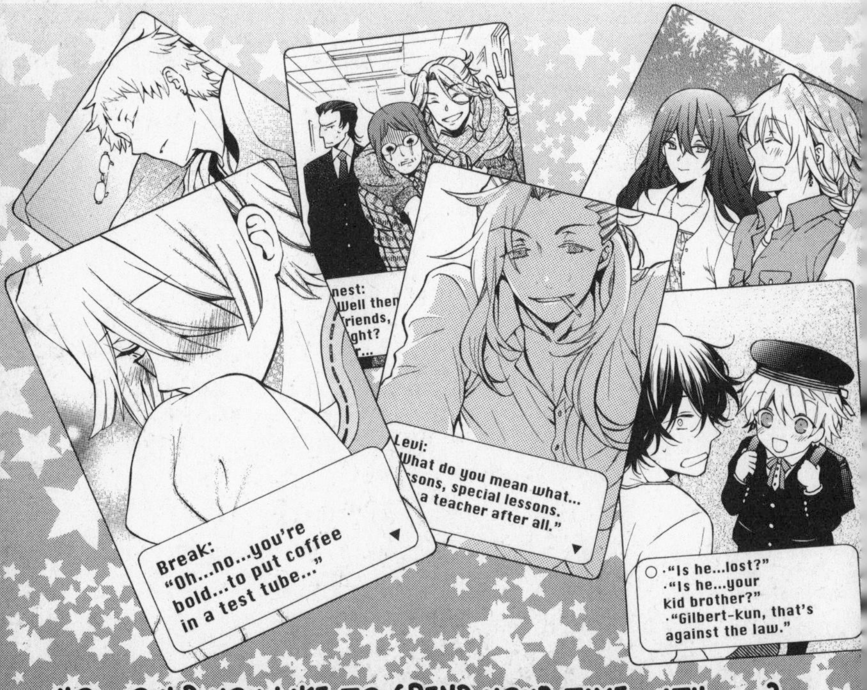
Break:
"Oh...no...you're bold...to put coffee in a test tube..."
Levi:
What do you mean what...
ssons, special lessons.
a teacher after all."
·"Is he...lost?"
·"Is he...your kid brother?"
·"Gilbert-kun, that's against the law."

WHO WOULD YOU LIKE TO SPEND YOUR TIME WITH......?

TRANSLATOR'S NOTES

COMMON HONORIFICS

no honorific: Indicates familiarity or closeness; if used without permission or reason, addressing someone in this manner would constitute an insult.

-san: The Japanese equivalent of Mr./Mrs./Miss. If a situation calls for politeness, this is the fail-safe honorific.

-sama: Conveys great respect; may also indicate that the social status of the speaker is lower than that of the addressee.

-kun: Used most often when referring to boys (though it can be applied to girls as well), this indicates affection or familiarity. Occasionally used by older men among their peers, but it may also be used by anyone referring to a person of lower standing.

-chan: An affectionate honorific indicating familiarity used mostly in reference to girls; also used in reference to cute persons or animals of either gender.

eight years
page 203

Japanese universities allow their students to spend up to eight years to graduate. If a student still cannot graduate after those eight years, they are expelled.

PandoraHearts

At long last, PandoraHearts has reached Volume 20. I really don't know what to write in this space anymore. Eep!

MOCHIZUKI'S MUSINGS

VOLUME 20

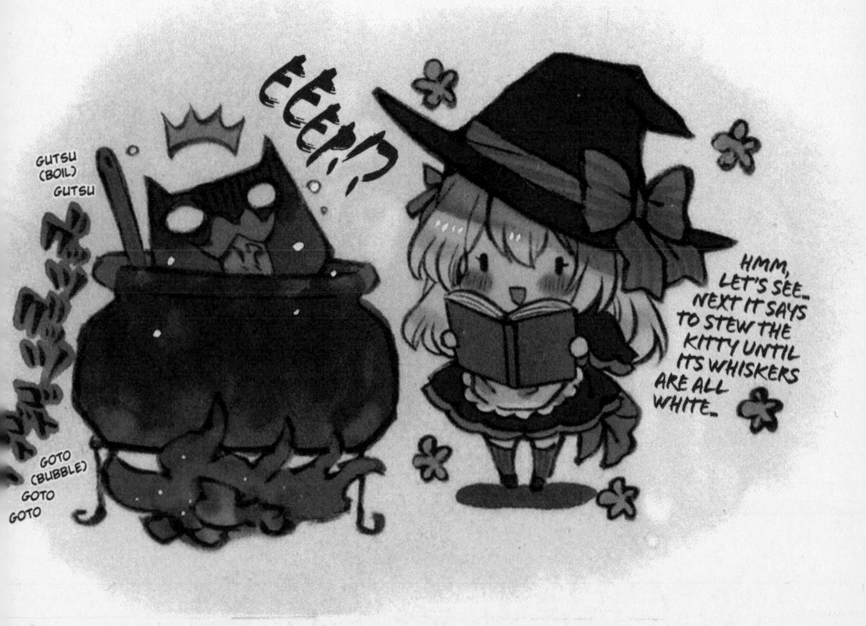
EEP!?
GUTSU (BOIL) GUTSU
GOTO (BUBBLE) GOTO GOTO
HMM, LET'S SEE... NEXT IT SAYS TO STEW THE KITTY UNTIL ITS WHISKERS ARE ALL WHITE...

PandoraHearts

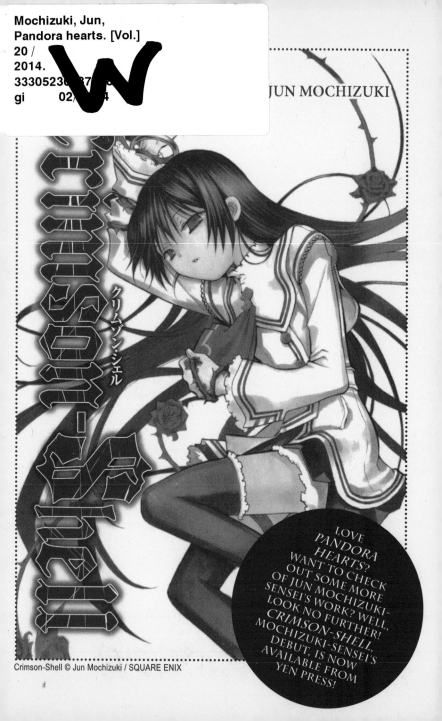

CRIMSON-Shell

クリムゾンシェル

JUN MOCHIZUKI

LOVE
*PANDORA
HEARTS*?
WANT TO CHECK
OUT SOME MORE
OF JUN MOCHIZUKI-
SENSEI'S WORK? WELL,
LOOK NO FURTHER!
CRIMSON-SHELL,
MOCHIZUKI-SENSEI'S
DEBUT, IS NOW
AVAILABLE FROM
YEN PRESS!

Crimson-Shell © Jun Mochizuki / SQUARE ENIX

Pandora Hearts

PandoraHearts ⑳

JUN MOCHIZUKI

Translation: Tomo Kimura • Lettering: Alexis Eckerman

PandoraHearts Vol. 20 © 2013 Jun Mochizuki / SQUARE ENIX CO., LTD. First published in Japan in 2013 by SQUARE ENIX CO., LTD. English translation rights arranged with SQUARE ENIX CO., LTD. and Hachette Book Group through Tuttle-Mori Agency, Inc.

Translation © 2014 by SQUARE ENIX CO., LTD.

Yen Press
Hachette Book Group
237 Park Avenue, New York, NY 10017

www.HachetteBookGroup.com
www.YenPress.com

Yen Press is an imprint of Hachette Book Group, Inc. The Yen Press name and logo are trademarks of Hachette Book Group, Inc.

First Yen Press Edition: February 2014

ISBN: 978-0-316-36908-4

10 9 8 7 6 5 4 3 2 1

BVG

Printed in the United States of America